ABUNDANCE

FOR A

PLANETARY

FUTURE

MAPPING ABUNDANCE FOR A PLANETARY FUTURE

KANAKA MAOLI AND CRITICAL
SETTLER CARTOGRAPHIES IN HAWAI'I

CANDACE FUJIKANE

'ŌLELO HAWAI'I EDITING BY C. M. KALIKO BAKER

DUKE UNIVERSITY PRESS *DURHAM AND LONDON* 2021

Designed by Aimee C. Harrison
Typeset in Arno Pro and Vectora LT Std by Westchester Publishing Services

Library of Congress Cataloging-in-Publication Data
Names: Fujikane, Candace, author.
Title: Mapping abundance for a planetary future : Kanaka Maoli and critical
settler cartographies in Hawai'i / Candace Fujikane.
Description: Durham : Duke University Press, 2021. | Includes bibliographical
references and index.
Identifiers: LCCN 2020021179 (print)
LCCN 2020021180 (ebook)
ISBN 9781478010562 (hardcover)
ISBN 9781478011682 (paperback)
ISBN 9781478021247 (ebook)
Subjects: LCSH: Environmental economics—Hawaii. | Water-supply—Hawaii. |
Globalization—Economic aspects—Hawaii. | Hawaiians—Economic conditions.
| Natural resources—Hawaii. | Land use—Hawaii.
Classification: LCC HC79.E5 F855 2021 (print) | LCC HC79.E5 (ebook) |
DDC 304.209969—dc23
LC record available at https://lccn.loc.gov/2020021179
LC ebook record available at https://lccn.loc.gov/2020021180

Cover art: Mealaaloha Bishop, *Kalo Paʻa o Waiāhole*, mixed media, 1999.
Image courtesy of the artist.

For the kūpuna who guided the way

For Tai and Kota

For all descendants

NĀ ʻAUMĀKUA

Nā ʻaumākua mai ka lā hiki a ka lā
    kau
Mai ka hoʻokuʻi a ka hālāwai
Nā ʻaumākua iā ka hina kua, iā ka
    hina alo
Iā ka ʻākau i ka lani
ʻO kīhā i ka lani
ʻOwē i ka lani
Nunulu i ka lani
Kāholo i ka lani
Eia ka pulapula a ʻoukou, ʻo ka poʻe
    Hawaiʻi
E mālama ʻoukou iā mākou
E ulu i ka lani
E ulu i ka honua
E ulu i ka pae ʻāina o Hawaiʻi
E hō mai i ka ʻike
E hō mai i ka ikaika
E hō mai i ke akamai
E hō mai i ka maopopo pono
E hō mai i ka ʻike pāpālua
E hō mai i ka mana.
ʻAmama, ua noa.

You ancestral deities from the
    rising to the setting of the sun
From the zenith to the horizon
You ancestral deities who stand at
    our back and at our front
You gods who stand at our right hand!
Breathing in the heavens,
Utterance in the heavens,
Clear, ringing voice in the heavens,
Voice reverberating in the heavens!
Here is your progeny, the Hawaiian
    people
Safeguard us
Growth to the heavens,
Growth to the earth,
Growth to the Hawaiʻi archipelago
Grant knowledge
Grant strength
Grant intelligence
Grant divine understanding
Grant intuitive insight
Grant mana.
The prayer is lifted; it is free.

—translation by Pualani Kanakaʻole Kanahele in *Kūkulu ke Ea a Kanaloa*

CONTENTS

have chosen not to italize ʻōlelo Hawaiʻi, which is now the convention for texts about Hawaiʻi. I use diacritical marks—the kahakō (macron) and ʻokina (glottal stop)—in the text, except in those places where the authors I cite have chosen not to use them. In a paragraph in which I discuss a particular moʻolelo (storied history) that does not use diacritical marks, I will not use them in names with which I have used diacritical marks elsewhere in the text. I have made this choice in these cases to leave open other possible meanings of names.

I use the kahakō to mark plural words (kupuna/kūpuna, wahine/wāhine). In the case of the term "Kanaka Maoli," I use the kahakō when referring to plural Kānaka Maoli or Kānaka (people), but not when using "Kanaka Maoli" as an adjective. Some words that are spelled the same way have the kahakō and others do not, depending on the meaning: for example, Māui the kupua/the island of Maui. Other words have dual spelling: Molokai/Molokaʻi.

Moʻolelo published in Hawaiian language nūpepa did not use diacritical marks, but when they occasionally did so for clarification, they used an apostrophe for the ʻokina instead of the glottal stop.

I use the terms "Kānaka Maoli," "Kānaka ʻŌiwi," and "Kānaka" in reference to people of Hawaiian ancestry. I also use the term "Native Hawaiian," regardless of federal definitions that rely on blood quantum classifications.

The translations are not meant to be definitive but are rather working translations. Where possible, I have noted other possible translations.

ACKNOWLEDGMENTS

In 2013, on a day of heavy rain clouds at the Laukapalili Laukapalala lo'i kalo (taro pondfields) deep in Punalu'u Valley, Daniel and Mealaaloha Bishop and I sit on a picnic table talking about the return of water to streams and the resurgence of kalo farming. I had been drawn to the Bishops' farm by Meala's painting entitled "Kalo Pa'a o Waiāhole," a glorious, epic portrait of the people of Waiāhole's struggle to protect the land and the waters that feed kalo. Kalo holds a special place in a Kanaka Maoli cosmology as the elder brother that they have a kuleana (responsibility, right, purview, privilege) to care for. Meala's painting is an exuberant study of kalo, depicting kalo leaves as maps of the ahupua'a, land divisions often, but not always, stretching from the mountains to the sea. These ahupua'a on the windward side of the island, in the Ko'olaupoko district, were the site of struggle for the people who stood for lands and waters depicted in the corm (root) of each kalo, all fed by the hard-won waters of Waiāhole. She illustrates the abundance of Kanaka Maoli economies of kalo cultivation, even at times when the state and corporate diversion and theft of water has made it difficult for kalo farmers to continue their practices as Kānaka Maoli.

As we sit there talking about restoration projects in Waiʻanae, Kalihi, and Waiāhole, Danny's bright eyes crinkle, and he laughs, saying, "You know what? There are so many struggles going on, so many people doing important work, and so many victories! We need to connect the dots." As the clouds release their rain and we run for cover, his words strike me with their full import. There are so many land struggles and restoration projects in Hawaiʻi connected to one another, both by their work against the occupying state and developer tactics to wasteland the earth and through the moʻolelo (historical stories), oli (chants), and mele (songs) that inspire those who stand for the land—but each struggle is often considered in isolation from the others. In each of these dramatically different lands, however, the people are all pili (connected) to each other through the akua, the elemental forms, who connect these places through fresh and saltwater waterways.

Six years later, in 2019, after returning to Oʻahu from two weeks of standing for Mauna a Wākea at Puʻuhonua o Puʻuhuluhulu to stop the contruction of the Thirty Meter Telescope, I am having a conversation with Meala at the Benjamin Parker Farmers Market run by her son Hanalē. She tells me, "I feel it now, all the hae Hawaiʻi, all the Hawaiian Kingdom flags flying from trucks all over the islands to support the struggle to protect Mauna Kea, to show everyone that the lāhui is still here. When they forced us to take down our flags after annexation, all of the women started making hae Hawaiʻi quilts so that their children could still fall asleep under their own flag. Now we are flying the flags all over. I feel like, today, we are finally connecting the dots." She completed the thought that her kāne Danny had raised those six years ago, that through the stand to protect Mauna a Wākea, we are seeing the fruition of a mapping of abundance.

These two quotations frame the work that I have done in this book to map the continuities among these struggles, to map the ways that they are inspired by the abundance people create for themselves, particularly in this era of global climate change. Kānaka Maoli have rooted their strategies of resurgence in the heroic actions of akua in the ʻike kupuna (ancestral knowledge) encoded in stories, chant, song, and riddles. The akua are the elemental forms who guide the people in their daily lives, and the lives of humans and the akua who embody the lands, seas, and skies are inextricable.

Those I thank here are a map of those dots.

My deepest gratitude goes to my greatest teachers, who have taught me about aloha ʻāina and a great love for the lāhui (the Hawaiian nation, people): Haunani-Kay Trask, Kū Ching, Kealoha Pisciotta, Pua Case, E. Kalani Flores, Walterbea Aldeguer, Alice Kaholo Greenwood, Lucy Gay, Danny and Meala Bishop, Puni Jackson, Hiʻilei Kawelo, Reny Aʻiaʻi Bello, Kalei Nuʻuhiwa, and Karen and Eiko Kosasa. I have learned so much from each of you.

I began this journey by following the movements of KĀHEA: The Hawaiian-Environmental Alliance. Attorney and then program director Marti Townsend has been a phenomenal force in mobilizing communities and protecting lands in Hawaiʻi, from her representation of KĀHEA in the contested case hearing against the Purple Spot in Waiʻanae, to the first 2011 contested case hearing against the Thirty Meter Telescope (TMT), to her representation of the Sierra Club in the Red Hill Jet Fuel case against the Department of Health and the US military. Lauren Muneoka has been the iwikuamoʻo (backbone) of KĀHEA's administration, holding us together with her administrative and technical skills. Shelley Muneoka has been the voice of aloha ʻāina for KĀHEA and has represented KĀHEA in community outreach events and before state agencies. Bianca Isaki has written key legal documents and findings of fact in the TMT case and has provided invaluable legal guidance. Past and present board members—Logan Narikawa, Kalaniʻōpua Young, Ikaika Hussey, Lucy Gay, Jonathan Kamakawiwoʻole Osorio, Christina Aiu, Jason Jeremiah, Koa Kaulukukui-Barbee, Miwa Tamanaha, and intern Tyler Gomes—have all played key roles in scrutinizing legislative bills, writing action alerts and sample testimony, and submitting grant applications, mobilizing communities in historic battles to protect lands and waters in Hawaiʻi.

The Concerned Elders of Waiʻanae have taught me so much about a loving commitment to community: Alice Kaholo Greenwood, Lucy Gay, Walterbea Aldeguer, Lori and John Nordlum, Kapua Keliikoa-Kamai, Pat Patterson, Georgia Campbell, Fred Dodge, Karen Young, Estrella and Joe Cabansag, Pearl Tavares, Elizabeth and Alan Stack, Everett Nakata, and others. I would also like to thank the farmers along Hakimo and Paʻakea Roads who shared their stories with us: Ryoei and Nancy Higa, Jerrol Booth, Pearl Tavares (mother), Pearl Tavares (daughter), Ken Mullen, Everett Nakata, Patsy Kaneshiro, Owen Kaneshiro. I thank also Kukui Maunakea-Forth, Gary Maunakea-Forth, Kamuela Enos, Cheryse Kauikeolani Sana, and the youth leaders at MAʻO Organic Farms. Thanks, too, to Kēhaulani Souza Kupihea, Fred Cachola, Chaunnel Pākē Salmon, Kamehaikana Akau, and Kuuleialoha Kauauakamakakuhauluakaukeano Ortiz for sharing their ʻike about Waiʻanae.

Thanks to the Kaʻala Cultural Learning Center water warriors Eric Enos and Butch DeTroye for teaching me so much about water in Waiʻanae. Kū Like Kākou has been holding it down in Waiʻanae with Momentum Mondays and Sustainable Sunday workdays at Kaʻala, and I have been fortunate to be able to join them: Kaukaʻohu, Noelani, Keola, and Hauʻoli Wahilani; Noe and Kawika Lopes; Kahili, Kapua, Meleanna, and Kaleo Keliʻikoa-Kamai; Kaleo Keliʻikoa, Kailana Moa-Eli, Kauluwehi Eli, Keke Manera, Kalaniʻōpua Young, Kaniela Cooper, Jessica Worschel, and many others.

I would also like to thank Nā Wāhine o Kunia for their lessons in the steadfast protection of Līhuʻe/Kunia and Pōhākea Pass: Sheila Valdez, Leilehua Keohookalani, Amy Kelly, and Mapuana Kekahuna. I learned about giving testimony from Summer Kaimalia Mullins-Ibrahim and Fred Mullins of the Kaʻena Cultural Practice Project, who defend Kaʻena with ʻike, poetry, and action.

I am grateful to the people who have made Hoʻoulu ʻĀina such a welcoming place. Mahalo palenaʻole to the reading group Hui Heluhelu Pū Alu: Kanoa O'Connor, Puni Jackson, Casey Jackson, Kaʻōhua Lucas, Kanoelani Walker, Pua o Eleili Pinto. Thank you to the steadfast people of Kalihi Calls, organized by Dawn Mahi: Mark Tang, Wanda Atkins, Cuddles King, Shawn Doo, Vicki Midado, Gordon Lee, Kēhaulani and Kāʻeiʻula Kupihea, Kupihea, Mary Lee, Naomi Sodetani, Ashley Galacgac, Glenda Duldulao, Innocenta Sound-Kikku, Jessica Aolani Higgins, Joey Miller, Nadine Noelani Aquino, and ʻAnakala Poni.

I am grateful to the Bishop family for inviting communities to work in restoring loʻi kalo in Waiāhole and Punaluʻu: Danny and Meala Bishop, Hanalē Bishop, Meghan and River Au-Bishop, and Kanaloa, Ikaika, and Kui Bishop. Onipaʻa Nā Hui Kalo has made these kinds of restorations possible all over the islands, and I thank Sharon Spencer, Gwen Kim, Kalamaokaʻāina Niheu, Danny Bishop, Penny Levin, and Earl Kawaʻa.

Mahalo to the mahi iʻa of Paepae o Heʻeia who have also welcomed me at workdays: Hiʻilei Kawelo, Keliʻi Kotubetey, Kanaloa Bishop, Keahi Piiohia, Kinohi Pizarro, Kealaulaokamamo Leota, Ikaika Wise, and Pūlama Long. I also thank the kiaʻi loko of Loko Ea, Buddy Keala, and Ikaika Lum.

Deep gratitude to the ever-expanding band of aloha ʻāina warriors I have worked with on Mauna a Wākea: Kealoha Pisciotta and Keomailani Von Gogh of Mauna Kea Anaina Hou, Kūkauakahi (Clarence Ching), Pua Case and E. Kalani Flores, Hāwane Rios and Kapulei Flores, Paul Neves, Deborah Ward, Marti Townsend; the petitioners in the contested case hearing I have worked with: Leinaʻala Sleightholm, Mehana Kihoi, William and

Cindy Freitas, Kalikolehua Kanaele, Hank Fergerstrom, Tiffnie Kakalia, Kahoʻokahi Kanuha, Dwight Vicente, Kualiʻi Camara; the Hawaiʻi Unity and Liberation Institute (HULI) organizers Kahoʻokahi Kanuha, Naaiakalani Colburn, Andre Perez, Camille Kalama, Kaleikoa Kaʻeo, Kahele Dukelow, ʻIlima Long; Mauna Kea kiaʻi Joshua Lanakila Mangauil, Kuʻuipo Freitas, Ruth Aloua, Laulani Teale, Earl DeLeon, Leilani Lindsey and Hiwa Kaʻapuni, Piʻikea Keawekāne-Stafford, Kainoa Stafford, Tammy and Isaac Harp, Elston Kamaka, Jojo Henderson, Leon Noʻeau Peralto, Haley Kailiehu, Kalama Niheu, Healani Sonoda, Shane Pale, Rhonda Kupihea Vincent, Ronald Fujiyoshi, Soli Niheu, Puanani Ikeda, Kathleen Lacerdo, Kaukaohu Wahilani, Māhealani Ahia, Kahala Johnson, Gino DʻAngelo McIntyre, Kupono Ana, Raymond Galdeira, and many more. To the attorneys who have represented the kiaʻi pro bono out of their love for Mauna a Wākea: Richard Naiwieha Wurdeman with the assistance of Brittni Waineʻe, Yuklin Aluli, Dexter Keʻeaumoku Kaʻiama, Lanny Sinkin, Gary Zamber, Aaron Kahauoliokuupuuwai Wills, and others.

To the kūpuna who were arrested on the front line of Mauna Kea to protect the mauna. I have named them all in the conclusion to this book, and I give special thanks here to those who have spoken with me about different parts of this book: Marie Alohalani Brown, Billy Freitas, Maxine Kahaulelio, Kalikolehua Kanaele, Pualani Kanakaʻole Kanahele, Leilani Lindsey-Kaʻapuni, Liko Martin, Jon Osorio, Loretta and Walter Ritte, and Noe Noe Wong-Wilson.

To the kiaʻi from whom I learn, holding space for the lāhui at Puʻuhonua o Puʻuhuluhulu on Mauna a Wākea: kumu hula Kekuhi Kanahele, Kaumakaʻiwa, Kauila and Tuhi Kanakaʻole, Ursula Uʻi Chong, Mililani Keliʻihoʻomalu, Noelani Ahia, Lauren Hara, Alika Kinimaka, Mahina Paishon, Kalama Niheu, Katy Benjamin, Keomailani Van Gogh, Presley Keʻalaanuhea Ah Mook Sang, Nalu OʻConnor.

My Huakaʻi i Nā ʻĀina Mauna ʻohana has taught me what Nelson Ho calls the "ground truths," the beauty of the land behind the theory: Kūkauakahi Ching, Baron Kahoʻōla Ching, Nelson Ho, Jennifer Ho, Kauʻi Trainer, Deborah Ward, Bryna Rose ʻOliko Storch, Tamsin Keone, and Christi Ching Maumau.

More recently, I have stood with longtime kiaʻi o Kahuku Kent Fonoimoana and Tēvita Kaʻili, who are taking a stand for Kahuku communities against massive 568-foot wind turbines whose low-frequency infrasound and flicker effect are causing debilitating health problems for the nearby schoolchildren and families. They are backed by an intergenerational group of leaders: Chantelle Eseta Matagi, Nakia Naeʻole, Shelly Beatty Mau, Isaac Silva, Rachel Kekaula, and Dayne Makanaokalani Kaawalauole.

Mahalo to the Papakū Makawalu and ʻAimalama researchers who have shared their knowledge with me: Pualani Kanakaʻole Kanahele, Kalei Nuʻuhiwa, Kuʻulei Higashi Kanahele, Malia Nobrega-Olivera, Roxanne Stewart, and Billy Kinney, as well as the scientists Noelani Puniwai, Rosie Alegado, and Kiana Frank.

I am also grateful to the aloha ʻāina activists who have shaped my political thinking about the occupation of Hawaiʻi and have articulated what an independent Hawaiʻi means: Kekuni Blaisdell, Haunani-Kay Trask, Mililani Trask, Walter Ritte, Noelani Goodyear-Kaʻōpua, Kaleikoa Kaʻeo, Kahele Dukelow, Andre Perez, Camille Kalama, Kahoʻokahi Kanuha, Kerry ʻIlima Long, J. Kēhaulani Kauanui, Keanu Sai, Pōmai Kinney, Pono Kealoha, and George Kahumoku Flores. Kyle Kajihiro and Terrilee Kekoʻolani of De-Tours, Ke Awalau o Puʻuloa, have taught me the complex politics of demilitarization in Hawaiʻi with clear and steady insights.

I would also like to thank the undergraduate and graduate students for their excellent feedback on my work in my spring 2019 Mapping Hawaiʻi's Literature senior seminar and spring 2014 and spring 2019 Mapping Moʻolelo against the Fragile Fictions of the Settler State graduate seminars. In particular, I would like to thank the students who gave me insights into and comments on parts of the manuscript: Kaleionaona Lyman, Wyatt Nainoa Souza, Emmanuel Kilika Bennett, Haupu Aea, Sabrina Kamakakaulani Gramberg, Billy Kinney, Samantha Ikeda, Joseph Han, Amy Vegas, Kim Compoc, Joy Enomoto, Katherine Achacoso, Maria Natividad Karaan, Noah Haʻalilio Solomon, Gregory Pōmaikaʻi Gushiken, Māhealani Ahia, Kahala Johnson, Aaron Kiʻilau, Kalamaʻehu Takahashi, Pono Fernandez, Koreen Nakahodo, Billie Lee, Janet Graham, Kelsey Amos, Ali Musleh, and Aaron Kiʻilau. I thank Keahi Lee in particular for introducing me to Meala Bishop's artwork.

The University of Hawaiʻi English Department has always been wonderfully supportive of my work, providing me with two semesters of research reduction, two sabbaticals, and a summer stipend for the research for and writing of this book. So many other University of Hawaiʻi colleagues have supported my writing over the years: Glenn Man, Valerie Wayne, Jonathan Okamura, Jeff Carroll, Kathy Phillips, Ruth Hsu, S. Shankar, John Zuern, Mark Heberle, Craig Howes, kuʻualoha hoʻomanawanui, Craig Santos Perez, Georganne Nordstrom, John Rieder, Paul Lyons, Shawna Yang Ryan, and Derrick Higginbotham.

C. M. Kaliko Baker has opened up new worlds for me through his lessons in translation, and I am so grateful that he has helped to edit my use of 'ōlelo Hawai'i. Thank you to Noenoe Silva, who also offered beautiful suggestions on the translations in chapter 5, and to Kalei Nu'uhiwa and Kahikina de Silva for their detailed explanation of the nuanced differences between Hawaiian language concepts.

Mahalo palena'ole to the scholars and activists who have read the manuscript in part or in full and have provided me with much needed feedback and support: Noenoe Silva, Kalei Nu'uhiwa, Noelani Goodyear-Ka'ōpua, Kī'ope Raymond, Erin Kahunawaika'ala Wright, Noelani Puniwai, Dean Saranillio, Gino D'Angelo McIntyre, ku'ualoha ho'omanawanui, J. Kēhaulani Kauanui, Maile Arvin, Marie Alohalani Brown, Eric Enos, E. Kalani Flores, Pua Case, Kealoha Pisciotta, Kūkauakahi Ching, Kaho'okahi Kanuha, Deborah Ward, Lucy Gay, Walterbea Aldeguer, Alice Greenwood, Haley Kailiehu, Johnnie-Mae Perry, Kēhaulani Kupihea, Kalani'ōpua Young, Hi'ilei Kawelo; Danny, Mealaaloha, and Hanalē Bishop; Billy, Cindy, and Ku'uipo Freitas; Mehana Kihoi, Leina'ala Sleightholm, 'Ohulei and Pumpkin Waia'u, Bianca Isaki, Vernadette Gonzalez, Hōkūlani Aikau, Paul Lyons, Ty Kāwika Tengan, Jamaica Heolimeleikalani Osorio, No'ukahau'oli Revilla, Kyle Kajihiro, Bryan Kamaoli Kuwada, Aiko Yamashiro, Uluwehi Hopkins, Jon Shishido, Nancy Fan, and Hetoevėhotohke'e Lucchesi.

I am grateful for so many other conversations with scholars who have helped me to clarify the arguments here: Aimee Bahng, Mary Tuti Baker, Ramzy Baroud, Kamanamaikalani Beamer, Jodi Byrd, Keith Camacho, Oscar Campomanes, David Chang, Mark Chiang, Kim Compoc, Jeff Corntassel, Noura Erakat, Alfred Peredo Flores, Annie Fukushima, Mishuana Goeman, Jairus Grove, Tēvita Ka'ili, Robin Wall Kimmerer, Tiffany Lethabo King, Evyn Lê Espiritu Gandhi, David Lloyd, Renee Pualani Louis, David Uahikeaikalei'ohu Maile, Brandy Nālani McDougall, Fred Moten, David Palumbo-Liu, Mona Oikawa, Kapā Oliveira, J. A. Ruanto-Ramirez, Cathy Schlund-Vials, Leanne Betasamosake Simpson, Alice Te Punga Somerville, Rajini Srikanth, Karen Su, Stephanie Nohelani Teves, Haunani-Kay Trask, Eve Tuck, Nishant Upadhyay, Robert Warrior, Patrick Wolfe, K. Wayne Yang, and Lisa Yoneyama. My writing group has inspired me in so many ways, and their incisive comments and questions have helped me to challenge myself in this book: Cynthia Franklin, Laura Lyons, Naoko Shibusawa, Monisha Das Gupta, Linda Lierheimer, Elizabeth Colwill, and Mari Yoshihara. Very special thanks to Cynthia, who has been my sprint-writing partner for the past five years. I am so grateful to her for her brilliant advice and the encouraging words that kept me going. Laura and Cristina Bacchilega have always supported me with keen insights on my work given with much love, and they have helped me to let the manuscript go out into the world.

I am deeply grateful to the editors at Duke University Press: Ken Wissoker for his support, and Elizabeth Ault for her warm encouragement and for deftly guiding the manuscript through the process. I am so glad that we had the chance to swim after beautiful uhu (parrotfish) together at Hanauma. My two anonymous readers read the manuscript carefully and thoroughly and provided me with wonderfully insightful questions that helped to sharpen the manuscript. I am grateful to Lisl Hampton, my project editor, who worked on this complicated manuscript with profound attention to detail and, more importantly, with so much care. Christopher Robinson was a pleasure to work with, and Aimee Harrison's design of the book cover surpassed my most extravagant imaginings, focalizing the beauty of Mealaaloha Bishop's artwork.

To my mother, Eloise Mitsuko Yamashita Saranillio, a Maui girl, for taking us on long drives to teach us to love places on Maui and their rootedness in moʻolelo. To my father, Kenneth Kiyoshi Fujikane, an artist who taught me to see beauty in the world and to have the courage to challenge the law when it is unjust. To my sister, Shelley, for her unwavering and loving support and for being my moral compass. To my brother Drew who fiercely fights for everyone in our family, always with a compassionate heart, and to my brother Dean Saranillio, who has been a true intellectual and spiritual companion in this journey of activism. To my sons, Tai and Kota, who have gone with me on many a huakaʻi, who get angry about stories of injustice, and who are learning how to do something about it. Finally, I would like to thank Glen Tomita: home is wherever you are, and I can take risks because you are my constant. Thank you for listening with love and patience, making me laugh, giving clear-sighted encouragement and advice, and taking care of our boys while I went off on workdays and huakaʻi. For all of this I give you my love.

ABUNDANT

CARTOGRAPHIES

FOR A

PLANETARY

FUTURE

One of the most visually stunning illustrations of a Kanaka Maoli cartography of climate change is the oral tradition describing the migration of the mo'o, the great reptilian water deities, from their home islands in the clouds to Hawai'i. In their lizard forms, the mo'o are formidable beings measuring thirty feet in length. In their Kanaka form, they are irresistibly beautiful women with great power, known to string yellow 'ilima flowers into lei while sunning themselves on rocks in pools of water. They are also desiring women, known to seduce men and to kill their lovers. If mo'o are depicted as elemental forms to be feared, it is also because they are the awe-inspiring protectors of water.[1] In the mo'olelo (storied history) of *Keaomelemele*, Mo'oinanea, the matriarch of mo'o deities, gathers her family of mo'o to accompany her from their cloud islands of Nu'umealani, Ke'alohilani, and Kuaihelani to O'ahu. They arrive in the 'ehukai o Pua'ena, the misty sea spray of the surf at the jagged lava cape in Waialua, and they make their way to the dark waters of the long and narrow 'Uko'a fishpond where the 'aka'akai (bulrushes) and the 'uki (sedge) stir with plentiful fish, then across the windblown plains of Lauhulu, perhaps to the Kaukonahua Stream, and from there to Kapūkakī:

> Ua hiki mua mai oia ma Puaena Waialua, aia malaila kona wahi i hoonoho pono ai i kana huakai nui, oia hoi ka huakai o na moo. Aia ma ke kula o Lauhulu ma Waialua, ua pani paa loa ia ia wahi e na moo. O ka hiki mua ana keia o na moo kupua ma keia paeaina, ma muli no ia o ka makemake o Kamooinanea, a penei e maopopo ai ka nui o na moo. Ua hoonoho palua ia ka hele ana o ka huakai, o ka makamua o na moo, aia i ka pii'na o Kapukaki, a o ka hope no hoi aia no i Lauhulu; a mawaena mai o keia wahi mai Waialua a Ewa, ua pani paa loa ia e na moo.[2]

> [Mooinanea] arrived first at Puaena in Waialua. There she arranged her great company of lizards. The plain of Lauhulu in Waialua was covered with them. This was the first time that the supernatural lizards arrived on these islands. It was through the will of Mooinanea. This is how we know of the number of lizards, she set them two by two in the procession. When the first of the lizards reached the incline of Kapukaki (Red Hill), the last ones were still in Lauhulu and between the two places, from Waialua to Ewa, the places were covered with lizards.[3]

From these words, we can imagine the stately procession of moʻo, their great tails sweeping from side to side, flickering between their reptilian forms as enormous lizards and their human forms as fierce men and women, making their way across the plains, with the Koʻolau mountains misted with rain to their left and the cloud-covered summit of Kaʻala in the Waiʻanae mountains to their right. The iwikuamoʻo, the continuous backbone of moʻo in this procession, foregrounds the moʻokūʻauhau (genealogy) of Moʻoinaneaʻs line as they surge across the island, making visible the continuities of water (see plate 1).

The migration of the moʻo may have taken place at a time when kūpuna (grandparents, ancestors) saw cascading changes in the natural world, perhaps an intensification of heat, a lessening of rainfall, shifts in the migration patterns of the ʻanae (mullet), in the health of the limu (seaweeds), in the numbers of ʻoʻopu (goby fish) who propel their way up waterfalls hundreds of feet high. One thing is certain: the arrival of the moʻo signals a historic moment when Kānaka Maoli began to pay greater attention to the care and conservation of water and the cultivation of fish. The moʻo became known as the guardians who enforced conservation kānāwai (laws) to protect the springs, streams, and fishponds, ensuring that water was never taken for granted.

Encoded in this moʻolelo is the art of kilo, keen intergenerational observation and forecasting key to recording changes on the earth in story and song, and such changes were met with renewed efforts to conserve, protect, and enhance abundance. The procession of moʻo teaches us cartographic principles of the pilina (connectedness) of the myriad ecosystems spread along the land and crossed by vast arteries of surface and subterranean waterways. A harmful event in one place ripples out to all others, and by the same principle, a restorative change catalyzes far-reaching and often unexpected forms of revitalization. In these stories, careful observance honors the akua, a word that kumu hula (hula master) Pualani Kanakaʻole Kanahele translates as "elemental forms," and enables adaptive responses that turn potentially devastating conditions into renewed possibilities for abundance.[4]

Capital tells a different story of a changing earth. Capital expands its domain through the evisceration of the living earth into the inanimacies of nonlife, depicting abundant lands as wastelands to condemn them and make way for the penetration of black snake oil pipelines under rivers, the seeding of unexploded ordnance in militarized zones, and the dumping of toxic wastes on sacred lands. As the effects of global climate change reverberate across the earth, we are seeing the consequences of capital's extraction and exhaustion through the expansion of deserts, the acidification of oceans, the rising seas, and the extinction of species. Cartographies of capital are processes of mapmaking that often rely on insistence rather than substance, on force and will rather than on ground truths. Such cartographies do not therefore merely depict the symptoms of a planet laid waste by late liberal settler states and globalization but are themselves a primary driving force of climate change.

The struggle for a planetary future calls for a profound epistemological shift. Indigenous ancestral knowledges are now providing a foundation for our work against climate change, one based on what I refer to as Indigenous economies of abundance—as opposed to capitalist economies of scarcity. Rather than seeing climate change as apocalyptic, we can see that climate change is bringing about the demise of capital, making way for Indigenous lifeways that center familial relationships with the earth and elemental forms. Kānaka Maoli are restoring the worlds where their attunement to climatic change and their capacity for kilo adaptation, regeneration, and tranformation will enable them to survive what capital cannot.

When we consider these stories about the earth, cartography manifests human articulations of our radically contingent relationships with the planetary. The cartography of the procession of moʻo frames vital questions for us: How are the exhausted cartographies of capital being transformed by the vibrant cartographies of Indigenous and settler ally artists, scientists, writers, and activists to restore more sustaining arrangements of life? How can abundance be mapped to show functioning Indigenous economies not premised on the crises of capital? How are lands mapped as having an ontology—a life, a will, a desire, and an agency—of their own? How can such cartographies help us to grow a decolonial love for lands, seas, and skies that will help to renew abundance on this earth?

Over and against the tactics of late liberal capital, *Mapping Abundance for a Planetary Future: Kanaka Maoli and Critical Settler Cartographies in Hawai'i* foregrounds more expansive, relational Kanaka and critical settler cartographies that sustain life. As I argue, cartography as a methodology is critical to growing intimate relationships with 'āina (lands and waters who feed) in ways necessary to our planetary future. In this way, mapping abundance is a refusal to succumb to capital's logic that we have passed an apocalyptic threshold of no return. Kanaka Maoli and critical settler cartographies in Hawai'i provide visual and textual illustrations of flourishing Indigenous economies of abundance. I argue that Kanaka Maoli cartographies foreground practices of ea—translated as life, breath, political sovereignty, and the rising of the people. Such ea-based cartographies teach us how to cultivate aloha 'āina, a deep and abiding love for the lands, seas, and skies through which undercurrents of Kanaka Maoli radical resurgence flow.

Mapping abundance is a profoundly decolonial act. David Lloyd has argued that it is precisely the fear of abundance that is inscribed in neoliberal capital. Abundance is both the objective and the limit of capital: the crisis for capital is that abundance raises the possibility of a just redistribution of resources:

> Perhaps, then, we need to recognize that precisely what neoliberal capital *fears* is abundance and what it implies. Abundance is the end of capital: it is at once what it must aim to produce in order to dominate and control the commodity market and what designates the limits that it produces out of its own process. Where abundance does not culminate in a crisis of overproduction, it raises the specter that we might demand a redistribution of resources in the place of enclosure and accumulation by dispossession. The alibi of capital is scarcity; its myth is that of a primordial scarcity overcome only by labor regulated and disciplined by the private ownership of the means of production.[5]

Capital depends on growth through the manufacturing of hunger; thus, capitalist modes of production manufacture the perception of scarcity to produce markets. To extend Lloyd's analysis, I argue that while capitalist economies proffer empty promises of imaginary plenitude, ancestral abundance feeds for generations. Writing from a Potawatomi perspective, environmental biologist and poet Robin Wall Kimmerer contends that recognizing true abundance erodes the foundations of capitalist economies: "In a consumer society, contentment is a radical proposition. Recognizing abundance rather than scarcity undermines an economy that thrives by creating unmet desires."[6] A Kanaka Maoli economy of abundance is one of māʻona, a fullness that comes from sharing, trading, gift-giving, conserving, and adapting. Economies of abundance create the conditions for people to see beyond the competition for scarce resources to our own regenerative capacity to cultivate abundance.

Capital produces a human alienation from land and from the elemental forms that constitutes a foundational loss. Humans compulsively try to fill this emptiness through an imaginary plenitude that commodifies land. In what I refer to as the settler colonial mathematics of subdivision, cartographies of capital commodify and diminish the vitality of land by drawing boundary lines around successively smaller, isolated pieces of land that capital proclaims are no longer "culturally significant" or "agriculturally feasible," often portraying abundant lands as wastelands incapable of sustaining life. Henri Lefebvre's articulation of a basic premise of geography holds true today: modes of production produce conceptions of space, and the process of urbanization in a capitalist economy is a trend toward the fragmentation, separation, and disintegration of space ad infinitum.[7] In David Harvey's words, capitalism is the "factory of fragmentation" that disperses production along multiple sites.[8] Such cartographies work to enclose and domesticate Indigenous places and their significance precisely because the seizure of land continues to be constitutive of the very structure of occupying and settler states. In Hawaiʻi, we can see the occupying state's logic of subdivision in a complex of state laws, ordinances, and policies, ranging from the tactics of phased archaeological inventory surveys to practices of urban spot zoning to definitions of thresholds of impact.

To map abundance is not a luxury but an urgent insistence on life. Envisioning and practicing abundance is a necessity in the face of the deadly consequences of occupation, settler colonial genocidal tactics, and corporate-induced climate change. Traditional Kanaka Maoli economies of abundance based on the cultivation of loʻi kalo (taro pondfields) were essential to recharging the aquifers and watersheds, but under colonial capital elaborate ditch systems diverted water away from valleys actively producing kalo to feed instead thirsty sugarcane. Parched streambeds lie in wait for the return of water, stones like bones bleaching in the sun. Many Kānaka Maoli were forced to leave their cultivation of kalo because of capital's accumulation by dispossession and privatization.

In the last thirty years alone, we have seen an 18 percent decline in rainfall.[9] As kūpuna remind us in an enduring ʻōlelo noʻeau (proverb), "Hahai nō ka ua i ka ululāʻau" (Rains always follow the forest).[10] Kānaka Maoli knew that the rains were dependent on healthy forests that attract the clouds and recharge the aquifers through capturing rain and fog drip, and there were kānāwai (laws) in place to protect the overharvesting of trees. Yet over the years since the introduction of a capitalist economy, the depletion of the ʻiliahi (sandalwood) and koa forests led to the explosive growth of invasive species that drink three times the water of Native species. The majority (90 to 95 percent) of dryland forests, once rich with the greenery of kauila, uhiuhi, kokiʻo, ʻaiea, and hala pepe trees, has disappeared.[11] Overdevelopment has also led to the massive expansion of impervious concretization, causing the more rapid depletion of groundwater resources. In the last two decades, water table levels have dropped by more than thirteen feet, allowing saltwater to enter and contaminate the lower water table.[12] The occupying state has focused on expanding watershed protections and removing invasive plant species while engaging in the reforestation of Native trees, yet despite these efforts, corporate and military diversions and water banking for future development projects continue to exacerbate these conditions.

To foreground abundance is not to romanticize a world seeing these changes in Hawaiʻi, or the catastrophic burning of the Amazon rainforests and the Australian bush, or the murders of hundreds of Indigenous land defenders.[13] In the work of Kanaka Maoli practitioners, we see generative ways of thinking of abundance in a time of climate change, neither through what Lauren Berlant has critiqued as "cruel optimism" nor through an antagonistic reading of the elements, but rather through Kanaka Maoli ancestral knowledges that value elemental forms in familial terms.[14] Practitioners strive to balance critical analyses of circuits of globalization with the moʻolelo about the currents of the oceans, winds, and rains that teach us an ethics of caring for the planet. In this commitment to restoring abundance, Kānaka Maoli stand with other Indigenous peoples who are on the front lines against global climate change.

Abundant-mindedness is a radical refusal of capitalist economies. "Abundance" is a word that grows out of Kanaka Maoli restoration projects, as practitioners assert their capacity to determine their own decolonial futures. Puni Jackson, program director at Hoʻoulu ʻĀina in Kalihi Valley, explains that so much energy is expended in deficit-thinking that strips Kānaka of agency and reduces them to victims when, instead, that energy is better spent culti-vating an abundant-mindedness as the foundation for building an inclusive lāhui, a broad-based collective of people committed to Kanaka Maoli land-centered governance.[15] She explains, "Because as a lāhui we need healing, all of us need healing, and it's easy to come to sort of a deficit-mindedness of 'no more 'nough' or 'poor thing Hawaiians' or 'we got all of this taken away,' but in the end we have each other, we have this 'āina, we have our babies, we have the heritage of our kūpuna that we are overwhelmingly blessed with, and so I hope to perpetuate that abundant-mindedness that I was raised with."[16]

Restoration projects show us that restorative events have outwardly cas-cading effects on ecological systems that are contingent on one other, and bottom-up cascades are as important in this era of global climate change as top-down cascades. If small, incremental adverse changes like a one-degree Celsius increase in global temperatures have exponentially harmful effects, other incremental changes to repair environmental damage, too, have expo-nential restorative effects that ripple out across ecosystems around the world. Mapping abundance offers us a way to rethink the scalar privileging of global corporate and state solutions over localized restoration movements. As Anna Lowenhaupt Tsing illustrates in her study of matsutake mushrooms, the dif-ference between scalable and nonscalable projects is not ethical conduct but the fact that nonscalable projects are more diverse: "The challenge for think-ing with precarity is to understand the ways projects for making scalability have transformed landscape and society, while also seeing where scalability fails—and where nonscalable ecological and economic relations erupt."[17] These moments of failure are the eruptions out of which unpredictable, entangled relationships are formed to enable unexpected conditions for life.

This book opens up another dimension to scalability by reconsidering the seeming precarity of relationships. Tsing's own project is one of tracking and mapping cultural formations globally that are like the filaments of fungal hyphae spread out into fans and tangles. What if these relationships have ac-tually been tracked for generations and adapted to by Indigenous peoples in ways that have enabled their own flourishing?

HOW WILL THE EARTH RECOGNIZE US?
A KANAKA MAOLI CARTOGRAPHY OF EA

Mapping abundance engages a different politics of recognition, one that centers not on the settler state's recognition of Indigenous peoples but on whether *the earth will recognize us*. To ask how the earth will recognize us entails a decolonization of the Anthropocene. Kyle Whyte (Potawatomi) has argued that Anthropogenic climate change is an intensification of the environmental devastation wrought on Indigenous peoples by colonialism, and we decolonize and denaturalize the Anthropocene by showing how it is driven by the carbon-intensive economics of colonial capital and its twinned engines of industrialism and militarization.[18] Macarena Gómez-Barris has also argued for decolonizing the Anthropocene by "cataloging life otherwise, or the emergent and heterogeneous forms of living that are not about destruction or mere survival within the extractive zone, but about the creation of emergent alternatives."[19] *Mapping Abundance* seeks to employ both of these strategies that critique the operations of what Elizabeth Povinelli terms "late liberalism," a periodizing that considers how neoliberalism's governance of markets is part of late liberalism's governance of difference, specifically its claims to authority over distinguishing life from nonlife.[20] As I argue, Indigenous peoples contest late liberal geontopower by speaking to the ways that we must listen to the laws of lands, seas, and skies in ways that will enable these elemental forms to recognize us in the reciprocal cultivation of abundance.

Against cynical critiques of anthropomorphism, arguing for the higher consciousness of the earth goes beyond the hermeneutics of human-centered logics. We are given enough observable indicators to discern what is in the best interests of the earth and the contingent life systems on it. Kānaka Maoli have long engaged in the practices of kilo, meticulously observing and identifying these laws of the natural order, and the moʻolelo give shape to the elements who take human form and voice their desires. Their words form the basis for the kānāwai that answer to the higher authority of the elements in the natural world. There are 400,000 akua, which points to the careful specificity with which elemental forms are distinguished from one another, and each elemental form is invoked in ceremony. Papakū Makawalu researcher Kalei Nuʻuhiwa explains that the prayer "Ka Pule a Kāne," for example, lists dozens of Kāne akua, from Kāneikeaolewalalo (Kāne in the cloud floating low) to Kāneikeaopaliluna (Kāne in the cloud resting on the summit), from Kāneikanoe (Kāne in the fog) to Kāneikaʻohu (Kāne of the mist) to Kāneikapuahiohio (Kāne of the whirlwind).[21] These akua were identified and named based on the ancestral insights into the optimal workings of interconnected ecological webs.

Adaptation to changes on the earth is not a resignation; it means intensifying movements against capital's devastation of the planet and *simultaneously* activating ourselves to enact an ethics of care.

Definitions of abundance ripen across these chapters. Kanaka Maoli cartographies look to ancestral knowledges in moʻolelo (stories/histories), oli (chant), mele (song), ʻōlelo noʻeau (proverbs), nāne (riddles), and pule (prayer) to renew the sources of abundance on the ʻāina momona (fertile and abundant lands). We can lay a foundation for an understanding of abundance here through the voices of the kūpuna (ancestors). Nineteenth-century historian Samuel Mānaiakalani Kamakau defines abundance based on the shining fishponds that hoʻohiluhilu (beautify, adorn) the land:

> he mea no ia e hoike mai ana i ka nui o na kanaka o ka wa kahiko, a o ka maluhia pu kekahi kumu i paa ai, ina paha he kaua pinepine, a he kue kekahi me kekahi poe, a pehea la auanei e lokahi like ai ka hana ana a paa keia mau hana nui o ka hana ana i na kuapa. Ina aole lakou e ai ana i ka hua o ka lakou mea i hooikaika ai. Pehea lakou i hooholo ai i ke awa a hiki i ke anana, a i ka anae hoi a hiki i ke iwilei, a i ka ulua hoi, he anana a muku, a i ke aholehole hoi, hele a koa ka lae, i ka oopu hoi, ua hele a like ka unahi me ko ka uhu. Ma keia mau kumu akaka loa. O ka maluhia o ke aupuni ke kumu i paa ai ka hana ana i na kuapa, a o ka maluhia ke kumu i nui ai ka ia, a o ka pakela nui i kanaka kekahi i hiki ai kela hana kaumaha.[22]

> This shows how numerous the population must have been in the old days, and how they must have kept the peace, for how could they have worked together in unity and made these walls if they had been frequently at war and in opposition one against another? If they did not eat the fruit of their efforts how could they have let the *awa* fish grow to a fathom in length; the *ʻanae* to an *iwilei*, yard; the *ulua* to a meter or a *muku* (four and one half feet); the *aholehole* [flagtail fish] until its head was hard as coral (*koʻa ka lae*); and the *ʻoʻopu* [gobey fish] until their scales were like the *uhu* [parrotfish]? Peace in the kingdom was the reason that the walls could be built, the fish could grow big, and there were enough people to do this heavy work.[23]

Kamakau's description of the dimensions to these fish are wondrous today as illustrations of abundance as an index of good governance. Such effective governance recognizes the hunger of war and the fullness of peace, and when the people are fed, they are able to work together to build and maintain the massive stone walls of the fishponds.

Taking broader movements for Kanaka Maoli political sovereignty into consideration, I also chart a mode of land-based governance that enables the cultivation of abundance: a mapping of ea. "Ea" is a word that brings together the layered meanings of life, breath, and political sovereignty, a rising—the rising of the people to protect the 'āina who feeds physically, intellectually, and spiritually. The word "ea" is likened to the birth of the living land itself. 'Ōlelo Hawai'i (Hawaiian language) scholar Leilani Basham describes a beautiful image of ea: "'O ke ea nō ho'i ka hua 'ōlelo no ka puka 'ana mai o kekahi mea mai loko mai o ka moana, e la'a me ka mokupuni."[24] In her introduction to *A Nation Rising: Hawaiian Movements for Life, Land, and Sovereignty*, Noelani Goodyear-Ka'ōpua sets the foundation for the collection by engaging Basham's words. She explains:

> Indeed, "ea" is a word that describes emergence, such as volcanic islands from the depths of the ocean. In looking to mele Hawai'i—Hawaiian songs and poetry—Basham points out that the term "ea" is foregrounded within a prominent mele ko'ihonua, or creation and genealogical chant for Hawai'i: "*Ea* mai Hawaiinuiakea / *Ea* mai loko mai o ka po." The islands emerge from the depths, from the darkness that precedes their birth. Basham argues that, similarly, political autonomy is a beginning of life.[25]

As the islands rise, ea is birthed, emerging from the fecundity of the ancestral realm of Pō. Goodyear-Ka'ōpua further explains that "ea is an active state of being. Like breathing, ea cannot be achieved or possessed; it requires constant action day after day, generation after generation."[26]

In such discussions of ea, the critical framework that has come to the fore is the analysis of occupation and the political status of Hawai'i as a sovereign nation-state under US occupation. Although the frameworks of occupation and settler colonialism are not necessarily mutually exclusive, activists have debated these different sets of discourses and outlined contrasting political processes for deoccupation and decolonization. Under the terms of international law that structure the occupation argument, "Indigenous peoples" refers to colonized peoples in a way that Kūhiō Vogeler argues is incommensurable with the occupation framework, which understands Kānaka Maoli as part of a multiethnic national citizenry under US occupation.[27] David Keanu Sai further argues that the US misrepresented Hawai'i as a "non-self-governing territory" in 1946 in order to disguise occupation under the cover of colonialism.[28] Others have argued, however, that occupation and settler colonialism are actually mutually constitutive. Goodyear-Ka'ōpua writes, "One might consider that a prolonged US occupation of Hawai'i enables the ongoing hegemony of a settler society—settler colonialism—with varying aspects and effects."[29] Analyses of settler colonialism are useful in illustrating how occupation has made possible state tactics that seek to legislate Kanaka Maoli traditional and customary practices out of existence. Settler colonial practices naturalize occupation to the point where the citizenry sees no alternative to citizenship in the occupying state. Dean Saranillio aptly describes this foreclosure of other potential futures through the settler colonial rearrangement of desire invested in what Edward Said has referred to as "a future wish." Saranillio writes, "Hawaiʻi's U.S. statehood movement functioned in particular as a 'future wish,' a kind of settler abstraction of what Hawaiʻi could become if it were a state, and the American lifestyle one would have as a 'first-class citizen,' all of which positioned Kanaka ʻŌiwi forms of sovereignty, governance, foodways, and relations in Hawaiʻi as outmoded and a less deserving power than the emerging liberal settler state."[30]

J. Kēhaulani Kauanui has broadened the implications of settler colonialism by arguing that it encompasses the logics of "Western civilization" adopted all over the world: "As Walter Mignolo argues in *The Darker Side of Western Modernity*, coloniality manifested throughout the world and determined the socioeconomic, racial, and epistemological value systems of contemporary society, commonly called 'modern' society. This is precisely why coloniality does not just disappear with political and historical decolonization, the end of the period of territorial domination of lands, when countries gain independence. Given this distinction, one can see that coloniality is part of the logic of Western civilization."[31] In other words, if Hawaiʻi were to be deoccupied today, there would still need to be an ongoing effort to decolonize not only the institutional structures of everyday life, but the settler colonial logics and capitalist economies of scarcity that structure the popular imaginary.

While I take as a premise the political status of Hawaiʻi as an occupied territory, a focus on US occupation as the sole analytic makes it difficult for us to engage in the broader decolonial analyses that challenge Western epistemological formations. Indigeneity continues to be a material positionality that connects Kānaka Maoli to Indigenous peoples around the world and one from which multipronged work against occupation and settler colonialism can be mobilized. For this reason, I will use the term "occupation" to refer to the political status of Hawaiʻi, "occupying state" to refer to the United States and the State of Hawaiʻi, and "settler colonialism" to refer to the social and cultural processes, regimes of rhetoric, and juridical arguments with which the occupying state naturalizes its governance. Patrick Wolfe reminds us that "settler colonialism is at base a winner-take-all project whose dominant feature is not exploitation but replacement . . . a sustained institutional tendency to eliminate the Indigenous population."[32] These considerations make clear that nonstatist organizing at restoration projects across the islands teach us that we do not have to wait for deoccupation or decolonization but rather that we can materialize that future beyond occupation and settler colonialism right now in the present. This mode of living a decolonial present is possible precisely because, as Goodyear-Kaʻōpua argues, ea as praxis provides a broad organizing foundation that defines "nation" as land based rather than state based, and that definition can be held productively open-ended, both in statist and nonstatist terms.[33]

In this way, Kānaka Maoli have joined a broader decolonial movement of Indigenous peoples who are not waiting for the dismantling of occupying or settler states or the return of their ancestral lands but are actively living that independent future beyond the occupying or settler state in the present. We live ea now, on a daily basis, in nonstatist ways that include the restoration of loʻi kalo (taro pondfields), loko iʻa (fishponds), ʻauwai (irrigation waterways), and ʻike kupuna (ancestral knowledge), as well as the cultivation of social relationships needed to grow a broad-based lāhui on the basis of Kanaka Maoli language, histories, knowledges, and practices. As Kānaka Maoli and other Indigenous peoples bring the land back into abundance, we see that this restoration of their land bases is key to the restoration of the planet.

FROM SETTLER ALLY TO SETTLER ALOHA ʻĀINA (SETTLER PROTECTOR OF LANDS AND WATERS)

Growing the lāhui, whether as a statist or nonstatist collective premised on Kanaka Maoli principles of land-based governance, has taken into consideration that settlers, too, can cultivate aloha ʻāina and a Hawaiian national consciousness, but aloha ʻāina for settlers must be informed by an understanding of settler positionalities and access to privileges under the operations of both occupation and settler colonialism. As we enlarge our tracking of global circuits of capital to a broader planetarity of interconnected life systems, non-Indigenous peoples around the world are following the lead of Indigenous peoples as land protectors. As a yonsei (fourth-generation) Japanese settler ally in Hawaiʻi whose ancestral lands are in Fukushima, Kumamoto, and Niigata, I have worked to move toward being a settler aloha ʻāina (land and water protector who affirms Kanaka Maoli independence) by engaging in synchronic, overlapping sets of practices: one set actively working to challenge the occupying state by making interventions into settler colonial operations of land seizure; and one that affirms Hawai'i's independence through the revitalization of waterways, food systems, and our relationships with 'āina and with each other.

More than twenty years ago, Kanaka Maoli scholar, activist, and poet Haunani-Kay Trask argued that it is settler colonialism itself as a set of political conditions that institutes the genealogical distinction between Natives and settlers. As she identified people of color as "settlers of color," she also opened up a space for settler allies by reminding us, "For non-Natives, the question that needs to be answered every day is simply the one posed in the old union song: 'Which side are you on?'"[34] Trask's question foregrounds settler agency in a world in which we can choose to identify with the lāhui. We know that occupying and settler states established on capitalist economies have no future, dissipating the humanity of and possibilities of life for Indigenous peoples, Blacks, migrants, Muslims, queer and transgender people, the poor, and anyone who represents a refusal of white supremacy, of capital, of late liberal forms of settler normativity, whereas Kanaka Maoli and other Indigenous economies centered around caring for the living earth see our differences as enabling in helping us to grow our capaciousness as collectives, drawing together our own inherited knowledges for all of us to flourish.

Recent setter colonial studies scholarship has turned to Chickasaw scholar Jodi Byrd's use of the term "arrivant," which she borrows from African Caribbean poet Kamau Brathwaite's work and extends to include "those people forced into the Americas through the violence of European and Anglo-American colonialism and imperialism around the globe."[35] They call for the use of the term "arrivant" to complicate what they describe as a settler-Native binary, but we should also remember that Byrd describes not only settler colonialism but also an "arrivant colonialism."[36] What are the implications and pragmatics of extending the term "arrivant" to other people of color? Brathwaite's use of the term "arrivant" for African Caribbean peoples works to differentiate what Trask herself distinguished as the violence of slavery from those lived by other peoples of color. Trask never extended the term "settler" to Blacks, and, as Tiffany Lethabo King points out, Trask "created opportunities to think about conquest and colonialism as fundamentally constituted by slavery as much as they were constituted by genocide."[37] Eve Tuck, Allison Guess, and Hannah Sultan further tease out the complexity of the term "arrivant" by pointing out that while it can help to highlight the complicity of all arrivants (including Black people) in the processes of settler colonialism, the term also conflates people of color in a way that can also erase the unique positionalities of Blacks under settler colonialism and the participation of people of color in anti-Black racism.[38] And that still brings us back to the question of our responsibilities to the lands where we live, whether we identify as settlers, arrivants, or otherwise.

As I see it, being a settler ally means an opposition to all forms of oppression mobilized by the occupying or settler state, whether anti-Black racism, racism against migrants, heteronormativity and heteropatriarchy, anti-trans discrimination, Islamophobia, or what Rob Nixon refers to as the "slow violence" of the environmentalism of the poor.[39] While different non-Native groups are mobilized under the operations of settler colonial capital, the United States—as a capitalist state, the occupying state, the settler state, the racial state, the carceral state, and the late liberal state and its heteronormative imaginary—takes on the multiple, overdetermined forms that compose the matrix of state power and assaults all who represent difference. I argue that considering relationalities under the conditions of settler colonialism requires our expansiveness in articulating the *simultaneity of overlapping positionalities*. We are always already simultaneously positioned, as both subjugated by settler state power and as settlers who often unwittingly support the state, and that's the kind of complexity I see Evyn Lê Espiritu Gandhi pointing out in her work: the simultaneity of "refugee settlers."[40]

While I will refer to the political status of Hawai'i as one of occupation, I call myself a Japanese settler ally or a settler aloha 'āina because I argue that these terms have their own capaciousness, one that grapples with settler colonialism and cultivates the seeds of a decolonial future. The descriptor "settler" roots us in the settler colonialism that we seek to dismantle so that we never lose sight of those conditions or the privileges we derive from them. At the same time, however, the term "settler ally" encompasses the *imaginative possibilities* for our collaborative work on ea and a land-based lāhui.

In 2012, Noelani Goodyear-Ka'ōpua and I had a conversation about the possibilities of the term "settler aloha 'āina," and she writes about the importance of settler allies who exercise settler kuleana (responsibilities, rights, privileges, purview) given to them but who do not lose sight of their settler privileges: "Perhaps, such a positioning might be thought of as a settler aloha 'āina practice or kuleana. A settler aloha 'āina can take responsibility for and develop attachment to lands upon which they reside when actively supporting Kānaka Maoli who have been alienated from ancestral lands to reestablish those connections and also helping to rebuild Indigenous structures that allow for the transformation of settler-colonial relations."[41] The term "settler aloha 'āina" recognizes that our work encompasses, and yet is about more than, being an ally; our work focuses on materializing decolonization itself.

This is why I call myself a Japanese settler aloha ʻāina: because being a settler and being an aloha ʻāina are not mutually exclusive; instead, we can break the category of settler wide open by taking our places on the front lines of movements for deoccupation and decolonization. When 65 percent of the Hawaiʻi State Legislature is constituted by Asian settlers who are making harmful decisions that undermine Kanaka Maoli traditional and customary practices and environmental protections, we have to recognize the millennia of mālama ʻāina (caring for the land) that enabled Kānaka to identify the laws of the elements.[42] We need to help shoulder the kaumaha (weight, burden, grief) of settler colonialism by doing the difficult work that Indigenous people do against and beyond the settler state. While we are watching and learning, catching up on generations of teachings, we must also step in, i kū maumau, i kū huluhulu, i ka lanawao (stand together, haul with all your might, under the mighty trees), and help to carry that tree to build the canoe.[43] More settler aloha ʻāina can take our places in toxic juridical state spaces, testifying against the ways that the occupying state breaks its own laws and standing on the front lines against law enforcement officers armed with tear gas. And more settler aloha ʻāina can help to grow the foundation for the lāhui by helping streams to flow once again so that the kalo can ripen and the fish can spawn, while supporting a form of Kanaka Maoli governance that will sustain us past the ruins of capital.

The challenge for us as settler aloha ʻāina is to recognize that we are all born of these lands and to love them, to act according to the laws of the akua while also recognizing the genealogical relationships to land that Kānaka have and that we do not. For me, it's loving the people I call ʻAnakē (Aunty) and ʻAnakala (Uncle), who are Kānaka and who are not related to me genealogically, and loving their kūpuna, knowing that there is one foundation of this earth and that my ancestral lands in Kumamoto, Fukushima, and Niigata are of that same foundation with these lands in Hawaiʻi. As the corporate agents of the Daiichi Nuclear Power Plant in my own ancestral lands announce that they will release unimaginable tons of wastewater contaminated with a radioactive isotope of hydrogen into the Pacific in ways that will enter into our flesh and bone in Hawaiʻi, I care for the lands, seas, and skies in Hawaiʻi, knowing that our efforts are necessary to healing the devastation caused by events elsewhere and that these regenerative effects will reach beyond in ways I cannot know. For all of these reasons, I love these lands without having to claim them, and I stand for them because they sustain me and my children.

Kimmerer contrasts the dangers of claiming to be "indigenous to place" with the necessity of becoming "naturalized to place":

> Immigrants cannot by definition be indigenous. *Indigenous* is a birth-right word. No amount of time or caring changes history or substitutes for soul-deep fusion with the land. . . . But if people do not feel "indigenous," can they nevertheless enter into the deeper reciprocity that renews the world? . . .
>
> Being naturalized to place means to live as if this is the land that feeds you, as if these are the streams from which you drink, that build your body and fill your spirit. To become naturalized is to know that your ancestors lie in this ground. Here you will give your gifts and meet your responsibilities. To become naturalized is to live as if your children's future matters, to take care of the land as if our lives and the lives of all our relatives depend on it. Because they do.[44]

Naturalization can pose potential problems as well, but Kimmerer is addressing the urgency of the ways that settlers, too, must grow this greater sense of reciprocity. Eighth-generation kalo farmer Jerry Konanui explains that we have to "wehe ourselves," open ourselves up to Kanaka Maoli ancestral knowledges and the wonder of what cannot be rationalized away.[45] As settler aloha ʻāina we can wehe ourselves to love the land, even as we are learning the way to best enact practices that are reciprocal. While part of our kuleana is to play a supportive role, that should not prevent us from actively challenging the occupying state or standing against law enforcement. And there are many settler aloha ʻāina and aloha ʻāina who are not Kānaka Maoli who have taken on this kuleana, including longtime and more recent activists Gwen Kim, Butch DeTroye, Dean Saranillio, Setsu Okubo, Cody Nemet Tuavaiti, Barbara Altemus, Imani Altemus-Williams, Kim Compoc, Jim Albertini, Joni Bagood, Gino D'Angelo McIntyre, Tēvita Kaʻili, Deborah Ward, Marion Kelly, Sylvia Thompson, Ben Manuel, Ronald Fujiyoshi, Ken Lawson, John Witeck, Mary Choy, Steven Takayama, Ed Greevy, Innocenta Sound-Kikku, Kyle Kajihiro, and many others.

A CRITICAL SETTLER CARTOGRAPHIC METHOD

To engage in the practices of critical settler cartography, I argue that being a settler aloha ʻāina is to grow an intimacy with land that brings about more pono (just, balanced, and generationally secure) arrangements of life. It is to open ourselves up to a different consciousness by which we receive land-based knowledge and by which we pass it on. I am slowly learning the beautiful intricacies and profound depth of ʻōlelo Hawaiʻi, to learn to think and write in Kanaka Maoli metaphors, to attend to the embodied theories that emerge organically from communities of practitioners. To walk these lands with the ʻAnakē and ʻAnakala who remember what their kūpuna saw and how they named places. To feel my hands blister and back ache from clearing the land of knotted hau thickets covering ancient loʻi kalo. To stand as a kiaʻi mauna (mountain protector) in a barricade of women against state police on Mauna a Wākea. To wade through thousands of pages of environmental impact statements and legislative bills. To feel my skin break out in rashes and hives in bodily responses to these documents. To feel my heart ache when University of Hawaiʻi attorneys attempt to discredit the kūpuna. To testify in support of Kanaka Maoli ancestral knowledges in juridical contexts. And to chant "E iho ana o luna, e piʻi ana o lalo" (What is above shall be brought down, what is below shall rise up) in unison from our jail cells, the voices of Kānaka Maoli and settler aloha ʻāina ringing across the halls when we are arrested for standing for the land. As a settler aloha ʻāina, I also join in the protocols of the lāhui. I give my aloha to the akua and the ʻāina by offering the hoʻokupu of my breath in pule (prayer), my body on workdays in loʻi kalo or at the loko iʻa, and the Kanikoʻo rains of my home in Heʻeia Uli whom I collect for the ahu of other places. All these practices honor and love the kūpuna who are not mine genealogically but are the kūpuna of this place where I live.

And I share in the joy, too, of these decolonial practices of growing ea and of striving to be in alignment with the akua. Kumu hula Pua Case reminds us that the mele "Mālana mai Kaʻū" teaches us, "Ohohia i ka hana ʻana aku e," we rejoice in the work, we move ourselves to the decolonial joy of standing together for the sacred mountain, Mauna a Wākea. Puaʻs words have inspired us with a profound sense of how much it is an honor to stand for the akua with other aloha ʻāina, as she tells us, "How I stand will not be shaped by who I stand against, but instead by who I stand for, and who I stand with."[46] This is the decolonial joy that we will pass on to our children so that our work will be intergenerational. Mapping abundance enables us to experience moments of wonder, even in the difficult work we do, and we grow the desire to return to this work again and again.

The critical settler cartography I engage in throughout this book is a methodology that is structured as a doubled praxis. Critical settler cartography first exposes the grandiose claims, contradictions, erasures, and ideological interests that drive settler colonial cartography. As I practice it in this book, that work begins with critiquing the toxic logics and imaginaries of late liberal settler colonial cartography. Exposing the political interests of settler colonial cartography is the foundation of our work to fulfill our kuleana as settler aloha ʻāina who stand against the occupying state. We can make use of our own personal areas of expertise and fluency in state logics to dismantle their regimes of rhetoric and their exploitative material practices. These settler colonial cartographies also present the evidence that leads to their undoing, palimpsests of what they seek to erase, enabling us to unlock interlocking systems of power.

The second part of a critical settler cartographic method is to move the critique into the expansiveness of Kanaka Maoli cartographies that map familial relationality among humans, lands, and elemental forms, plant and animal ʻohana (family). As Renee Pualani Louis notes, "Kanaka Hawaiʻi cartographic practices are a compilation of intimate, interactive, and integrative processes that expresses Kanaka Hawaiʻi spatial realities through specific perspectives, protocols, and performances. It is distinctive from Western cartographic practices in that Kanaka Hawaiʻi recognize the forces of nature and other metaphysical elements as fundamental spatial relationships."[47] Kanaka Maoli cartographies of ʻiʻini (desire) and leʻa (pleasure) trace these lands with great tenderness and profound aloha ʻāina, planting this love for land, seas, and skies in those not from these places so that we will grow to care about their flourishing. Rather than reproducing the settler imaginary in the rhetorical abstractions and figures of the occupying state, we can learn how to think in ʻōlelo Hawaiʻi (Hawaiian language). Katrina-Ann R. Kapāʻanaokalāokeola Nākoa Oliveira describes the sensuality of Kanaka geographies as intensely physical and personal modes of relating to place, time, ancestry, and history. She argues that such a sensual knowledge of ʻāina grows out of five "sense abilities" and goes beyond them to include the "sense ability of naʻau [guts, mind, heart, seat of knowledge, or visceral core]," the intuitive, visceral responses to supernatural phenomena that deny "rational" explanation; the "sensibility of kulāiwi," a rootedness to the place of one's ancestry where the bones of the kūpuna reside; the "sense ability of au ʻāpaʻapaʻa," life according to ancestral time, measured in the lunar cycles, the seasonal cycles, and the life cycles of the earth; and the "sense ability of moʻo," the culmination of knowledge gained over generations in moʻokūʻauhau, a genealogical line remembering the lessons of ancestors and the ordering of space and time.[48]

This doubled praxis is inspired by an argument that Mishuana Goeman has made regarding the recovery of Indigenous lands through mapping. As a cautionary point, she reminds us that "(re)mapping is not just about regaining that which was lost and returning to an original and pure point in history, but instead understanding the processes that have defined our current spatialities in order to sustain vibrant Native futures."[49] By deconstructing settler colonial logics, I foreground the ways that there are both precolonial and anticolonial forms of Kanaka Maoli cartography, and our understanding of both is necessary for abundant futurities.

MOʻOʻĀINA AS A KANAKA MAOLI CARTOGRAPHIC METHOD

The image of the moʻo procession helps us to envision relational Kanaka Maoli cartographies in a key concept: "moʻoʻāina." The word "moʻo," used to reference land, had surfaced repeatedly in my research on 1851 Land Commission Awards, and I began to see how it provides a powerful challenge to settler colonial mathematics of subdivision as well as the representation of land as nonlife in capitalist economies. Moʻoʻāina are the smaller land divisions that are part of a larger land base, genealogically connected to one another across ahupuaʻa, as the long iwikuamoʻo (backbone) formed by the moʻo akua in Moʻoinaneaʻs genealogical line. What is deeply telling and beautiful about maps of moʻoʻāina is that they are defined by their relationality with that which lies on their edges, borders that are not boundaries of separation but seams of relationality. Tracing these relationalities becomes a method of grasping the integrity of land, the ways that the shapes of moʻoʻāina are defined by the rising and the setting of the sun, their locations in relation to the seas and the mountains, their relationality to larger ʻiliʻāina land divisions on their borders. Moʻoʻāina also teach us about the ways that elemental forms are shaped by the specific topography of each ahupuaʻa. Makanilua (Two winds, echoing with the word lua, the art of hand-to-hand fighting) is an ʻiliʻāina enclosed on two sides by low ridges of hills in Waiāhole where the Kiliua wind of Waikāne wrestles with the winds of Waiāhole. Keaomelemele is the golden cloud that gathers in the sea spray of Puaʻena, blown by the Moaʻe northeasterly trade winds across the face of the setting sun in Waialua that outlines the cloud in gold, and then is carried to her home in the cloud forest at the summit of Puʻu Kaʻala. They remind us, too, that landforms are often ʻohana (family) to each other, ecological continuities remembered through genealogy.

My focus on moʻoʻāina builds on the work being done on the larger ahupuaʻa land division, foregrounding the ways that smaller landforms are related to one another not only within a single ahupuaʻa but also across ahupuaʻa. Kamanamaikalani Beamer and Lorenz Gonschor define ahupuaʻa

FIGURE I.1 Hawaiian Studies Institute, *O'ahu: Pre-Māhele Moku and Ahupua'a*, Kamehameha Schools, 1987.

as "a culturally appropriate ecologically aligned and place specific unit with access to diverse resources" (see figure I.1).[50] Beamer and Ka'eo Duarte have further illustrated that the ahupua'a were mapped by early Kanaka Maoli surveyors in efforts to secure the international recognition of Hawai'i as an independent nation-state and to retain Kanaka Maoli control over lands.[51] S. P. Kalama's *Hawai'i Nei* (1839) map is a monumental document that named and color-coded the ahupua'a of each island, preserving a complex system of Kanaka Maoli knowledge that continues to be used in mapping lands today.

As children in Hawai'i, we are taught the ecological continuities of ahupua'a. The clouds water the mountaintops with rains that travel down in streams; then the Kanaka-built 'auwai carry some of the stream water to lo'i kalo (terraced taro pondfields) and then return the water from the lo'i to the stream, now enriched with the nutrients from the lo'i kalo. These enriched waters travel down to the muliwai (estuaries), where the mixing of fresh and saltwaters provides nurseries for the pua (baby fish) cultivated in the fishponds that open into the seas. Water vapor from ocean waters and aerosol particulates from wave action against the coastlines then seed new clouds to recharge the hydrological cycle.

The beauty of moʻoʻāina is that they remind us that water moves not just from the mountains to the sea but also laterally across ahupuaʻa, often in inexplicable ways. Clouds do not abide by man-made boundaries, traveling across them to water the land. They also remind us that there are intricacies in subterranean worlds that we cannot see, and moʻoʻāina enable us to think more expansively about the lateral relationality of ecosystems and the far-reaching impacts of settler colonial overdevelopment, as well as Kanaka Maoli movements for ea.

REFUSING THE OCCUPYING STATE, HONORING THE LAWS OF THE AKUA

In tracing an epistemological shift to Indigenous economies of abundance, I am also addressing the ontological turn in new materialist work that asks fruitful questions about the imagined distinctions between life and nonlife. Much of that theorizing has grown out of Jane Bennett's work on vibrant matter and her generative conclusion that we must "devise new procedures, technologies, and regimes of perception that enable us to consult nonhumans more closely, or to listen and respond more carefully to their outbreaks, objections, testimonies, and propositions."[52] The work of Bruno Latour, Mel Chen, Donna Haraway, and Kath Weston has been critical to accounting for the agency of more-than-human subjects, the earth as the distributed intentionality of all agents (human and nonhuman), the fragile divisions between the animate and inanimate, the importance of making kin in multispecies worldings, as well as the intimacies of visceral engagements and configurations of life at the molecular level.[53]

Even as these discussions challenge our conceptions of the distinction between life and nonlife, what is becoming more visible globally are the ways that regimes of settler late liberalism have used such distinctions as a tactic of control. Povinelli argues that, unlike biopower, which operates through the governance of life and the tactics of death, geontopower is "a set of discourses, affects, and tactics used in late liberalism to maintain or shape the coming relationship of the distinction between Life and Nonlife."[54] Under late liberal governance, geontopower authorizes itself with the capacity to regulate what constitutes life and nonlife and attributes to Indigenous peoples an inability to make such distinctions.[55] Yet the figurations of the "carbon imaginary," the scarred space between life and nonlife, Povinelli argues, is tenuous at best, for "the more we press on the skin of life the more unstable it feels for maintaining the concept of Life as distinct from Nonlife."[56]

I build on Povinelli's work by amplifying her argument that Indigenous people are rejecting the very regimes of geontopower. Kānaka Maoli argue that it is not state recognition that they seek, but that, instead, the akua—the elemental forms of the natural world—have laws of their own and a higher claim to authority than human forms of governance. As Kanaka Maoli and Indigenous scholars and activists elsewhere have argued, federal recognition, as it has been defined by occupying and settler states, has proven to be the very means to consolidating their political authority. On June 23, 2014, the US Department of the Interior (DOI) held the first of fifteen meetings in Hawai'i and across the United States, raising five threshold questions regarding federal and state facilitation of a federal process to recognize a Native Hawaiian government. These meetings can be understood as part of a sequence of events dating from 1993, when President Bill Clinton signed the joint resolution that is now Public Law 103-150, thereby apologizing for the US military support of the 1893 overthrow of the Hawaiian Kingdom government and calling for a "reconciliation between the United States and the Native Hawaiian people."[57] Over time, multiple revisions of what became known as the Akaka Bill left many convinced that federal recognition of Hawai'i as a domestic dependent nation under the Department of the Interior would only ensure continued US occupation.[58]

At the DOI meetings, Kānaka 'Ōiwi and their allies gave overwhelming public testimony, with a resounding "A'ole!" (No!), to a federally driven form of recognition, calling instead for an end to US occupation and the restoration of Hawai'i's independence. Maile Arvin describes the powerful way in which these testimonies quoted testimony from kūpuna in the 1890s who refused the US annexation of Hawai'i.[59] As the Movement for Aloha No ka 'Āina (MANA) summarized in a public statement, "Throughout these packed hearings we witnessed an outpouring of love and patriotism as testimony after testimony rejected the proposed rule change, rejected federal recognition and reaffirmed over and over that the Kingdom of Hawai'i still exists as a subject of international law. And it is through international law that we expect to move forward to restore justice to our people, lands, and government."[60]

This refusal articulates with other Indigenous rejections of recognition politics. Dene scholar Glen Coulthard elaborates, "I argue that instead of ushering in an era of peaceful coexistence grounded in the ideal of reciprocity or mutual recognition, the politics of recognition in its contemporary liberal form promises to reproduce the very configurations of colonialist, racist, patriarchal state power that Indigenous peoples' demands for recognition have historically sought to transcend."[61] Kanaka Maoli scholar J. Kēhaulani Kauanui further points to one irreducible condition: "The US government prohibits Native governing entities from securing international legal status as independent states."[62]

In stark contrast to the way that these hearings were actually about the settler state's demand for recognition, Leanne Betasamosake Simpson shows us how it is reciprocal recognition between people and Earth that matters for Indigenous peoples: the ways they recognize plant and animal nations, and the ways they are recognized in turn. She writes:

> Reciprocal recognition is a core Nishnaabeg practice. We greet and speak to medicinal plants before we pick medicines. We recognize animals' spirits before we engage in hunting them. Reciprocal recognition within our lives as Nishnaabeg people is ubiquitous, embedded, and inherent. Consent is also embedded into this recognition. When I make an offering and reach out to the spirit of Waawaashkesh before I begin hunting, I am asking for that being's consent or permission to harvest it. If a physical deer appears, I have their consent. If no animal presents itself to me, I do not.[63]

These acts of recognition constitute radical resurgence, a resurgence that refuses settler colonialism and instead locates Indigenous peoples in broader governing systems based on laws of the natural world that transcend human laws.

Kanaka Maoli cartography takes familial relationships with the akua, the elemental forms, as a premise, and cultural practices are grounded in chants and practices that ask the akua for their consent. There are protocols in place for asking permission to enter into a place and to gather. The elemental forms respond to these requests and recognize us through hōʻailona (signs). Sometimes the signs are elemental: a sudden rush of wind, the flick of a fish tail, a flock of nēnē flying overhead, or the mists that kolo (creep) in to hide a place from our eyes. At other times, kūpuna explain that they feel in their naʻau (seat of knowledge or visceral core) whether their actions are pono (morally right, just, balanced).[64] But to even know how to ask permission or to read hōʻailona, it is important to trace kilo practices of observation back to genealogical relationships.

Kānaka ʻŌiwi trace their origins to several genealogies, one of the most well-known of which is the Kumulipo, a mele koʻihonua (chant of creation) that traces the genealogy of Kānaka Maoli back to the emergence of life out of Pō, the deepest darkness out of which all things emerge. Out of fiery heat and the walewale (primordial slime) of Pō emerges Kumulipo (Source of life) and Pōʻele (Dark night), then the coral polyp, the shellfish, the seaweeds and the grasses, the fishes, the vines, trees and shrubs, the birds and insects, the reptiles, the animals of the sea and the land, the landforms and cliffs, and the stars hung in space. Kānaka are descended from Papahānaumoku (She who is the foundation birthing islands) and Wākea (He who is the wide expanse of the heavens), who appear in the thirteenth wā or era.[65] This genealogy also appears in "Mele Hānau no Kauikeaouli," a mele hānau (birth chant) for Kauikeaouli, Kamehameha III:

> ʻO Wākea ke kāne, ʻo Papa,
> ʻo Walinuʻu ka wahine,
> Hānau Hoʻohoku he wahine,
> Hānau Hāloa he aliʻi,
> Hānau ka mauna,
> he keiki mauna na Kea.

> Wākea was the husband, Papa,
> Walinuʻu was the wife,
> Born was Hoʻohoku, a daughter,
> Born was Hāloa, a chief,
> Born was the mountain,
> a mountain child of Kea.[66]

From their union is born a daughter, Hoʻohōkūkalani, and from the union of Wākea and Hoʻohōkūkalani is born a keiki ʻaluʻalu (premature baby) who is buried and from whose body unfurls the kalo (taro plant) named Hāloanakalaukapalili, the long rootstalk with the trembling leaf.[67] A second child is born, and he is Hāloa, the first aliʻi (chief). In this genealogy, Kānaka Maoli are genealogically descended from the land and are the younger siblings of Mauna a Wākea and the kalo. Through these genealogical connections, Kānaka grow aloha ʻāina and a responsibility to mālama ʻāina (care for) their kūpuna and elder siblings.

The range of our intimate relationships with land shifts across time and place. Sometimes the love is for a mother or grandmother, for Papa, the earth, and yet at other times aloha ʻāina is a lover's passion for a place, as Poliʻahu's cinder cones are embraced by Kūkahauʻula's pink glow at sunrise and sunset on Mauna a Wākea, or it is the tender love for a child, as the love that Protect Kahoʻolawe ʻOhana activists felt for Kahoʻolawe, an island bombed for decades by the US military for target practice. We can see desire for the land in the mele "ʻO Pāʻauʻau" by John U. Iosepa, which conveys the ʻiʻini (desire, yearning) underlying the love that the people have for the sea of Polea called Pāʻauʻau (at Puʻuloa, also known as Pearl Harbor): "Pau ʻole koʻu hoʻohihi i ka nani o Pāʻauʻau / Na wai e ʻole ka ʻiʻini ua noho a kupa i laila?" (I am endlessly entangled in desire for the beauty of Pāʻauʻau, / Who would deny the desire, those who have dwelled there until they have become intimately familiar with that place?).[68] This entanglement in desire for land is rooted in the kilo (observations) of one who has lived in a place until deeply well-versed in the expressions of the land.

I want to press against the limitations of heteronormative conceptions of desire that privilege cisgender and heteronormative imaginaries. This desire for ʻāina is a desire for lands who often embody both female and male elements. As kumu hula Pualani Kanahele Kanakaʻole teaches us, Mauna a Wākea, the sacred mountain, is both male and female.[69] For this reason, I have chosen to refer to lands with the gender fluid pronoun "they" and with the living pronoun "who." As we see in the moʻolelo of *Keaomelemele*, the desire that Hina and Kū feel for each other as a wahine (woman) and a kāne (man) seeing each other for the first time is based not on binary gender identifications but on the ways that the land has tutored them in lessons of beauty. Human physical beauty is defined by the poetic descriptions of lands: Hina is compared to "he maikai Waipio he alo lua na pali" (the elegance of Waipiʻo with its matching cliffs) and Kū is compared to "he ohia la e noho mai ana i ka malu o na lau laau o ka waokele" (an ʻōhiʻa lehua tree standing out amid the leafy shade of the forest).[70] The land is the primary referent for beauty, desire, and pleasure. These accounts of land enable what Kalaniʻōpua Young describes as a restorative condition of queerness that rearticulates "cissettler" colonialism, a queer love ethic that activates the transformation of violence and "disarms and indeed tenderizes the people to care again to wake up and act upon that intuition."[71]

LEARNING THE ARTS OF KILO TO MAXIMIZE ABUNDANCE

In Hawaiʻi, the occupying state invests minimally in climate change solutions with shortsighted goals. Instead of viewing the health of entire systems, "sustainability" models are often designed as quick fixes. As limu (seaweed) gathering practitioner Billy Kinney explains, "We should be working toward creating and sustaining systems of holistic health and productivity that aid in the revitalization of ancestral abundance, in all our communities, instead of trending on possible quick fixes that require an unrealistic amount of scaling up. Thinking you can heal mother earth with only a sustainability mindset is pulukeke."[72] What Kinney focuses on here is a broader restoration of the earth based on the reciprocity between people and the earth, including long-term relationships that are being built between practitioners of both Kanaka Maoli ancestral scientific knowledges and decolonized STEM (science, technology, engineering, and mathematics) knowledges.

Vital to understanding climate change is the Kanaka Maoli art of kilo, the intergenerational observation of elemental forms that has been recorded in story and song. Kilo is a practice of reading omens in the elements, in cloud formations, moon phases, ocean currents, politics. Practices of kilo engage in observing, forecasting, adapting, and activating ourselves to respond to climate events and their impacts on all areas of life. Papahulilani researcher Kalei Nuʻuhiwa explains, "When you kilo, when you observe closely, you are no longer afraid of the natural events that are happening in the world. You cultivate that relationship that our kūpuna had with the natural world."[73] Only when we have tracked the fine patterns of daily and seasonal changes for baseline recordings can we recognize the anomalies that are hōʻailona (signs). Kilo is not adaptation as resignation; it is an active analytic that enables us to anticipate change and to act to maximize their potentially abundant effects.

When Kanaka Maoli scientists kilo, they refuse an antagonistic framing of global climate change events; rather, they see the elemental forms as ancestors in a changing world. At a Lāhui Hawaiʻi Research Center keynote panel titled "Kāne and Kanaloa Are Coming: How Will We Receive Them? A Kanaka Talk (Take) on Climate Change," Noelani Puniwai, Kiana Frank, Oceana Puananilei Francis, Rosanna ʻAnolani Alegado, and Kealoha Fox described the rising sea level as the return of the akua Kanaloa (deity of the deep consciousness of the ocean) and the flood pulse events as the return of Kāne (deity of fresh waters and hydrological cycles).[74] In her work, Puniwai, a Hawaiian studies professor who specializes in natural resources and environmental management, explains,

> If you know your akua, if you are pili to your akua, if you have aloha for your akua and understand their functions, you will know how to work with them and how to respond to them. We, too, must change. We have to adapt to the elements. The first adaptation is that we must know who

the akua are; the akua are different on each island, and we have to know the akua of our places. When we know our akua, we can call their names and activate them and ourselves.[75]

The 400,000 akua are identified by the places where they dwell, and we are being called upon to fine-tune our kilo skills to the point at which we can distinguish their land-based characteristics from one another so that we can see for ourselves how they are related to specific atmospheric, oceanic, or reproductive convergences and cycles. The akua also interact with one another so that Kāne's freshwater presence helps to mitigate the acidification of Kanaloa, and the moʻolelo teach us about their elemental relationships with one another.

In one of the most beautiful expressions of ea, kiaʻi o Keʻehi and cultural anthropologist Kēhaulani Kupihea explains that kilo makes it possible for her to activate herself on a "kupuna vibration." In ceremony and protocol, the chanters' voices vibrate as they call out to the akua for guidance, protection, and knowledge, and when their voices align with ancestral vibrations, this becomes a catalyst for events to occur, as I discuss in chapter 5.[76] Similarly, in chapter 4, Kealoha Pisciotta describes the way that we are "brought into alignment with the akua" in order to move action.

Researchers from the Edith Kanakaʻole Foundation have designed Papakū Makawalu as a methodology for the art of kilo by categorizing and organizing the natural world. It is based on a methodical, holistic view of the Hawaiian universe and is the foundation of knowledge for understanding and becoming intimately involved with the systems of natural phenomena and their life cycles.[77] As Kanahele explains, Papakū Makawalu appears in wā ʻumikūmākolu (thirteenth era) of the Kumulipo, beginning with Palikū and Palihaʻa, the male and female ancestors of Haumea. Kanahele identifies Haumea as the ancestor who teaches Kānaka about the three houses of knowledge that comprise Papakū Makawalu: Papahulilani, Papahulihonua, and Papahānaumoku. Kanahele defines these houses in this way:

> Papahulilani is the space from above the head to where the stars sit. It is inclusive of the sun, moon, stars, planets, winds, clouds, and the measurement of the vertical and horizontal spaces of the atmosphere. It is also a class of experts who are spiritually, physically, and intellectually attuned to the space above and its relationship to the earth.
>
> Papahulihonua is inclusive of earth and ocean. It is the ongoing study of the natural earth and ocean and its development, transformation, and evolution by natural causes. It is also a class of experts who

are spiritually, physically, and intellectually attuned to this earth and its relationship to the space above and the life forms on it.

Papahānaumoku is the embryonic state of all life forces. It is the birthing cycle of all flora and fauna inclusive of man. It is the process of investigating, questioning, analyzing, and reflecting upon all things that give birth, regenerate, and procreate. It is also a class of experts who are spiritually, physically, and intellectually attuned to things born and the habitat that provides their nourishment and growth.[78]

Kanahele uses the word "attunement" to describe the intimate relationship between Kānaka and ʻāina, similar to conceptions of a kupuna vibration and an alignment with the akua. It is the pilina (connectedness) of all life-forms that governs these ecological systems.

Papakū Makawalu practitioners established Hui ʻAimalama in 2013 to revive practices of Kaulana Mahina (the planning of planting, fishing, and other practices by the lunar calendar) as a climate change tool. Organizers Kalei Nuʻuhiwa, Olani Lilly, Malia Nobrega-Olivera, and Micky Huihui focus on traditional Hawaiian educational pedagogies, and they bring together experts, practitioners, and scientists to teach Kaulana Mahina as an adaptive strategy for survival and flourishing, "to revive and enjoy the privileges of living in the season with the natural cycles of the environment, track natural occurrences around us by the lunar cycles and control the human responses to a changing climate with the intent of surviving."[79] The understanding of ʻaimalama is that kilo practices approach what appear to be the precarities of climate change and, instead, ground those changes in observable data regarding the interconnection of moon phases with the growth of plants, the spawning of fish, coral, and shellfish, the propagation of limu (seaweed), the patterns of winds, rains, and stream and ocean currents.

As much as this book honors the careful practices of kilo that are specific to each place, I do not reveal the specific locations of sacred places. I map the moʻolelo on the ground only when they are wahi pana (celebrated places) that are well-known and are noa (freed) from kapu (sacred prohibition), those that are either discussed in previous publications or that I have been given permission to share. In other cases of wahi kapu (forbidden places), I do not speak their names.

The image of the procession of moʻo forms the iwikuamoʻo (backbone) for this book, one that takes us from the moʻoʻāina lands of Waiʻanae to the lands of Moʻoinanea on Mauna a Wākea. I trace the moʻo topographies in chapter 1 to identify the Kanaka Maoli relational cartography of moʻoʻāina as itself a methodology from our recovery of the birthplace of the kupua (supernatural being) Māui in Waiʻanae, a method of tracking continuities that we can use against settler colonial mathematics of subdivision. Chapter 2 expands on the movement of moʻo across the land by considering maps in motion in huakaʻi (embodied, relational journeys) that teach us how to grow aloha ʻāina for lands in their many kino lau (bodily forms). In Waiʻanae, on an environmental justice bus tour first organized to protect the birthplace of Māui, Kanaka Maoli and critical settler cartographies map the continuities of resource extraction and industrial dumping emblematic of the larger settler colonial processes driving climate change, while foregrounding Kanaka Maoli maps of abundance used to protect these places.

Chapters 3 and 4 take us to the waters and stones of Mauna a Wākea and the stand that Kānaka Maoli and settler aloha ʻāina have taken against the construction of the proposed Thirty Meter Telescope (TMT). Chapter 3 considers the ways that the occupying state sets up rhetorical regimes to shore up "thresholds" between what it deems life and nonlife, specifically in the occupying state's denial of standing to Moʻoinanea, a reptilian water protector in the contested case hearing against the telescope. Against these degradation thresholds, Kānaka and their allies map the continuities of the waterways of Mauna a Wākea recorded in chants, songs, and the moʻolelo of Kamiki. Chapter 4 looks more closely at the life of pōhaku (stones) as ancestors who stood with eight hundred people against the TMT on June 24, 2015. In a visual illustration of the genealogical continuities of the Kumulipo, as well as of Kanaka Maoli genealogical pilina to the moon and the stars, row upon row of water protectors lined up on the mountain in ways that recall for us the procession of moʻo, spiraling their way back to the piko (the umbilicus) of Mauna a Wākea.

Chapters 5 and 6 are paired by tracing the corridor of the hau flowers that mark the footsteps of Haumea along the waterways across the Koʻolau mountains. In chapter 5, I follow the moʻo and manō (shark) movements in subterranean waterways that have enabled Kānaka to map vertically the papa (strata of the earth). As Haumea gives voice to the higher consciousness of the sovereign land, she illustrates a profound knowledge of the waterways traveled by the moʻo and the manō into the mountains. These waterways are now threatened by subterranean monsters in the theater of militarized neoliberalism in the Pacific: storage tanks filled with 187 million gallons of jet fuel one hundred feet above the aquifer. At the nearby Hoʻoulu ʻĀina and Hoʻōla

Keʻehi restoration projects, children are learning about the sovereign land and about long-term reciprocal relations. Chapter 6 maps the yellow hau flower paths of the moʻo blooming from one restoration project to another. In the continuation of the love story of Haumea and Wākea, Haumea multiplies her moʻo body forms as beautiful women who pack the plains of Kualoa to battle the army of Kumuhonua, just as the people have fought to restore Waiāhole stream waters and the Hale o Meheanu Fishpond in Heʻeia. On the cover of this book, we see how Mealaaloha Bishop maps these water struggles in the rhythms of her painting, while her son Hanalē plants kalo by the moons. The path of yellow flowers reminds us that the hau has long protected ancient kalo terraces and fishponds where regenerative effects unfold, opening up the possibilities that each ʻāina momona (fertile lands) project affords the other.

In this book, mapping abundance in Kanaka Maoli and critical settler cartographies is an embodied experience of the land on huakaʻi (physical, spiritual, and intellectual journeys), where we bear witness to the wonders of the akua. We understand mapping abundance as a sensual experience, as when Kānaka Maoli and settler aloha ʻāina stand with the Waimānalo Limu Hui to haku (braid) the deep red-brown limu manauealoa (seaweed) into lei limu that we drape around our necks and swim out to wrap around pōhaku (stones) along an ancient pāhonu (turtle enclosure). The spores from these lei limu are carried by the currents to seed new limu gardens along the coast of Waimānalo and in unexpected places we may never see. In this way, mapping abundance restores, imagines, and grows a sovereign present for an abundant planetary future.

CHAPTER ONE

MOʻOʻĀINA AS CARTOGRAPHIC METHOD

Recovering the Birthplace of Māui in Waiʻanae

In bitter irony we now sing, describe in dance, in the most beautiful poetic expressions, of wahipana that no longer exist, that have been totally destroyed by modern man. In another irony Tūtū Pele who "destroys" or eats the land, leaves in her wake cultural kīpuka, little pockets of old growth forest, untouched by fire, that become the seed bank to re-vegetate the barren lava fields which over time re-new as rich cultural habitats. Is this a lesson for us today? Are we able to leave behind us a place able to re-new itself in a healing environment?—ERIC ENOS, director and cofounder of the Cultural Learning Center at Kaʻala, testimony against the proposed Nānākuli B Composting and Solid Waste Landfill Facility (2010)

Puʻu Heleakalā in Waiʻanae rises up in massive, ridged brown columns above the kula pili, the yellow grassy plains below. When I look at it, I imagine Māui lassoing the kukuna o ka lā, the rays of the sun, his muscles straining as he struggles to break them to slow the sun's traversal across the sky. Māui sought to lengthen the days so that kalo farmers could tend to their loʻi kalo (taro pondfields) and his mother Hina could dry her kapa, cloth beaten from the bark of the wauke. The land shimmers with the heat of the sun that has teeth in Lualualei, the sun that bites my feet. Behind me winds Ulehawa Stream. As I stand looking at this great hill, the clouds pass across intensely blue skies, and the shadow in the crevice where the columns meet darkens and pulses. The ridged curves sharpen into view as the thighs of Hina and the shadow above as the maʻi that birthed Māui. In this mapping of the moʻolelo, the waters of Ulehawa appear as birth waters rushing out into the seas where Māui would later try to fish up the islands with his fishhook, Mānaiakalani.

In fall 2010, Waiʻanae communities were locked in a struggle with developers to protect the birthplace of Māui from being developed into a light industrial park. Yet as I read through the environmental impact statement prepared by the developer, Tropic Land LLC, I could not recognize Lualualei in their descriptions. Where the developer characterized the land as a "wasteland," I saw neighboring truck farms with vast green fields of Mānoa lettuce, basil, and green onions. The developer had desiccated the living land through stark line drawings paralyzed in time, two-dimensional documents that abstract, compartmentalize, and encode the intimacies of land into a "parcel" and a "project area," into lines, dots, grids, letters, and numbers, into state-regulated tax map keys, zoning codes, soil classifications, and productivity ratings. I see these conditions of cartographic depletion replicated again and again in Hawaiʻi and in other Indigenous places in the world: the corporate manufacturing of wastelands through the processes of exhausted settler colonial cartographies.

At the time, the kūpuna (elders, grandparents) from a group known as the Concerned Elders of Waiʻanae and I were poring over maps trying to locate the birthplace of the hoʻokalakupua (supernatural being) Māui on the conservation lands proposed for the industrial project at the base of Puʻu Heleakalā in Lualualei. The developer had demanded that we provide documentation of the specific location of Māui's birth, and as I made my way through the registered maps, I realized that I was not just looking for that one place but for a broader land-based principle encoded in ʻōlelo Hawaiʻi (the Hawaiian language) that conveys the idea of the integrity of land as a traditional Kanaka Maoli value. I wanted to show that places on the land could not be isolated from each other but that, instead, the entire valley must be viewed as a complex of land formations that are actually Māui's mother and sisters.

As we had witnessed over and over again, developers deployed the settler colonial mathematics of subdivision, cartographies that dismember land into smaller and smaller pieces isolated from one another, to the point where each fragment is, according the occupying state, either no longer "culturally significant" or small enough to be given a token easement. This diminishing of land is part of the larger project of the occupying state that must repeatedly, compulsively seize land through a piecemeal process precisely because it never completely captures the occupied territory, and there is always the possibility that the territory will escape its grasp. In the process, entire ecological systems become fractured, creating a devastating cycle whereby the cartographic fracturing of ecological systems actually produces wastelands.

I remembered that one of the Concerned Elders, Walterbea Aldeguer, had given a beautiful account of the ways that the kūpuna who were the kupa ʻāina, the people born from the land, had used the term "moʻo" to describe their lands. The developer had claimed that there was no water for farming on the land, but Walterbea knew that the kūpuna's reference to their land as moʻo had to have a connection to water. On one of our political bus tours of environmental injustice hotspots in Waiʻanae, she explained, "Aunty [Alice] did the research: she went into the Bureau of Conveyances and she found old documentation showing land claims that the tūtūs [grandparents] back here had to actually make for their ʻāina. And they would refer to their ʻāina as their 'moʻo.' You know, 'I have this moʻo with that many kalo ponds.' And it just brought tears to my eyes as they described their ʻāina and the water, the streams that used to run through their properties. And then you think, if there were that many loʻi, *there was plenty of water*."[1] The kūpuna's use of the word "moʻo" is striking and suggestive. The very definition of the word "moʻo" is central to Kanaka Maoli worldviews and runs counter to settler co-lonial practices of subdivision because it illustrates principles of genealogical continuity. "Moʻo" is a base word that Mary Kawena Pukui and Samuel Elbert define as, among many other things, a "lizard" or "water spirit," a "succession, series, especially a genealogical line," a "story, tradition, legend," a "narrow strip of land, smaller than an ʻili," and a "ridge, as of a mountain."[2] We can see from these definitions the origins of the word "moʻolelo" as a "succession of talk," a story that is part of a larger story, "moʻoʻāina" as a small land division that is part of a larger land base, and through "moʻokuʻauhau" (genealogy), the lines that connect kūpuna (grandparents) to moʻopuna (grandchildren). The term evokes all these things; moreover, "moʻopuna" are "grandchildren," fed by their kūpuna, both words rooted in "puna" as "spring" and also meta-phorically as a "wellspring of knowledge."[3] For the kūpuna to refer to their smaller, interconnected land divisions as moʻo, then, evokes the importance of protecting these watered lands so that there would be water, knowledge, and abundance to pass on to their grandchildren.

Moʻoʻāina also illustrate traditional practices of kālaiʻāina, or carving the land up into divisions, but these divisions were contiguous or nested one inside the other in ways that were connected to each other on the larger land base.[4] In moʻoʻāina continuities, palena (boundaries) do not diminish the meaning of places as they stand in relation to one another.

Alice's research and Walterbea's memories direct us to the deeper significance of these moʻoʻāina of Waiʻanae as beloved lands through which coursed the abundance of water that flowed down from Mauna Kaʻala.[5] Pukui, with E. S. Craighill Handy and Elizabeth Green Handy, provides an expanded definition of moʻoʻāina that is rooted in the cultivation of kalo: "Long strips of arable land within an ʻili were called moʻo (strips) or moʻo ʻāina. We judge it to be primarily associated with wet-taro planting in valley bottoms where strips of loʻi extend along the streams and ditches, although dry-taro and sweet-potato plantings were also termed moʻo. Moʻo ʻai, however, specifically refers to a strip where taro was planted; and a long row of loʻi is spoken of as moʻo kuapapa loʻi. It was the practice of planters to give individual names to their moʻoʻāina."[6] Running alongside streams and ditches, moʻoʻāina resonate with the great moʻo lizards who are water protectors, and the loving way that each moʻoʻāina is named attests to the intimate relationships that the kūpuna cultivated with the land and elemental forms around them. As cultural practitioner E. Kalani Flores explains, naming the lands and elemental forms allows Kānaka Maoli to recognize the land and invoke the land by name in ceremony. This would enable the land to respond through hōʻailona (signs), either through growing abundance or other astonishing events.[7]

Through Walterbea's words, I found what I was looking for: a wondrous moʻoʻāina map in the form of Land Commission Award 3131 claimed by Kuapuu. This map gives us a glimpse into the kūpuna's world in transition, following the 1848 Māhele that marked the privatization of land and the entry of a Kanaka Maoli system of land stewardship into a capitalist economy of private property ownership. These Land Commission Awards were recorded in volumes of *Native Testimony* and *Foreign Testimony*, and I saw that as each kupuna came forward in Waiʻanae, they mapped their moʻoʻāina, testifying to knowing the land, mapping the land in relation to other lands. And they were defined also by human relationalities as other Kānaka stepped forward as well, bearing witness to having seen and known those moʻo to be cared for by the claimant.

This chapter maps abundance in Hawaiʻi through a method of identifying Kanaka Maoli *relational* cartographies of moʻoʻāina, smaller land divisions pili (connected to) a larger land base representing the interconnectedness of land formations from mauka to makai, from the mountains to the sea, across ahupua'a, and beyond to the seas and skies. Mo'o'āina evoke the magnificent procession of mo'o that I discuss in the introduction, genealogically connected mo'o and lands that present an image of the iwikuamo'o (backbone) of the land. Mo'o'āina embody the critical concept of the integrity of land and the ways that land cannot be dismembered. The mo'o'āina stretch across the layered papa (strata) of land, and all places are connected as one land base.

These references to "mo'o" as land also mark resonant topographies of the mo'olelo of the reptilian mo'o water guardians, their genealogical continuities, and the shape of water. Mo'o'āina emerge as an organic principle of life that reminds us that distant places on the land are connected by vast networks of surface and subterranean waterways. In the epigraph to this chapter, Eric Enos describes kīpuka as oases or islands of seed banks that survive lava flows, and mo'o'āina are kīpuka of knowledge that seed a decolonial future. They provide a way of tracing through more expansive ways of knowing and mapping land.

In this chapter, I illustrate the ways that mo'o'āina as a relational cartographic method challenges cartographies of capital and their settler colonial mathematics of subdivision. To foreground this land-based economy of mo'o'āina, I consider a land struggle in Lualualei, where the largely Kanaka Maoli community mobilized people against a development project that became known as the Purple Spot, a project coded purple on maps representing the industrialization of a green agricultural district, as well as other land struggles taking place all over the islands. I return to the procession of the mo'o to track the hydrological cycles that unfold along the mo'o'āina and to show that mo'o'āina mapping has enabled the restoration of lo'i kalo at the Ka'ala Cultural Learning Center. Against the desiccating forces of capital, Kanaka Maoli practitioners are working to restore and cultivate abundance on the mo'o'āina continuities of lands and waterways.

CRITICAL SETTLER CARTOGRAPHY:
MAPPING THE MATHEMATICS OF SUBDIVISION

In this chapter, a settler mathematics of subdivision takes the form of urban spot zoning now eroding agricultural districts and, with Hawai'i's current rate of import (90 percent of our food), greatly diminishing our very capacity to feed ourselves. Developers purchase inexpensive agricultural lands that they then represent as "wastelands" incapable of sustaining life so that they can be speculatively rezoned to urban use for profit. Once one spot is rezoned, it is then used as a reference point by other developers to petition for the rezoning of adjacent lands, based on the argument that their proposed urban use is "consistent" with the "existing" uses. Urban spot zoning, in effect, makes urban creep possible and is facilitated by deeply problematic city land use ordinance laws that identify waste disposal, resource extraction, and biofuels processing facilities as "acceptable" activities for conditional use on agricultural lands.[8]

In 2009, the people's fight against urban spot zoning became iconic in the struggle against the Purple Spot. The Honolulu Department of Planning and Permitting has designated Waiʻanae as a region for a "sustainable communities plan" designed to sustain modest growth and rural character, in contrast with "development plans" for the Primary Urban Center and urban fringe areas. In past versions of the "Waiʻanae Sustainable Communities Plan," Waiʻanae communities had been adamant that urban development should not be allowed to intrude into the agricultural district and instead should be focused alongside the already existing urbanization along Farrington Highway.[9] Tropic Land LLC, however, had begun a process to petition the State of Hawaiʻi Land Use Commission for a boundary amendment to reclassify 96 acres of land from the agricultural district to the urban district for a light industrial park in Lualualei.[10] If rezoned I-1 for "limited industrial use," permitted uses would include a light industrial park—initially proposed as a trucking baseyard—light manufacturing, and processing in enclosed buildings. The director of the planning commission decided that this proposal would provide what he called "economic opportunities" for the people of Waiʻanae, and so, in an executive decision, he inserted a map in the sustainability plan that featured a purple spot representing industrialization deep in the green agricultural district of the valley (see plate 2).[11]

The proposed site, however, lies along the foot of the great hill Puʻu Heleakalā and is well known in moʻolelo as the birthplace of Māui. Māui is "he keiki āiwaiwa" (a marvelous child), whose supernatural abilities and resourcefulness showered the people with his ua (rain, gifts), which include fire, ʻawa, and longer days.[12] In Kaaia's account of Māui's attempt to join the islands, Māui and his brothers paddle out to the seas of Ulehawa, and Māui looks to his mother Hina's place at Puʻu Heleakalā to gain his bearings.[13] The brothers see a kaliu, a bailer made from a gourd curved like a woman, floating on the water, and Māui puts it in the canoe. He directs them to paddle to Pōnahakeone, and when they turn to look back, they see that the bailer has turned into a beautiful woman, Hinaakekā. When they arrive at the fishing grounds, they turn around again, only to find that the beautiful woman has disappeared. Māui then lets down his famed fishhook, Mānaiakalani. Hinaakekā grasps the hook, then approaches Unihokahi, who is identified in other moʻolelo as a one-toothed shark.[14] She tells him that she and Māui are having an argument about how many teeth he has, and she asks him to open his mouth so that she can count them. When he does so, she quickly hooks Unihokahi's mouth and tugs on the line. Māui ties the line to the back of the canoe and calls on his brothers to paddle without looking back. They paddle powerfully, and after a while they are exhausted and out of breath. Māui urges them on and grasps a paddle himself, but then, overwhelmed with curiosity, the brothers turn to look back and see the massive islands drawn up behind them, rising above the seas, and they shout out in surprise. When this happens, Mānaiakalani is loosened from the mouth of Unihokahi, and the islands drift back to their original places.

Embedded in this moʻolelo are the lessons of kilo practices regarding the kaulana mahina (moon phases). Since Hina's many manifestations include Hinaʻaikamalama (Hina who devours the moon), and Hinaikamalama (from whose food calabash the moon and stars escape to the heavens), Martha Beckwith suggests that accounts of Hina refer to the planting calendar by moon phases and the fishing calendar by the rising and setting of the stars.[15] When Māui looks to his mother Hina's place of beating kapa on Puʻu Heleakalā, he may also be looking to Hina's moon phases. There are many other considerations here, such as the time of year and the different places where the moon rises along the ridgeline of Puʻu Heleakalā. We can look to nineteenth-century historian Kepelino's words about the moons for receding tides. If Māui fished at night, the Hilo moon would give him an entire night of low tide when the land could be said to rise up from the seas.[16] By contrast, the Kūkolu and Kūpau moons were days of low tide when, as Pukui notes, "he kai pueone" references "a sea so low as to expose the sandy bottom."[17] Perhaps, as Kalei Nuʻuhiwa suggests, on such a night or day of low tides, Māui hooked the islands as the tides receded and the land was exposed, but as Māui's brothers raced against time, the high tides returned, covering over the land.[18]

The irony here is that as the developer sought to isolate the Purple Spot from the famed places in the Māui moʻolelo, that moʻolelo is *precisely* about the integrity of land and the pilina (connectedness) of each place in the pae ʻāina (archipelago). Māui is the great navigator who knew that the islands were already connected underwater in one great papa (foundation).[19] "He

Inoa o Kualii" also describes Māui baiting his fishhook Mānaiakalani with the ʻalae a Hina, the mud hen of Hina, and raising the islands by pulling up the papa, the foundation.[20] The Kumulipo, too, emphasizes that this moʻolelo of Māui is not the bringing together of land, which is already one land mass under the seas, but the joining of the ancient ocean:

Ono i ka ia na Hinaakeahi,
Ao i ka lawaia, kena Hina
E kii oe i ko makuakane,
Aia ilaila ke aho ka makau,
O Manaiakalani, o ka makau ia,
O ka lou ana o na moku e hui ka moana kahiko.[21]

Then he longed for fish for Hinaakeahi,
Learnt the art of fishing, was sent by Hinaakeahi.
Go hence to your father;
'Tis there you will find line and hook;
That is the hook, 'tis called Manaiakalani.
When the hook catches land 'twill bring the old seas together.[22]

In Liliʻuokalani's translation, the last words, "hui ka moana kahiko," focus on the joining of the ancient seas, allowing Māui, as the master navigator who travels ma ke ala moana (on the pathways of the sea) to raise the islands above the surface of the water. As Shelley Muneoka, the outreach coordinator of KĀHEA: The Hawaiian-Environmental Alliance, suggested to me, Māui is drawing together nā kai ʻewalu, the celebrated eight channels that run between the islands, into the single ocean of a time before Papahānaumoku birthed islands.[23]

As intervenors in the contested case hearing, the Concerned Elders of Waiʻanae and their KĀHEA attorney, Marti Townsend, were also aware that the urbanization of this Purple Spot would pave the way for settler colonial expansion in the form of an urban corridor cutting across Lualualei Valley. Townsend had found a proposal in the Waiʻanae Sustainable Communities Plan to build a secondary access road through Pōhākea Pass, in the mountains that rise up inland behind the Purple Spot, and Kyle Kajihiro located the same road as Project 57 in the Oahu Regional Transportation Plan 2030.[24] As Lucy Gay, one of the Elders, pointed out at an Environmental Justice in Waiʻanae Working Group meeting, the Purple Spot was actually part of a line drawn through Pōhākea: "A line on a map is never just a line. It represents the dreams and desires, the vision of the developer. So the Purple Spot isn't on the map in isolation—it's connected to the line on the map that now represents the developer's desire for a road. And when you have roads, you also have the other things that roads attract: gas stations, restaurants, housing, people. And over time, these roads become urban and industrial corridors into rural or agricultural communities."[25] The symbol of the Purple Spot took on a life of its own in community organizing, emblematizing the infrastructures of capital made possible by settler colonial urban spot zoning taking place all over the islands.

What the Tropic Land developers were ultimately proposing was the condominiumization of land, the practice of subdividing land into a condominium property regime, where parcels of the land are sold off to individual owners. Tropic Land proposed to carve up the land into forty-one lots, averaging two acres each, to be sold off piecemeal as $2 million condo units (see figure 1.1). The developers were manufacturing terra nullius, clearing the ground for their own creation narrative, a narrative about jobs in an economically depressed and underdeveloped region, a narrative about the industrial park providing "business incubators" that illustrates how settler colonial corporate interests attempt to reproduce the conditions of their own production.

Such a mathematics of subdivision recalls Kamana Beamer and Kaʻeo Duarte's arguments regarding lands in Kaimukī on Oʻahu that were overlain with numbered street names, a checkerboard gridding technique that was used in 1785 by Thomas Jefferson to subdivide public land into one-square-mile lots.[26] Such subdivisions, while presumably producing a more egalitarian division of space, also functioned to erase Indigenous knowledges of place.

These subdivision tactics are continuous with what Marx analyzed as the late fifteenth-century forcible expropriation of the agricultural population, which sharpened into the widespread practice of enclosure in sixteenth-century England and later juridical practices in the eighteenth century. Bills for the enclosure of commons were passed by Parliament as the laws by which large landowners seized the peoples' communal property as their own private property. Then, as now, accumulation by dispossession and the reduction of communal property to private property depended on the construction of wastelands, as we can see reflected in a 1785 essay titled "A Political Inquiry into the Consequences of Enclosing Waste Lands."[27] David Chang points to the continuities between these enclosure laws and the 1887 General Allotment, or Dawes Act, which divided up the common lands of American Indian tribal nations as private property and made possible the

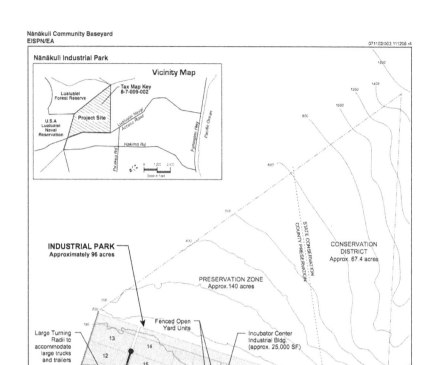

Figure 3
Site Plan
November 2008

2-4

FIGURE 1.1 Tropic Land LLC's site plan map, showing gridded condominium units. From the *Nānākuli Community Baseyard: Final Environmental Impact Statement*, April 2010. Archived at the Office of Environmental Quality Control (OEQC) Library, State Department of Health, Honolulu.

settler state's seizure of these lands through sale, defaulted mortgages, and tax forfeiture sales.[28]

Although Kanaka Maoli traditional and customary practices are accorded protections in the Hawai'i State Constitution, the agents of the occupying state deploy the mathematics of subdivision to circumvent these protections by instituting artificial boundaries that isolate traditional sites from much larger complexes. Article 12, section 7 of the Constitution states, "The State reaffirms and shall protect all rights, customarily and traditionally exercised for subsistence, cultural and religious purposes and possessed by ahupua'a tenants who are descendants of native Hawaiians who inhabited the Hawaiian Islands prior to 1778, subject to the right of the State to regulate such rights."[29] Occupying state law acknowledges that Kānaka Maoli have a unique political status in Hawai'i. The occupying state goes on to insist that Native Hawaiian rights are, as the passage continues, "subject to the right of the State to regulate such rights," but, as Native Hawaiian Legal Corporation attorney Camille Kalama points out, "The state does not have the right to regulate such rights out of existence."[30] To skirt this law, developers characterize lands proposed for urban rezoning as "wastelands," even when adjacent lands are deemed culturally significant. In the particular case of the Purple Spot, the cultural impact assessment for bordering land that features places recognized in the Māui mo'olelo is 145 pages long, while the cultural impact assessment completed for the Purple Spot was only 11 pages long, precisely because the investigator contracted by Tropic Land only recorded findings within the red property boundary lines.

In one particularly emblematic cartographic moment that encapsulates the mathematics of subdivision, the developer's attorney swept into the Land Use Commission hearing room with an orange five-gallon bucket of dirt, which he entered as Petitioner's Exhibit 67. During his cross-examination of a planner from the Hawai'i Department of Agriculture, the attorney gestured toward the bucket of dirt and asked, "Do you consider land that contains rocks of this size to be good farmland?"[31] The attorney was trying to establish that the stoniness of the land supports the conclusion in the final environmental impact statement that "agricultural activity on the property is not sustainable."[32]

This iconic moment visually enacts the sleight of rhetoric by which developers reduce land down to a bucket of dirt in an all-too-familiar allegory for a settler colonial form of mapmaking. The attorney sought to assert the *self-eviden*ce of the dirt, its capacity to represent only itself. In this moment, the attorney reduced lands to their most isolated, molecular state, to dirt held in suspension, isolated away from the histories, stories, material practices, and people of the place from which the dirt was taken. In this way, life itself is endlessly subdivided and subtracted. The mathematics of subdivision eviscerates lands, renders them devoid of meaning in the manufacturing of terra nullius, land belonging to no one, erasing twenty years of farming on the land. The dirt was instead made to represent the deficiency of "property" in its most abject state. In this way, developers map land as buckets of dirt or as core geological samples, committing forms of epistemic and material violence to the lands and the people they sustain. In the most stunning of ironies, however, the attorney chose to represent the worthlessness of the land with a stone, not knowing that in the national antiannexation song of protest, "Mele 'Ai Pōhaku" (Stone-eating song), stones are "ka 'ai kamaha'o o ka 'āina" (the astonishing food of the land) that sustains Kānaka physically and spiritually.

KANAKA MAOLI TESTIMONY ON THE FAMILIAL
RELATIONSHIPS AMONG LAND FEATURES

In his own testimony, noted Wai'anae kupuna Fred Keakaokalani Cachola explains that when developers argue for the significance of one site over another, that action violates the cultural and historical integrity of relationships between places:

> So you see, our ancestors didn't limit themselves to just one site. You cannot isolate one site and say, "That's significant; anything outside of it is not significant." I think you gotta look at the historical significance of the entire area because from the cultural context, that's what makes sense, not "Well, we can only look within the red boundaries." This is an arbitrary line, drawn by somebody. When you consider historical integrity, you cannot use these artificial boundaries to stop investigations. These boundaries were not known to our ancestors. These are western-created boundaries for political-economic purposes, not for cultural purposes. Yeah, they're all related. We all related. You cannot look at Hina's Cave as isolated—Hina's Cave is relative to the entire mountainside, to Ulehawa, to Māui and all the activities that occurred with Māui.[33]

This process illustrates that settler colonial erasures are authorized by the occupying state's land use laws, which prevent archaeologists from looking at the relationality of places in historic complexes that cross red boundary lines.

Like the procession of mo'o, the mo'o'āina lands in Lualualei are genealogically connected to one another as members of Māui's family. After interviewing the kūpuna of Lualualei and Nānākuli regarding lands seaward of the Purple Spot at the site of an earlier proposed project, the Nānākuli B Solid Waste Landfill Facility, cultural anthropologist Kēhaulani Souza Kupihea writes in the cultural impact assessment,

> Māuiakalana was born of Hina right below her cave at Ulehawa. Māui's sisters are the valleys of Lualualei and Nānākuli (Nānāikuʻulei). The body of Māui is impressed in the rocks of Puʻu Heleakalā and the ridgeline of Palikea, only viewed in the first rays of the sun or by full moon light. . . .
>
> Community members were adamant that one piece of the cultural landscape cannot be cut off from another. Each part of the landscape exists in relationship to each other, just as the *ohana* of Māui as landforms are in relation to each other: the mother is in the cave above, the son born below near the ocean, the sisters as surrounding valleys.[34]

In this beautiful testimony, the community shows us the integrity of lands as they metamorphose into the figures of Māui's mother and sisters, and we see the wonder of the land features coming to life as we imagine Hina embracing her children. Their words welcome us into their intimate vision of the vitality of that place of Māui's birth with a wonder that can begin to grow our own transformation.

The developer, however, further sought to reduce the birthplace of Māui to one small spot that could be cordoned off and built around. In his closing arguments before the Land Use Commission, the Tropic Land attorney referred to landmark Hawaiʻi Supreme Court cases to argue that the land in question in Lualualei is an "ephemeral" cultural landscape as opposed to a location for physical practices like gathering; thus, he argued, Hawaiian customary and traditional rights were not affected by the development of an industrial park:

> The Intervenors have claimed that Lualualei Valley and certain features in Lualualei Valley including Pohakea Pass, Ulehawa Stream, and Puu Heleakala played prominent roles in the moolelo of Maui. We're not disputing this at all. But we believe that the Supreme Court cases, particularly the Ka Paakai o ka Aina case, which chided the Land Use Commission for failing to consider the impact of development on customary and traditional rights of Native Hawaiians, and the PASH case which recognized the rights of Native Hawaiians to exercise traditional and customary rights over undeveloped land, both address traditional

and customary rights that are physical in nature: the right to cross over undeveloped land to get to the ocean for gathering of salt, of fish, to go fishing, to worship in mountain areas, to go and gather flowers for halau. These kinds of rights are the rights that the Supreme Court recognized. But here we have a situation where claimants are saying that the cultural landscape, which is more of an ephemeral concept, it's not something that you can go on the ground and say, "This is the exact spot that Maui was born in." Or, "This is the exact route of the path— the path to Pohakea Pass." So we're not in a position where we know that we have to set aside a certain path. And for that reason we believe that the Commission, while taking cognizance of the cultural significance of the area, cannot point to any one thing that it can set aside and say, "Petitioner, you should allow a 10-foot path along this route for gathering."[35]

Here, the attorney explicitly states his intent: to isolate a sacred place to a "10-foot path" so that development can commence around it, but, since sacred places cannot be isolated in this way, he argues that it is the *lack of specificity* that invalidates cultural practices on that land. Furthermore, he argues that a cultural landscape is an "ephemeral concept," willfully dismissing thousands of years of Kanaka Maoli practices. Ultimately, the Tropic Land attorney himself was attempting to erode the definition of what constitutes "practice," challenging the very foundation of the Hawai'i State Constitution's recognition of Native Hawaiian customary and traditional rights.[36]

As Walterbea Aldeguer responded in her testimony, however, Māui's body can be seen slumbering along the ridgeline of Pu'u Heleakalā. She explains, "The kupua Māui was not born at a street address. Look at how his body spans the whole landscape of a mountain ridge. When we are told he is born at Ulehawa, that means he was born out of the entire area of Ulehawa, which stretches from Pu'u Heleakalā to the sea."[37] As shape-shifting kupua take the form of mountains, the mo'olelo exceed beyond the attempts of developers to diminish cultural places into enclosed easements.

RECOVERING THE BIRTHPLACE OF MĀUI:
MO'O'ĀINA AS METHOD

Our work, then, was to return the dirt in the developer's bucket back to Lualualei and to recover the continuities of land obscured by purple spots, red boundary lines, and orange buckets. As Walterbea, Alice Kaholo Greenwood, and I were searching for documentation of the birthplace of Māui, we looked to their memories for guidance. Alice was a long-time activist in Waiʻanae, well known for her skilled advocacy for houseless communities.[38] As a genealogist and a descendant of the great nineteenth-century historian and educator John Papa ʻĪʻī, Alice had assembled a thick black binder with photocopies of every Land Commission Award (LCA) for Waiʻanae, which she took with her to public meetings concerning land use. Her LCA records turned out to be the key that unlocked our case.

At a meeting of the Environmental Justice in Waiʻanae Working Group, the Elders combed through Tropic Land's final environmental impact statement and saw that historian Samuel Mānaiakalani Kamakau had identified the birthplace of Māui as Ulehawa and Kaolae in the October 21, 1869, issue of the Hawaiian-language newspaper *Ke Au Okoa*.[39] First, Kamakau cites Māui's ʻUlu genealogy. From ʻUlu and Kapunuʻu descend Akalana who lived with Hinakawea, and from them, Māuiakalana.

> O Ulehawa me Kaolae ko lakou aina hanau, ma ka aoao hema o Waianae. Ke waiho la kana mau mea kuhikuhi a pau loa, a me na mea kaulana ke ana kuku a Hina, ka makau o Manaiakalani, ke kipuka helela, na kahua koi a Maui, a me na oihana a pau loa.[40]

> Ulehawa and Kaʻōlae, on the South side of Waiʻanae, Oʻahu, was their birthplace. There may be seen the things left by Māui-akalana and other famous things: the tapa-beating cave of Hina, the fishhook called Mānai-a-ka-lani, the snare for catching the sun, and the places where Māui's adzes were made and where he did his deeds.[41]

Alice then recognized the name "Kaolae" as one she had seen on an award in her binder, and she was able to identify LCA 3131 as mapping the location of Kaolae.[42] Alice explains, "What had happened was that I was doing a lot of land research, and I had the land deeds for cultural sites in Waiʻanae. Then, at a meeting, Lucy was talking about the cultural impact statement mentioning Kaolae and when she said that name, I turned around and said, 'Oh, that's the land where Māui was born at!' And I showed her the land deed I was working with. LCA 3131 was given to Kuapuu, and Kaolae is mentioned in it."[43]

Alice had made a copy of the typewritten *Native Testimony* entry that listed Kuapuu's claim to three ʻāpana (sections), and Kaolae is listed there as an ʻili ʻāina (land division larger than a moʻoʻāina) near the Ulehawa River (see figure 1.2).[44]

```
Lauhulu sworn he has seen his 2 moo lands Puniaikane and Makamai in the ili of
Leleaekoae in Waianae, Oahu - 31 patches and a pasture in 1 section.
Section 1   Mauka                Kukuilaukahuli in Punokapu ili
            Ewa                  Kukuilaukahuli and Lelekoaeiki ili    *Pg.404
            Makai                Kaaikanaka koele patch
            Waianae              Water stream
Section 2 - Uluhawa, a River.
            Mauka                Kawakea pali
            Ewa                  Kaolae ili land
            Makai                Government road
            Waianae              Puuohulu pali
Section 3 - A wauke valley toward the mountain.
            Mauka                Pali
            Ewa                  Kiilauhulu pali
            Makai                Kaole ili land
            Waianae              Pili pasture
Sections 1,2,3 to Kuapuu from Kahele at the time of Kaomi, no one objected.
Kanepaina sworn he has known in the same way as Lauhulu.
```

FIGURE 1.2 *Native Testimony* entry for Land Commission Award 3131, Government of the Hawaiian Kingdom, 1850.

Jason Jeremiah, director of the Natural and Cultural Resources Department at Kamehameha Schools, explained to us the structure of a land claim: "In general, each Land Commission Award had two to three ʻāpana. One ʻāpana was for a loʻi [taro pondfield] claim, a second one for a house lot, and sometimes a third ʻāpana was for an upland planting or resource gathering plot. In this case ʻĀpana 1 was one that featured 31 loʻi, ʻĀpana 2 was perhaps for the house lot, and ʻĀpana 3 was an upland wauke patch. Looks like only ʻĀpana 1 was awarded to him."[45] Jeremiah located LCA 3131 for us on Registered Map 2108, but ʻApana 1 with the two moʻoʻāina named Puniaikane and Makamai (Kamai) is located in Waiʻanae Valley.[46]

ʻApana 2 of LCA 3131 identifies the ʻiliʻāina of Kaolae on its ʻEwa border, the place-name "ʻEwa" designating the rising of the sun in the east. On the Waiʻanae side of the moʻoʻāina—the place-name "Waiʻanae" designating the setting of the sun in the west—stands the pyramid-shaped "Puuohulu Pali" (Cliffs of Puʻuohulu). On the Mauka side (inland toward the mountains) are the dark green "Kawakea Pali" (ka pali a Wākea, or the cliffs of Wākea, today contracted as the "Palikea" cliffs), the ridgeline that joins Puʻu Heleakalā to the Waiʻanae mountains. On the Makai (seaward) side is Government Road.

Using these guidelines, Alice and I scanned several maps until we finally found Lualualei Registered Map 2040, surveyed in 1901, where we could trace the "Government Road" that is now Farrington Highway in the ʻEwa direction (see figure 1.3).[47] We did not recognize the spelling of the name at first, but there it was—"Ka Olai"—on the map.

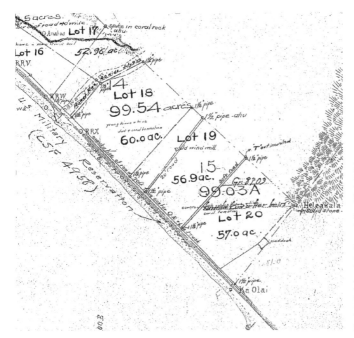

"Ka Olai" is located on the beach on the border between Nānākuli and Lualualei, at a point directly in line with "ka ʻōlae" (the promontory) of Puʻu Heleakalā pointing makai, between what are now Helelua and Haleakalā Streets.

This evidence seemed to locate the birthplace of Māui near the ocean, away from the Purple Spot, but Walterbea and Alice remembered being told that Kaolae was located inland at the location of the proposed development. The developer's demands for documentation took us back to the archival sources in the Land Conveyance Bureau. I cross-referenced the typescript of LCA 3131 with the original handwritten script in the *Foreign Testimony* volume, and I was finally able to map the entirety of Kaolae through the relationality of *two moʻoʻāina* on its borders that are not easily identified in the typescript but can be seen in the ambiguities of the looping handwritten script. Land Commission Award 3131 in volume 9 of *Foreign Testimony* presents the original map: a beautiful hand-written map from 1850 depicting Kuapuu's "mooaina" (see figure 1.4):

3131 KUAPUU CLM [CLAIMANT]

Lauhulu sworn, the land of clm consists of 2 mooainas, called Puniai-kane and Kamai in the ili Lelekoae W. O. [Waiʻanae Oʻahu] It contains 31 loi and a kula in one piece

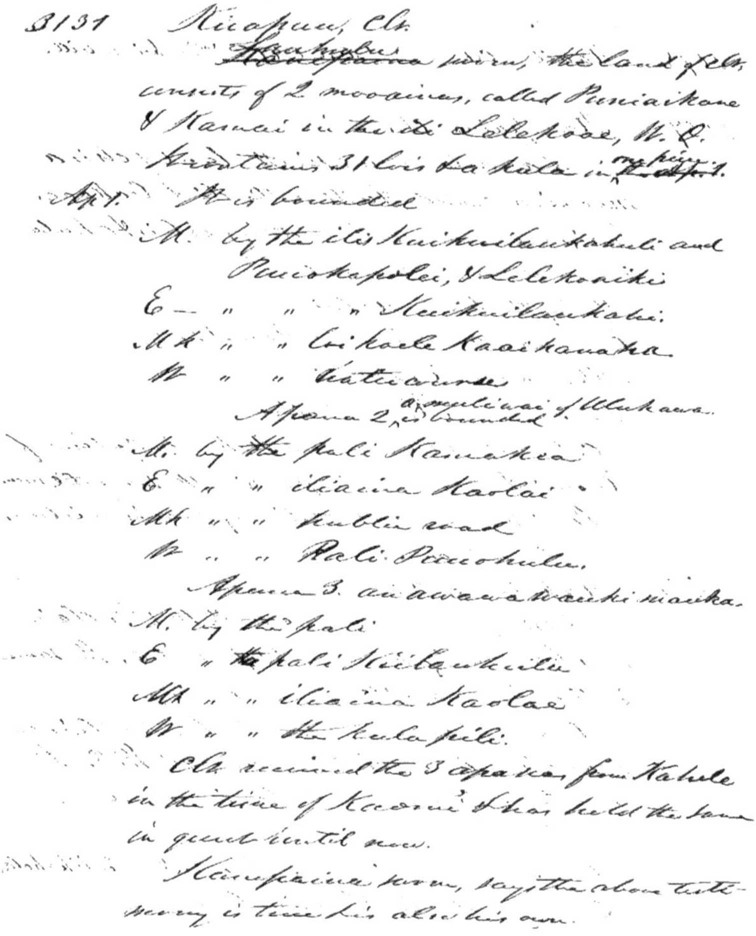

FIGURE 1.4 *Foreign Testimony* entry for Land Commission Award 3131, Government of the Hawaiian Kingdom, 1850.

Ap 1: [Apana (Section)]: It is bounded
M [Mauka]: by the ili Kuikuilaukahuli and Puuokapolei, Lelekoaiki
Mk [Makai]: " " loi koele Kaaikanaka
E [Ewa]: " " Kuikuilaukahi
W [Waialua]: " " watercourse

Ap 2: a muliwai of Uluhawa is bounded
M [Mauka]: by the pali Kawakea
E [Ewa]: " " iliaina Kaolai

Mk [Makai]: " " public road
W [Waialua]: " " Pali Puuohulu

Ap 3: an awawa wauke mauka
M [Mauka]: " " by the pali
E [Ewa]: " " pali Kiilauhulu
MK [Makai]: " " iliaina Kaolae
W [Waialua]: " " the kula pili

Claimant received the 3 apana from Kahele in the time of Kaonui and has held the same in quiet until now. Kanepaina sworn, says the above testimony is true and is also his own.

February 26, 1850.[48]

We see here both ʻĀpana 2 and "Kaolai" as we had found it on Registered Map 2040. It is, surprisingly, ʻĀpana 3 that featured "Kaolae" in handwritten script, which had been recorded as "Kaole" in the typescript. ʻĀpana 3 is a moʻo that is a well-watered "awawa wauke mauka" (inland wauke valley) abutting the pali that rises up in the back of Lualualei Valley, bordered in the ʻEwa direction by brown columns of the "pali Kiilauhulu" (cliffs of Kiilauhulu), in the Waialua direction by the fragrant "kula pili" (grassy plains), and the seaward direction by the ʻiliʻāina of Kaolae.[49] It is the combination of two moʻoʻāina in this land claim, then, that shows us the extent of Kaolae as a long ʻiliʻāina that stretches from deep in the valley along the base of Puʻu Heleakalā to the sea, from the wauke valley to the seas of Ulehawa.

Moʻoʻāina mapping in *Foreign Testimony* provides archival evidence that the Purple Spot is indeed located on the larger ʻiliʻāina of Kaolae where Māui was born, illustrating the epic dimensions of Māui's birthplace as he takes the form of a giant, his profile the ridgeline spanning the entire length of Puʻu Heleakalā itself. In this way, a more expansive moʻoʻāina understanding of the integrity of ancestral lands poses an epistemological and material challenge to the settler colonial mathematics of subdivision.

I further extend that LCA depiction of moʻoʻāina maps to a visual cartography of the genealogy of these two moʻoʻāina we had found. At the Puʻu Heleakalā Headstart Preschool in Nānākuli, the children learn of the wondrous gifts of Māuiakalana as mapped in a mural (see plate 3) painted by Joseph Momoa, father of *Game of Thrones* and *Aquaman* actor Jason Momoa. Momoa painted this mural in 1978, five years after graduating from Nānākuli High School, and it is a visual portrait of the genealogy of the land that has become etched into the community's collective consciousness. In this mural, we see Hina beating her kapa on Puʻu Heleakalā, using the wauke she gathered from the valley below on the lands of Kaolae. Hina has tucked a yellow hau flower behind her ear, plucked from the tree below, the flower beloved by the reptilian moʻo. Her son Māui is born at the foot of Puʻu Heleakalā. The birthwaters of Ulehawa stream down to the seas of Ulehawa, where Māui fishes in a canoe with his brothers. Māui gains his bearings by looking to the place where Hina is beating her kapa on Puʻu Heleakala, and then he and his brothers lower his fishhook Mānaiakalani to capture Unihokahi, to pull up the islands from the eight channels in order to join the ancient ocean. These Māui moʻolelo unfold in other murals in schools in Waiʻanae, but Momoa's mural is striking in its cartographic depiction of the moʻoʻāina continuities of the topography of Lualualei, which enables us to see places and people in relation to each other through genealogy and kinship ties.

Momoa's map traces what Katrina-Ann R. Kapāʻanaokalāokeola Nākoa Oliveira refers to as the "sense ability of au ʻāpaʻapaʻa," life according to ancestral time, which brings the past, present, and future together on one temporal plane where we see the lives of the akua (elemental forms) as indistinguishable from the lives the people.[50] Momoa explains, "I wanted to show Hina and Māui, but I also wanted to show the people of Waiʻanae who live here swimming in the waters, learning to paddle canoe. I painted things that I grew up with. These are the things that inspired me, that would have inspired others. I was inspired by the branches of the hau tree that my uncle had in his yard, and my uncle was a fisherman, so I liked the way the manini looked and decided to paint them."[51] The men paddling the canoe could be Māui and his brothers pulling up the islands or they could be young men growing up on Hakimo Road who are part of Momoa's canoe club. This collapsing of time shows how the people who continue to enact these practices can see their lives reflected in the living action of the akua and kupua, flickering between the present and time immemorial.

HYDROLOGICAL CONTINUITIES OF MOʻO,
CLOUDS, AND TOPOGRAPHY

Moʻoʻāina gives us a cartography of life, a way to map the continuities of lands joined by waterways. As the guardians of the elemental forms of water, the moʻo reflect the seductive beauty, healing properties, and often deadly currents of these bodies of water, and their presence is known through the yellowing leaves of the hau and other plant life around the edges of a pool.[52] As Marie Alohalani Brown explains, knowledge of moʻo itself is elusive. She writes, "Predominantly female, moʻo deities embody the hoʻōla (life-giving) and hoʻomake (death-dealing) properties of the element they were most associated with, water. Replicating the elusive nature of moʻo, fragments of knowledge about these reptilian water deities lurk here and there, sometimes in unexpected places, often hidden deep within our epic moʻolelo."[53] Brown's extensive, monumental study provides the genealogies of moʻo and the complexities of their natures, so here I will focus on the continuities they represent as moʻo are mapped on the land.

In her discussion of Kanaka geographies, Oliveira explains that a "moʻo sense ability" in relation to land is one that recognizes that ʻike kupuna, ancestral knowledge, flows genealogically from the kūpuna, the ancestors who are the "kū" (to stand) and "puna" (spring), to the moʻopuna, or grandchildren, who are the "moʻo" (continuous) and "puna" (spring).[54] She writes, "Moʻo is a series, a culmination of insight gained and traditions practiced by the Kanaka community. We follow in the many footsteps of our ancestors; we know because our ancestors knew. For Kānaka and other indigenous peoples, culture, the moʻo of footsteps taken by our kūpuna, is a cornerstone of our societies. Each succeeding generation builds upon our culture, creating a solid foundation for the next."[55] Moʻo sense ability traces how knowledge is accrued over generations through the observation of phenomena, and we can see how such kilo practices deepen the lessons of the procession of moʻo across multiple registers.

We can look to *Keaomelemele* to provide a broader context for both the procession of moʻo water protectors and the meaning of moʻoʻāina. As each moʻo pair lined up in the procession, they stretched across the island like moʻoʻāina land divisions, all linked by the coursing streams fed by the rains of each place they pass through. There are thousands of rain names, as Collette Leimomi Akana and Kiele Gonzalez carefully document, each rain distinct in color, duration, intensity, path, sound, scent, meaning, and effect.[56] The clouds from which the rains fell were also carefully categorized and named. Embedded in *Keaomelemele* are the hydrological lessons of kilo practices that enabled kūpuna to identify 37 distinct clouds and 405 subcategories of these clouds.[57] Keaomelemele is the golden cloud of a girl whose childhood home in the cloud islands niniu (twirls) in the wind:

> Eia mai ke kaikamahine eueu a hookalakupua o ka lewanuu, ka mea nana i lele mai e like me ke o ana o ka uwila ma ka Hikina a holo aku kona malamalama ma na welau o ka honua, ka mea nana i hehi ku i na ale o ka moana Pakipika, ka mea nona na onohi alii i hoopuni ia e na ao

polohiwa, a nona hoi ka hale e niniu mau ana i na welelau makani i ka po a me ke ao, a he Hiena hoi no ia mau la i napoo aku la.[58]

Here is the bold and magical girl of the rarified atmosphere, the one who flew here like a lightning strike in the east and whose brilliance ran to the edges of the earth, the one who treads the Pacific Ocean's billows, whose royal eyes are adorned by dark clouds and whose dwelling twirls night and day on the fringes of the wind, and who was a noble one of those days of yore.[59]

Keaomelemele flies like a lightning strike in the east, where Kānehoalani (the deity of the sun) rises and warms the ocean waters. In the mo'olelo, clouds form as they are blown by the northeasterly Moa'e trade winds into the cloud forests on the kuahiwi, the O'ahu mountaintops of Kānehoalani, Lanihuli, Paliuli, and Ka'ala. Keaomelemele's guards are the horizon clouds: Kaopuahikikakahiaka (The horizon cloud that appears in the morning), Kaopuahikiahiahi (The horizon cloud that appears in the evening), Kaopuahikiaumoe (The horizon cloud that appears late at night), Kaopuakiei (The peeping horizon cloud), Kaopuahalo (The peering horizon cloud), Kaopuakii (The leaning horizon cloud), Kaopuahele (The moving horizon cloud), Kaopuanohomai (The sitting horizon cloud), Kaopuamelemele, (The yellow horizon cloud), Kaopualani (The heavenly horizon cloud), Kalaniopua (The line of horizon clouds), Kaopuaikamakaokala (The horizon clouds before the face of the sun), and Kawelelauopua (The end of the horizon clouds).[60] Kukeaoloa (Ku of the long cloud) is set as the guard of the door of the cloud house. Mo'oinanea then designates Kaopuaola (The living horizon cloud) as the cloud she teaches to read omens. The power of clouds and the elemental force of water to erode mountains and to carve out great valleys is also told as an account of the power of Keaomelemele's chanting that splits the mountain of Konahuanui apart from Waolani, creating Nu'uanu valley.[61]

While the vision of this procession of the hauntingly beautiful mo'o marks a great historic event, the reenactment of this procession in their elemental forms can be seen on a daily basis as the clouds make their way across the land and shape-shift in alignment with the topography. The mo'o first land in Hawai'i at the northwestern lae (cape) of Pua'ena in Waialua. The sharp, salt-encrusted a'ā (lava) juts out into the deep blue waters of Waialua, and from this point, we can see across the bay the stretch of blue-green mountains rising up from Waialua to the tip of Ka'ena Point (see plate 4).

FIGURE 1.5 Clouds captured in fog drip on the lashes of fern and moss on Mauna Ka'ala, September 29, 2017. Photograph by the author.

As we stand in the 'ehu kai o Pua'ena (the sea spray of Pua'ena), we can see how sea spray particulates seed clouds.[62] Kūpuna observed the natural cycles of the sea spray and the formation of clouds that are blown by the trades directly to Mauna Ka'ala, whose multistoried cloud forests attract the ua of Kolowao, the rain described in 'ōlelo no'eau (proverbs) as accompanied by mists that creep among the trees.[63] Drops of moisture from the mist are captured as fog drip in the lashes of 'ākolea, uluhe, and kihe ferns and mosses that cling to 'ōhi'a trees (see figure 1.5). At the summit of Ka'ala, Keaomelemele and her kāne (man) Kaumaili'ulā eventually make their home.

At Pua'ena, the mo'o may have landed at the protected sandy cove of Māeaea and, from there, made their way inland to the loko wai (freshwater fishpond) of 'Uko'a, where the last mo'o in the procession, Laniwahine, now makes her home. Manu tells us,

O Laniwahine a me Alamuki, o laua na moo nana i pani mai ka huakai a ua poe moo nei, aia keia mau moo ma Waialua, a o Laniwahine, aia oia ma ke kula o Lauhulu ma ka loko o Ukoa, a no keia loko ka olelo kaulana, "Pupuhi ka i'a o Ukoa, naue ke Uki." O Alamuki hoi, aia oia ma ka uwapo nui ma kela muliwai e waiho la ma Waialua, e pili pu la me Kamooloa, a no keia huakai nui o ka moo, ua oleloia ma keia moolelo, oia ka mea i kapaia ai kela wahi o Kamooloa, a me ke Kulaokamoo ma Waialua a hiki i keia la.[64]

Laniwahine and Alamuki were at the end of the procession of lizards. These lizards dwelt in Waialua. Laniwahine remained at the plain of Lauhulu, at the pond of Ukoa. A famous saying is of this pond, "The fishes of Uko'a blow, the rushes are stirred." [Pukui's footnote: "Fishes are so numerous, that their breath stirs the rushes. M. P."][65]

An underwater tunnel is said to have given Laniwahine passage to bathe in the sea, and when the waters of the seas were rough, the waters of the fish-pond were also disturbed.[66]

The abundance of 'Uko'a is legendary, but the beautiful descriptions of the curious fish that belong to Laniwahine also illustrate how abundance is measured in the commingling of multiple lines of genealogy. Kamakau writes,

he loko ia kupanaha no nae a Ukoa aia ma ia loko na ia kupanaha, he ku-mu kekahi aoao, a he anae kekahi aoao, he weke pueo kekahi aoao he anae kekahi aoao, a he moa lawakea, a he ano nui o ka ia a i ka unaunahi ana, he onionio moelua ka onionio o ka ili maloko, a o ke ano kupanaha o na ia pela, a ua maopopo i na pulapula a pau, aia na Lahiwahine kela mau ia, a he mau ia kupono ole io no ka ai ana, aka, o ka anae o Ukuoa [sic], ua piha i ka momona, aole nae e piha mau i ka momona, aole no he ia ke hiki i kekahi manawa, a e lilo no he mea wiwi a poo laau ka ia, a i kekahi manawa e nalowale loa no ka ia, aole e ike ia, a he mea maa loa ma na loko a pau, aia no a hana ia, aia no a hoomanao ia ka poe kiai kamaaina o na loko, alaila, e piha no na loko i ka ia, a e piha no i ka momona ka ia.[67]

Uko'a was a very strange fishpond—extraordinary fishes lived there. A fish might be a *kumu* fish on one side and an *'anae* mullet, on the other; or one side might be a *weke pueo*, and the other an *'anae*; or a fish might be silver white like a white cock and when scaled the flesh might be striped and variegated inside. It was understood by all Laniwahine's descendants that these strange fish belonged to her, and that it was not right to eat them. The mullet of Uko'a were usually full of fat, but sometimes they were not—and sometimes the fish did not come at all. Sometimes they were thin, with woody heads, and sometimes they disappeared altogether. That was the customary thing in all fishponds, and then the thing to do was to do honor to (*ho'omana'o*) the *kama'aina* guardians of the ponds. Then the ponds would fill with fish, and the fish would be fat.[68]

When we look at the weke pueo, it is a fish that looks to be caught itself in an evolutionary midstream, with the silvery back of a mullet, segmented spots and stripes, and orange and yellow mottling. 'Uko'a is now a marshland choked with California grass, and the people who are restoring the adjacent loko pu'uone, Loko Ea, dream of clearing Laniwahine's home at 'Uko'a as well.

The procession may have traveled to the point where the Poamoho Stream meets the Kaukonahua Stream, all watered by Līlīlehua, the delicate, fine rain of Waialua that falls on the chilled lehua flower. The procession then made its way across the plains of Lauhulu, and then across Kamo'oloa (Long line of lizards) and Kulaokamo'o (Lizard plain), place-names on maps today.[69] The mo'olelo asks us to see the procession of mo'o akua as a connected line of water across the 'āina, a procession that travels across the ahupua'a of Pa'ala'a, across Kamananui and the area known as Kemo'o watered by the Pō'aipuni encircling rain and the Nāulu plains showering rains.[70] The streams of the Wai'anae and Ko'olau mountain ranges meet in the Kaukonahua Stream, the longest stream in the archipelago, where waters are carried along a geological erosional unconformity, the seam between the Wai'anae and Ko'olau volcanic series.[71] Proceeding along this stream, the mo'o may have walked on the 'Ewa plains along the Waikele Stream that marks the joining of 'Ewa and Wahiawā Districts.

Because these struggles for water continue today, the principle of mo'o'āina is key to cultivating an aloha 'āina understanding of the continuities of land. As readers, we, too, are swept "i ka wiliwai a ka makemake" (into the whirlpool of desire) for these places relationally described in the mo'olelo. *Keaomelemele* teaches us this decolonial desire by remembering the mo'o guardians and mapping their homes.[72] After dwelling with Kāne and the others of their family in Waolani for some time, Mo'oinanea left to make her home in the clay pits of Pu'unui at Kunawai.[73] Eventually, the mo'o spread throughout all of the islands to dwell in springs, ponds, streams, and other bodies of water across ko pae 'āina o Hawai'i (the archipelago). Starting from their home at Waolani, 'Ālewa lives below Pu'unui in upper Kapālama, and Kunawai and Koleana live at Moanalua. Kānekua'ana lives in the lochs of 'Ewa (now known as Pearl Harbor), and it is this mo'o who is said to have brought the pearl oyster to the sea of 'Ewa and to have taken it away. Maunaua lives above Līhu'e, and Pūhāwai at upper Wai'anae. Alamuki,

Kamoʻoloa, and Kemoʻo are lizards who served under Laniwahine, and they live in places in Waialua now named after them. Punahoʻolapa lives in Kahuku in a deep pool just in back of Kahipa Point. Laniloa chose to live in the pool of Kapuna at Lāʻiewai in Koʻolauloa, a source of water for the loʻi kalo there. Mokoliʻi lives at Kualoa in Koʻolaupoko where "its tail is always stirring up the sea behind it." Pākole lives at Kahuluʻu, Māʻelieli at Heʻeia Kea, Luluku at Kāneʻohe, Olomana and Kalapawai at Kailua. These are only a few of the moʻo that Manu lists on Oʻahu and on other islands. The moʻolelo reminds us that we, too, are held accountable to the elemental kānāwai (laws) protecting water, and the lands are filled with moʻo guardians who continue to watch over the waterways.

MOʻOʻĀINA MAPPING TO RESTORE
WATER TO LANDS IN WAIʻANAE

Keaomelemele, the yellow cloud lined with gold when blown gently across the setting sun, makes her home with her kāne (man) of the twilight, Kaumailiʻulā, at the summit of Mauna Kaʻala. Dwelling with them there is the lovely moʻo Kamaʻoha, who takes the form of the gray cloud-capped hill, Puʻu Kamaʻoha. It is said that there was once a freshwater fishpond on the plateau of Kaʻala called the Luakini fishpond, where fish were well-stocked for the exclusive use of the aliʻi (chief). Hoʻokala has provided oral testimony that his father often went to this freshwater fishpond for shore fish that included hīnālea (wrasse), wuwoa (perhaps uouoa, sharp-nosed mullet), mullet, and others.[74] The "ʻelemihi of Kaʻala" was a red freshwater crab also known to inhabit this fishpond.[75]

The cold waters of Kaʻala continue to feed the loʻi kalo below. The abundance of these lands was evident in 1800 when there were at least 50,000 acres in wetland kalo cultivation in Hawaiʻi and more still in dryland cultivation.[76] It was the 1893 overthrow of the Hawaiian Kingdom government, and then the subsequent US occupation of Hawaiʻi and its operations of settler colonialism that made possible the twinned seizures of land and water. By 1900, there were only 1,279 acres in kalo cultivation; today, it has shrunk to 400 acres.[77] This dramatic decline in traditional kalo farming is the visible sign of other effects of settler colonialism: introduced diseases and the population collapse of Kānaka Maoli from one million to forty thousand at the time of the 1893 overthrow, changes in land tenure from stewardship to the institution of private property in 1848, and economic shifts to capitalism and dispossession through the taxation of land.[78]

The walls of the ancient loʻi kalo, however, remain, and their locations are remembered in state registered maps that mark lands that were "Formerly in Taro." Older maps also become blueprints for the restoration of water because they map the old moʻoʻāina along waterways. These water memories are important today for kalo farmers, who are fined by the state for what the state claims are "water diversions." In places like Waiʻanae, lands that were once considered the ʻumeke or calabash that fed the island with kalo had by the 1970s become identified as economically depressed regions, and the US war on poverty led to a model cities program that funded a Waiʻanae RAP Center for youth.[79] A nonprofit organization, the ʻŌpelu Project, leased from the state 97 acres of what used to be land used by Waiʻanae Ranch for the youth to reconnect to the land.

Eric Enos, whose words open this chapter, is currently director of the Kaʻala Cultural Learning Center, and he explains that, in 1976, the young people made an amazing discovery. They realized that there was a series of 300- to 600-year-old rock wall terraces in Waiʻanae Valley, the remains of loʻi kalo on lands formerly in kalo cultivation that had since gone fallow.[80] Because the kalo pondfield complex was so extensive, they also knew that there was at one time water in abundance to feed these pondfields. The youth and Enos enlisted the help of ʻAnakala Eddie Kaanaana from Hawaiʻi Island to restore the loʻi kalo, grounding the project in ʻike kupuna of kalo cultivation practices. They found one of the old plantation flumes and piped the water back to the loʻi that they had restored. Enos, the kūpuna, and the youth were able to restore 3 acres of the 250 acres that were formerly in kalo cultivation.

Settler colonial maps are always marked in some way by persistent historical traces that can never be completely erased. These traces evoke entire histories of past abundance, the corporate theft of water, and most importantly the possibility for reclaiming water. Butch DeTroye, who helps to run Kaʻala Farms, tells me the story about the importance of a settler colonial map that helped to establish their claim to water.[81] When the young people began to pipe water from the stream to the loʻi they were restoring, the occupying state considered their pipe a "diversion of water." To refute the state's claim that they were illegally diverting water, researcher Marion Kelly found a map, Registered Map 2372 of the "Forest Reserve Waianae Valley, Waianae Kai, Oahu," drawn by surveyor M. D. Monsarrat in 1906 (figure 1.6).[82] This map locates the old "tunnels" that diverted water away from streams to the Waiʻanae Ranch. These older maps are invaluable for the marginalia that tell the story of water in Waiʻanae. This map in particular includes a 1924

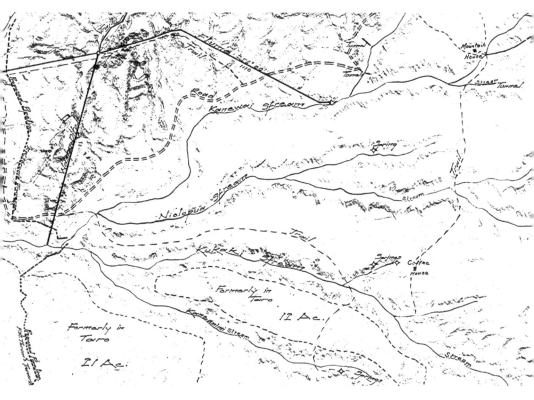

FIGURE 1.6 A 1906 map of the Waiʻanae Valley Forest Reserve by M. D. Monsarrat, Registered Map 2372. Cartographic evidence of the settler colonial theft of water, marking lands "Formerly in Taro" cultivation and water diversion "Tunnels."

notation summarizing that 289 acres were "formerly in kalo cultivation," and that there had been twenty-six "springs" and eighteen water "tunnels," providing evidence of the historical cause and effect of the diversion of water to ranches. This map proves that the kalo terraces found by Enos and the youth lie on lands that are cartographically marked "formerly in taro." The return of the water back to the loʻi kalo is a *restoration* of water, not a diversion of water.

Kapua Sproat, professor of Native Hawaiian law and environmental law, has had to remind the state repeatedly that its own water code provides for the fact that kalo farmers do not need permits to use water from streams. The code specifies, "Traditional and customary rights assured in this section, shall not be diminished or extinguished by a failure to apply for or to receive a permit under this chapter."[83] Central to these struggles to return water is the definition of "diversion," which is a Western concept oriented toward profit. Earl Kawaʻa, a Hawaiian Resource Specialist at Kamehameha Schools, has presented testimony before the State Commission on Water Resource Management to support the Duey family on Maui who had been threatened with fines for not having a permit for the structures they used to *move* water to their loʻi kalo. He explains,

> So that day, I asked the Water Commissioners, "Ua lawe nā poʻe Hawaiʻi i ka wai? Did Hawaiians divert water?" When they said they didn't know, that was the answer I was looking for. I said, "Hawaiians did not divert water. We used water." I explained that diversion is not a Hawaiian tradition. Hawaiians never diverted water. There is only discussion of "hana," of "use," not of diversion. Diversion is a Western concept. We build the ʻauwai and we move water from the river to a poʻowai to the ditch to the taro patch, and then we hoʻihoʻi i ka wai, return the water back to the stream again. That's "use," as opposed to "diversion." Diversion is what happens when you take the water, it goes somewhere, and that's translated into money, and the money goes into their pockets. Diversion means that there is no hoʻihoʻi back into the stream. All those rivers are dry.[84]

These are the definitions that kūpuna map for the settler state that must be documented to show that kalo farmers' use of water is not the same as diversions by corporate agribusinesses.

We track these waters on a huakaʻi (physical journey to feed the naʻau, one's visceral core) organized by Hui Kū Like Kākou, an aloha ʻāina network in Waiʻanae organized by Kaukaohu Wahilani, Noe Lopes, and Kapua Keliʻikoa-Kamai. Enos takes us across former cattle ranch lands to a beautiful and deceptively small spring. We trace the path of the stream that winds down from the spring and find that it feeds a loʻi bursting with green abundance. At one time, the young people of Kaʻala planted this loʻi, and it is now cared for by a lineal descendant of those lands. In the quiet, with only the faint sounds of the ʻowē nahenahe a ka wai, the soft murmur of the water flowing into the loʻi, we stand gazing at this spring-fed loʻi.

The loʻi takes us to a different time, and it reminds us that any one part of the story will not suffice; it is the continuities of the moʻoʻāina and moʻolelo that we see mapped on Papahānaumoku, she who is the foundation birthing islands. We see these moʻoʻāina continuities as we move along her contours, and the story of these reciprocal relationships continue between the moʻoʻāina and their moʻopuna descendants. That is the vision of abundance that we must recover and cultivate in this world of changing climate.

CHAPTER TWO

MAPS IN

MOTION

Mapping Wonder

in Waiʻanae on

Huakaʻi Aloha ʻĀina

As the moʻo in chapter 1 surge across the land "ma keia huakai nui a ua poe moo nei" (in the great procession of moʻo reptilian water deities), we are reminded that the practice of huakaʻi is an embodied one; we walk the land in a physical, spiritual, and intellectual journey to celebrated places in what Kūkauakahi describes as "a cultural and spiritual walk in the footsteps of our ancestors that allows us to see the land through their eyes."[1] In this way, huakaʻi is a piko (umbilical cord, junction of stem and leaf) that connects past, present, and future generations through the collapsing of temporalities (see plate 5). The moʻolelo are not just relegated to the mists of the distant past but are enacted with the brilliant clarity and wonder of ongoing phenomena, enabling those on the huakaʻi to grow aloha ʻāina, love for the land, seas, and skies that comes with the kuleana (right, responsibility, privilege) of caring for them. It is this practice of huakaʻi that enables us to seed and to grow our own intimate relationships with land, whether as descendants of the kūpuna who walked the land and passed on the moʻolelo, or as settler allies learning this intimacy so that we can grow a new aloha ʻāina consciousness of our relationship with Papahānaumoku, she who is the foundation of the earth.

As we move across the land, we see the land assume its many kino lau (bodily forms), whether terrestrial, elemental, plant, animal, or human. When we are on huakaʻi with those who are kupa ʻāina, grown from that land, their stories teach us to see the metamorphosing expressions of the land, the shifting silhouettes of ridgelines that enable the moʻolelo of time immemorial to unfold in the present as the akua (elemental forms) go about their daily lives.

In the spectacular emergence of Pele herself in the eruptions of Kīlauea in 2018, we see the land itself, alive, moving. We are reminded of the moʻolelo of Pele's union with Kamapuaʻa, the pig god who provokes Peleʻaihonua, Pele who is the lava eating the earth. After a provocative exchange of verbal insults, she pursues the handsome kupua down to the seas. As the deity runs down the sides of the crater home of Pele in his pig form, we see the greenery that are his kino lau sprouting from his every footstep, the ʻamaʻumaʻu fern, uhaloa grass, and kūkaepuaʻa grass springing up in his wake, and his final leap into the sea where he takes his kino lau as the humuhumunukunukuāpuaʻa, the pig-snouted fish.[2] Pele pours forth in her form as lava, burning the verdant vegetation and leaving kīpuka (oases of seed banks) for the regeneration of the forests in her wake, cascading into the sea in clouds of steam. We also see this moʻolelo of desire each day as the pele (lava) eats the land and the ʻōhiʻa forests, making its way to the sea, birthing new lands that are then revitalized by Kamapuaʻa's sister, the raincloud Leialoha, who waters the pāhoehoe and makes it rich for renewal by the seeds carried by the birds and blown from the kīpuka.

Kānaka observed the unfolding of these moʻolelo on the lands while traversing them on foot or paddling past them in canoes, but there are also many wondrous ways that Kānaka traveled, aided by their moʻo, animal, or plant ʻohana (family). In the moʻolelo of Lāʻieikawai, the great moʻo Kihanuilūlūmoku bears Lāʻieikawai and ʻAiwohikupua's sisters away on his tongue to dwell in the uplands of ʻŌlaʻa.[3] The sisters Lāʻieikawai and Lāʻielohelohe also have "ka mana noho iluna o ka eheu o na manu" (the mana to sit on the wings of birds).[4] In the moʻolelo of Hiʻiakaikapoliopele, Kānemilohae travels to Hawaiʻi on his cowry shell, as do Kaulanaikapōkiʻi and Kilikilipua in the moʻolelo of Keaomelemele.[5] Hiʻiaka's attendant Pāʻūopalaʻā extends her fern fronds to kolo aʻe (creep) forward, providing a shielded moving path for Hiʻiaka and Wahineʻōmaʻo so that they may travel safely through an attack by Pāʻieʻie.[6] Moʻokini traveled to Hawaiʻi on the great whale Hamumu, and the riders of Keʻehi lagoon raced across fishponds on sharks.[7]

Kānaka in motion were able to see new dimensions to lands as they assumed their various kino lau. To map the unfolding of the moʻolelo on the land, we need to be able to see the lands in their many manifestations under the shifting shadows of clouds, in the slanting afternoon light that illuminates crevices never seen before, the high sea spray mist on a windy day of rough seas that makes it possible to see the nuances between hills, the constantly, fluidly metamorphosing expressions of the land.[8] In just the right moment, under just the right light, the moʻolelo emerge. We see Wākea making love to Papa when the rain creates waterfalls down the steep slopes of the Koʻolau mountains, the peaks resembling the broad, heart-shaped leaf of the ʻape, ʻopi i ka lau, i ʻapu (folded over to form a cup for drinking water), vaginal shapes, illustrating the procreative movements of water fertilizing Papahānaumoku.

For Kānaka Maoli and settler aloha ʻāina, the work of deepening the dimensions of maps is to set those maps in motion through the third dimension of space and the fourth dimension of time. In a historic land struggle in Lualualei, a kupuna realized through kilo observation that the the birth of the kupua Māui takes place along the ridgelines of the Waiʻanae mountains every time we travel past them, as described in the fifteenth wā (era) of the Kumulipo. Kūpuna in Waiʻanae take people from all over the world on the Huakaʻi Kākoʻo no Waiʻanae Environmental Justice bus tours to show people the moving map of the Māui moʻolelo in Lualualei to plant the seeds of aloha ʻāina for Lualualei in bus riders and to move that aloha ʻāina to direct action.

In this chapter, I consider the ways that huakaʻi has become a foundational strategy in Kanaka Maoli cartography, remapping developers' wastelanding by inviting decision makers to travel across the land and experience wonder for themselves. The practice of wastelanding, as Traci Brynne Voyles has argued, is one whereby colonial epistemologies *constitute* lands through racial and spatial politics as bodies that are "pollutable."[9] Against the developer's claims, the kūpuna work on the Huakaʻi Kākoʻo no Waiʻanae bus tours to show the living nature of the moʻolelo by moving people across the land. On this tour in Lualualei, they weave together their childhood memories of growing up in Lualualei, the histories of environmental injustice, the processes of extractivism linked to the dumping of toxic waste juridically authorized by city and county ordinances and occupying state laws, as well as the continuities and vitality of the moʻolelo and community-based organizing.

Under the economies and cartographies of occupation, settler colonialism, and global capital, many people in Hawaiʻi have grown alienated from living lands, the wahi pana (celebrated places) and wahi kapu (sacred places) that have over time become commodified and urbanized. For many people, place-names in ʻōlelo Hawaiʻi (Hawaiian language) have no meaning, or places have been built over and their names changed in ways that obscure generations of kilo observations that teach us about the gifts these places were known for. Yet ʻāina never ceases being the land that feeds even when covered with concrete, and as we see a resurgence of ʻōlelo Hawaiʻi and other Kanaka Maoli forms of knowledge, we recover the moʻolelo of these lands that continue to feed us intellectually and spiritually in ways we are often not even aware of.

As the occupying state and developers represent wondrous lands as wastelands to pave the way for urban and industrial development, kūpuna and cultural practitioners are currently building a broad, widespread movement throughout the islands to mobilize moʻolelo in huakaʻi aloha ʻāina to protect wahi pana and wahi kapu from overdevelopment. On these huakaʻi, Kānaka Maoli are engaging in the traditional practice of kaʻapuni mākaʻikaʻi, sightseeing tours taken as occasions to view, remember, and teach the moʻolelo of the akua, the kupua (supernatural beings), the aliʻi (chiefs), and the people of these places. Moʻolelo are part of the radical resurgence of Kanaka Maoli ways of knowing, along with the critical decolonial effects they create as they illustrate that what the occupying state designates as wastelands are actually ʻāina momona (fat, fertile, abundant lands) and ʻāina kamahaʻo (wondrous lands). Growing aloha ʻāina has the doubled meaning of growing love for the land as well as growing the people who are the aloha ʻāina, the patriots who sustain a love for the ʻāina and the lāhui, the broad-based collective of people committed to Kanaka Maoli land-centered governance.

Political mobilizing also has its own cascading effects. As speakers on the Huakaʻi Kākoʻo no Waiʻanae environmental justice bus tours map out the conditions of occupation, settler colonialism, and racism manifested in environmental injustice hotspots in Waiʻanae, they not only educate but enlist the aid of activists from other social and political movements. Supporters are called "multipliers," who take the knowledge that they gain back to their home communities to share struggles on a broader base of support for each other. While occupying states articulate the logics of settler colonialism with other settler states, we also see decolonial and international solidarities against settler colonialism. Political tours of the West Bank show activists and educators the conditions of Israeli occupation of the Palestinian territories and the impact of Israeli apartheid policies on Palestinians.[10] Kanaka Maoli activists have traveled to Palestine and have worn keffiyah in their stand to protect Mauna a Wākea and have stood in solidarity with Palestinians when former Secretary of State John Kerry visited Honolulu in 2014.[11] Palestinians in the Boycott, Divest, and Sanction movement have traveled to stand with kia'i mauna (mountain protectors) at Mauna a Wākea and have learned about settler colonialism in Hawai'i on our bus tour in Wai'anae. My understanding of political bus tours is also shaped by my own experiences with Black Taxi tours in Belfast. In 2007, I traveled to Belfast with my friend Laura Lyons, who arranged for two Black Taxi tours for a group of Hawai'i-based scholars so that we could bear witness to the deadly historical struggles between the loyalists, who want the six counties that make up Northern Ireland to remain a part of the United Kingdom, and the Irish nationalists, republicans who believe the island should be one united, independent republic of Ireland. The taxis took us to see the murals of the paramilitary Ulster Volunteer Force and the Ulster Defense Association in the loyalist neighborhoods on Shankill Road and the republican murals commemorating the hunger strikes of Bobby Sands and other political prisoners who have sought national liberation. Similarly, on huaka'i, the kūpuna in Wai'anae are very clear about their strategy to invite others into their struggles and to ask them to take on the kuleana (responsibility, right, privilege, purview) of testifying to protect these places.

The bus tours enact the storytelling conventions in the composition of mo'olelo that take readers on huaka'i to cultivate a pilina (connectedness) with the places in the mo'olelo. The haku mo'olelo (story composer) will often intensify the wonder of one place by comparing it with another. In ku'ualoha ho'omanawanui's discussion of meiwi mo'okalaleo (traditional poetic devices), she cites Hiapo Perreira's terms "kōkua" (help, or an authorial aside) and "kīkahō kualehelehe" (an "interjection that imposes the writer's thought or further explanation") to identify the moments when the haku mo'olelo calls on the reader to recall another related incident elsewhere.[12] In some cases the narrator will stop and describe "ko'u hali'a," his or her sudden remembrance or fond recollection of another notable moment in history or mo'olelo. The two places are then bound by the wonder of the event, and the listeners, who may not be kama'āina (native-born) to the place in the mo'olelo, will be able to grow aloha 'āina for that place through other famous places they know.

The affective, emotional quality of a place is conveyed in kaona, the concealed reference to a person, thing, or place that intensifies the haku moʻolelo's narration. These connections are built on what Lilikalā Kameʻeleihiwa describes as four possible levels of kaona: (1) the face value of the story; (2) allusions to "ancient events, myths, gods, and chiefs who have become metaphors in their own right"; (3) chants and proverbs; and (4) a hidden meaning known only to the haku moʻolelo and the special members of the audience.[13] As she concludes, kaona "includes the use of place names and the symbolism attached to the names of winds, rains, plants, and rocks, evoking a certain emotional quality on many levels."

Places themselves come to define the beauty and mana of the people who sprout from the land: in Puna, it could be the fragrance of hala; in Waiʻanae, the cooling Kaiāulu breeze; in Waiāhole, the kalo paʻa (variety of hard taro) that is like the obstinate people. In this way, people themselves become portals who transport others to the places they are from. In *The Epic Tale of Hiʻiakaikapoliopele*, Hoʻoulumāhiehie describes Hiʻiaka and Kaʻanahau making love in a way that shows how a lover embodies the wonders of their birth sands:

Ua ike iho la o Hiiaka i ka nani o Kailua—ua hoopapa i ka oopu maka peke o Kawainui—ua ike kumaka i ka ui o Makalei, a ua eha Kaukaopua i ka eha lima ole a ke aloha, ke wili la i ka wili wai a ka makemake.

A o Kaanahau hoi, ka ui o Kailua, ua inu ʻo ia i ka wai koo-lihilihi o Puna—ua nowelo i ka pua lehua o Panaewa—ua ike i ka nani o Aipo—ua maeele i ke anu o Hauailiki—A pela iho la i hookoia ai na makemake elua i holo like ke kaunu i Waiolohia.[14]

Hiʻiaka came to know the splendor of Kailua, fondled the tiny-eyed ʻoʻopu fish of Kawainui, witnessed the beauty of the magical Mākālei tree, and Kaukaʻōpua was hurt by the unintended pain of love, spinning in a whirlpool of desire.

As for Kaʻanahau, the most handsome man of Kailua, he drank the droplets of Puna's own lashes, delved into the lehua blossom of Panaʻewa, experienced the glory of ʻAipō, and was numbed by the chill of Hauaʻiliki.[15]

From these brief yet deeply layered and suggestive allusions and wordplay, we are swept to Kailua and Puna and asked to envision this passionate love-making through the levels of kaona, from the physical pleasures of their union to the references to wahi pana that evoke for audiences the pleasures of recognition. The magical Mākālei tree is both the majestic image of Kaʻanahau's erect stature and the allusion to the abundance of this wondrous tree that attracts fish. The flowers of this tree fall into the water and attract the phallic fish, ka ʻoʻopu maka peke (the tiny-eyed goby) that Kawainui is well-known for. Kaʻanahau, in turn, drinks from Hiʻiaka, entranced with the fragrant hala of Puna before delving like a bird into her lehua flower. The complexity of this short passage is rooted in the names of Kaukaʻōpua, ʻAipō, and Hauaʻiliki, which take us to other moʻolelo. Kaukaʻōpua is a mountain in Hanalaei, Kauaʻi known to dwell "i ka hau o Kaukaʻōpua," the dense hau forests evoking for us the way that Hiʻiaka's body is tightly guarded by her older sister Pele's words forbidding her to sleep with a man and the pain of Hiʻiaka's initiation into love-making with a man.[16] But the hau forests of Maui were also known as secretive places for love affairs.[17] Kaʻanahau is attuned to Hiʻiaka's sense of foreboding in anticipation of Pele's wrath. Here, we see how Hiʻiaka and Kaʻanahau are each transported to the other's lands, while yet other place-names are evoked to convey complex undercurrents in the event of their union.

And this desire is not just a desire between men and women but between women and between men. In her dissertation, "(Re)membering ʻUpena of Intimacies: A Kanaka Maoli Moʻolelo Beyond Queer Theory," Jamaica Heolimeleikalani Osorio describes in the most exquisite terms the way that the lands teach us about pleasure, particularly how women learn to pleasure each other, like birds sipping nectar from lehua flowers:

> Only when we read these moʻolelo carefully, and enjoy the pleasure of these encounters, do we fully realize that ʻāina provide an opportunity for deploying kaona to mask yet celebrate sexuality and intimacy. Being intimate and pili with our ʻāina teaches us how to be intimate and pili to each other. Like Bush and Paaluhi, the composer of the famed "Manu ʻŌ'ō" [ʻŌ'ō Bird] does not choose to describe an ʻōʻō sipping the nectar from a lehua blossom because of shame, or a desire to conceal the experience of one wahine [woman] sipping the wai koʻo lihilihi from another. Rather, it was from watching our manu mūkīkī their lovers that we kānaka learned to care for, cherish, and enjoy our lovers. . . . Being raised by our ʻāina, experiencing its flourishing and loving our ʻāina, informs how we practice aloha and pleasure with each other. When we deploy kaona sexually, as when we playfully compare ourselves to manu ʻōʻō and our lovers to lehua, it would be good for us to reflect on the pilina these metaphors are

(re)membering for us kānaka today. They are lessons in love, pleasure, care, and consent.[18]

In Osorio's words, the ʻāina is our first and most enduring teacher, teaching us that aloha is not bound by settler colonial heteronormativity, that pleasure travels beyond these bounds with care and consent.

In much the same way, the peoples across the world are drawn together on the bus tour, transformed by the kūpuna's profound aloha for Lualualei. When the kūpuna on the bus tour tell the moʻolelo of Māui, they are asking the bus riders to extend their love for their homes to Lualualei through the stories of Māui, which are particularly expansive as a meeting point for people because Māui stories abound across the Pacific. Māui not only fishes up and attempts to join the islands, but as the quintessential navigator he joins all of the islands in the Pacific through teaching the people how to navigate by the stars.

I myself am not kamaʻāina, Native-born, to Waiʻanae. As a yonsei, a fourth-generation Japanese settler aloha ʻāina, I grew pili to the ʻāina of Waiʻanae, closely bound to that land, through the bus tour and the moʻolelo of Māui that I learned growing up in my childhood home on Haleakalā, Maui.[19] In 1976, my family lived in a new working-class subdivision below Pukalani Terrace. I was in the fifth grade, growing up in the midst of Kanaka Maoli activism to protect the island of Kahoʻolawe from US military bombing and stands taken by kalo farmers against urbanization in Kalama Valley and Waiāhole. I remember riding the school bus to the Eddie Tam Gym in Makawao to see a reenactment of the epic stories of Māui slowing the path of the sun over Haleakalā. Sitting cross-legged on the floor of the basketball court, we listened as Hina tells her son Māui that the days are not long enough to dry and bleach her kapa. We watched Māui standing at the summit of Haleakalā, lassoing the sun's rays, muscles straining as he pulls at the coconut husk rope to break the rays of the sun. I later imagined these stories unfolding at the summit of Haleakalā as we drove up the highway that cuts through the green fields of sugarcane that brought my Japanese great-grandparents here from Fukushima, Niigata, and Kumamoto. The sugarcane, and the circuits of global capital it represents, frames the way that moving to Pukalani was also the beginning of my own education in settler colonialism, as our family entered into the controversies over suburban development in Pukalani and the desecration of iwi kupuna, the bones of Kānaka who had lived there long before us. The moʻolelo of Māui defines who I am as a settler aloha ʻāina who grew up on Haleakalā, and it is the seed that helped me to grow aloha ʻāina for Waiʻanae and the people who live there.

It was another performance of the Māui moʻolelo that drew me into Waiʻanae land struggles. On April 26, 2010, the Kumu Kahua Theatre featured "Māui the Demigod," directed by Wil Kahele, for a fundraiser for the American Friends Service Committee (AFSC)–Hawaiʻi Chapter, a demilitarization organization led by Kyle Kajihiro and Terri Kekoʻolani. At the end of the performance, with the images and scenes from Māui's adventures still fresh in our minds, Alice Kaholo Greenwood, a descendant of the nineteenth-century historian and political leader John Papa ʻĪʻī, rose with her cane and spoke to the audience about the ongoing struggle in Lualualei Valley to protect Māui's birth sands. On this land, Tropic Land LLC had begun a process to petition the state Land Use Commission for a boundary amendment to reclassify 96 acres of land from an agricultural to an urban district for the proposed construction of a light industrial park.[20] Greenwood invited the audience to the Huakaʻi Kākoʻo no Waiʻanae Environmental Justice bus tour organized by the Concerned Elders of Waiʻanae (an organization of more than two hundred kūpuna and cultural practitioners), KĀHEA: The Hawaiian-Environmental Alliance, and the AFSC. The bus tour was designed to help people from Waiʻanae and beyond to testify at the upcoming Land Use Commission hearings, the first of which was slated for September.

The Māui stories of wonder are particularly important in Nānākuli, Lua-lualei, and other places along the Waiʻanae coast that have been depicted in the media as arid wastelands, both geographically and culturally, racialized as Hawaiian places of poverty, houselessness, substance abuse, and violence, despite the abundance grown by Waiʻanae farms and the waiwai (wealth) of Kānaka Maoli in their familial relationships and ancestral knowledges and practices. Waiʻanae is also a distinctively Hawaiian place because Hawaiian Homestead lands were established there by the occupying state, thereby moving Kānaka away from the increasingly lucrative land markets in the metropole of Honolulu and the tourism-driven economy of Waikīkī. Settler colonial regional planning has led to a proliferation of environmental injustice hotspots that have had devastating effects for Kānaka Maoli and others living in Waiʻanae who consequently suffer from the highest rates of health problems, including cancer and respiratory diseases. The Concerned Elders of Waiʻanae worked with KĀHEA program director Marti Townsend, executive director Miwa Townsend, outreach coordinator Shelley Muneoka, and media and technical administrator Lauren Muneoka to foreground Kanaka Maoli and community activism in the face of environmental injustices and to educate communities about land use laws.

Two weeks after the Kumu Kahua play, many of us board a bus together at MAʻO Organic Farms in Lualualei Valley. The KĀHEA organizers have compiled a folder with handouts entitled, "Land Use 101: How We Decide What Land Is Used for What Purposes." One handout features a breakdown of the occupying state's four land categories: "Urban," "Rural," "Agricultural," and "Conservation." The handout also lays out the tactics that developers use to recruit community buy-in for landfills on agricultural lands through community benefits packages devised to divide and overcome communities. Another handout outlines the "Principles of Environmental Justice," as adopted by the 1991 First National People of Color Environmental Leadership Summit. A fact sheet titled "'Purple Spot' Plan Threatens Oʻahu's Remaining Ag Lands" explains that in past Waiʻanae Community Sustainability Plans the community has been adamant that urban development "shall not be allowed to intrude into the Agricultural area."[21] The huakaʻi shows bus riders ways that they can participate in the struggle by signing the "Petition in Support of a Truly Sustainable Plan for the Waiʻanae Coast," urging the Honolulu City Council to adopt the version of the Waiʻanae Community Sustainability Plan update that does not feature the Purple Spot industrial zone.

The bus tour takes us along a roadmap of the Elders' activism over the years, and each of the three speakers focuses on a different facet of the struggle. Walterbea Aldeguer recounts for us the stories of her childhood and the moʻolelo of Lualualei, Alice Greenwood speaks about social justice and her advocacy for the people of Waiʻanae, and Lucy Gay describes environmental injustices and community organizing. All three of their voices move in and out of the narrative to haku (braid) together their accounts of community organizing along with their analyses of the political and corporate forces they stand against, all bound together by the wonders of the moʻolelo of Māui. As they share the traditional moʻolelo of Māui, they also weave in their own stories and histories so that we see a lei that twists together strands of the past and the present, from the actions of the kupua (supernatural beings), the akua (the elemental forms), and the people to their descendants' struggle against environmental injustices today.

As the bus travels across these lands, we see the effects of decades of settler colonialism on the very contours of the land. We turn off Farrington Highway and drive into Lualualei Valley toward the green Waiʻanae mountains. The road runs along the dry concrete channel built to contain the waters of Māʻiliʻiliʻi Stream.[22] Walterbea contrasts the bare concrete with the stream of the past, full of flashing silver schools of ʻamaʻama (juvenile mullet) (see figure 2.1). As she tells us, she grew up in the malu (shelter) of Mauna Kaʻala, which is always in the clouds:

> Why did we have so much water? Well, you have to remember that our tallest mountain on this island happens to be Kaʻala. And when I was a little girl, I always remember, every morning the mountain was always covered with clouds—rain clouds. There are streams from Māʻiliʻili, and all the way to Maipalaoa the streams would connect, and it was like a moat, and so we'd be back there playing, swimming with the baby fish, the ʻanae [mullet] and the moi [threadfish]. You had that environment where they could actually come in to spawn.
>
> So now when you go up to the mountain, what happens is that you find that the water has been capped, there's not enough water going to our streams. They put canals where we used to have marshlands. And so when you remove the water, and you start to change things, you change the ʻāina. These canals we're going to pass, they would drain the backlands and that way people could develop the land. So in place of the marsh and the main plants that used to grow in these areas, you have more kiawe [invasive algaroba] trees than you would have your wauke [paper mulberry] and your other native plants.[23]

After the Army Corps of Engineers concretized the channel to prevent flooding, the concrete itself prevented the stream from recharging the aquifer and the movement of nutrients from the soil to the muliwai (estuaries) that serve as nurseries for the pua (baby fish). The Elders tell us that their very own City and County of Honolulu compounded the problem by illegally dumping concrete into the Māʻiliʻiliʻi stream. The Elders documented the dumping in 2008, reported it to the Department of Health, and the city was fined $1.3 million.

In the larger picture, the Elders are working toward a future of stream restoration. As we look out over the concrete channels that are dry in the summer but run with water in the rainy season, Walterbea tells how this stream can be abundant again if the concrete is broken up and covered over with metal mesh that will hold the concrete in place while allowing the

FIGURE 2.1 Walterbea Aldeguer on the bus tour, Lualualei, February 21, 2015. Photograph by the author.

water to recharge the aquifer and streams to flow to the ocean to restore the muliwai.

The bus turns east, and to our right we begin to see the ways that the land is hollowed out, excavated for resource extraction, and then filled with toxic waste. Along Pa'akea Road, we stop at the limestone quarry. Pa'akea means "white hardness" and is a word used for limestone, sedimentary rock made up of the skeletal fragments of marine life, primarily corals and mollusks. In the ko'ihonua (cosmogonic genealogical chant) the Kumulipo, one of the very first ancestors is the 'uku ko'ako'a (coral polyp). The Kumulipo recounts how Pō, the deep dark night, births the male Kumulipo and the female Pō'ele, and to them, we are told, "Hanau ka Uku koakoa, hanau kana he akoakoa puka" (A coral insect was born, from which was born perforated coral).[24] The makai (seaward) portions of Lualualei were once underwater coral beds and limu (seaweed) gardens. As we look out over the white limestone quarry, we see the exposed bones of the land that are ground up and used in cement to build the hotels in Waikīkī.

Statehood and capital's increasing hunger for raw materials had its own indelible impact on Lualualei. Lucy explains that, prior to 1959 and statehood, cement was shipped in from the continent, but Henry J. Kaiser anticipated the buildup of hotels in Waikīkī after statehood and was able to acquire a permit for a quarry and cement plant (see figure 2.2). Quarries then create

FIGURE 2.2 Lucy Gay describing community strategies against corporate environmental degradation. Lualualei, February 21, 2015. Photograph courtesy of Christina Aiu.

large holes that extractive capital sees as lucrative opportunities for landfills. She explains:

> So these quarry puka [holes], they were excavated as deep as fifty or sixty feet below grade. The owner of the quarry thought it would be really wonderful if they could plug up the holes with waste, right? So he got a permit from the Department of Health and a contract with a multinational energy-generating enterprise. They would take coal that comes from Indonesia and burn it at the power plant. Then they are left with this coal bottom ash, the residue. In this ash, there's a lot of toxic stuff, including arsenic and mercury. Well, they were taking the ash by truckloads and depositing the ash in these cells that were big as

a football field. When they measured the arsenic in the ash, they found that it was at an acceptable level for an industrial park, but it was not acceptable for a residential area. So what did the Department of Health do? They raised the acceptable threshold![25]

This strategy of increasing acceptable thresholds to accommodate increasing contamination resonates with other settler colonial uses of thresholds that I discuss in chapter 3. Bottom ash itself is highly toxic and can contain, in addition to arsenic, heavy metals like lead, mercury, cadmium, chromium, and selenium. The ingestion of bottom ash can cause damage to the nervous system, cognitive defects, developmental delays, and behavioral problems, along with lung disease, heart damage, kidney disease, and gastrointestinal illnesses. As Alice points out, "The most terrible thing we found was, what had happened was, the children who live in the neighborhood would sneak in and go swimming in the cells, and they would come out all white, covered in ash. Nobody knew what it was."[26]

The waters of these turquoise storage lagoons are known to enter into the hydrological cycle. Although the Concerned Elders could not determine if the groundwater was affected, they did learn from neighboring farmers that the waters in the cells were actually connected to the sea. Lucy tells the bus riders that the quarry had given the chicken farmers permission to dump their chicken droppings into the cells, and the farmers noticed that the water levels in the cells were rising and falling with the tides. The cells had broken through to the saltwater table, and the toxic material was being leached into waters traveling through perforated limestone tunnels to the ocean. When the landowner petitioned for a permit for a landfill, the Concerned Elders were able to stop it by bringing this bottom ash issue into the public arena. Because of their investigative work, the Department of Health did not renew the landowner's permit for accepting bottom ash, and they were able to stop the quarry from being repurposed as a landfill.[27]

Moʻoʻāina as a principle reminds us that the industrial activities at landfills trigger far-reaching ripple effects. As practitioner Michael Lee explains, kūpuna knew that the flowers that fall into the streams in the mountains are carried down through the underground Karst limestone caves down to the muliwai (estuary) where the fish feed on them. Spring waters that emerge in the sea nurture limu (seaweed) gardens. Far down at the shores, toxic waste materials become a part of the food chain within such ecological continuities, causing even more harm to communities already struggling upland with the respiratory impacts of the bottom ash dust and the toxic particulates blown across residential communities from the landfills.

When we look out of our bus windows toward the dark green mountains, we see flat yellow plains behind barbed wire fence. This was once the kula pili, the grassy plains noted on the moʻoʻāina map of Māui's birthplace. The militarization that sustains US occupation and makes tourism possible spreads out across 10,000 acres in this agricultural valley. The Lualualei Naval Radio Transmitter Facility (NRTF), once the primary Department of Defense long-range transmitter installation in Hawaiʻi, occupies 1,729 acres and transmits high- and low-frequency radio signals for the navigation of Navy vessels throughout the Pacific. Nearby is the Naval Magazine Lualualei, an 8,105-acre area where 255 above-ground storage structures are capable of housing 78,000 tons of ammunition and explosives.[28]

Pūhāwai is the powerful moʻo of the sacred Pūhāwai spring located on the military base, which continues to be inaccessible to the public. In 1884, there were at least 163 loʻi (taro pondfields), in addition to dryland crops, on the plains of this land fed by Pūhāwai.[29] On June 4, 1934, Kalihi Contracting Co. was contracted by the US Navy in Lualualei Valley to build a water diversion tunnel on the north bank of Pūhāwai Stream. The Pūhāwai spring had an estimated flow of 20,000 to 60,000 gallons of water a day, and at one point 800 feet from the portal of the tunnel the water flow was 450,000 gallons of water a day.[30] In 1935, the construction plans show that a concrete plug with a valve was to be installed to water-bank the flow in the dike complex in the months when the water was not needed by the military. Since then, many of the military operations at Lualualei have downsized to a staff of thirty-five, and families have long moved away, but the waters have not been restored.

As we make our way inland on the Lualualei Naval Road, we see the ridged columns of Puʻu Heleakalā. The kūpuna direct our attention to the PVT Integrated Solid Waste Management Facility to our left. They tell us how Waiʻanae is the site of Oʻahu's only major municipal landfill (the Waimānalo Gulch Sanitary Landfill) and the only construction and demolition landfill that accepts asbestos and petroleum-contaminated materials (PVT). The ninety-foot-high mountain of trash at the PVT facility has been dubbed its own topographic feature by the community, Puʻu ʻŌpala (Trash hill). The dust created by the landfill and the adjacent cement-recycling facility gets into the schools and homes of the largely Kanaka Maoli communities of Coral Sands and Princess Kahanu Estates Homestead. Lucy, a master strategist, tells the bus riders that in 2010 PVT sought to expand its footprint, and at a community meeting hosted by the Department of Health on PVT's application, the Concerned Elders submitted their own response: they argued that if PVT's Puʻu ʻŌpala grew any higher than its ninety feet, the landfill should be mandated to grade a green belt a thousand feet wide around their landfill to protect the residents from the dust. As a result of the Elders' work and community opposition, PVT did not apply for an expansion at that time.

On the bus tour the kūpuna then turn to the possibilities of Kanaka Maoli organizing and affinity activism. They stop at the location of the Purple Spot, the lands under consideration for the proposed light industrial park. As we look out over the chain-link fence to the gently sloping expanse of waist-high green grasses and kiawe trees nestled against Puʻu Heleakalā, we see a microcosm of Hawaiʻi's history of US occupation. In 1848, at the time of the Māhele, the land in Lualualei valley was designated Crown land; after the overthrow and illegal annexation, Land Grant 4751 was sold in 1903 to H. M. Von Holt, who was associated with the provisional government, a group of thirteen settler businessmen and politicians who could only overthrow Queen Liliʻuokalani illegally and with the help of the US military.[31] This land was later purchased by Lincoln McCandless, notorious for his diversion of water from the windward side of the island to the sugar plantations on the central plains, thus drying up loʻi kalo and forcing kalo farmers from their farms. In 1967, seventeen acres on the Purple Spot were leased to Tadashi and Kazuto Araki, who farmed it until 1978.

The developer's attempts to represent the land as a wasteland are haunted by public memories of abundance and by personal archives of photographs that provide evidence of the history of abundance on the land. Alice shows us photographs in her black binder of Walterbea's family members who used to work on what was once the Araki farm. The 1968 photos show us the Araki brothers proudly holding up fat watermelons, workers standing thigh-deep in fields of leafy greens on their farm (see figure 2.3). In an interview with journalist Samson Reiny, Tadashi Araki describes with pride his famous sweet Waiʻanae onions, green onions, eggplants, bell peppers, tomatoes, lettuces, cucumbers, papaya, watermelons, and cantaloupe. He also raised hundreds of goats for milk.[32] We kept these photos of his ʻāina momona (fat and fertile land) projected on the wall of the Land Use Commission hearing room, where it was particularly effective, especially at times when the developer's attorney insisted on the unfeasibility of farming on this land.

The Arakis farmed that land from 1967 to 1978. By 1978, they had increased the acreage under cultivation by half an acre a year but were forced to leave all they had worked for when the McCandless heirs proposed to

FIGURE 2.3 Alice Kaholo Greenwood on the bus tour sharing photos she has collected in her research. Lualualei, February 21, 2015. Photograph courtesy of Christina Aiu.

increase the rent and to take a percentage of their crop yields.[33] Ryoei and Nancy Higa then moved onto the land and farmed it from 1978 to 1988. In 1988, the land was sold to Kabushiki Kaisha Oban, one of many Japanese corporations who sought to develop golf courses in Hawai'i.

Higa was given a notice of eviction, which ignited a firestorm of protest in the context of other historic cases of the eviction of farmers in places like Kalama Valley and Waiāhole-Waikāne Valleys. Wai'anae communities rallied at Higa's farm, where he told everyone, "NO CAN EAT GOLF BALLS!" In a massive community gathering, a thousand people wearing T-shirts emblazoned with Higa's words rallied at his farm. As a result, the Wai'anae Neighborhood Board voted unanimously against the golf course. Years later, in 1996, the City Planning Commission voted to rezone the land, but the developer was unable to secure city water for the golf course. The lands then lay fallow until Tropic Land LLC purchased them in 2005.

To help bus riders understand what is at stake for the kūpuna and families in this struggle, Walterbea shares a Kanaka Maoli cartography in motion that tells the story of Māui's birth along the ridgeline of Puʻu Heleakalā and Palikea. As we drive back to Farrington Highway, she tells us that although she had heard the stories of Māui since her childhood, she learned about the profile of Māui in 1998 from Fred Cachola, her former seventh-grade teacher. He shared with her the story about how he and Josiah "Black" Hoʻohuli had learned of Puʻu Heleakalā's silhouette of Māui from a night watchman at the construction site of what is now the Garden Grove townhouse complex.

Walterbea went on to discover not only Māui's profile, but the land features that replay the moʻolelo of his birth each time we travel toward Kaʻena along the coastline of Lualualei. She remembers,

> In 2009, I was reading the Kumulipo, that section pertaining to Māui, and I came across the part that told the story of Māui's hatching from the egg and his mother hearing him coo, how he became a full grown rooster, and then how his mother Hina referred to him as her brave child.
>
> So what I did was I drove from Ulehawa on Farrington Highway and followed the Kumulipo as I read. And I started to see, oh, my, it's in our landscape. Keaulumoku was the one, the haku [composer], who created this chant. And I thought, well, how wise, how knowledgeable this person was to have known that this story actually exists—the features, everything, this is in Waiʻanae still."[34]

Composed by Keaulumoku in 1700, the Kumulipo is based on ancient genealogies and was published in the Hawaiian language in 1889 by King Kalākaua. Queen Liliʻuokalani's 1897 translation of the fifteenth wā (era) of this text reads:

Hanau Maui a kamalo,
O ka Malo o Akalana i humea,
Hookauhua Hina, a keahi hanau he moa,
He huamoa ke keiki, a Hina i hookahua,

FIGURE 2.4 Māui's profile, his head to the left, as seen from Hakimo Road, Wai'anae, June 22, 2013. Photograph by the author.

Aohe hoi he moa o ka moe ana.
He moa ka ka hanau ana.[35]

Maui with a malo was born.
The malo with which Akalana girded his loins
From which Hina became pregnant, and by fire brought to life a fowl.
An egg was that child, which Hina brought forth.
Her husband was not a fowl.
Yet a chicken was brought to life.[36]

Walterbea directs our attention to the mountains that rise up at the back of Lualualei. She begins by pointing to the great dome of Pu'u Heleakalā that is an egg lying on its side. We see the land shifting, metamorphosing, and from the composite of mountain ridges, two peaks that form a beak emerge as a chick hatches from the egg. As we turn off the coast mauka toward the mountains, up into the Princess Kahanu Estates on Hawaiian Home Lands, the beak and the body shift again as Pu'u Heleakalā extends out to the Palikea ridgeline, becoming the silhouette of a beaked man with a wattle. As we continue up Hakimo Road, the silhouette finally transforms into the rugged facial planes of a handsome man (see figure 2.4).

The land, as Walterbea shows us, is a living map in motion, teaching us a different logic of movement, the continuity and fluidity that we would need to use against the static maps of capital. She explains, "One thing about Waiʻanae is we want to save our view-planes because that's where our stories are."[37] Walterbea's recovery is itself a story of wonder, drawing from the ridgeline of Puʻu Heleakalā that stands as a "kīpuka"—a seed bank of memory, as Eric Enos describes it in the epigraph to chapter 1—one that allows for a renewal of knowledge and regrowth. As Walterbea's account illustrates, Māui's profile had been forgotten by many, but the night watchman could look to the mountain and recall the memory from which the telling of the story was renewed. Walterbea's own recovery of the genealogy and birth of Māui recorded in the Kumulipo shows us how the land maps memories of these moʻolelo and ensures that the telling of these stories continues on into the present, grounding the people of Lualualei in the stories of their kulāiwi (ancestral lands).

Walterbea has also taught me nuanced lessons about the agency of lands who have their own desires. One night, after a long meeting of the Environmental Justice in Waiʻanae Working Group, Walterbea asked me, "Have you ever seen Māui under the full moon?" I had not, so we drove to Hakimo Road and looked out across the outline of Maui illuminated by the bright Akua moon. I will never forget that as we stood there together, Walterbea breathed, "Oh, look at him! He is *so* handsome, so beautiful. He is one handsome brotha, you know what I mean?"[38] I saw Māui for the first time in Walterbea's desire for the kupua, a well-built man with curling hair, a high forehead and strong brow and angular jaw. At that moment, I could see Māui through my being pili to Walterbea, my kumu (teacher) and my friend. The mana, the life force of Walterbea's breath, showed me what I would not otherwise see: Māui rising to his feet not only to ensnare the rays of the sun but to enfold a lover in his arms.

The Māui moʻolelo can be considered an example of what Cristina Bacchilega calls a "genre of wonder," one that presses against the limits and conditions of the possible. Bacchilega explores what she refers to as a "poetics and politics of wonder" that are "activist responses" and "potentially transformative. . . . I say 'potentially' because their effects depend on our reading practices, our openness to forming a different *habitus*."[39] These genres of wonder ask us to challenge the limits of our conceptions of what is possible and to deepen our imaginative capacities. It is the wonder of the Māui moʻolelo that draws us back again and again to Lualualei. It is in the moments of kamahaʻo or kupaianaha, the marvelous, strange, and wonderful, that the metes and bounds of settler colonial borders are transgressed—and by extension, the conditions of occupation and settler colonialism that are contingent on the foreclosure of possible worlds beyond them.

The moʻolelo of Māui resonate with the bus riders who see how wonder is being transformed into direct action and how Māui's resourcefulness is being enacted by the Concerned Elders today. The people themselves, like Māui, have been incredibly resourceful not only in protecting land in Waiʻanae but in offering their own gifts to future generations in Waiʻanae. The Kumulipo describes Māui's gifts with a beautiful word: they are referred to as "ua" (rain), translated by Queen Liliʻuokalani as "showers." As Mary Kawena Pukui and Samuel H. Elbert explain, "Rain was beloved as it preserved the land; it was called kāhiko o ke akua, adornment of deity."[40] The people of Waiʻanae offer here the ua of new moʻolelo, ones that tell of their transformative activism and organizing for future generations, moʻolelo that fall on the land like rain for renewed abundance.

The huakaʻi ends with a story of regeneration at MAʻO Organic Farms. MAʻO is an acronym for "Mala ʻAi ʻŌpio," which has a doubled meaning as both "the youth food garden" and "the place that grows young people." As the developer's environmental impact statement describes the soil of the land as "unsuitable for cultivation," across the valley, less than two miles away, MAʻO Organic Farms manager Kamuela Enos speaks about the fertility of the Lualualei Vertisol soils, A and B rated soils of of highest productivity according to the University of Hawaiʻi Land Study Bureau's ratings. He showed us how the surface of the gray clay soil cracks in the heat of the sun, turns over, and tills itself. The young people of Waiʻanae learn that the Lualualei Vertisol soil is among the richest soils for planting in the world, as evidenced by the abundance of fruits and vegetables MAʻO supplies to high-end restaurants, in addition to its community-supported agriculture program and the Waiʻanae Farmers' Market. Kamuela describes how MAʻO has developed a two-year Youth Leadership Training College internship program through which interns learn the ways in which kūpuna created microclimates through biodiversity, the moʻolelo of Lualualei Valley, the names of its mountains, winds, rains, and the akua associated with different places, all of which helps them to engage in farming methods rooted in an ʻŌiwi knowledge base.

In September, the bus tours inspired many to come out to the Land Use Commission hearings to testify against the boundary amendment. For five months of hearings, residents of the valley, kūpuna, cultural practitioners, farmers, environmental justice activists, demilitarization activists, young people interning at the nearby MAʻO organic farm, university professors,

cultural experts on the Māui moʻolelo in Hawaiʻi and across the Pacific testified to the significance of this land. The developer's attorney asked each
person who testified whether she or he had been on the property, and every
single one could affirm that they had. They had been on the bus tour, had
seen the land and heard the moʻolelo that expanded well beyond the con-
fines of his orange bucket.

THE IMPERMANENCE SYNDROME AND
THE MISMAPPING OF WATER

During the Land Use Commission hearings, Earl Yamamoto, a planner from
the Department of Agriculture, described how urban spot zoning adversely
affects agricultural production. He described the "impermanence syndrome" as a devastating cycle in which farmers facing urban encroachment
find it difficult to invest in the expensive equipment and structures necessary for operating their farms.[41] Farmers cannot invest in expensive equipment without the protection of agricultural lands. It's not difficult to see why
farmers are critical of the state's lack of commitment to an agricultural future.
Jerroll Booth, Araki's neighbor, explains that because he believed in an agricultural future for Lualualei, he was able to invest in expensive greenhouses
that house 40,000 square feet.[42]

The struggle to see these lands remain in agriculture is part of a long-
standing fight between developers and farming communities that has been
ongoing for over seventy years. Alice, Lucy, and I walk door to door along
Hakimo Road, talking with farmers about the proposed urban spot zoning,
encouraging them to come out to the hearings, and in turn they tell us stories
about a pattern of urbanization that displaced them from places like Kalihi,
Kaimukī, Hawaiʻi Kai, and Kalama Valley. As Yukiko Kimura documents in
her book Issei, in 1955, the Honolulu City Planning Commission ordered the
removal of piggeries from Kalihi, forcing many farmers to relocate east to
Koko Head and west to Waiʻanae.[43] From 1949 to 1959, farmers were forced
to move from Waiʻalae and Kāhala to Koko Head, but then from 1966 to 1968
they were all evicted once more by Bishop Estate to make way for the Hawaiʻi
Kai housing subdivision project being developed by the Kaiser Land Development Company. The story picks up in Lualualei Valley, where many of the
farmers relocated their farms. Pearl Tavares, who owns a pig farm on Hakimo
Road, remembers, "We used to have our pig farm at Koko Head, but we got
chased out of there. Our leases from Bishop Estate expired. One hundred
and fifty farmers had to move, and a lot of them moved to Waiʻanae."[44]

The struggle Pearl recounts of evictions in Kalama Valley has been described by scholar-activist Haunani-Kay Trask as a landmark case in the "birth of the modern Hawaiian movement."[45] Trask elaborates on the post-statehood shift in the economy from sugar and pineapple plantations and military expenditures to tourism, land speculation, and commercial development. Landless farmers had been pushed out of places rezoned for suburban and commercial development, and they felt Kalama Valley was their last stand. Joined by antiwar students from the University of Hawai'i demanding an ethnic studies program, Kanaka Maoli leaders Pete Thompson, Kīhei Soli Niheu, and Kalani Ohelo formed the Kōkua Kalama Committee to protect Kalama Valley. By June 1970, the tenants received "certificates of disposs-session." Protectors stood in front of bulldozers to stop the demolition of homes, but they were arrested for trespassing. The Kōkua Kalama Committee organized rallies at the state capitol that were attended by thousands of supporters. The group saw their purpose as broader than just Kalama Valley, so they renamed themselves Kōkua Hawai'i and were joined by The Hawaiians, an association of Hawaiian homesteaders. Inspired by the Black Panther Party, their slogan was "Huli!" (Overturn!). One of the iconic images from this movement is a photo of three dozen protectors standing on the roof of the home of farmer George Santos, the last unbulldozed house in Kalama Valley.

Tropic Land's final environmental impact statement, then, had to be based on a sleight of evidentiary hand to provide scientific documentation of the inability of the land to grow food, belied by the twenty-year history of abundance on that very land. That is, Tropic Land's *Nānākuli Community Baseyard: Final Environmental Impact Statement* (2010) based its findings on a partial truth. The "Agricultural Feasibility Report" states that

> Approximately 80% of the project site has an overall agricultural productivity rating of E—as determined by the University of Hawai'i Land Study Bureau. Lands rated in this low category are characterized by soils in their native state having serious limitations relative to agricultural productivity. Because much of the parcel is stony, agricultural options for the project site, without amendment or modification, are considered to be minimal. A small portion of the site is accorded an overall agricultural productivity rating of B if it is irrigated.[46]

I tracked the developer's source for their maps to the Land Study Bureau publication *Detailed Land Classification: Island of Oahu* (1972), which provided classifications of the soils all over O'ahu, and I found that Tropic

FIGURE 2.5 Map no. 159, "Waianae, Schofield Barracks," in the Land Study Bureau's *Detailed Land Classification: Island of Oahu* (1972), by Tamotsu Sahara, on which I have outlined the petition area. The map shows that E ratings for unirrigated lands become B ratings when irrigated.

Land was once again minimizing the "small portion" that was classified as B-rated lands.[47]

For my own testimony, I designed a series of maps based on the principles of critical settler cartography that exposes the tactics of capital. I used the 1972 aerial maps from *Detailed Land Classification* as the base map to remap the project site, and we see the lands there in neat rows of variegated shades of green, showing us exactly where the land was in active agricultural cultivation (see figure 2.5). More importantly, my map highlights the fact that to make the Purple Spot look like a wasteland, Tropic Land reported the rating of land in its *unirrigated* state to argue that the petition site is unproductive. On the *Detailed Land Classification* map, E63 designates lands at the proposed site that are not irrigated. As the surrounding farms show, irrigated lands are identfied by an "i" following the "land type" number, such as "B62i." With irrigation, the overall productivity rating of the lands in the petition are improved to B63i, the same "highly productive" rating as soils at MA'O Organic Farms across the valley.

In their own cartographic work, the Concerned Elders again used the land itself as a map to render visible the abundance of the valley. Lualualei Valley comprises deep two-acre lots with farming often hidden behind the homes. Alice painted signs that read "green onions," "round onions," "Mānoa lettuce," "squash," "melons," and "piggery," and the farmers posted them on the fences that line Hakimo Road for the land use commissioners to see as they made their own tour of the valley. In this way, the Concerned Elders threw into relief the small, family-owned farms that are often eclipsed by the developer's conception of successful farming as necessarily a large-scale corporate enterprise. Truck farming, the cultivation of vegetable crops that are transported to local markets, is actually a much more sustainable form of farming than corporate farming, which often depends on exploiting Southeast Asian migrants for labor.

In the end, we won the case, and it was a tremendous victory for the people of Wai'anae. But we did not win the case on the cultural grounds we had argued. One cultural practitioner who was to receive a portion of the the community benefits package had argued that the land was a wasteland, and because of this testimony the land use commissioners asserted that there was "no consensus" on the significance of that land. Instead, they denied the developer's petition for a boundary amendment based on the fact that the Navy owned the only road leading to the property and that Tropic Land had failed to secure a long-term easement for access to their property.

Yet this land struggle was about much more than the one case against the industrial park. It was about the growing of aloha 'āina for Lualualei through the education of entire communities about the wonders of Lualualei, both through the Māui mo'olelo and the power of Kanaka Maoli community organizing. In the end it was more important that we shared the mo'olelo as it is mapped on the land with the 'ōpio (young people) who attended the hearings and with the community activists who have taken the strategies we used in Lualualei to protect other places in Hawai'i and beyond.

Years later, on December 15, 2017, I received a stunning letter from Kukui and Gary Maunakea-Forth, the executive director and farm operations director of MA'O Organic Farms. They announced that their nonprofit organization, the Waiʻanae Community Re-Development Corporation, was going to purchase the lands of Māui's birth for organic farming, and they were able to complete the purchase in April 2019. They wrote,

> We have already started clearing the neighboring 21-acre parcel of invasive weeds, and the soil is remarkable, exceptionally deep and fertile Lualualei Vertisol series soil. We recall with a smile the attempts by the developer's representatives to portray the soil as infertile and poor for growing food. We start planting there in the spring.
>
> This purchase is vital to the community's future for three reasons: youth, food and sustainability. First, we will quadruple the number of youth we can support with on-farm internships and tuition support as they pursue a college education and become our new leaders in the community; second, we will grow food production from 85 tons to 1,400 tons per year, feed our communities, create new jobs, and help to tackle our vulnerability in the face of poverty and climate change; and third, we will secure MAʻO's organizational sustainability by expanding earned revenue to account for more than 90% of the operating budget (up from 36% currently), ensuring that this work will be perpetuated.[48]

The reclamation of the land by the farming community is a tremendous victory for all aloha ʻāina across the islands, and MAʻO will multiply these abundant effects through the farmers they are seeding who are learning to engage in kilo (observation) practices to meet the challenges of climate change. This is exactly what Alice, Walterbea, and Lucy had envisioned for the land, and the struggle itself proved to be one that drew the community together and equipped them to materialize these conditions of possibility.

The bus tours have continued. Alice passed away in 2017, but she is with us every time we tell stories about her carrying her black binder to meetings and the recovery of Land Commission Award 3131 that helped us to locate the birthplace of Māui. Lucy, Walterbea, and I tell the moʻolelo of Māui to map wonder on the ground, weaving in environmental injustices and community organizing that has since taken place. On more recent huakaʻi, bus riders step out of the bus to look out across the windswept grassy plains of the lands where Māui was born, listening to the voices of kūpuna mapping the moʻoʻāina.

CHAPTER THREE

MOʻOINANEA'S

WATERWAYS ON

MAUNA A WĀKEA

Beyond Settler Colonial

Thresholds in the Wao Akua

The Kumulipo is a koʻihonua, a cosmogonic chant that maps out the genea-logical descent of Kānaka Maoli and all things out of the deep, ancestral darkness that is Pō. Kānaka have observed lands, seas, and skies as ancestors for hundreds of generations, and they have cultivated a sense of integrated wholeness from these familial arrangements of life. This genealogical connect-edness to lands and elements forms a foundation for Kānaka Maoli to refuse late liberal capital's imaginary. They can do so because they have inherited from their ancestors the pleasures of true abundance in the pilina, the con-nectedness, of Kānaka with the ʻāina and with the akua. By invoking the names of the akua, Kānaka Maoli have been able to grow intimate relationships of aloha with the elemental forms around them. As capital's imaginary plenitude eludes humans, it is elemental and human relationalities that make for true abundance.

Such differences between Indigenous economies of abundance and capitalist economies of scarcity have been thrown into sharp contrast in the struggle that Kānaka Maoli and their allies have taken to protect the sacred mountain lands of Mauna a Wākea from the construction of the Thirty Meter Telescope (TMT). In chapter 1, I discussed the moʻolelo of Moʻoinanea setting into motion the migration of her moʻo descendants to Hawaiʻi. In the moʻolelo of Mauna a Wākea, Moʻoinanea makes her home in Lake Waiau, a pool of water shaped like a kalo leaf, a map in motion of the stars and the constellations (see plate 6).[1]

Mauna a Wākea is "ka makahiapo kapu na Wakea," the sacred first-born of the union of Papahānaumoku, she who is the foundation birthing islands, and Wākea, he who is the wide expanse of the heavens.[2] As the highest point in the Pacific and, from its underwater base, the tallest mountain in the world, Mauna a Wākea is "ka piko o ka moku," the piko of the island in the many senses of the word.[3] In the study of Kanaka Maoli human anatomy, there are three piko: the first piko is the fontanel, the connection to the aumākua (deified ancestors); the second piko is the navel, the umbilicus that connects Kānaka to the kūpuna (elders, past generations); and the third piko is the maʻi (genitals), which connect Kānaka to the ʻōpio (youth, future generations). The mauna embodies all three of these piko.[4] The Edith Kanakaʻole Foundation explains, "When we understand the three *piko* of the human anatomy, we may begin to understand how they manifest in Mauna Kea. Mauna Kea as the fontanel requires a pristine environment free of any spiritual obstructions. Mauna Kea as the umbilicus ensures a definite genealogy of indigenous relation and function. Mauna Kea as genitalia ensures that those who descend from Wākea (our heaven), Papahānaumoku (our land-base) and Hoʻohōkūkalani (the mother of constellations) continue to receive the physical and spiritual benefits entitled to those who descend from sacred regions."[5]

Genealogically, the mauna is the piko or summit, the child born of the meeting of Papahānaumoku and Wākea, the earth and the sky. Mauna a Wākea is thus the elder sibling of both the kalo plant and of Kānaka, all fathered by Wākea. These verses from "He kanaenae no ka hanau ana o Kauikeaouli" recount the genealogy of Mauna a Wākea:

O hanau ka Mauna a Wakea
O puu aʻe ka mauna a Wakea
O Wakea, ke kane,
   o Papa, o Walinuu ka wahine

Hanau Hoohoku, he wahine
Hanau Haloa, he ʻlii

Hanau ka Mauna
    he keiki mauna na Wakea[6]

Born of Kea [Wākea] was the mountain,
the mauna of Kea budded forth.
Wākea was the man,
    Papa Walinuʻu was the woman.

Born was Hoʻohoku, a daughter,
Born was Hāloa, a chief,
Born was the mountain,
    a mountain child of Kea.[7]

Through this moʻokūʻauhau (genealogy), Mauna a Wākea is the piko that binds the people to their ancestors and to all their pulapula, the seedling descendants: all those who came before and all those who will come after. Mauna a Wākea thus embodies the profound sense of familial connectedness of Kānaka Maoli to the past, present, and future.

The genealogy of water on Mauna a Wākea also speaks of currents of connection and abundance. Water that collects on the piko of the kalo plant, which refers to the junction of the stem and kalo leaf, is sacred because it has not yet touched the earth, and water on Mauna a Wākea is most sacred because it is the highest source of water that flows to feed the island.[8] Kāneikawaiola, Kāne of the life-giving waters, loves the summits of the mountains, and from this love were born the water deities of Mauna a Wākea: Poliʻahu, the woman wrapped in the snow mantle of Mauna a Wākea; Līlīnoe of the fine mist that gently meanders across the mauna; Waiau of the swirling waters; and Kahoupokāne, master kapa maker who beats the brilliant, snow-white bark cloth. Kahoupokāne tosses water on her kapa, which become the heavy rains, beating her kapa thunderously, and when she flips the bright new kapa over, this is the lightning flashing in the skies. In the winter months of hoʻoilo, the sisters wear the kapa hau, the mantle of snow, and in the summer months of kau wela, they wear the kapa lā made from the beaten gold kukunaokalā (rays of the sun).[9] Moʻoinanea is the reptilian water guardian who watches over Poliʻahu when she resides in Waiau during the warm summer months.

I begin with these genealogies to foreground the abundance of water forms on Mauna a Wākea. In the face of this abundance, the occupying state has historically represented Mauna a Wākea as a wasteland, a barren desert. Through these representations, it has sought to profit from the construction of observatories. In 1968, the land board issued a lease for the construction of a single telescope, but, since then, that one telescope has multiplied to become thirteen observatories—or twenty-two, if we consider that some observatories house multiple telescopes.[10]

More recently, in 2010, the University of Hawai'i at Hilo (UH) filed a conservation district use application on behalf of the Thirty Meter Telescope (TMT) Corporation for the proposed construction of what would be the most massive observatory yet.[11] The TMT would be 180 feet, or about eighteen stories, high—taller than any existing structure on the island of Hawai'i—and would extend over a footprint of more than five acres, a plan which would require excavating twenty feet into the northern plateau of the sacred mountain, removing 1,782,000 cubic feet of pāhoehoe lava and earth.[12] Two 5,000-gallon tanks, each capable of storing eighteen tons of chemical and human wastewater, are proposed to be located underground over the Waimea aquifer that feeds a large portion of the island.[13] The state agency should have immediately denied the permit, since NASA's prior environmental impact statement (EIS) for the proposed Outrigger Telescope had determined that existing telescopes were already causing an impact that is "substantial, adverse and significant" on conservation land, a determination that stopped the construction of that telescope.[14] The *Final Environmental Impact Statement* for the TMT itself states, "From a cumulative perspective, the impact of past and present actions on cultural, archaeological, and historic resources is substantial, significant, and adverse; these impacts would continue to be substantial, significant, and adverse with the consideration of the Project and other reasonably foreseeable future actions."[15]

Astronomers and the occupying state have argued for the need for the TMT based on a grand and sweeping vision of discovering the origins of life and lush inhabitable planets that lie waiting to be discovered. It's not difficult to see where such arguments are going. If humans have destroyed this planet, the TMT project provides a fantasmatic vision of a planetary Garden of Eden out there that promises an escape from the creeping sands of the desert on earth.

To expedite the environmental review process, the UH applied for the conservation district use permit (CDUP) on behalf of the TMT, in what for all intents and purposes is a conflict of interest, since the university manages the Mauna Kea Science Reserve and subleases the land to the observatories. Under these conditions, the State Board of Land and Natural Resources approved the CDUP for the TMT in February 2011, and it did so before holding the contested case hearing requested by six petitioners, an action that the Hawai'i Supreme Court later ruled a procedural error. Those six petitioners became known as the Mauna Kea hui (collective) and went on to stand for the mauna in two contested case hearings and the Hawai'i Supreme Court case against the TMT: Kealoha Pisciotta of Mauna Kea Anaina Hou, E. Kalani Flores and B. Pualani Case of the Flores–Case 'Ohana, Kūkauakahi (Clarence Ching), Paul Neves, Deborah J. Ward, and Marti Townsend representing KĀHEA: The Hawaiian-Environmental Alliance, assisted by Bianca Isaki, Lauren and Shelley Muneoka, and Miwa Tamanaha.

On May 13, 2011, E. Kalani Flores, a Mauna a Wākea cultural practitioner and a Hawaiian studies professor at Hawai'i Community College, submitted a petition for standing in the contested case hearing on behalf of Mo'oinanea, the reptilian water guardian of Waiau. In a prehearing meeting, Flores testified,

> First of all, Haw. Admin. R. §13-1-31 states that persons can be admitted as a party if they have "some property interest in the land, who lawfully reside on the land," and it continues on. "Lawfully reside on the land," those who are adjacent property owners, or who otherwise can demonstrate that they will be so directly and immediately affected by the requested action that their interest in the proceeding is clearly distinguishable from that of the general public, shall be admitted as parties on timely application. So we contend that, one, Mo'oinanea does have property interest in the land, and she does reside on the land on the summit of Mauna a Wākea also referred to as Mauna Kea.[16]

While Flores was carrying out the will of Mo'oinanea, he was also putting the occupying state on trial for its failure to recognize the elemental deities and the guardians who reside on the mountain as parties with an interest in the land.

In this chapter, I trace the discourses of "thresholds" in the case. The occupying state went on to assert what Elizabeth Povinelli terms "geontopower," or the authority to distinguish between life and nonlife, a threshold that the occupying state also manipulates to argue that Kānaka Maoli, too, have crossed a threshold of colonial impact that makes them so thoroughly colonized that they are unable to continue the traditional practices of their kūpuna with any "authenticity."

As I argue in this chapter, Kānaka Maoli assert that the laws of the akua, the elemental forms, take precedence over human laws, an argument that resonates with Indigenous peoples all over the world facing global climate change. Kealoha Pisciotta, a party in both contested case hearings and the

Hawai'i Supreme Court case against the TMT, has successfully protected Mauna a Wākea from the construction of new telescopes for over twenty years. She explains, "Mauna Kea holds a special place on earth, therefore the cultural tradition as a temple is dedicated to peace and aloha. When we walk on the sacred ground and in the sacred realms, we are bound by the laws of the akua, not our own." As she concludes, state laws have "no jurisdiction in the wao akua."[17] As I show in this chapter, Kānaka reframed the hearings to show that when the occupying state refused to recognize the elemental forms, Kānaka refused to recognize the occupying state. This refusal underpins Kanaka Maoli reclamation of political agency in ongoing movements for ea—life, breath, and political sovereignty.

As a water protector, Mo'oinanea also stands for the protection of waters across the earth. From the standpoint of a critical settler cartographic method, we can track the mathematics of subdivision and the rhetorical regimes of "containment" that the TMT and the occupying state reiterated to argue that the massive industrial complex of the TMT would not contaminate the aquifer. I consider first the maps presented by the settler state and TMT attorneys to argue that Mauna a Wākea is a wasteland, before turning to the maps drawn by Kanaka practitioners who based their own maps on centuries of kilo practices evident in 'ike kupuna (ancestral knowledge) of Mauna a Wākea encoded in the mo'olelo of Poli'ahu, in chants, and the mo'olelo of Kamiki. 'Ike kupuna tracks the waters as they flow down Mauna a Wākea to illustrate the mo'o'āina continuities of waterways that stretch out across the pu'u (cinder cones) studded plains of Pōhakuloa to Hualālai.

The kia'i (protectors) on Mauna a Wākea are water protectors who foreground the interconnectedness of our global struggles. The kia'i have formed alliances with First Nations peoples in the Idle No More movement in Canada to protect water and have traveled to stand with more than three hundred Native nations in solidarity at Oceti Sakowin Camp at Standing Rock against the North Dakota Access Pipeline.[18] They stand with all peoples facing threats to water in what Chadwick Allen describes as trans-Indigenous future worlds.[19]

AN ELEMENTAL LOVE STORY

The mo'olelo, mele, and oli of Mauna a Wākea are all love songs that provide lessons in the ecological continuities necessary for the vibrancy of life on the mountain. We see these laws in the mo'olelo of Kūkahau'ula's courtship of Poli'ahu. It is the mo'o guardian of Waiau, Mo'oinanea, who is the pilina (connection), the enabling relationality, bringing the elemental lovers together.

As an aliʻi (chief) and a historian, Emma Ahuena Davison Taylor provides an account of Kūkahauʻula's courtship of Poliʻahu, a story about the elemental consciousness of the water forms on the mauna. Kūkahauʻula (the Pink-Tinted Snow's Arrival) has heard of Poliʻahu's great beauty and travels on the first ray of the sun from the eastern gateway at Kahiki to Mauna a Wākea. When he attempts to approach her, her attendants Līhau (the chilling frost), Kīpuʻupuʻu (the hail), and Kuauli (the biting rains) drive him away, and the mists of Līlīnoe hide Poliʻahu from view.[20] Each day he returns but is forced to flee. One day, as he retreats across the sky, his pink kapa reflects the sunlight and creates a glorious rainbow. Moʻoinanea sees the rainbow as a hōʻailona (sign) of Kūkahauʻula's devotion and calls out to him to return the next day. At dawn Kūkahauʻula returns, and when Poliʻahu sees his beautiful feather cloak, she calls out to her mother Hina, asking her to invite him to come closer so that she may chant her aloha to him. Hina is alarmed and sends the biting cold rains after him, and Līlīnoe cloaks Poliʻahu in her mists.

Moʻoinanea then instructs him to conceal his cape until he reaches Waiau and then permits him safe passage across the lake. The sun's rays reflect the hues of his cloak, a rainbow arches over the pool, and the silvery waters become a shimmering pink. He approaches Poliʻahu, who is reclining on a bed of snow and little white hinahina flowers: "He advanced slowly, his pink robe outspread, radiantly gilding the brow of Mauna-kea with its glorious hue, until it was almost noon, chanting softly to her of his love, in the stillness of God's acres until he was close enough to throw his brilliant pink toga over her shoulder. Drawing her within his arms, he wrapped the robe entirely around her until they both were concealed within its folds."[21] In her own testimony to protect the mountain, cultural practitioner Kuʻulei Keakealani, concludes, "So for us, we bear witness to them, to this loving. Sunrise and sunset, Mauna a Wākea is going to turn colors . . . hues of pink and purple, some say red. . . . We are watching Kūkahauʻula, who is this man who has traveled from afar and has seen this dream and comes in search of this woman. So Kūkahauʻula is embracing her like no other man could, as he loves Poliʻahu two times, every day, no nā kau ā kau, forever and ever."[22] When the snow or the red dirt of the mauna glows with the rising or the setting of the sun, we see Poliʻahu's lover Kūkahauʻula embracing her, his cloak wrapped around her puʻu (cinder cones) (see plate 7). In this moʻolelo the kūpuna emphasize the visual impact of seeing the mauna come alive as the akua traverse the entire summit.

FIGURE 3.1 Aerial photo of Waiau and overflowing waters from the *Archaeological Inventory Survey of the Mauna Kea Ice Age Natural Area Reserve*, 2013.

This moʻolelo of the meeting of the lovers is also about the waters produced by the union of the sun's warmth and the snows. As Kūkahauʻula's "pink Sun's beam / Embraces and kisses the snow," the snows melt into the waters on the mountain. In the story, the kupuna explains to her moʻo (grandchild) that the "heart of the goddess melts and overflows with love and feeds the mountain streams": "You have heard of the waters of Poliahu that our ancient and noble chieftains of that great island preferred to any other, to quench their thirst with, and how their faithful retainers would have to travel for miles each day, getting up at early dawn, carrying the water gourds all the way up the steep slopes of Mauna-kea, to a place called Pohaku-loa, to fetch the drinking water from the melted snow accumulated there, bestowed by the goddess, for their feudal lords."[23] When we look to Waiau, we can see clearly the path of waters that overflow the puʻu to carve out Pōhakuloa Gulch (see figure 3.1). Waiau is said to feature an impermeable clay layer that makes possible this wondrous body of water on Mauna a Wākea, but the moʻolelo records the fact that "confined" bodies of water on the mountain overflow like Poliʻahu's heart overflows with the melted snows, the waters that travel underground to emerge as the springs Houpokāne, Waihūakāne, and Līlīnoe.

Despite thousands of years of moʻolelo, oli, and mele about Mauna a Wākea as the principle source of water for the aquifers on the island, the occupying state has historically represented Mauna a Wākea as a wasteland. An early 1891 map by American surveyor C. J. Lyons inscribed the summit with the words, "Barren Rock and Sand," illustrating American perceptions of this sacred place as land incapable of producing life.[24] A decade later, a 1901 Hawaiʻi Territorial Survey map labeled Mauna a Wākea as a "Waste Land" with "No Vegetation" (see figure 3.2).[25]

In the larger context of US occupation, this "wasteland" designation is reminiscent of Ngũgĩ wa Thiongʻo's words about the cultural bomb that extends occupation into the social processes of settler colonialism by representing Native pasts as wastelands: "The effect of the cultural bomb is to annihilate a people's belief in their names, in their languages, in their environment, in their heritage of struggle, in their unity, in their capacities and ultimately in themselves. It makes them see their past as one wasteland of non-achievement and it makes them want to distance themselves from that wasteland."[26] In Hawaiʻi, settler colonial depictions of the land as "lying in waste" were aimed at seizing political control over both people and land and erasing a vast Kanaka Maoli knowledge base.

Late liberal settler colonial wastelanding of the summit of Mauna a Wākea persists in the TMT case. In the 2017 contested case hearing of the TMT, UH and TMT International Observatory (TIO) attorneys falsely argued in their joint findings of fact that nineteenth-century Kanaka Maoli historian Davida Malo had called Mauna a Wākea "a wasteland." They write, "He made no mention of traditional or historic practices atop the summit of Mauna Kea and reported that it was considered wasteland or the realm of the gods."[27] This citation seemed deeply problematic to me, so I tracked the quotation they cited and found that they had only consulted Nathaniel Emerson's English translation from *Hawaiian Antiquities: Moʻolelo Hawaiʻi*. The phrase "waste places" appears not in the text itself but in the translator's footnote: W. D. Alexander's introduction to the volume clarifies that the footnotes were written by Emerson and not Malo.[28] This is Emerson's translation of Malo's text: "12. The belt below the *wao-eiwa*

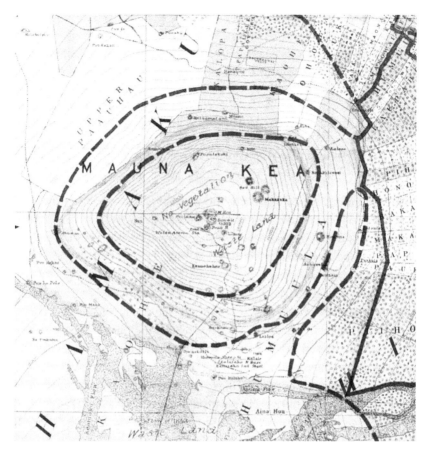

FIGURE 3.2 John M. Donn, detail of *Hawaii Territory Survey: Hawai'i, Hawaiian Islands*, 1901.

was the one in which the monarchs of the forest grew, and was called the *wao-maukele*, and the belt below that, in which again trees of smaller size grew was called *wao-akua*,[6] and below the *wao-akua* comes the belt called *wao-kanaka* or *mau*. Here grows the *amau* fern and here men cultivate the land."[29] "Footnote 6," written by Emerson, reads as follows: "Sect. 12. In the phrase wao-akua, which means wilderness of the gods, we have embodied the popular idea that the gods and ghosts chiefly inhabit the waste places of the earth." It is therefore through a settler colonial imaginary that Emerson describes the realm of the gods as the "waste places of the earth," but, as I show in chapter 5, Kānaka themselves described the wao akua as a place of abundance, where food grows wild under the care of the elements.

Malo's text is not even specifically about Mauna a Wākea; it provides an account of "Ke Kapa Ana i Ko Loko Mau Inoa o ka Moku" (The naming of what is found on the islands), a description of the different realms on the islands. Here is the text in ʻōlelo Hawaiʻi:

> 12. O kahi o na laau loloa e ulu ana makai mai o ka wao eiwa, ua kapa ia aku ia, he wao maukele ma ia poai, ao kahi makai mai, o ka wao maukele e liilii hou iho ai na laau, ua kapa ia aku ia he wao akua, ma ia poai kahi makai mai o ka wao akua e ulu ana ke amaumau, he wao kanaka kahi inoa, he mau kahi inoa oia poai, kahi a na kanaka e mahiai ai.[30]

Malo contrasts the wao akua with the wao kanaka, the realm of humans, where vegetation must be cultivated by Kānaka who farm. The fact that the university and TMT attorneys only consulted an English translation illustrates the dangers of their inability to read ʻōlelo Hawaiʻi and their disregard for Kanaka Maoli knowledges.

From these contrived depictions of Mauna a Wākea as a wasteland emerge one of the most egregious logics of the occupying state: the construction of a "threshold of impact." In 2009, the multinational corporation Parsons Brinckerhoff Americas Inc. was contracted as a consultant to prepare the environmental impact study for the TMT. Despite the material ways that the project would be devastating to the conservation district, the waters on the mauna, and Native Hawaiian cultural practices and knowledges about stewarding that water, Parsons Brinckerhoff project manager James T. Hayes argued in his written direct testimony in both contested case hearings that "the addition of the Project will result in only limited, incremental impacts, and will not result in any new significant or adverse impacts.[31] To make this claim, Parsons Brinckerhoff manufactured the figure of a "threshold of impact" to argue that the mountain was already so irrevocably degraded that the addition of an even larger telescope would not tip the balance from a "less than significant impact" to a "significant impact."[32] The TMT EIS states,

> In general, the project will add a limited increment to the current level of cumulative impact. Therefore, those resources that have been substantially, significantly, and adversely impacted by past and present actions would continue to have a substantial, significant, and adverse impact with the addition of the Project. For those resources that have been impacted to a less than significant degree by past and present actions, the Project would not tip the balance from a less than significant level to

a significant level and the less than significant level of cumulative impact would continue.[33]

Despite this nonsensical rhetoric, the Board of Land and Natural Resources (BLNR) approved the conservation district use permit. In 2018, four Hawai'i Supreme Court Justices upheld the BLNR decision.

In his dissenting opinion, Justice Michael Wilson points to the ways the majority opinion is "fraught with illogic," authorizing a dangerous new "degradation principle." Wilson rightly argues, "The degradation principle dilutes or reverses the foundational dual objectives of environmental law—namely, to conserve what exists (or is left) and to repair environmental damage."[34] The articulation of this degradation principle by the other justices undermines environmental law by presenting a view of the mauna as being degraded beyond repair, precisely the apocalyptic view that the earth, too, has passed a threshold of no return, thus foreclosing the possibilities of restoration and regeneration.

Late liberal capital has crafted these rhetorical regimes of "thresholds of impact" in a way that sets up a catch-22 for the earth that entraps it in a human-crafted paradox. The "degradation principle" hinges on the construction of a "threshold" and employs an untenable logic for conditions on both sides of the threshold that lead to the same conclusion: the impacts of a project either do not degrade land enough to have crossed the threshold of impact, or lands are already too degraded past such a threshold: in both cases projects are permitted to move forward. The absurdity of this formulation is that the threshold itself creates a condition where there is no basis for the denial of permits. As a multinational corporation, Parsons Brinckerhoff (now agglomerated as part of the even larger multinational firm WSP) extends over five hundred offices across forty countries, and echoes of this rhetorical regime are repeated all over the world in capital's wastelanding of the earth.

I would dispute Parsons Brinckerhoff's analysis by pointing to the exponential nature of what they refer to as a limited increment of environmental impact. Miniscule impacts trigger large-scale cascades that multiply outward and catalyze other effects. We are seeing now incremental increases in global temperatures—toward a mere two-degree Celsius rise above preindustrial levels—that are triggering the melting of glaciers and ice sheets, thermal expansion of seawater, increased frequency of storm surges and flooding events, saltwater contamination of aquifers, and king tides that rise higher each year. In the case of the TMT, cultural practitioners and environmentalists testified to the fact that the incremental impact is by no means even a small impact, and that such a massive industrial complex would have tremendous natural impacts within what is currently designated as a conservation district.

Kānaka Maoli challenge settler colonial fallacies about the insignificance of incremental impact. Pisciotta argued in the first TMT contested case hearing in 2011 that it is precisely this "increment" that would not only cause irreparable harm to the mauna and to the people, but that the actual enormity of the TMT itself will expose and crush the fragile juridical underpinnings of the occupying state: "The TMT is not only the straw that breaks the camel's back, it's the elephant that will cause the entire system to break down."[35]

MOʻOINANEA TESTIFIES IN THE CONTESTED CASE HEARING AGAINST THE TMT

From the very outset of the prehearing deliberations, the UH and TMT attorneys were representing not only the interests of the Thirty Meter Telescope but the occupying state's authority to adjudicate the very thresholds between life and nonlife that has now put us in planetary jeopardy. By contrast, Kanaka Maoli practitioners sought to redefine the quasi-juridical process by calling our attention to the importance of recognizing the higher authority of the laws of the akua, the elements. E. Kalani Flores opened up the contested case hearing by petitioning for standing in the case for Moʻoinanea, the moʻo guardian of Waiau. To meet the occupying state's condition that "person" be defined as human, he presented Moʻoinanea's human genealogy: "We also say Moʻoinanea, who lives on the mountain, does have human blood in her. She does have a genealogy. We have a genealogy for Moʻoinanea that extends back four generations. So she does have a human physical characteristic connected to her. She has a physicality to her."[36] Flores responded to the contention that Moʻoinanea is a disembodied spirit by explaining that she takes human form: "She can transform into a full human form at times, or she can transform into a full moʻo form at times, or other times she can also transform in part human and part moʻo form."[37] Flores further challenges the occupying state's extension of standing to "corporations," arguing that water guardians with human form and genealogies should also be recognized as "persons."

The UH attorneys made the question of Moʻoinanea's standing what they identify as a "threshold issue" and proceeded to align Moʻoinanea with nonlife, defining "spirit" as "not a living organism." The UH attorney argued, "We point to the definition of person. We point to the precedents in terms of whether or not a spiritual being, or a being that is not a living organism, or legal entity such as any of the other entities he's described. . . . Again, this is a threshold hearing here whether or not that entity falls into the definition of a person. If it does not, then it doesn't matter about the property interest, doesn't matter about impact. So we believe it's a threshold issue."[38] Clearly the attorneys were attempting to establish this particular threshold between life and nonlife to foreclose the question of "property interest." Yet property interest is at the very heart of the problem in the case precisely because Mauna a Wākea is on former Crown lands and because the occupying state has no legitimate title to the 1.8 million acres of Crown and government lands seized at the time of the 1893 overthrow of the Hawaiian Kingdom government—lands that the occupying state now designates as "public trust lands." As Hawaiian studies professor and sovereignty activist Kaleikoa Kaʻeo states succinctly, "No consent. No treaty. No title. No TMT."[39]

The occupying state was particularly threatened by the possibility of Moʻoinanea gaining standing because the state itself is premised on naturalizing the belief that settler colonialism, too, has also crossed the threshold of impact. This formula of a "threshold of impact" has larger implications as an assertion of settler colonialism as a foregone conclusion. Like the trope of the "vanishing Indian," this argument isolates colonization to a past point in time as a threshold that has already been crossed, and in this way, the occupying state and its agents seek to foreclose the possibility of decolonization.[40] As a petitioner in the contested case hearing, Pua Case explains, "To allow Moʻoinanea to testify would open the door to Hawaiian beliefs that they want to say existed only in the past before Christianity."[41] The Office of Mauna Kea Management actually takes it upon itself to determine what "modern practices" are appropriate and more often deems contemporary efforts of Kānaka to engage in the practice of building ahu (shrines) as examples of "vandalism" and has them dismantled.[42]

On May 27, 2011, the hearing officer Paul Aoki issued Minute Order No. 6, "Order Regarding Standing," recommending that "the BLNR deny the request for Moʻoinanea to appear as a party in the contested case, because the information provided indicated that Moʻoinanea is a spirit, not a person, and as such does not meet the requirements of Haw. Admin. R. §13-1-31 and 13-1-2 to be admitted as a party."[43] On June 23, 2011, the BLNR voted unanimously to adopt the hearing officer's recommendation. Joseph A. Salazar concludes in his analysis of this case, "Moʻoinanea emerged as an absent other, both expendable yet necessary, not unlike Kanaka Ōiwi more generally in such discourses requiring their presence insofar as their enlistment and appropriation affords the state, scientific, and capitalist imperatives varying degrees of legitimacy; yet, simultaneously requiring their disenfranchisement, silencing, and absence in order to continue the unethical displacements of settler colonialism."[44] The occupying state performatively recognizes Moʻoinanea and Kanaka Maoli belief systems in their evidentiary documentation because it depends on this representation of itself as a liberal, multicultural nation state, but it fails to accord Kānaka Maoli true recognition because to do so would ultimately challenge the very foundation of the occupying state.

I want to extend this analysis to consider Elizabeth Povinelli's arguments about the ways that US geontopower relies on sustaining the figure of the "desert" in the "carbon imaginary" to maintain the distinction between life and nonlife. We can look to Povinelli's discussion of the Belyuen Aboriginal community's struggles to protect the sacred place of Two Women Sitting Down, where a corporation sought to develop the Bootu Creek manganese mine. She argues: "Take the Desert and its central imaginary Carbon. The Desert comprises discourses, tactics, and figures that restabilize the distinction between Life and Nonlife. It stands for all things perceived and conceived as denuded of life—and, by implication, all things that could, with the correct deployment of technological expertise of proper stewardship be (re)made hospitable to life. The Desert, in other words, holds on to the distinction between Life and Nonlife and dramatizes the possibility that Life is always at threat from the creeping, desiccating sands of Nonlife."[45] In the discursive strategies of the TMT, the late liberal vision of settler colonialism is obsessed with the origins of life, how life began, and "discovering" planets that are hospitable to life, now that humans have wastelanded this earth. Mauna a Wākea is both the ground that promises this capability of discovering life on new planets to colonize but itself must be deemed incapable of sustaining life.

Kānaka responded to the occupying state by rejecting its regime of geontopower. Despite the occupying state's efforts to silence Moʻoinanea and Poliʻahu's testimony, *they did indeed testify*. Through his written direct testimony, Flores presents the voices of Poliʻahu and Moʻoinanea as part of a multipronged strategy. First he addresses the occupying state within the terms of its own laws governing conservation land use, meticulously enumerating the ways that the BLNR and the university were violating state laws. He then regrounded the hearings in Mauna Kea's realm of the wao akua, where the laws of the akua are preeminent and the akua have the authority to grant permission for access to the mountain. In his testimony, he explains, "Poliahu serves as caretaker and guardian for the mountain and grants permission to certain spirits coming to the mountain. She is a part of the landscape features with a highly evolved consciousness."[46] He then presents us with the voices of Poliʻahu and Moʻoinanea:

> I have been present at times when she [Poliʻahu] has shared her concerns about the existing and proposed further desecration on the mountain. She has explicitly remarked that she does not want the existing and any new observatories on this sacred mountain. They are blocking the *piko* on the summit. If she is dislocated due to the new telescope, it might create new problems and affect the weather patterns on the mountain as well as other areas on the island.
>
> I have been present at times when Moʻoinanea has shared her personal accounts about herself and her family as well as described the types of cultural traditions our *kūpuna* of old practiced on Mauna a Wākea including pilgrimages to the top of the mountain. In addition, she has expressed her concerns about the existing observatories and proposed further desecration on the mountain with the new project . . . She has shared that the existing observatories have created obstructions and hazards for those who reside on Mauna a Wākea. Likewise, the proposed new observatory will adversely impact Moʻoinanea and others who dwell on the summit.[47]

Flores's attunement to the guardians and the elements on the mauna makes possible the identification of the laws of the akua that stipulate no obstruction on the summit region that includes the northern plateau. We hear the guardians and the elements providing the elemental logic behind these natural laws. The environmental impact statement for the TMT presents extensive documentation of Mauna a Wākea as a piko that requires a pristine environment free of spiritual obstruction. Moʻoinanea's and Poliʻahu's testimonies attest to the fact that building a massive telescope industrial complex on the piko of Hawaiʻi Island would have extreme consequences for the natural elements, which include the water that travels across and within the mauna and the weather patterns that not only produce that water but are stabilized by the mauna.

Flores emphasized that elemental forms have a consciousness, and each akua was named so that Kānaka could become attuned to the consciousness of each element:

> I can say personally we've encountered many things from the spirit realm in many different ways, and that our ancestors understood this very clearly, that when we talk about akua, our akua, in the context, they

are the natural elements around us. That's why our kūpuna, our ancestors, gave them names. So it's not just the rain or the snow or the ocean and the waters; these elemental forms were the akua of our people. And it's not just elements, these elements have a consciousness. And when I say a consciousness, they have the ability to interact with us as humans. They have the ability to listen and receive what we have to offer in a chant or a song, and they have the ability to respond back.[48]

Flores describes the capacity of the elemental forms to recognize humans and to respond back to us. This attunement to the akua is central to the relationships that Kānaka have grown with 400,000 elemental forms, such as the different kinds of mists that feed Mauna a Wākea's aquifers, from the kiliʻohu (fine, misty rain) to the kilinoe (fine, misty rain heavier than the kiliʻohu) to the noe kolo (creeping mist). Kānaka are able to invoke these elements by their names to honor them or to make a request, and the elemental forms respond back by showing us hōʻailona (signs) that communicate consent or dissent.

When we look to Kanaka Maoli cartographies, we see that asking for the land's consent is part of the protocol for that cartography. The protocol of asking the ʻāina for recognition and permission is the foundation in oli kāhea (chants requesting permission to enter into a place). When practitioners chant an oli kāhea, they recognize that each person is taking on a kuleana (responsibility, right, purview, privilege) to be responsible and respectful in this place. If there is a person receiving the visitors, that person will chant an oli komo if the visitors are welcome. If there is no person receiving us, we must be able to read the signs that are provided by the lands, seas, or skies. When we travel on huakaʻi into the forest or into the wao akua, the realm of the akua, we wait for a hōʻailona, listening to the lands, the winds, the waters, to discern if we are welcome to enter. At times, we will see Lilīnoe descending, her mists covering the land from view, or the winds will be so strong that we must double over, and we know these are signs that we are being asked not to enter, either because we do not have the proper intentions or because conditions are dangerous. On other days, the winds will blow gently or the mists will open up a path, and we know we have been given permission to enter.

If we look back to the moʻolelo of Poliʻahu and Kūkahauʻula, we see that Kūkahauʻula did not request permission to approach Poliʻahu, and he is repeatedly denied entrance into her presence by her attendants and by her mother, Hina, who ward him away with the force of the elements. It is only when Moʻoinanea sees the rainbow he created that she recognizes his love for Poliʻahu. She calls out to him in recognition, and he, in turn, recognizes the moʻo and appeals to the water guardian for help. It is through Moʻoinanea, who embodies the moʻo principle of connectedness and relationality, that Kūkahauʻula is able to join Poliʻahu.

Throughout the hearings, Flores shifted authority from the occupying state to the court of the elemental forms. Flores asked each of the university's witnesses, "Have you asked permission or consulted with the ancestral akua connected to Mauna Kea whether this project of such massive size and scope is compatible with this sacred landscape?"[49] None of the TMT representatives had sought permission from the mountain or the elemental forms for their consent to the TMT project. Through their communication with Moʻoinanea, the Flores-Case ʻohana (family) was able to document the protocol for consultation of the guardians and deities of the mauna: "According to Moʻoinanea, kahuna would go for their chief to gather water from the lake as an offering for chiefs or places they travel to. First, they would have to state why they wanted to collect this water and their purpose for it. They also needed to state how much water was needed. Then a $lā'ī$ (tī leaf) was put on the lake. If permission was granted, lāʻī floats. If not, lāʻī sinks."[50]

Because the representatives had failed to ask permission for the construction of the TMT, the hōʻailona from Moʻoinanea in opposition to the project was visibly striking to everyone. In 2013, when the BLNR affirmed its approval of the TMT's conservation district use permit, Waiau shrank from three hundred feet in diameter to twelve inches. Flores and Case write, "[In 2013], Moʻoinanea left the land and Lake Waiau dried up to almost nothing. And the change shook everyone."[51] Moʻoinanea returned in the following year, but the water guardian had made it clear that the TMT is not to be built on Mauna a Wākea.

THE OCCUPYING STATE'S ISOLATION OF WATER

Mountain lands are protected by state laws as conservation districts because they are the sources of water for aquifers.[52] The 11,288 acres of the Mauna Kea Science Reserve leased by the University of Hawaiʻi from the Department of Land and Natural Resources (DLNR) is located over five delineated aquifer systems: the Waimea, Onomea, Hakalau, Paʻauilo, and Honokaʻa aquifers. What the occupying state has named the "Astronomy Precinct" is located entirely above the Waimea aquifer.

The threats posed to the water sources on Mauna Kea include accidental spills of chemical and human wastewater as they are loaded onto trucks and transported down the mountain. The EIS describes a process whereby mirror-washing wastewater would be collected and trucked off the mountain. There would be two 5,000-gallon underground tanks, each holding eighteen tons of liquid, one for chemical waste storage and one for domestic sewage waste storage. There would also be a 2,000-gallon diesel tank above ground.[53] The EIS claims that all potentially chemically impacted wastewater, such as the mirror-washing wastewater, would be drained in double-walled pipes and captured in a double-walled underground storage tank equipped with leak monitors. The EIS estimates that once a month, when the tanks reach 2,000 gallons (or seven tons of liquid), the tanks would be emptied onto trucks that would transport the waste down the steep, curving, unpaved roads of the mountain. The EIS notes that there is an increased risk of spills at the points of loading and transporting the wastewater: "Although transportation of the mirror washing wastewater off the mountain will alleviate concerns regarding the degradation of water resources, it will increase the chance that an accident could occur as the wastewater was transported from the TMT Observatory to the treatment and disposal facility."[54]

On December 13, 2016, the TMT expert witness in hydrology, Tom Nance, claimed that the TMT project would not have a significant or adverse impact on groundwater. Nance presented a map of the "Mauna Kea Groundwater Schematic" in his testimony, a map that only serves to highlight what hydrologists do not know about Mauna a Wākea (see figure 3.3).[55]

From a critical settler cartographic perspective, I would call this map an "empty" map of the land. The very fact that the map depicts the "south flank" of Mauna a Wākea, not the *northern* plateau that is the proposed site for the TMT, emblematizes the ways that settler colonial cartography obscures evidence of impact. Even as a schematic, the map oversimplifies the complexity of the ways that water moves in Mauna a Wākea. The map illustrates a gray blank space marked by notes at elevations and the misspelled names of the springs. The map shows us nothing of the presence of the dikes and sills within the mountain, the possibilities of perching waters overflowing, or the topographical details of the numerous puʻu (cinder cones) that capture water. The map oversimplifies water sources on the mountain, attributing water to rainfall with no acknowledgement of the importance of fog drip that saturates the entire mountain.

The hydrology expert attempted to isolate and contain the problems posed by accidental spills by denying the continuities of these waterways

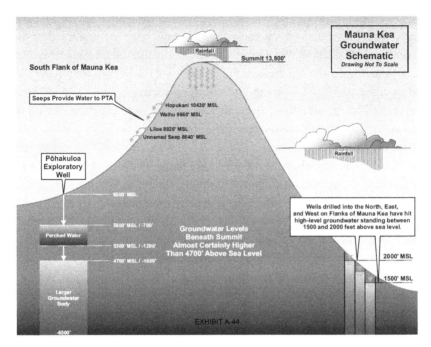

FIGURE 3.3 "Mauna Kea Groundwater Schematic," University of Hawai'i at Hilo exhibit A-44 in the second TMT contested case hearing, 2016–17.

and the potential for the contamination of aquifer. Upon cross-examination, however, Kūkauakahi asked, "Now, what happens if a perched bunch of water is added upon beyond the capacity of the perch to hold it, what happens to the extra water?"[56] Nance admitted, "Well, depending on the nature of the perching mechanism, it could either discharge at the surface as a spring, which is what PTA taps into, or it could actually leak laterally and and go down to the groundwater that exists beneath it." Kūkauakahi then asked, "So now that we have talked about dikes, what is the sill? . . . Are you saying that there are mechanisms in the ground, in this case subsurface, that can move water both vertically and horizontally?"[57] Nance replied, "It will move vertically by gravity. Horizontally, it will move downgradient." Here, Kūkauakahi directed our attention to the sills that move water laterally across the mountain in ways that Nance was not accounting for, pointing to the potential conditions of a toxic spill contaminating groundwater. All that Nance's map can say is that groundwater level is "almost certainly higher than 4,700 feet above sea level," but that could be anywhere up to the 13,800-foot summit.

Nance further argued that a spill of chemical wastewater would not have an impact on groundwater because the mountain has a "natural trickling filter effect." He testified, "Should an accident occur and should the wastewater start moving downward through the unsaturated lava, which we call the Vadose Zone, it would traverse thousands of feet vertically downward before it ever reached the underlying groundwater, maybe by 6, 7,000 feet. We don't know for sure what that distance is to the groundwater, underlying groundwater, because beneath the summit *we don't know exactly where the groundwater is.*"[58] Nance clearly admits that they do not know where the groundwater is. Moreover, to support his claim about the trickling filter effect, he presented an example that actually refutes his claim. He presented exhibit c-37 on the Kealakehe Wastewater Treatment Plant in order to show that 1.8 million gallons of secondarily treated effluent is dumped into a pit and that "no definable adverse impact is occurring from this otherwise what people think [*sic*] is an alarming way to be discharging effluent."[59]

Nance's claims that the water would be "filtered" were soon proven false. Upon cross-examination, KĀHEA attorney Dexter Keʻeaumoku Kaʻiama asked Nance if he was aware of the fact that in 2008 Chip Hunt, a groundwater hydrologist for the US Geological Survey, found anthropogenic sources of contamination of ocean waters from that sewage treatment facility. Kaʻiama asked, "Are you aware, sir, that in 2014 a draft report prepared by the Hawaii Department of Health designated the nearshore waters outside of Honokōhau as impaired under Section 303, Subsection D of the Clean Water Act?"[60] Nance replied that he was not aware of that. In his cross-examination, Lanny Sinkin, representing the Temple of Lono, pressed this point, asking, "Are you aware that more than 20 scientists signed on to a statement issued by Hana Consulting in August of 2014 that said, we request an end to the dumping of effluent at Kealakehe that is having a negative impact on the nearshore marine environment?"[61] Nance replied he was not aware of that fact.

KANAKA MAOLI MAPPING OF WATER
ON THE NORTHERN PLATEAU

The empty maps that represent the state's knowledge of the hydrogeology of Mauna a Wākea contrast with the wealth of knowledge provided in the cultural impact assessment interviews with Kanaka practitioners and long-time residents of the area, who recount detailed observations of the underground caves flowing with water or the puʻu that capture water, such as Puʻu Pōhaku and the flush of puʻu below the northern plateau.

Kuʻulei Higashi Kanahele is the lead Papahulihonua researcher with the Edith Kanakaʻole Foundation's Papakū Makawalu team who focuses on earth and ocean sciences, the development, transformation, and evolution of the earth by natural causes. In her work, she interprets traditional Hawaiian chants that document centuries of environmental observations. In her written direct testimony for the second 2016–17 TMT contested case hearing, Kanahele writes that Mauna a Wākea is a pahuwai (water container) in the hydrological cycle.[62] She explains that the chant "E Ō E Maunakea" describes Maunakea's role in gathering the clouds to recharge the aquifer and names the water deities of Maunakea: Poliʻahu (snow), Lilinoe (mist), Waiau (lake), and Kalauʻākōlea (fog drip).

Kanahele directs our attention to the elemental form Kalauʻākōlea and her particularly significant role in the hydrological cycle. She points out that fog drip feeds the streams that flow inside and down the sides of mountains. Kūpuna knew this and honored fog drip in the form of the elemental deity Kalauʻākōlea. She explains, "Kalauʻākōlea is one of the names found in that chant, 'E Ō E Mauna Kea,' that I referenced earlier, and Kalauʻākōlea, if you translate it literally, ''ākōlea' is the fern and 'ka lau 'ākolea' refers to the leaf blade of that fern. And the leaf blade attracts or collects the water, the mist in the atmosphere, and that water then becomes fog drip."[63] In the moʻolelo of *Keaomelemele*, Kalauʻākōlea is Poliʻahu's younger sister who sings for her a song that is the basis for the mele, "Kahuli Aku, Kahuli Mai."[64] In that song, the kāhuli snails in the forests call out to the kōlea birds, asking them to fetch for them the water from the 'ākolea fern.

The TMT's EIS makes no mention of the importance of fog drip, and this is a notable omission because recharge source studies of neighboring Mauna Loa have confirmed that fog drip is a primary component of the water balance of mountain areas on Hawaiʻi island, exceeding rainfall during the spring and summer months.[65] Fog drip is key because it shows us how the mountain is saturated with water.

Although there is no 'ākōlea fern at the high altitudes of the northern plateau, Kalei Nuʻuhiwa suggests that another term for fog drip is kēwai (dew-laden),[66] and Kūkauakahi Ching provides insights into the ways that it is the pōhaku (rocks) who capture the kēwai in their nono (pores). He explains, "You don't need vegetation for fog drip because rocks can collect it. And this is why the lichens grow under the rocks. The moisture collects under the rocks and feeds the lichen."[67] There are also unexpected 'upena nananana a Papa (spiderwebs of Papa) that capture fog drip (see figure 3.4). In chapter 5, Puni Jackson describes how Papahānaumoku holds out her web

FIGURE 3.4 Mauna a Wākea fog drip captured in an ʻupena nananana a Papa (Papa's spiderweb), June 26, 2016. Photograph by Nelson Ho.

of stars to help Kānaka to track celestial bodies, a phenomenon noted in the Kualiʻi chant that references "O Papa la hoi ka nananana" (Papa is the spider).[68] Referencing the complex system of string coordinates marking the stars in the sky and tied across the ipu hoʻokele waʻa (navigational gourd), here the ʻupena nananana a Papa is part of the hydrological cycle on Mauna a Wākea.

On our own huakaʻi across the mauna, we have seen what I think of as the kapuaʻi o Poliʻahu (footsteps of Poliʻahu), illustrating the ways that Mauna a Wākea is a pahuwai. The traces left by Poliʻahu's movements across the land resemble rivulets that run down the slopes, sweeping larger, multicolored pebbles into lovely hills and ridges of tiny pōhaku. This is the living earth, the diurnal freeze-thaw cycles and frost heave, which creates delicate geomorphological mōʻali (furrow) patterns of little pōhaku (see plate 8). When moist soil experiences sudden freezing temperatures, the water freezes in the soil. Thermomolecular and capillary action draws water from deeper in the soil upward toward the colder temperature, where it solidifies as ice crystals on the cold mornings of the rainy hoʻoilo season. The crystalline ice needles push through the lepo (soil), up toward the sun, rolling the pebbles into the mōʻali between the raised rows. When the ice crystals first emerge, they refract the sunlight into prismatic wonders, tiny rainbows. When the ice melts, the finer brown soil sinks back into the ground in rivulet patterns. This is the elemental wonder of Poliʻahu's footsteps. It is, however, Kealoha Pisciotta's words that breathe aloha into the ʻāina: "If you are there on the mauna early enough, just as the sun rises on a cold night—you can see how the ice crystals form from the moisture below to form icicles that push up through the ʻāina to form this pattern. The crystals shine rainbows as the sun hits them. Just for a moment you can see them. It is so beautiful that tears flow from one's eyes. So humbling . . . kupaianaha [wondrous]!"[69]

ʻIke kupuna defines the sacred in terms of elemental lessons that ensure the flourishing of the people and the islands. Kuʻulei Kanahele concludes, "Our ancestors knew the importance of designating Maunakea as sacred and keeping the summit area pristine to maintain the purity of our water."[70] Kanahele further argues that the problem in this modern world is that humans take a "reactive approach" to protecting resources. Efforts focus on recovering ecosystems after they have been damaged, saving forests by reforestation, saving endangered animals by raising them in captivity. The lesson of ʻike kupuna is to protect ecosystems from harmful human activities so that they are not damaged in the first place.

WALKING IN POLIʻAHU'S FOOTSTEPS: HUAKAʻI I
NĀ ʻĀINA MAUNA AND THE MOʻOLELO OF KAMIKI

If we listen for water, we will hear the elemental forms of water speaking in the moʻolelo of water. In 2013, Kūkauakahi plotted the path for Huakaʻi i Nā ʻĀina Mauna to travel to the sacred springs on Mauna a Wākea remembered in the moʻolelo of Kamiki. I have walked with Kūkauakahi, our alakaʻi (leader), and others on the ancient kuamoʻo (trails) of Mauna a Wākea since 2012. We walk across the mountain lands in the Kanaka Maoli practice of kaʻapuni mākaʻikaʻi as described in chapter 2. On these huakaʻi, we walk in the footsteps of Poliʻahu, Kamiki, the warriors of ʻUmi, the kupua Māui, and Queen Emma to different parts of the mauna, all of which are sacred and related to other land formations both through view-planes and genealogies. As Kūkauakahi explains, walking across Mauna a Wākea changes us: "We go up there to learn about the mountain and how we can learn to live with its most intimate moods and attributes. We go up there to discover who we are and to learn about our special inner workings—and each other. The lines of sight and the land formations you see will become mapped in your naʻau. Being able to experience the intangibles, to experience the experiences of the ancients, brings the kind of special intimacy of real feelings and identification. It's all beautiful."[71] The mauna is mapped in the naʻau, the gut, the deep visceral core of our knowledge and emotions, for all of us, as Kānaka Maoli and as settler aloha ʻāina.

Kanaka Maoli cartography in the moʻolelo of Kamiki tracks the waters of Mauna a Wākea. The moʻolelo of Kamiki was published in the Hawaiian-language newspaper *Ka Hoku o Hawaii* between 1914 and 1917 by John Wise and J. W. H. I. Kihe, telling of the travels in the 1300s of the two supernatural brothers, Kamiki (The quick or adept one) and Makaʻiole (Rat eyes), on a huakaʻi around Hawaiʻi island—along the ala loa and ala hele, the ancient trails and paths—competing along the way with ʻōlohe, experts in running, fishing, debating, or solving riddles.[72] They were empowered by their kupuna, Kauluhenuihihikoloiuka (The great entangled growth of uluhe fern which spreads across the uplands), who instructed Kamiki to travel along ke ala kapu (the sacred path) to the home of Poliʻahu, one of their elder relatives, to collect the sacred water of Kāne for ʻawa. Kamiki goes and dips his ladle into the Waihūakāne spring to fill the ʻawa bowl Hōkūʻula. Along his journey, the water overflows the sides of the bowl to form the numerous springs below the mauna. In this beautiful moʻoʻāina map of Mauna a Wākea, we see how the waters on the plains are derived from the interconnected waterways. Here is the moʻoʻāina map in the moʻolelo of Kamiki:

> O ka lele aku la no ia o Ka-Miki a nalo aku la iloko o ka ohu kolo iluna o ka laau, a pela no hoi o Ma-Kaʻiole a nalo aku la iloko o ke ehu o ka lipo e kuehu ala i ke kula o Waikoloa. I ka oili ana o Ka-Miki a lele, pupuu a hoolei loa, kioʻe ana keia i ka wai Kapu a Kane iloko o ke kanoa i kapaia, o Hoku-ula, a ia wa i ike mai ai na wahi akua kiai i ka ale o ka wai a hu ae la mawaho o ka punawai, a ia laua i holo mai ai, o ka maalo o ke aka ka laua i ike a nalo aku la a ua kapa ia ka inoa o ua punawai ala o "Ka Wai hu a Kane," a hiki i keia la, no ka hu ana o ke kioʻe ana a Ka-Miki i ka wai iloko o ke kanoa awa o ke akua.[73]

> Kamiki then leapt and vanished into the creeping mists of the forest, and in this way, too, Makaʻiole vanished into the onset of darkness on the plains of Waikōloa. When Kamiki burst through the mist, quick as a flash, he began ladling the sacred water of Kāne into the ʻawa bowl named Hōkūʻula, and at that time, the guardians [Pōhakuakāne and Pōhakuloa, the aforementioned "akua kiai"] saw the water rippling and overflowing from the spring. As they approached, they saw a shadow pass them by and disappear, and the spring came to be called Kawaihūakāne (The overflowing waters of Kāne), until this day, because

of the overflowing from Kamiki's scooping the water and pouring it into the 'awa bowl of the god.[74]

The mo'olelo reminds us that Kanaka Maoli cartographies illustrate inter-generational knowledge about the overflowing of water, against the TMT's insistence that water is contained in "perched" and "impermeable layers." We recall, too, the story of Kūkahau'ula and the overflow of water down Pōhakuloa Gulch.

The water that Kamiki collects from the springs is then carried by the Waikōloa winds to form the other springs:

> Holo aku la keia a kiei aku la i ke kula o Waikoloa no ka nana ana i ke kaikuaana ia Ma-Ka'iole, a ike aku la keia ma ke alo iho o na puu o Ho-loholoku iloko o ke ehu pohina o ka lepo e kahili ia mai la e ka Waikoloa, a oia ko ianei wa i huli ae ai a holo maluna o na puu, a ale ae la ka wai a maninini iho la, a kahe aku la a ki'o, a lilo i punawai, a kapaia ia o Waikii a hiki i keia la, no ke kii ana o ka pohaku a Kane, e puai ala i ke kumu o ka pali o ke kuahiwi o MaunaKea, e huli ala ilalo o ke kula lehu lepo o Pohakuloa e nana aku la i ka waiho lakee ae a na puu Kekee.
>
> Pupuu a hoolei loa, ku ana keia i Hanakaumalu, ke kupunawahine o Hiku-i-kanahele, ai kapaia o ke "Ana o Hiku," a hiki i keia la, a aia no keia ana ke waiho la ma ke alo iho o Hainoa a me ka puu o Honuaula, ma ka aoao Hema Komohana o ka piko o Hualalai a me ka wai o Kipahee.[75]

This one [Kamiki] went and peered at the plains of Waikōloa to watch his older brother Maka'iole, and he could see out to the brim of the cinder cones of Holoholokū, inside a hazy cloud of dust swept up by the Waikōloa wind, and at this time, he turned and ran along the tops of the cinder cones, the water splashed over the brim of the awa bowl and flowed down to a pool, becoming a spring called Waiki'i to this day, because Pōhakuakāne fetched some of the water, water that flows out from the base of the cliffs of Mauna Kea, water flowing beneath the dusty plains of Pōhakuloa, water that spreads along the crooked topography of the Keke'e cinder cone.[76]

Quick as a flash, he arrived at Hanakaumalu, the grandmother of Hikuikanahele, called "Keanaohiku" today, and this cave remains at the brim of Hainoa and at the hills of Honua'ula and on the west-south side of the piko of Hualālai and the water of Kipahe'e.[77]

In this passage, the waters of Waiau are carried by the akua, the cold wind Waikōloa, to form the springs that extend from Mauna a Wākea to Hualālai.

Hōkūʻula is also the name of a hill in Waimea said to have been lifted out of the sea by a turtle, where nearby Waikōloa Reservoir 1 is now located. Water collects in puʻu, and Pua Case remembers that, once, she went to the rim of that puʻu at night and saw Hōkūʻula (Mars) reflected in the water in the puʻu.[78] Across the plains of Pōhakuloa the springs extend, waters flowing through intricate underground waterways from Waikiʻi near Puʻu Kekeʻe to Keanaohiku and Kīpaheʻe at Hualālai. The moʻolelo connects these distant moʻoʻāina, from Mauna a Wākea across Pōhakuloa, which is currently leased by the state of Hawaiʻi to the US military for live-fire training. Through careful practices of kilo, kūpuna studied the continuities of these flows, and their ʻike continues to stream to us today through this moʻolelo like the flows of water down Mauna a Wākea.

MAPPING THE GENEALOGY OF ALOHA
ʻĀINA ON MAUNA A WĀKEA

Haley Kailiehu captures the genealogical continuities of these waters of Mauna a Wākea in a community-painted mural on the University of Hawaiʻi campus as a part of an arts festival sponsored by *Ka Leo o Hawaiʻi*, the university newspaper. On October 12, 2013, she sent out a call to students, staff, faculty, and community members to join in painting the mural to call attention to the university's role in supporting the construction of the TMT and to mobilize the community against the DLNR's renewal of the university's general lease for the Mauna Kea Science Reserve. Over a hundred people gathered over the course of the weekend to add their brushstrokes to this mural (see plate 9).

Kailiehu's community mural provides a rich cartography of the genealogical abundance of the life-sustaining waters of Kāneikawaiola on Mauna a Wākea. The painting shows us the sacred water streaming down the mountain from Waiau, home of Moʻoinanea, feeding the Kānaka as kalo people, siblings of the kalo, their leafy arms outstretched to Wākea, Sky father. Their malo is the corm of the kalo rooted in the lepo, the rich soil of the earth, painted like the living, pulsing cells of the pōhaku on the land. At the center of the mural is a visual illustration of the genealogical chant at the opening of this chapter, beginning with Papahānaumoku (The foundation of the earth-birthing islands) and Wākea (Expansive sky father). To the right of them is their daughter, Hoʻohōkūkalani, holding a baby in her arms. Her first child by Wākea was born as an unformed fetus and, when buried, grew into the kalo plant Hāloanakalaukapalili, whose leaves tremble in the wind. The second child she carries in her arms is Hāloa the aliʻi, the younger sibling to the kalo and also to Mauna a Wākea.[79] These ancestors fill the land in the mural, reminding us of the genealogical descent of Mauna a Wākea, of kalo, and of Kānaka from Papa and Wākea, all fed by the life-giving waters of Kāne at Waiau. The mural is a map that restores the land to its embeddedness in the moʻolelo, oli, and mele of abundance and the kuleana given to Kānaka to care for their elder siblings.

The text accompanying the mural calls our attention to the contradictions between the university's mission of being a "Hawaiian place of learning" and its actions demanding the construction of the TMT: "UH CANNOT BE A / HAWAIIAN PLACE OF LEARNING / WHILE LEADING THE DESECRATION / OF MAUNA A WAKEA. / HEY UH . . . BE ACCOUNTABLE. / BE A HAWAIIAN PLACE OF LEARNING. . . . / STAND WITH THE PEOPLE. . . . / STOP THE DESECRATION. . . . / STOP THE THIRTY METER TELESCOPE!" After the completion of the mural on Sunday, however, a *Ka Leo* staffer painted over the message with the words "Ka Leo Arts Festival."

In response to this act of censorship, HauMANA, the student arm of the Movement for Aloha No ka ʻĀina (MANA) led by Kerry Kamakaokaʻilima Long and Andre Perez, quickly organized a march attended by more than two hundred students, faculty, and staff, visually reminiscent of the procession of moʻo water protectors making their way across Oʻahu. Like the moʻo, the Kānaka form an iwikuamoʻo, a continuous backbone of genealogy, supported by settler allies, all marching in the procession to protect the lands and waters of Mauna a Wākea, activating a new generation of water protectors. They rallied outside the *Ka Leo* office building, where they spoke out against the university's act of censorship. Kailiehu reflects on the power of the mural:

> I feel an overwhelming sense of hope. I can remember the people, the keiki with parents, friends with more friends, and the kūpuna, who we were all there painting together. Our Mauna a Wākea mural was an attempt to convey our message to the rest of society, to bring awareness to a concern that we felt all people should understand and know fully. Our Mauna a Wākea mural was a venue where people from within the scope of consciousness and others, not so much aware, could come and learn and actively engage in taking a stance.[80]

The gathering of hundreds of students to stand for the mauna attests to the power of this ancestral map. The abundance that had been eviscerated from the 1901 Territorial Survey map is restored in this mural, which maps the pilina between Kānaka and Mauna a Wākea, and it helped to activate the students in the stand to protect the mauna.

———————————

In the quiet stillness of Mauna a Wākea, with only the sound of the Kīpuʻupuʻu mountain winds whipping our jackets and the crunch of our footsteps on the lava cinders, we make our way down loose, flat rocks, stacked tiles of gray, blue, red, and gold, shifting ground beneath our feet. We look out over the mountain lands, the steeply sloping terrain of rocks, and we see the land open up to a stunning vista as the late afternoon sun casts a golden light on the slopes clothed in yellow mountain grasses, the pili uka (upland grasses) of the heʻupueo, seedheads blowing in the wind. We can see Poliʻahu and her sisters, Līlīnoe, Waiau, and Kahoupokāne wearing the golden kapa pounded from the rays of the sun. We can see the red puʻu (cinder cones) below us, rising out of a rolling surf of clouds like Kānehūnāmoku, the twelve hidden islands of Kāne guarded by Moʻoinanea.

The settler state has desecrated the springs by fencing them in and building concrete reservoirs that divert their sacred waters to pipes that carry the water down to the Pōhakuloa Training Area and to state park bathrooms.[81] Yet the water from one spring contines to stream down from a massive moss-covered boulder, the breast of Kāne, as it has done for millenia. From there, we look out over the plains of Pōhakuloa to imagine the springs that stretch out across military-occupied lands all the way to Hualālai.

Kūkauakahi teaches us the cultural practice of huakaʻi to enable us to bear witness to extraordinary beauty, but he also teaches us that this practice of ea comes with the kuleana of taking direct action to testify against the exploitation of these places and to mobilize people in the stand to protect the mauna. Kūkauakahi has been a petitioner in both contested case hearings and in the Hawaiʻi Supreme Court case against the TMT, and he is a plaintiff in a case against the renewal of the BLNR permit to the US Army and its use of Pōhakuloa for live-fire training exercises at the base of Mauna a Wākea, 133,000 acres across which the springs extend from Waiau.

On these huakaʻi, we walk the lands of Mauna a Wākea in the practice of ea, growing our alignments with the mauna, the akua, and each other as we remember the moʻolelo. From these places, we visualize the moʻoʻāina, the continuities of the many places celebrated in moʻolelo of the waters of Kāne. It is the mapping of this abundance in our naʻau that sustains us in our daily practices of ea as we stand to protect Mauna a Wākea and seek to bring into being a rich and fertile decolonial future for the pulapula, the seedling descendants.

CHAPTER FOUR

KŪPUNA
PŌHAKU
ON MAUNA
A WĀKEA

Spiraling Back
to the Piko

Pōhaku (stones) are manifestations of Pāpahānaumoku, she who is the foundation birthing islands, the ʻāina who feeds. Following the 1893 invasion of Hawaiʻi by the US military and the overthrow of Queen Liliʻuokalani by settler businessmen, the Provisional Government asked the Royal Hawaiian Band to sign an oath forsaking the queen and her government. As ʻōlelo Hawaiʻi and Indigenous politics professor Noenoe Silva recounts, when the band refused, they were told that they would be fired and that they would have only rocks to eat.[1] Ellen Kekoʻaohiwaikalani Wright Prendergast heard their story and composed for them the song "Mele Aloha ʻĀina," also known as "Mele ʻAi Pōhaku" (Stone-eating song) and "Kaulana Nā Pua" (Famous are the flowers). In this song, the aloha ʻāina patriots insist,

> ʻAʻole mākou aʻe minamina,
> I ka puʻukālā a ke aupuni
> Ua lawa mākou i ka pōhaku
> I ka ʻai kamahaʻo o ka ʻāina

We do not value
the government's sums of money
We are satisfied with the stones
Astonishing food of the land.[2]

Here, the aloha ʻāina reject the "hills" of money, proclaiming that they will be fed by food of greater substance, the pōhaku, "ka ʻai kamahaʻo o ka ʻāina" (the wondrous food of the land). "Ua lawa mākou i ka pōhaku" (We are satisfied with the stones) has become a popular rallying cry in the face of occupation and settler colonialism: the stones of the ʻāina are lawa (enough) to sustain the people. We recall from chapter 3 that the nono (pores) of stones collect the fog drip on Mauna a Wākea, feeding the aquifers that sustain the island, and pōhaku form the structures that feed: the fishponds, kalo terraces, heiau (places of worship), and ahu (altars). Kuʻualoha Hoʻomanawanui shares the meaning of being satisfied with stones as it is passed down from kūpuna Eddie Kaanaana and Lydia Hale to Kawika Winter, who writes: "It is with stones that we build our terraces to grow kalo—the staple food of the Hawaiian people. It is with stones that we cook the kalo in the imu. It is with stones that we pound our kalo into poi. It is with stones that we carve the poi board. It is with stones that we carve our canoes to go fishing, And it is with stones that the foundations of our houses are made."[3] Winter concludes, "What it is really saying is that it is our traditions as a Hawaiian people that will carry us on as people." The mana (the divine life force of stones) and the action of standing for the land feed the people, whereas they would starve on paper money that does not provide spiritual sustenance. Abundance here is defined as the living stones of the ʻāina who feeds.

Those who have testified to protect Mauna a Wākea are ʻai pōhaku (stone eaters) whose words have the gravity and weight of stones. They speak the truth, building walls of words, solid as stones, around the sacredness of the mauna. ʻŌlelo Hawaiʻi scholar Kahikina de Silva describes Kanaka Maoli sovereignty activist, scholar, and poet Haunani-Kay Trask as an ʻai pōhaku and elaborates on the aloha ʻāina who stand for the land:

The term ʻai pōhaku is not used lightly. . . . The eating of stones is not smooth and easy. Gleaning sustenance from them does not make you fat like the kōlea bird that visits Hawaiʻi each winter. But as such unyielding, solid creatures, pōhaku are also the hardened, congealed essence of Papa herself and of the land that makes us kānaka. . . . Those who do, whose mouths eat rock, consequently speak with the solidity and mana of the pōhaku they have absorbed. And, when appropriate, they may even spit those rocks at deserving audiences. The voices of such ʻai pōhaku, Haunani-Kay Trask included, are unmistakable. In an age of dislocation they remind their peers and their pōkiʻi that land is not simply a locale; it is our connection to each other, to ancestors gone and descendants to come. And they work endlessly to convince others to politically acknowledge this connection.[4]

The kiaʻi mauna (mountain protectors), too, are the ʻai pōhaku who have come forward to do the difficult work of speaking out against the desecration committed and proposed by the occupying state. Kahikina's father, Kīhei de Silva, explains the resonance of the term "ʻai pōhaku" with moʻo: "a piliamoʻo, a mea hoʻopōhaku, an ʻai pōhaku—one who clings, lizard-like, to rocky cliffs, one who remains immovable, rock-like, in one place; one for whom stones are spirit food."[5] Such ʻai pōhaku, he writes, build walls of stone, "one stone at a time, an embankment over which the profane cannot step and within which the sacred and the life-giving thrive once more."

This chapter honors the ʻai pōhaku who continue to protect the ʻāina and their descendants. The mapping of these ʻai pōhaku shows us an intergenerational spiraling back to the piko that is Mauna a Wākea, to the pilina that connects Kānaka Maoli to the akua (elemental forms), the kūpuna, and the many other ʻaumākua (deified ancestors) who stand for Mauna a Wākea. On June 24, 2015, eight hundred ʻai pōhaku gathered at the mid-elevation mark in an intergenerational human blockade against the construction crews who tried to make their way to the northern plateau to build the Thirty Meter Telescope (TMT). In their testimony against the TMT, Kānaka had testified to the importance of the ahu (stone shrines) on the northern plateau and their connection to the stars. The lines of pilina from Mauna a Wākea extend out across the islands in maps of sight lines, astronomical alignments, and pathways of energy. These view planes remind us of the ways that Mauna a Wākea is connected to distant kūpuna islands in the northwestern Hawaiian islands and to the sun, moon, and constellations. This abundance of Mauna a Wākea has become the source for what kiaʻi mauna Kahoʻokahi Kanuha terms "EAducation," an education in ea, history, politics, and sovereignty as manifested in the struggle to protect Mauna a Wākea. Cartographic artwork by Haley Kailiehu maps the kiaʻi spiraling back to the piko of Waiau, resonating with the visual image of the procession of moʻo water protectors and bringing the kiaʻi in alignment with the akua.

The stand to protect Mauna a Wākea has become a focal point of movements for ea in Hawaiʻi. Leon Noʻeau Peralto, a scholar-activist who founded Hui Mālama i ke Ala ʻŪlili (huiMAU) and whose work traces the histories of the Hāmākua district, describes the wordplay in references to Mauna Kea as the ʻōpuʻu, alluding to the "budding forth" of the mountain as well as comparing the mauna to the lei ʻōpuʻu, the whale tooth pendant that must be recovered in the struggle for ea. He writes,

> In 1959, the United States transferred control of these ʻāina [these lands of Mauna a Wākea] to the state of Hawaiʻi, establishing the Public Land Trust. Since this seizure occurred and American occupation began in these islands, control of the allodial title to these ʻāina mauna has framed the ongoing struggle by Kānaka Maoli and many others to mālama [care for] this keiki mauna na Wākea [mountain child of Wākea], in the face of increasing pressure to impose further desecration upon its summit. Thus . . . our struggle to recover the ʻōpuʻu that is Mauna a Wākea parallels our enduring struggle to reestablish our ea as a lāhui in these islands.[6]

He cites Hawaiian studies scholar Kekuewa Kikiloi, who explains that the genealogy of Mauna a Wākea tells not only of the "ʻbirthing' of the archipelago but also the ʻbirthing' of a unified Hawaiian consciousness."[7]

Kānaka Maoli have stood as protectors of Mauna a Wākea even before the construction of the first telescope in 1968. Shelley Muneoka, a board of member of KĀHEA: The Hawaiian-Environmental Alliance, reminds us that the genealogy of the stand for Mauna a Wākea goes back much further than the struggle against the University of Hawaiʻi's representation of the Thirty Meter Telescope: "The moʻokūʻauhau, the genealogy of this movement doesn't start with people fighting UH, but with people loving Mauna Kea, which extends even further back than that."[8] Although the media has sought to cast the protectors of the mauna as "protestors against astronomy," "telescope detractors," or "foes," each phrase narrowly centers astronomy and positions people against it. The people who stand for Mauna a Wākea have made it clear that they are kiaʻi (protectors) who center the mauna, and as protectors, they stand with land and water defenders all over the world.

Such a movement to protect Mauna a Wākea is built on a strong foundation of kapu aloha. Kapu aloha is a commitment to pono (morally right, just, balanced) actions and the highest form of aloha extended to everyone, including one's opponents. Kumu hula and Mauna Kea hui petitioner Pua Case further explains that while kūʻē (resistance) is important, the sacredness of the mauna and the changing times require a return to kapu aloha as an ancestral protocol of conduct: "Kapu aloha, that means that no matter where you stand on this mauna, you come here in complete aloha, in firm commitment to pono, upright and just. We understand that the time has shifted, and we understand that we need to gather here at this point in time in a different way, in an older way based on what our kūpuna taught us, based on the values that they have left for us, based on the values that still live."[9] Kapu aloha has enabled the movement to grow, and as a guiding protocol it has been a way of inviting everyone, allies and opponents, to join in the movement.

Mauna Kea protector Kealoha Pisciotta further explains kapu aloha as the action of being in alignment with the akua and their laws. Pisciotta learned star knowledge from her aunt, noted expert Kamakahukilani von Oelhoffen, who descended from an ancient navigational line, as well as from the distinguished scholar Rubellite Kawena Johnson, and she explains that the mauna teaches us kapu aloha through the laws of the akua: "Encoded in the very landscape of the mauna are the great wisdom songs of creation. The first songs of aloha. These were the songs sung for us by the akua to bring us into being and to help bring us into alignment with them."[10] These alignments move events and make possible ʻāina momona (fertile lands), as she elaborates:

> Kapu aloha is aloha in motion. It's how we move aloha. When the akua roam the land, they're invoking the kāhelahela, translated as the summation of the life of the sea and the land. We invoke kapu aloha so that we can be in alignment with akua to make the ʻāina, ʻāina momona [abundant lands]. When we are in alignment with akua then the mauna miracles happen, the ʻāina flourishes and everything is restored to the sacredness of the day it was created.
>
> When you see nature respond with us, then we know we're in alignment. The classic story is about the symbol of the aliʻi that is the rainbow. There were special people who used to kāhea [call out] to create the alignment, to call forth the rainbow for the aliʻi. They were aligning things so that the aliʻi were walking in alignment. Aunty Kamaka used to say, "Throw the rainbow!" And we were like, what do you mean, Aunty? "You gotta line it up, Kealoha, do the oli [chant], call it out!" I really didn't know what she was talking about. But she had us practice

in the water, and she'd say, find the sound that resonates in the water, like the pū [conch shell], she would say, [blow] one pū, two pū, they create a third sound that is beyond the resonance of each of the two. "Find the resonance, find the resonance." So in the water, you go and practice, just try hakalama [syllabary], "a–e–i–o–u." Just try to find the sound that resonates with the water. I was practicing and practicing, kept trying, kept trying, and then all of a sudden, I hit that point, the resonance. It goes "WHOOOOH!" across the water. My aunty heard it, too. And once you find it, you try to figure it out for all of the elements, where is the resonance? That's how we determine that we are in alignment. We're going to see the hōʻailona [sign].[11]

In this powerful description, we see kapu aloha as the movement of sound and vibration, a condition that makes pono (right, balanced) action happen. Pisciotta teaches us that we chant to send out the kāhea with an aloha that reverberates, setting up alignments among the elements with our voices so that the sun and the rain can come together to form the rainbows or other wondrous phenomena.

Kapu aloha has strengthened the people who have stood for the mauna like the ancestral moʻo water protectors. In June 2015, as attorneys for the TMT and the Mauna Kea hui were preparing for the August 27 Hawaiʻi Supreme Court hearing on the validity of the Board of Land and Natural Resources's approval of the conservation district use permit (CDUP) for the TMT, the kiaʻi mauna learned that the TMT was planning to commence construction, despite the fact that the court case had not yet been resolved. Two months earlier, on April 2, there had been thirty-one arrests of kiaʻi who took a stand to protect Mauna a Wākea from construction crews. Construction had been halted then, but the protectors learned that construction was scheduled to begin once more. They sent out the kāhea (rallying call), and many of us flew to Hawaiʻi island. On June 24, at 4:00 in the morning, hundreds of us, Kānaka, settler aloha ʻāina, Black, American Indian, First Nations, Palestinian, and Muslim aloha ʻāina, Maori and other Pacific cousins, gathered at Hale Pōhaku under the dim glow of lights from the Mauna Kea Visitor Center.

The kiaʻi leaders turned to ʻike kupuna to structure the action that was to take place that day. ʻŌlelo Hawaiʻi kumu (teacher) and kiaʻi mauna Kahoʻokahi Kanuha mapped out the strategy of forming lines of people across the access road to the summit, in order to set into motion the structure of the Kumulipo, the koʻihonua chant detailing the genealogical connectedness of all things, from the land, seas, and skies to Kānaka Maoli. He later explains, "We try as much as possible to ground our resistance in cultural understanding. I wanted sixteen lines of kia'i on the state road to represent the 16 wā [eras] of the Kumulipo. The county and state officers would have to get through the seven wā of Pō, night, before they got to other wā of Ao, day, hence the idea of sixteen lines and sixteen alaka'i."[12] The lines would start at what has become known as the "Legendary Crosswalk" or the Aloha 'Āina Checkpoint, the crosswalk in front of the visitor center where kia'i are asked to "check our aloha" to be sure that we are all in kapu aloha. Sixteen lines, each with an alaka'i (leader), would then be positioned above the paved county road on the graded state road, fifty feet apart. The county police and state officers would have to explain their rights to every line of protectors before any arrests could be made. As Kanuha spoke, I could see in my mind's eye a vision of the Legendary Crosswalk multiplied sixteen times up the mauna on the state road.

The kia'i called for volunteers to be legal observers to document the arrests and the treatment of the people, to ensure that the state Division of Conservation and Resources Enforcement (DOCARE) officers were following procedures. Although I was willing to be arrested, as an older Japanese woman I would be more useful as a legal observer who would remind the DOCARE officers of their aunties and schoolteachers. My work would be to try to ensure that the officers were taking the time to follow their own protocols and to prevent any violence from being inflicted on the protectors. As a legal observer, I planted myself with the first line of kia'i on the state road.

Hawai'i County police arrived at the Aloha 'Āina Checkpoint at 7:00 in the morning, where rows of kia'i had spontaneously organized themselves below the state road, chanting, in successive lines twenty feet apart up the quarter-mile of county road to the state road. The officers were greeted by children who extended kapu aloha to them with lei lā'ī (tī leaf lei) to ensure that all would be safe. For three hours, police talked with multiple lines of hundreds of protectors who stretched across the expanse of the county road, explaining their rights to them as kia'i continued to chant in ceremony. There was only one arrest during this time.

At 10:00, we saw protectors making their way up to the state road. We all watched as DOCARE Chief Lino Kamakau approached Lākea Trask, the alaka'i of the first line. Trask, Haunani-Kay Trask's nephew, stood kūpa'a (steadfast) for the mauna in respectful conversation. At this time, cultural practitioner and educator Luana Busby-Neff directly addressed Kamakau with compassion: "You have a beloved name of ours that we cherish and honor: Kamakau, one of our great historians. We know the battle is not with you, and we're in a system that is dividing and separating us. The kapu aloha that we hold is for you specifically, because of how they have chosen you to come forward to us. It's hard."[13] Kamakau was visibly moved and replied, "The feelings are mutual. Trust me. I have a hard time. But I gotta do my job." When the line finally dispersed, protectors moved up to the second line of protectors behind them. At the second line, Kanuha stated clearly, "I give you my word. I will not block traffic. I *will* block desecration."[14] When the DOCARE officers realized that there were more lines ahead, they pushed forward and began arresting the kia'i.

Line after line, the protectors stood with red kīhei tied over one shoulder and with red "Kū Kia'i Mauna" ("Stand, mountain protectors," or "Stand like the mauna") shirts, holding their ground on the mauna as long as they could. In the mana wahine line, Kaleinohea Cleghorn, Nohea Kawa'a-Davis, Alohilani Keohuloa, Mehana Kihoi, Ku'uipo Freitas, Naaiakalani Colburn, Hōkūlani Reyes, and many more women stood with arms linked, holding the length of a lei lā'ī, chanting "Mālana mai Ka'ū" in powerful unison, calling together the peoples of the different districts of Hawai'i island in the building of a canoe sealed together by Mauna a Wākea (see plate 10).[15] Long after this stand, this photo continues to be circulated to rally kia'i at times when Mauna a Wākea is most in need of protection. In the 'ōpio line, Movement for Aloha No ka 'Āina (MANA) organizer Kerry Kamakaoka'ilima Long led the young people who were growing into their own leadership kuleana (responsibility, right, purview, privilege). The DOCARE officers moved forward, arresting eleven people along the way, including Kanuha, Kaleikoa Ka'eo, Hualalai Keohuloa, and Andre Perez, leaders in the Hawaiian independence movement. These leaders dropped to the ground when arrested, and as the DOCARE officers carried them away, as the people wailed "Auwē!" out of grief and concern, Kaleikoa said to the officers, "I love you guys more than you guys know! This is for our keiki o ka 'āina [children of the land]! We have to fight for our people! We will be gone if we don't work together! We must show the world we love this place!"[16]

With the mists of Līlīnoe enveloping us and the icy, biting Kīpu'upu'u and Kuauli rains warding the crews away from the summit as they once did to Kūkahau'ula, Poli'ahu's suitor, the state officers and the construction crews were stopped at the eleventh line where 'Ohulei Waia'u led the kia'i who chanted and danced to "Mele Hānau no Kauikeaouli," asserting the genealogies of Mauna a Wākea and Kānaka.[17] The kia'i who stood in that line, Pumpkin Waia'u, Leialoha Kaleohano, Winter Ho'ohuli, Kini Kaleilani Burke, and

Michelle Tomas, chanted in rhythmic powerful unison, their voices ringing strong and clear in the mist and the rain.

This powerful moment illustrates the fullest expression of ea, an upsurging of a sovereign people aligned with the elemental forms. The mana or life forces converged as they chanted their genealogy: the ua, the rains, and the mists watering the Kānaka, the pulapula (seedlings) of Papahānaumoku and Wākea; the pōhaku planted in the road, standing as kūpuna with their descendants; the Kānaka who chanted their genealogical relationship to the mauna, standing in the malu o ka mauna, the sheltering protection of the mauna. In this powerful moment, the kiaʻi faced a contemporary threat but stood for Mauna a Wākea firmly rooted in their ancestral knowledges, offering their leo (voices) up to the akua of the mauna.

The alignments were so powerful that the convoy of state officers and the construction crews could not proceed. Chief DOCARE officer Kamakau announced that they were calling off construction for the day. He approached the eleventh line and was brought to tears, "Aloha everybody. From myself . . . I apologize to you guys. . . . You understand what I gotta do. And you may not accept it, but I gotta do my job. I'm really, really sorry. Our number one thing right now is public safety. We're not going up."[18] The kiaʻi hugged this Kanaka and expressed their aloha for him, one of their own people who had been sent by the occupying state to divide Kānaka Maoli from each other but who was instead courageous enough to show everyone the transformative power of kapu aloha.

The administrators of the occupying state gave different reasons for calling off construction that day. First, they said that the rain and the lack of time would make it difficult for construction crews to work. Then they said that the pōhaku that had been planted in the road were the deterrent. They refused to acknowledge the power of the people's leo in unison and the ancestral elemental forms that stood with them that day in kapu aloha.

OCCUPYING STATE TACTICS OF TELESCOPING
AND KANAKA MAOLI STAR MAPS

Kūpuna pōhaku are present on Mauna a Wākea in the many ahu that form the Ring of Shrines on the mauna. The TMT environmental impact statement (EIS) identifies more than 263 historic properties in the Mauna Kea Summit Region Historic District, including 141 ancient shrines in the Mauna Kea Science Reserve.[19] Yet instead of considering how all of these historic sites in the district are related to one another as a complex, the TMT's use permit application isolates only *three* sites as "traditional cultural properties" (TCPs): Puʻu Kūkahauʻula, Lake Waiau, and Puʻu Līlīnoe. By isolating these three sites, the university argues that the TMT is removed from "significant" TCPs and does not have an adverse cultural impact on them.

The archaeologist who testified as a UH witness in the 2011 contested case hearing stated that the TMT project would not have a direct impact on historic sites or their immediate surroundings.[20] Her argument was that, since there was an "empty space" in the middle of the historic shrines, the archaeologists had determined this to be the optimal site for the TMT. Upon cross-examination, the archaeologist admitted that she does not read ʻōlelo Hawaiʻi and has access only to translations and works printed in English.[21] In the case of the TMT, the final EIS selectively relied on non-Hawaiian evaluations of sites on the northern plateau to produce the desired findings to support the TMT.

Because capitalist regimes read "space" as "empty"—and so ostensibly not utilized to its "highest and best use"—the archaeologist failed to acknowledge that the proposed site for the TMT sits in the middle of an entire complex of shrines. In his cross-examination, Mauna a Wākea practitioner E. Kalani Flores asked the archaeologist, "Do you know if these particular sites that we see here surrounding the TMT site, if there is an energetic spiritual connection between these sites and the other sites within here?"[22] She replied, "I can't make that determination."

Flores pointed out that the occupying state used cartography to minimize the appearance of impact through omitting key sites. In October 2010, the University of Hawaiʻi at Hilo submitted the CDUP application on behalf of the TMT, and the site map the university submitted showed only three historic shrines and one terrace in the vicinity of the TMT: a "single upright stone with several support stones" (SIHP No. 16172), "one, possibly two uprights placed in a bedrock crack" (SIHP No. 16167), a "multi-feature shrine with total of eight, possibly nine uprights arranged in two groups" (SIHP No. 16166), and a "terrace of unknown function" (SIHP No. 21449) (see figure 4.1).[23]

Flores drew our attention to a contrasting map from the *Archaeological Inventory Survey of the Mauna Kea Science Reserve* (August 2010) that provided a fuller picture of the northern plateau. Flores showed us that the CDUP application map failed to depict two historic properties and five "find spots": SIHP No. 16169, SIHP No. 21447, and "find spots" 1997.034, 2005.05, 2005.06, 2000.7, and 2005.08.[24] "Find spots" are defined as those findings that are modern or cannot be defined as historic sites because of an uncer-

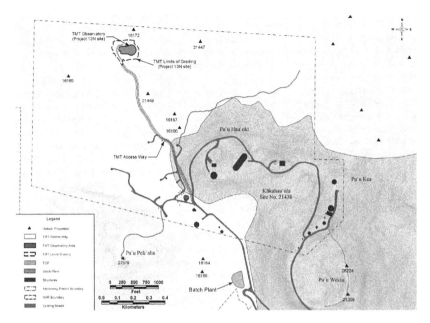

FIGURE 4.1 Map of historic properties in the vicinity of the TMT project site. Presented in the TMT Conservation District Use Permit Application.

tainty regarding their age, but they attest to the contemporary continuation of traditional practices on the northern plateau.[25] The sheer number of 263 historic sites and find spots on the *Archaeological Inventory Survey* map proves that the TMT would be located at the very center of intensive traditional practices.

Flores went on to describe the "telescoping effect," yet another iteration of a settler colonial mathematics of subdivision that reduces the field of vision. Flores elaborates, "What they have done is they have minimized. They gave us the telescoping effect. Telescoping effect, you know what it is? You take a look at the telescope, you zoom in so you only can see this and you don't see everything else. According to the state and federal law in the assessment of sites, there's a need to look at all the sites in their integrity."[26] Flores then presented a map of the Ring of Shrines illustrating that the entire summit of the mauna is a sacred district (see figure 4.2).

Archaeologists have devised recommendations for what they call "distributional archaeology" to address tactics like telescoping. In her testimony as an expert witness, archaeologist, anthropologist, and ethnohistorian Kēhaunani Abad argued that the archaeological inventory survey for Mauna

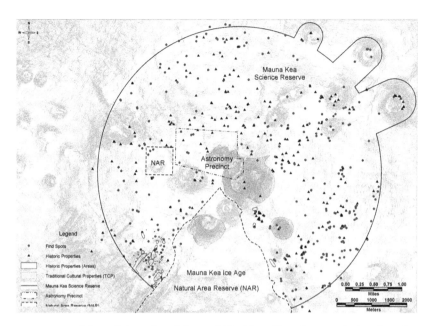

FIGURE 4.2 Map of Macro-Level Site and Find Spot Distribution, *Archaeological Inventory Survey of the Mauna Kea Science Reserve*, 2010.

a Wākea exemplifies a foundational problem in archaeological studies: the failure to evaluate individual sites as parts of regional complexes. She writes, "A body of archaeological literature referred to generally as distributional archaeology argues that studies using smaller-sized sites as the units of analysis lack rigor and fail to glean the full explanatory potential from the archaeological record, especially as it relates to surface artifacts (as opposed to artifacts found in excavations), a scenario especially applicable to finds at Maunakea."[27] Because Western-trained archaeologists deem modern cultural practitioners as "not credible," they refuse to consult them about the purposes of the shrines, leading to their conclusions that the purposes of these shrines are "unknown," even as knowledge of these shrines continues to be passed down among Kanaka Maoli practitioners.

Flores testified that far from being an "empty space," the shrines on the northern plateau form an intricate star map. In his written direct testimony, Flores cited an ancestral guardian connected to a pōhaku near the TMT site: "This guardian explained the significance of many of the sites on the northern plateau as they are interconnected like a large star map. Individuals from certain family lines were guided to come up to the mountain during certain times of the year to reestablish, construct, align, activate, and/or maintain these sites."[28]

An understanding of the configuration of shrines as a map illuminates the astro-architectural star knowledge that the archaeologists were unable to access because they refused to consult the body of Kanaka Maoli practitioners who continue their practices today. The "empty space" is in fact a nexus of energetic lines that Flores described as "aka." He explained, "On the northern plateau, many of the sites have both visual and energetic alignments with each other as well as with other noted natural features such as the surrounding puʻu. Due to the massive height and size of the TMT observatory, it would cause significant visual, physical, and energetic obstructions amongst these sites."[29] The shrines that make up the Mauna a Wākea star map continue to activate the Kānaka who are learning the intergenerational knowledge of the stars and the spiritual alignments created by the shrines.

Yet despite this testimony, the Hawaiʻi Supreme Court majority ruling in 2018 concluded that "the BLNR found no Native Hawaiian cultural resources or traditional or customary practices within the TMT Observatory site and Access Way areas."[30] The egregious nature of the Supreme Court's majority opinion was fully contested in the petitioners' motion for reconsideration, which points to numerous expert witnesses who testified to their cultural practices at the proposed site of the TMT: in addition to solstice and equinox ceremonies at shrines on the northern plateau and other practices tracking celestial bodies in space, there are medicinal items that can only be collected on the northern plateau and ceremonies honoring iwi kupuna (ancestral remains) buried there.[31]

While the Flores-Case ʻOhana presented testimony on the sacredness of the northern plateau, they emphasized that the entire mountain is sacred as a piko. Flores cites Pua Kanahele's description of Mauna a Wākea embodying the three piko on the human body and expands on her words to explain the damage the construction of telescopes and their presence has caused on the mountain:

> It is this *piko* on top of the summit where energies and life forces flow from higher dimensions and the Creator and are then transferred into the Earth. . . . However, when the piko of the summit is obstructed with the physical excavation of the landscape, asphalt and cement pavement, metal posts implanted in the ground, buildings, and construction, it curtails or prevents this flow of energy. Thus, the development on the summit is causing adverse impacts and significant obstructions of the life forces that flow into these islands through this *piko*.[32]

If we think of the ways that the pōhaku in ahu channel energy, Mauna a Wākea itself is the greatest ahu that channels energy upward, reverberating into the heavens, connecting the mauna to other mountains and to the stars in the sky.

MOʻOʻĀINA LINES OF ENERGY AND SIGHT

As the attorneys for the TMT were employing a telescopic optic to enclose and diminish expansive Kanaka Maoli views of Mauna a Wākea in relation to other bodies in space, ʻike kupuna documents the genealogical relationships between Kānaka and the ancestors in the skies. In the Kumulipo, we see the expansiveness of Kanaka relationships with the sun, moon, and stars who are also akua, celestial ancestors with whom they have intimate relationships. The stars are listed in "Wa Umikumamaha" (The fourteenth era) of the Kumulipo where we are told,

> Paa na hoku kau i ka lewa,
> Lewa kaawela lewa Kupoilaniua
> Lewa hai aku lewa hai mai,
> Lewa ka hai lewa ka haihai,
> Lewa ka ua ka puuhoku wahilaninui,
> Lewa ka pua o ka lani Kauluaihaimohai,
> Lewa puanene ka hoku hai haka.[33]

> The stars secured were hung in space.
> Streaks of dawn were hung up with Kupoilaniua in space.
> Rocking here and rocking there
> Hung the bunches of swift offerings,
> Hung the bunch of stars that rained in Wahilaninui,
> Hung the flower of the heavens Kauluaihaimohai,
> Hung the little stars of fighting omen.[34]

What follows next is a list of the stars and constellations, including Nahuihui (Orion) and Makaliʻi (Pleiades).

These genealogical lines are also traced in the moʻolelo. The Milky Way is compared to fish, and one name for it is Kaiʻauiokalani. Rubellite Kawena Johnson refers to the Milky Way as a moʻo, and she also references the prayer "Pule Hoʻowilimoʻo." Moʻo here could be a path or succession of stars but also resonates with lizard, and Moʻoinanea's genealogical line extends to the moon and the stars, as is documented in the moʻolelo of ʻAukelenuiaʻīkū.[35]

In this moʻolelo printed in the Hawaiian-language newspapers, Kamoʻoianea weaves together the strands of her genealogy by arranging the meeting of ʻAukelenuiaʻīkū and Nāmakaokahaʻi. In the Kaunamano version of the moʻolelo, we see that the moʻo Kamoʻoʻīnanea (Kamooianea) is the sister of Kaukihikamalama, the kupuna pōhaku who is the moon.[36] Kamooianea is the mother of Haumea and the grandmother of Nāmakaokahaʻi, who rules over her relatives, including the sun, moon, and stars. Kamooianea is also the mother of Kapapaiākea, ʻAukelenuiaʻīkū's mother. ʻAukelenuiaʻīkū is the favored son of the aliʻi ʻĪkū, and, one day, his jealous older brother throws him into the pit of Kamooianea to be devoured. Instead, ʻAukele's younger brother calls out to her that ʻAukelenuiaʻīkū is her grandson, and so Kamooianea recognizes ʻAukele by giving him a map. She devours two men and then vomits or discharges (luaʻi) them onto two large ʻape leaves to form a map, passing on words of instruction to her grandson: "[O] keia mau aina elua e ku nei ma ke alo o kaua la, o Holaniku a me Holanimoe he mau aina maikai loa keia, he nui na wahi pono i ke kanaka e noho ai, he nui ka ai, ka awa, ke ko, ka maia, na mea ai no a pau e ola ai ke kanaka" (These two lands that stand before us are Hōlanikū and Hōlanimoe; these are very beautiful lands with many good places for people to live, abundant vegetable food, awa, sugarcane, bananas, everything people need to live).[37]

She gives him other gifts as well. She gives him a god, Lonoikaʻoualiʻi, the laukahi leaf that satisfies hunger for four months, an ax, and a knife that can cut into anything. Then she cuts off her tail (huelo), and she says to her grandchild, "O kuu kino maoli keia" (This is my real body).[38] Through her tail, Kamooianea passes on to her grandson the knowledge of his genealogy that he will use to pass through her brothers and sisters to the place where guards protect the waters of Kāne. Moʻolelo scholar ʻIolani Antonio extends this gift of genealogy to the ways that the moʻo teaches us lessons of regeneration: Kānaka can grow aloha ʻāina for lands and places in Hawaiʻi and elsewhere that are not their ancestral lands: "In the same way that Kamooianea has the potential, as a moʻo, to regenerate her tail, we Kānaka Maoli who have been violently severed from our kulāiwi can regenerate connection and meaningful relationships through the resurgent practices of aloha and mālama ʻāina, regardless of whether or not we are genealogically connected to the places for whom we fight."[39] Aloha ʻāina is regenerative, and seeds can be planted in new lands, as ʻAukelenuiaʻīkū learns when he voyages to the lands of Nāmakaokahaʻi.

In this moʻolelo, we see one account of the pilina between Kānaka and the moon. When ʻAukelenuiaʻīkū goes in search of the waters of Kāne,

Nāmakaokahaʻi tells him to fly straight to the sun, but, falling astray to the left, ʻAukelenuiaʻīkū hurtles into deep space and survives only by catching hold of Kaukihikamalama.[40] The moon tells him that even his grandchild Nāmakaokahaʻi has never climbed his back and asks in irritation, "Na wai oe?" (Whose [child] are you?). ʻAukelenuiaʻīkū responds, "Nau no, oi ana, o ke keiki au a Kapapaiakea laua o Iku" (Yours, above all, I am the child of Kapapaiakea and Iku).[41] ʻAukelenuiaʻīkū knows his genealogy, and he can claim that he is the moon's. The moon further queries, "O ka hanai no oe a ka Poino laua o Kamoemoea?" (Are you the one raised by Poino and Kamoemoea?). When ʻAukelenuiaʻīkū affirms this, we are told "maopopo iho la i ka mahina he moopuna ia nana" (the moon understood that he was a grandchild of his), that ʻAukelenuiaʻīkū is a "keiki a Kapapaiakea laua o Iku, hanai a Poino laua o Kamoemoea, moopuna a Kamooianea" (child of Kapapaiakea and Iku, raised by Poino and Kamoemoea, grandchild of Kamooianea).

The lines of flight in the moʻolelo of ʻAukelenuiaʻīkū from this earth to the moon and the stars can be mapped as view planes from Mauna a Wākea. Kealoha Pisciotta explains that Mauna a Wākea is the fulcrum of solstice and equinox ceremonies and of different kinds of navigational practices because it is the highest point for sight lines to and from sacred places. To illustrate these sight lines, Pisciotta submitted a map that depicts traditional Hawaiian cultural view planes as exhibit c-5 in the contested case hearing in 2011 (see plate 11). A planning group from the University of California at Berkeley called Community by Design worked with Pisciotta to map the star knowledge of her aunt, Kamakahukilani Von Oelhoffen, her Oniha family, and her own kilo hōkū (star practices), including that of the solstice and equinox ceremonies conducted on the mauna.[42] In contrast to the occupying state's diminishing cartographies of telescoping, this more expansive mapping of view planes extends out from Mauna a Wākea, connecting to heiau on Kauaʻi, to the kūpuna islands (the northwestern Hawaiian islands), and further out to Polaris and Pleiades at the New Year, and to the Southern Cross. Pisciotta writes:

> On this view-plane map, you can see that the TMT will be in direct line of sight of Maui and the NW plane which is used for ke ala ao (solstice and equinox ceremonies). There are also lines that represent the relationship between Mauna Kea and Poliʻahu Heiau on Kauaʻi, Ahu a ʻUmi Heiau situated between the three great mountains (Hualālai, Mauna Loa, and Mauna Kea) on Hawaiʻi Island, the Puʻukoholā Heiau in Kawaihae, Hawaiʻi Island, and Motu Manamana (Necker Islander) of

the North Western Hawaiian Islands which marks the great turnaround of the sun during the ke ala polohiwa [solstice] time.[43]

The view planes look out from and to Mauna a Wākea from these different places across the island and extend across the archipelago and into the skies. The view planes chart channels of energy that run between alignments of the mauna with heiau and other sacred places.

True to form, the University attorneys' interpretation of this expansive view planes map attempted to contain these continuities once more by actually *subdividing practice*. Arguing that the view-planes map presented the views from a single spot on the summit, the UH attorneys argued that Kanaka practitioners only engage in practices at a single place at the summit, despite the Mauna Kea hui's repeated testimony that practitioners engage in practices all over the mountain lands, with the evidence of 263 shrines all over the summit region.[44]

REBUILDING THE AHU

The pōhaku are the kūpuna (ancestors) who feed their descendants. Stones are passed hand to hand, from Kanaka to Kanaka, to build fishponds, loʻi kalo and heiau, places of sustenance and ceremony. When Kamehameha I built Puʻukoholā Heiau, a line of thousands of Kānaka stretched across fourteen miles, passing rocks hand to hand, from Pololū Valley in North Kohala to Kawaihae. Kānaka continue to halihali pōhaku in restoration projects today.

Kānaka have also continued to engage in traditional practices of constructing ahu, a practice that requires deep knowledge of and attentiveness to the life force of rocks. On June 21, 2015, a group of Kānaka Maoli gathered at the site of the proposed TMT with a truckload of heavy pōhaku to build an ahu. Among those who had gathered was William Freitas, an uhauhumu pōhaku or kāne pōhaku (stonemason) who works with stones. He begins his story by saying, "The pōhaku is the piko, the umbilicus, that led me to Mauna a Wākea."[45] On April 2, 2015, the day that thirty-one protectors of Mauna a Wākea were arrested for protecting the site of the proposed TMT from construction crews, a photograph of Freitas confronting county and state law enforcement officers on Mauna a Wākea went viral on social media. He sat in the roadway to the summit, immovable as a pōhaku, in a way that resonated worldwide with other images of Indigenous elders who are the stones standing for their descendants (see figure 4.3). That image was a powerful galvanizing force that rendered visible the asymmetrical power

FIGURE 4.3 William Freitas, a pōhaku kupuna for Mauna a Wākea. April 2, 2015. Photograph by Kuʻuipo Freitas.

relations between the occupying state and Kanaka Maoli protectors, as well as the unbounded aloha ʻāina of the protectors who were willing to be arrested to protect the mauna. His daughter Kuʻuipo pulled his hands down before he could be handcuffed, and he agreed to step aside, only to find that she was later arrested at the summit.

William Freitas has always worked with stone, recognizing stones and asking them for their permission to be moved and used to build. He reflects, "As we come forth daily into the world, we're always taking, taking, all that Papahānaumoku has. As soon as men open their eyes, they first thing they going to do is take, take from the land, so we ask permission to harvest, we ask permission to take, we ask permission for everything, to even enter, to even walk into the space."[46] The chanting for permission is part of an exchange: the voice is a gift that possesses mana, the life that comes from a person in the breath, the chanting, and the thoughts. He explains that when he builds ahu, he asks permission of each stone whether they want to be a part of the ahu: "When I feel the stone, the mana of the stone resonates with my naʻau [visceral core], and they tell me if they want to come with me or not."[47] Many stones have asked him to take them home with him, and he finds later that their homes at Kohanaiki, Heʻeia Bay, and Honokōhau Harbor have been destroyed by overdevelopment.

Three months later, on June 21, the protectors built an ahu on a site that the TMT had desecrated. The original pāhoehoe lava trail had been made into a jeep road and was bulldozed by TMT crews to broaden the roadway to the proposed site. When the kiaʻi arrived at the TMT site, the security guards told them that their trucks could not enter. The protectors climbed out of their trucks and lined up, stretching everyone out as far as they could go. And then, as their ancestors had done for millennia, they worked to halihali pōhaku, passing the stones hand to hand. The second ahu was built on June 23, and Ke Ahu o ka Uakoko was built on June 24, the day that the construction crews tried to make their way to the proposed TMT site. William remembers:

> I was not there, but they built it because while they were standing there waiting for the parade of TMT to come up, their naʻau [visceral core and seat of knowledge] started talking to them. These young ones did it themselves. I had showed them how to do it from the beginning. There's a piko of the area we are going to build the ahu in. We're going to lay the layers spiritually from the beginning. Before we start there's a pule [prayer], and as we build, as we go around each stone, we pule until we reach the top. But the items that were in the hoʻokupu [offering], those are the items that protect that ahu. The hoʻokupu sat there until it disintegrated and went into the ahu.

When the protectors successfully warded off law enforcement and the construction crews that day, the protectors agreed to take down two of the ahu with the understanding that the third ahu, Ahu o ka Uakoko, would remain because it did not block the road. Yet on September 13, 2015, protectors found the ahu had been bulldozed to the ground. Under investigation, it appeared that a Mauna Kea Support Services employee had removed the ahu to access "fill material" for repairs to a road.

The desecration of the ahu was one that filled the people with kaumaha, a heavy grief, yet the protectors redirected their energy to focus instead on kapu aloha and the joy of standing with other aloha ʻāina for Mauna a Wākea. Pua Case teaches the kiaʻi that we cannot be driven to anger or colonial despair, because our children will look to us in these movements, and we have to teach them that we rejoice in the privilege of standing for the mauna. This movement will have longevity, and ea will be intergenerational for our children. She writes,

> Although we are seriously strengthening ourselves and standing steadfast . . . we honor the healing, the joy, and above all the laughter . . . for

we must remain healthy and our children must see that we are in harmony and balance and as we stand as leaders and in service, and as we work hard we remain in peace within ourselves and we breathe the same breath as Mother Earth . . . and we will not let anyone drive us to anger or rage, to depression. For our children, let us remain light-hearted, in peace as we move onward and forward. . . . Idle No More. . . . Eo![48]

In the face of colonial despair, the protectors of the mauna have chosen life and joy in their collective celebration of their relationship with the mauna.

One of the mele that has come to represent this collective effort of protecting Mauna a Wākea is "Mālana Mai Ka'ū," a song excerpted from a longer chant and sung to celebrate the voyaging canoe Hōkūle'a. "Mālana Mai Ka'ū" is a map that describes the people and places of the different districts of Hawai'i island, from Ka'ū, Puna, and Hilo, to Kona, Kohala, and Hāmākua, to Waipi'o, Mahiki, Waimea, and Kawaihae. The places are themselves the parts of a canoe, and Mauna a Wākea is the pala (sealant) that binds together the different districts:

Mālana mai Ka'ū
Mālana mai Ka'ū, me Puna, me Hilo,
Hele mai Kona me Kohala me Hāmākua,
He ka'ele 'o Waipi'o, he pola 'o Mahiki,
He uka 'o Waimea, he awa Kawaihae,
He kupe no ka wa'a o Poli'ahu,
He pala Mauna a Wākea i luna
Pa'a kuahiwi ke ali'i i ka wa'a
Ohohia i ka hana 'ana aku ē

Buoyant Comes Ka'ū
Buoyant comes Ka'ū and Puna, and Hilo,
Traveling from Kona, Kohala and Hāmākua,
Waipi'o is hollow like a hull, Mahiki, flat like a platform,
Waimea is a highland, Kawaihae, a harbor,
An end piece for the canoe is Poli'ahu,
Mauna Kea, there above, is a sealant for the wood,
The forest is secured by the chief who cuts down the wood
Rejoicing at the activity.[49]

When Case teaches this chant to those who stand for Mauna a Wākea, she focuses on the final line of the chant: "Ohohia i ka hana 'ana aku ē." She tells us, "The most beautiful word is in that last line. The word 'ohohia' [to rejoice] is going to remind us what feeling, what spirit we are in. We are in the joy of being in the mauna, in the joy of being aware, conscious enough to know that we remember our mauna is sacred and the joy in that."[50] What becomes clear is that ohohia is an integral part of kapu aloha: it is what sustains people in struggle, what brings them together again and again as a lāhui.

MAPPING ABUNDANCE THROUGH EADUCATION

We are now seeing a great flowering forth, an awakening throughout the islands and across the globe that has been brought about by Mauna a Wākea and the abundance of intergenerational leadership. Kānaka Maoli and settler aloha ʻāina are engaged in statist and nonstatist forms of organizing on the mountain and across the islands. As more and more people travel to Mauna a Wākea to support the kiaʻi mauna, we have seen the emergence of what Hawaiian medium preschool teacher Kahoʻokahi Kanuha has termed "EAducation," a philosophy of education that directs educational projects on the Hawaiian historical and cultural foundations for political autonomy. Kanuha organized the Hawaiʻi Aloha ʻĀina series of EAducation workshops on the mauna that have grown into a widespread movement across the islands to educate people about ea (political sovereignty), Hawaiian history, and politics. Kanuha explains the importance of education as a foundation for movements for ea:

> "EAducate" is a word that I used at the beginning of the Mauna Kea movement. On September 20, 2014, I started Hawaiʻi Aloha ʻĀina, a monthly series of free presentations for the community in Kona. I made Aloha ʻĀina messaging on t-shirts to support this series financially. Our first shirt was "ā hiki i ke Aloha ʻĀina hope loa" (until the very last Aloha ʻĀina). These were the words spoken by James Keauiluna Kaulia in a speech against the annexation of Hawaiʻi by the United States where he famously stated that Kānaka would stand for Hawaiʻi's independence until the very last aloha ʻāina, the very last patriot of the lāhui, the nation. The idea was to EAducate, a philosophy of education that would give the lāhui the ability to rise, to ea. EAducation is about learning your culture, your history, your language, your stories. That is what will empower the lāhui.
>
> EAducation is what will return breath and life to our lāhui; it will give us the ability to have sovereignty, rule, and independence over all the decisions we make and over the future of our lāhui.[51]

Kanuha's focus on EAducation is critical to a strong foundation for the lāhui and for the next generation of Kānaka who will carry on the work of cultivating ea.

Kanuha planted the seeds of ea and a new consciousness at the very site of struggle, teaching students at Hale Kū Kiaʻi Mauna, the structure and ahu built near the Legendary Crosswalk in the year after the 2015 stand. He speaks to the haumāna (students) about the reason why the kiaʻi are standing for Mauna a Wākea within the larger context of US occupation in Hawaiʻi. He explains,

> The reason for our being here, for all these pilikia, development, not just on Mauna Kea . . . is due to the fact that we are not able to govern ourselves and determine for ourselves what is pono and unpono for our people and our ʻāina. So I'm going to get into a political realm, but it's not so much politics as ʻoiaʻiʻo, as it is the truth of the matter. And so we determined that instead of trying to pick the fruits of the tree, instead of trying to trim the leaves and the branches, let's huki this whole kumu out of the ground, and let's get the roots out of it. The source of this pilikia is an illegal occupation by the United States of our people dating back to the overthrow in 1893.[52]

As he explains to the students, we must plant new trees, Native trees, the knowledge of effective governance that is based on ancestral knowledge, as we are able to see flourishing now at Puʻuhonua o Puʻuhuluhulu at the base of Mauna a Wākea, as I discuss in my conclusion. Ea grows out of an education in ʻoiaʻiʻo, truth, and that kind of education must question the very foundations of education in occupied Hawaiʻi. An EAducation is one that is rooted in ʻike kupuna, bearing the fruit of children who will be able to choose a future that is pono: right, balanced, and sovereign.

Artist and educator Haley Kailiehu's piece "Huliau" depicts EAducation as a turning point, an unfurling, as children join their parents and families in the struggle, raising the hae Hawaiʻi that billows in the wind, the Hawaiian flag that was lowered at the time of the overthrow and cut to pieces when Hawaiʻi became a republic (see figure 4.4). The children are the huli (kalo tops) who are planted in the Legendary Crosswalk. "Huliau" also refers to an overturning, one based on recalling the past (see figure 4.5). Kailiehu illustrates this in the image of the children being EAducated, huli taking root, their young green shoots bursting through the asphalt of the crosswalk, the institutional structures of settler colonial education. The huli

FIGURE 4.4 "#WarriorsRising," Mauna a Wākea, April 10, 2015. Photograph courtesy of Naaiakalani Colburn.

represent ea itself, the rising of the people of the lāhui. Such abundance cannot be contained, covered over, or stifled. Kailiehu writes in her artist's statement for the piece, "The huli has already been planted, and it will continue to grow. This one is for the poe aloha aina maintaining a continuous presence at the aloha aina crosswalk checkpoint. Mahalo for planting the huli for the huliau in us all."[53]

The huli being planted in the crosswalk also illustrates the horizontal, outward cascades of EAducation from the mauna. 'Ohulei Waia'u, the alaka'i who led the kia'i in the eleventh line in chanting "Hānau ka Mauna," the line that stopped the convoy of law enforcement and the construction crew, maps the abundance of leadership on the mountain in a way that corresponds to the teeth of shark 'aumākua or guardians. She explains:

FIGURE 4.5 Haley Kailiehu, *Ka Huliau*, July 2015. Image courtesy of the artist.

> We were in line eleven and from our perspective, we could see all of the lines below us, and we heard about what was happening. Once they got past one row, the next row would come up. We heard that our strong leaders Kaleikoa, Kahoʻokahi, and Hualālai were taken and that everybody was afraid because we knew they had been handpicked for arrest as our leaders, but I said to them, "Don't worry, we're like the teeth of the manō. When one shark's tooth falls out, there's always another to replace it." Not like, watch out, we're going to bite you. No, what we realized is that there are always many, many rows behind that front, many, many leaders who are coming into their own and are willing to step up to lead us.[54]

The lines of protectors, then, were rows of shark's teeth, plentiful, resilient, and regenerative. Sharks tear their prey so vigorously that they break or lose their teeth daily. New teeth are continuously growing in rows that move forward, up to seven rows of replacement teeth and as many as thirty thousand teeth in a lifetime. The teeth are as the lehulehu, the multitudes that stand for Mauna a Wākea, the 400, the 4000, the 40,000, the 400,000 protectors that are being regenerated in the ʻōpio on the mauna. In this way, this image illustrates what Kūkauakahi describes as the *decentralization* of organizing on Mauna a Wākea, the suppleness of such an organizing structure.[55] When the leaders have been arrested, others have stepped in to take their places, including the ʻōpio who have come into their own as leaders, and still others who have taken the lead in organizing ʻAha Aloha ʻĀina gatherings in their own communities across ka pae ʻāina o Hawaiʻi, to grow relationships, economies, systems, and structures for independence. This nonhierarchical, horizontal leadership is mapped on the land, the rows and rows of protectors lined up the mauna like the rows of shark teeth, illustrating a land-based conception of the lāhui. Waiaʻu's words present us with an example of Kanaka Maoli cartography that illustrates the visual mapping of the independence movement premised on Kanaka economies of abundance through regeneration.

RETURNING TO THE PIKO: STANDING
WITH THE KŪPUNA PŌHAKU

Kailiehu represented this image of the lines of kiaʻi on Mauna a Wākea in a way that presents a Kanaka Maoli cartography of a genealogical return to the piko as the source of ea, one resonating with Kanahele's and Flores's words about the piko that is Mauna a Wākea. In July 2015, Kailiehu depicted the lines of kiaʻi in a piece titled ReKALOnize Your Naʻau (see plate 12). In this image, Kailiehu inverts the process of colonization by calling on us to plant the kalo in the naʻau, reclaiming the naʻau—the guts, the seat of knowledge, the visceral core—from colonization. The kiaʻi hold the lei lāʻī, the open tī leaf lei, before them, in lines extending up to Waiau, which is depicted as the leaf of the kalo. This image brings together the piko as the point where the stem attaches to the kalo leaf from which veins radiate out, the piko as the summit, and the piko as the umbilicus that connects past generations of kiaʻi to present and future generations. Kailiehu writes,

> This image depicts our kiaʻi mauna standing in lines up on the mauna walking together to the piko of our ea, ka piko o Wākea, at Waiau. The shape of Waiau, I often see as similar to that of the kalo leaf. And like the piko of the kalo leaf, the piko of the mauna connects us to our ʻāina and akua, the sources of our ea. It is thus in our returning to the piko to strengthen these ancestral connections that the consciousness of our lāhui is re-kalo-nized, re-centered, and re-born.[56]

Thus, reKALOnizing the naʻau is an act of indigenous resurgence that turns inward. Waiau is the poʻowai, the place from which the headwaters and ʻike (knowledge) flow to the people and to which the people return to regain ea.

The spiral is an image that reaches far back into the ancestral past, mai nā kūpuna mai, even as it represents an unfurling, a blossoming forth. As Pisciotta explains, the kupu pattern is one example of a spiraling fern that represents many meanings, including "to sprout, germinate, grow, increase, blossom, and is symbolic of genealogy or the pathway back to the ancestors and the supernatural realms.... It is meant to acknowledge, inspire and evoke the sacred meanings of the sacred pattern—to reconnect us to the sacred realms."[57] Pisciotta further explains that the word "ho'opōhuli" evokes "a complex set of meanings, which is to blossom, burst forth as a plant does to break through the ground and sprout, or put another way, the act of unfurling, as does the kupu or the eye of the giant hapu'u fern when it unfurls its arms (beautiful fronds) to reach up towards the light." To ho'opōhuli resonates with the activation of the children breaking through the asphalt and sprouting, the unfurling of the hae Hawai'i in trucks on the streets of Hawai'i, or again with Kailiehu's kalo Kānaka discussed in chapter 3, with their leafy arms reaching up to receive sunlight or rains.

The lines of kia'i also reverberate with the image of the procession of the mo'o akua that I describe in the introduction, a procession of the mo'o two-by-two across the land, imaging the waterways that spread across the ahupua'a. Here the kia'i stand in lines in a procession of protection going up to Waiau, the sacred waters of Mauna a Wākea. The kia'i (protectors) are the mo'o in the multilayered senses of the word: they are the mo'o as descendants, the mo'opuna tracing their way back to the kūpuna and back to the ancestral knowledge of Pō in the waters of Waiau, standing like the mo'o water protectors. They are the mo'o'āina or unbroken succession of lands. Their stories become the mo'olelo, the succession of stories that emanate from and lead back to Pō.

No'eau Peralto writes about the return to the piko that is Waiau and the convergence of akua, 'āina, and Kānaka there. Peralto draws from and elaborates on the work of Kīhei and Māpuana de Silva and their eloquent reading of "A Maunakea 'o Kalani," the last of eight mele composed to commemorate Emalani Kaleleonālani Naea Rooke's 1881 journey from Mānā to Mauna a Wākea. Queen Emma had faced the great pain of losing her son Albert Edward Kauikeaouli Kaleiopapa a Kamehameha in 1862 and her husband, Alexander Liholiho (Kamehameha IV), in 1863, and she had lost the 1874 election to King Kalākaua. The lāhui struggled to maintain their political independence under increasing American political influence. The mele tells of the momentous occasion when Queen Emma bathed in Waiau:

A Maunakea 'o Kalani
'Ike maka iā Waiau
Kēlā wai kamaha'o
I ka piko o ke kuahiwi

The Queen was at Maunakea
To see Lake Waiau
That remarkable body of water
At the peak of the mountain.[58]

The de Silvas explain that the seemingly simple lines are rich with profound meaning:

> When we know the backstory and eight-mele context, we recognize that "'ike maka iā Waiau" means a good deal more than "[she] saw Lake Waiau." It means that Emma immersed herself in the healing water of Waiau. It means that she knew and experienced Waiau completely. Once we're on the lookout for embedded clues, we can also recognize that "wai kamaha'o i ka piko o ke kuahiwi" means considerably more than "remarkable body of water at the peak of the mountain." The phrase resonates, instead, with sacred, regenerative signficance. Piko is not just "peak"; it is "umbilicus, navel, genital, center." Kamaha'o is not just "remarkable," it is "wondrous, inexplicable, transforming." When Emma immersed herself in Waiau, she entered the piko wai kamaha'o of her ancestor-gods, the wondrous, liquid point of union from which all kānaka descend. She was reconnected; she was nourished; she was reborn. Pēlā nō i ho'okamaha'o ai kēlā wai iā ia. Thus did the water transform her.[59]

Queen Emma's return to the meeting point of past, present, and future generations speaks of her renewal of her commitment to the lāhui despite great difficulties. Peralto adds, "The generations before us who engaged tirelessly in this struggle have essentially led us to the edge of Waiau's sacred waters. As we gaze at our own reflection on her placid surface, just as Kaleleonālani did over a century ago, we are confronted with a timeless reminder of where we come from, who we are, and who our grandchildren will grow to become."[60] Kailiehu's image of the water protectors, then, speaks to the way that they, too, stand in a procession that leads back to ancestral relationships that renew the people spiritually, intellectually, imaginatively, and physically.

On June 24, the kia'i were not alone: their kūpuna pōhaku made their way down to the road to stand with their descendants. As the state officers began arresting people to speed up the ascension of the work crews, one of the kia'i, Kaukaohu Wahilani from Puea, Wai'anae, was above the eleventh line and describes what he saw: "Lïlïnoe covered both our lāhui and DLNR;

FIGURE 4.6 Jada Anela Torres with the kūpuna pōhaku, Mauna a Wākea, June 24, 2015. Photograph by Ehitu Keeling. Courtesy of Torres and Meleana Smith.

however, where we were higher up, it was clear and sunny. We could only hear the chanting and cries of our lāhui. We were all waiting for our lāhui to join us, and that is when this 'anakala [uncle] spoke and said, 'Hui lāhui! Looks like nā kūpuna are ready to come down the mauna and join us!' As soon as those words left his mouth the lāhui started to halihali the pōhaku and place them on the road! It was amazing. From pōki'i to kūpuna, everybody was doing the hana lima!"[61] The pōhaku were planted in the road, some here and there and others in low rock walls that formed a labyrinth through which people, but not the vehicles of settler colonial capital, could pass. As the kūpuna, the pōhaku formed the last impenetrable line. Their immovable presence reminds us of the image of William Freitas planted on the road, refusing to allow law enforcement officers to pass. Kailiehu's image, then, is also a mapping of moʻokūʻauhau, or genealogy, from the keiki in the first line on the county road, through to the 'ōpio line and other lines up the mauna, and finally to the kūpuna pōhaku above, the pōhaku the last in the genealogical line standing for Mauna a Wākea.

In one unforgettable photograph taken that day, Jada Anela Torres sits in the lap of the kūpuna pōhaku as beloved children do (see figure 4.6). She was planted there on Mauna a Wākea with her older brother Jonah and her parents, Meleana Smith and Kaleo Torres, as an 'ohana, a family, standing with their kūpuna pōhaku that day. As she looks into the camera, we see that one day, she will be a kupuna who will share this image with her moʻopuna (grandchildren), and she herself, like William Freitas sitting on the road, will be as the kūpuna pōhaku surrounding her, an 'ai pōhaku, standing for the piko of Mauna a Wākea.

As Kānaka stood with their elemental kūpuna and settler aloha ʻāina, the construction crews did not reach the summit that day. Richard Naiwieha Wurdeman, the attorney for the Mauna Kea hui, is also our beloved pōhaku, and he submitted a request for a stay of construction that was issued by the Hawaiʻi Supreme Court in November 2015.

In the conclusion to this book, I look at the ongoing stand people are taking at Puʻuhonua ʻo Puʻuhuluhulu on Mauna a Wākea, which continues to draw more and more people in through the embrace of kapu aloha. One thing we know: we will continue to fight for Mauna a Wākea, ā hiki i ke aloha ʻāina hope loa (until the very last aloha ʻāina). We stand steadfast, kūpaʻa, knowing that the kūpuna pōhaku, the ʻaumakua, and the myriad other forms the kūpuna take are protecting the mountain and that we will stand there with them when the construction crews try to make their way back up the mountain.

The lines of kiaʻi mauna standing on Mauna a Wākea extend out to other front lines in the movement against the capitalist economies driving climate change. Kānaka Maoli have joined other Indigenous climate warriors around the world in trans-Indigenous alliances foregrounding the impacts of settler colonial industrialization and extractivism on the global crises we face. The kiaʻi mauna have traveled to Standing Rock to stand in unison with the tribes there against the construction of the Dakota Access Pipeline. Kanaka Maoli protectors Pua Case, Hāwane Rios, Malia Hulleman, Camille Kalama, Andre Perez, Sam Keliʻihoʻomalu, Earl DeLeon, Kalaemano Michael Keyser Jr., Kalamaokaʻāina Niheu, and many others have made it clear that it is time we all stand together on the front lines of the struggle to protect the earth. As Case told NBC News, "I went to Standing Rock because it is the time for all of us who are committed to protecting the water, the earth and our life ways to align in our efforts, to strengthen one another. We are not alone, and in these times of serious impact, desecration, construction and destruction we have no choice but to unify not just for ourselves, our people and all people, but for the next seven generations . . . before it is too late, we stand."[62]

CHAPTER FIVE

VERTICAL MAPS

OF SUBTERRANEAN

WATERS IN KALIHI

The Laws of Haumea

and Kānemilohae

M apping abundance must also map the hydrostratigraphy of mo'o'āina vertically across different papa (strata) of the earth, seas, and skies. As we follow the epic procession of great mo'o in *Keaomelemele* in chapter 1, their huaka'i along waterways and bodies of water across the land may have taken them beneath the ground to subterranean worlds where volcanic lava tunnel systems interbed with extensive limestone cave systems, joining waterways from the farthest points on the island below what often seem to be waterless plains.

As the first pair of mo'o make their way along the Hālawa Stream, their great tails curve past the crater of 'Āhuimanu up the incline to Kapūkakī. Today, it is at Kapūkakī that the mo'o engage in battle with monsters that lie beneath the surface of the land. The Red Hill Bulk Fuel Storage Facility, one of the largest underground fuel storage facilities in the United States, houses twenty underground jet fuel storage tanks that lie buried like eggs of catastrophic potential. The US Navy stores 187 million gallons of jet fuel only one hundred feet above the Southern Oʻahu Basal Aquifer, which supplies 25 percent of the drinking water on the island of Oʻahu.[1] In January 2014, the US military reported a 27,000-gallon leak of jet fuel from tank 5 into the earth.[2] These storage tanks were built in 1941, and over the years the steel liners have corroded to a thickness of two millimeters. In the event of an earthquake, there could be a flood of millions of gallons of fuel into the earth, reaching the groundwater aquifer.

Kanaka Maoli cartography, born out of generations of kilo (observation) of the subterranean movements of water, has tracked the pathways of water. The Kīhoʻihoʻi Kānāwai collective of Kanaka Maoli practitioners presents such a map of the vertical papa in a beautifully conceptualized plan for the restoration practices of island stewardship.[3] Kumu hula (hula master) Pualani Kanakaʻole Kanahele and her Papakū Makawalu team of researchers at the Edith Kanakaʻole Foundation identify twenty-two wao, or horizontal positionings, organized around mauna (mountains) for the stewardship of each wao (realm). There are six divisions for Wao Lani, the heavenly strata, ten divisions of the Wao Honua, the island land base, and six divisions of the Wao Kanaloa, the ocean divisions. For these divisions, there are various kānāwai (laws) that they have asserted based on chants and songs regarding the care of these divisions and their natural processes. In this chapter, I focus on the wao kanaka, seaward of the wao akua and the laws of this wao that focus on the care of freshwater sources:

KĀNĀWAI PAHULAU—the edict of 400 chambers; concerning the care of aquifers and their relationship to ocean health and reef ecosystems

KĀNĀWAI PAHUKINI—the edict of 4,000 chambers; concerning the care of aquifers, water tables, glaciers, snowcaps, caves, watersheds; recognition of all manner of watersheds in all stratums

KĀNĀWAI KĀNEMILOHAE—the edict of passage; ability for groundwater and underground water to have uninterrupted passage; for the health of ocean creatures in the freshwater areas; for the health of the island as fresh cool waters deter hurricanes from decimating islands.[4]

Kānāwai Kānemilohae, in particular, is the law that evokes the akua Kānemilohae. Pualani Kanakaʻole Kanahele describes Kānemilohae as the elemental form of the vertical movement of magma. Born from the right palm of Haumea, Kānemilohae "is the movement of magma vertically from its sources to the earth's surface, weaving and twisting its way through many layers of earth."[5] He also takes the form of a shark who navigates through these strata of the earth. Kānemilohae moves action in the moʻolelo, gifting his sister Hiʻiaka with the power to break through the strata of the earth and to threaten their sister Pele with the ocean waters that would extinguish her fires.[6]

So many of the great moʻolelo teach us about this vertical cartography as subterranean sources of water are brought forth from the land through acts of aloha by the akua (elemental forms) out of their love for Kānaka. Kāneikawaiola (Kāne of the living waters), like Wākea, is seen as a source of life and procreative principles.[7] He and Kanaloa, the deity of the deep consciousness of the sea, are described as water finders who travel throughout the islands. Kanaloa is the desiring principle, and Kāne enacts the fulfillment of that desire by thrusting his ʻōʻō (digging stick) into the earth to create gushing springs for their ʻawa, a ceremonial drink.[8]

Other deities open up the earth to reveal the waterways of Kāne flowing beneath. When the people of Keawaʻula in Waiʻanae tell Hiʻiakaikapoliopele that they live on a waterless land, Hiʻiaka states emphatically, "He aina wai keia" (This is a land of water).[9] She explains that they must dig into the "papa kumu one manoanoa" (the thick stratum of sand) to reach the wai ʻono, the sweet water beneath. Hiʻiaka gathers her paʻū uila (lightning skirt), raises it above her right shoulder, and strikes the sand.[10] The earth rumbles and begins to naue (shudder), and a deep gaping pit opens up where her paʻū has struck, revealing the waters that course beneath.

When Hiʻiaka battles her sister Pele, it is their older brother, Kānemilohae, who empowers her to break through the strata of the land, where different forms of life dwell, from the strange insect people on the third stratum to the bird feather home of Papa and Wākea on the fifth stratum.[11] Hiʻiaka threatens Pele's home in Kīlauea by attempting to break through the eight strata of Kīlauea, reaching to the freshwater table, and then the sea below it, to drown out Pele's fires. After stomping her foot and bursting through the first four papa, Hiʻiaka maps the strata for her attendant, Pāʻūopalaʻā:

> Ua hele ia mau haku ou e noho mai la—la, a luuluu ka makaʻu maluna o lakou no kuu wawahi i na paku pale o ka lua o Kilauea, oiai hookahi no paku i koe iaʻu, pii ka waipuna, wai huʻihuʻi iloko o Kilauea; hoea au i ka papaku eono, pii ka wai kai, huai iloko o ka lua; hoea au i ka walu o na papa, hulihia o Kilauea holookoa.[12]

> Those [chiefs] of yours are overwhelmed with fear about my destruction of the shielding layers of Kīlauea Crater, for I have only one shield left and then cold spring water will flow into Kīlauea, and when I reach

the sixth level, sea water will rise, and flood into the crater; when I arrive at the eighth level, all of Kīlauea will be demolished [or overturned, overthrown].[13]

This vertical mapping of the strata helps us to imagine the subterranean complexities we cannot see that are present on all islands.

This chapter expands on these strata in the context of the principle of ke ea o ka ʻāina, the sovereignty of the land, the consciousness of the land, and the ways that the lands recognize us. Joseph Mokuʻōhai Poepoe's "Ka Moolelo o ko Wakea ma Noho ana ma Kalihi—Ka Loaa ana o ke Akua Ulu o Kamehaʻikana" teaches us about reciprocal recognition and a vertical mapping that gifts the people with water. This moʻolelo is taught at Hoʻoulu ʻĀina, a restoration project in Kalihi Valley, to provide children, their families, and volunteers with the foundational knowledge of Haumea. Haumea possesses knowledge of the different layers of the land, something the great shark deities knew, too, as they made their way high up into the mountains of Kalihi, Moanalua, and Mānana (Pearl City). These shark deities remind us that there is much the occupying state does not know about the movement of water across the land. The effects of jet fuel tank leakages will radiate outward in ways they cannot predict, but so too do the restorative effects of the cultivation of abundance.

Far down on the shores of Kalihi, kiaʻi o Keʻehi and cultural anthropologist Kēhaulani Souza Kupihea speaks of ea as our capacity to achieve a "kupuna vibration" that enables the lands to recognize Kānaka. We see these hōʻailona (signs) of kupuna vibration in the wondrous events recorded in the cartographic work of Kēhaulani and her kāne, the artist Kupihea, who show us the continuities of the uplands with the larger complex of the lau papa, the reef flats at Keʻehi.

HAUMEA AS POTENTIALITY

Haumea is preeminently the consciousness of the earth. She is the akua (elemental form) of abundance, the great deity known for having many kino lau (bodily forms), transforming herself from old age to youth as beautiful women across generations. Kanahele tells us, "Haumea is the Hawaiian dominant matrix of all things born."[14] She continues, "In the Kumulipo creation chant, Haumea is the most significant female form, endowed with fertility and procreative power."[15] In the thirteenth wā or era of the cosmogonic chant the Kumulipo describes this great deity:

O Haumea kino pahaohao,
O Haumea kino papawalu,
O Haumea kino papalehu,
O Haumea kino papamano,
I manomano i ka lehulehu o na kino.[16]

Haumea of the wondrous forms,
Haumea of the eightfold forms,
Haumea of the four hundred thousandfold forms,
Haumea of the four thousandfold forms,
Whose myriad forms took multitudinous shapes.[17]

Haumea is the name of her spirit form; in her Kanaka form, she is a woman, Papahānaumoku (She who is the foundation birthing islands). Haumea can multiply her body into thousands of women, and she also takes the form of multiple moʻo reptilian water guardians. Historian and life-writing scholar Marie Alohalani Brown points to one genealogy of Haumea being both punalua (two lovers sharing a third) and daughter or granddaughter to Moʻoinanea, the great matriarch of moʻo.[18]

Kalei Nuʻuhiwa describes Haumea in the most profound and beautiful imagery as potentiality. Nuʻuhiwa is a Papakū Makawalu researcher whose primary discipline is Papahulilani, the study of the atmosphere, including its phenology, energies, and cycles from a Hawaiian perspective. In describing the centrality of Haumea to establishing sacred space, Nuʻuhiwa explains that chants like "Nā ʻAumākua" (quoted in full as the book's epigraph) show us how Haumea sets up her sacred space in multiple meridians, from the rising to the setting of the sun, from the zenith to the horizons where the earth and the sky hālāwai (meet).[19] She describes the ways that Haumea sets up a spherical space similar to the honua (earth) to establish sacred space at heiau (places of worship) and to create the conditions to enable action:

> Haumea is really the potential for something to happen. One of the things that she does is called "ka hei a Haumea." The term "hei" has many meanings: to ensnare or to make string figures. So we take those same terms for "hei," and we put them onto another structure that's built called the heiau. What we're doing on the heiau is we ensnare "au," time is au, or current, or energy, at the heiau where all of these different meridians gather. We are creating our cosmos. Our universe is being created on that heiau so that we can actually create that potential, the proper energy that needs to happen so we can move action.

The hei a Haumea is actually a net that she took care of, and what she would do is she would cast it into the sky so she could plot things. She plots genealogy. She is the one who creates that potential. So if you imagine the image of the net, and it's bringing together four different strands, what do you have in the middle there? The hipu'u, the image of the knot. That is the imagery of potential. That is the honua that's being created for the proper thing to happen. So one of the things she does is she casts that net into the sky, and she plots out all the stars in terms of time. It's providing the potential for all of us to move forward, for all that needs to be done. We replicate it in the net that is stretched over the 'umeke as there's water on the inside so we can plot out the stars, because each of those hīpu'u, those potentials, will line up with stars that are up in the sky. That's the ipu maloha [net filled with food] that is often found in different ceremonies.[20]

Creating the cosmos on the heiau moves action, which evokes for us Kealoha Pisciotta's words about the importance of being in alignment with the elemental forms in chapter 3. Nu'uhiwa goes on to explain that Haumea is both the careful plotting of known factors, like the genealogy of kūpuna and the changing positions of the stars in the sky to mark time, but the "hei a Haumea" (Haumea's string figure) is also about the potentiality of future generations. The hei map the star lines used by navigators. Heiau or sacred altars are positioned in relation to the stars, and as I explained in chapter 4, these navigational star maps show how, astro-architecturally, heiau were positioned in alignment with the stars in order to enable events to happen, to focus the energy generated by these alignments.

Ho'oulu 'Āina program coordinator Puni Jackson describes a similar concept that arises in the mo'olelo of Wākea and Haumea living in Kalihi of the 'upena nananana a Papa, the spiderweb of Haumea in her form as Papa. The mo'olelo recalls for us that the wonders of Haumea are remembered in the Kuali'i chant, "O Papa la hoi ka nananana / O Papa unoa awa'awa'a kua" (Papa is the spider, / Papa of the burning, muscular back).[21] Jackson explains, "Rubellite Kawena Johnson talks about the way that Papa holds the web of the stars and all cosmology, like the tracking of the sun. It's basically a spider's web that the heiau are aligned to, every ahu is aligned a certain way so they can be true directionally. The spider's web is tracking; it's helping us to track celestial bodies."[22] Both the hei and the 'upena nananana provide us with a striking visual imagery for Haumea's emplotment of potentialities, what Johnson describes as Kealaakeku'uku'u (Pathway of the spider;

"ku'uku'u" means to let down, as a net): "The pathway of the spider is shown on the navigation gourd of Hawai'i. . . . Across this sphere was graphed, in the form of a net woven over the calabash of mesh squares, a grid numbering twenty-four to thirty-six spaces."[23] I discuss this ipu ho'okele wa'a (navigational gourd) net in greater depth later in this chapter.

Haumea is described as an elemental form who presides over birthing, and from the different parts of her body she herself births the deities, some of whom are landforms who lie in Kalihi Valley below her home at the mountain peak of Kilohana. Kanahele explains that the chant "Haumea lāua 'o Moemoe'ali'i" describes these births.[24] In addition to birthing Pele "ma kahi mau e hānau 'ia ai ke kanaka" (from the usual place of people), she births her daughter Kapō'ulakīna'u from her knees, a lele (a land division) named "Kapo" that is part of Kapālama but who "flies" to Kalihi and now lies deep in Kalihi Valley.[25] Haumea's son Kamohoali'i (also known as Kānekamohoali'i) is the eldest child born from her fontanel; he is Pele's brother who is the initiator and navigator, the heat in the Hearth and the sky, the high cliff of a caldera.[26] He is also the great shark akua who also takes the form of a mo'o and a hill in the back of Kalihi Valley.[27]

The love and desire between Haumea and Wākea is told as a mo'olelo of the abundance of Kalihi, mapped across the ahupua'a (land divisions) that extend out over both sides of the Ko'olau mountain range. Their home at the green peak of Kilohana sits along the iwikuamo'o, the backbone of the mo'o, the seam of relationality between the ko'olau (windward, northern) and the kona (leeward, southern) sides of O'ahu, straddling the 'ōmo'omo'o (ridgeline). When they look out over one side of the pali or cliffs, they see the sweeping breadth of Kalihi Valley, the mountain waters that flow down in a waterfall to the Kalihi Stream. On the other side of the mountains are the sheer cliffs with numerous waterfalls that make their way down to He'eia Stream in Ha'ikū. When Wākea and Haumea look out behind the curve of the ridgeline of 'Ioleka'a on the windward side, they see the distant blue cliffs of Palikū that are Haumea's ancestors. If they look to the leeward side, they can even see the path of the mo'o procession across O'ahu, from Waialua to Kapūkakī.

Although the 'āina is largely covered with concrete from the lowlands of Kalihi Valley to the seas, the land continues to feed our imaginations and our na'au (visceral core). We can trace the story of water traveling along the mo'o'āina in this valley down through what used to be multistoried canopies of koa (acacia koa), 'iliahi (sandalwood), 'ulu (breadfruit), kukui (candlenut tree), hala (pandanus), hau (a species of hibiscus), 'ōhi'a (a species of Myrtaceae), palapalai (a species of bracken fern), and maile (a member of the periwinkle family), now given way to invasive species: the albizia, monkeypod, pine, haole koa (white leadtree), and strawberry guava trees. Kalihi Stream makes its way down the sweeping valley through lands that were once in cultivation of kalo and ʻuala (sweet potato). Hawaiian families were moved off their ancestral lands to live on Hawaiian Homesteads on seized Hawaiian Kingdom Crown and government lands in Waiʻanae. In the 1960s, local Japanese developer Herbert Horita built up much of Kalihi Valley for working-class families, and many residents now work in the tourism industries in the iconic example of conspicuous capital, Waikīkī.

THE ABUNDANCE OF HAUMEA AND WĀKEA AT KALIHI

In the valley that sweeps out below Haumea and Wākea's home at Kilohana lies Hoʻoulu ʻĀina, a 100-acre nature preserve in the ʻiliʻāina of Māluawai and ʻŌuaua, both names remembering the waters and the rains that Kalihi is well known for. Hoʻoulu ʻĀina works to restore the health of the land and the people, guided by the ʻōlelo noʻeau that reminds us that the land breathes: "ʻO ka hā o ka ʻāina, ke ola o ka poʻe" (The breath of the land is the life of the people).[28] Thousands of volunteers work at Hoʻoulu ʻĀina to restore the ancient sites and sacred places on the land, remove invasive trees, support organic reforestation and agroforestry, and cultivate Pacific food and medicinal plants in community gardens.

In 2014, it was in the planning room tucked away at Hoʻoulu ʻĀina, under the malu (shelter) of Kilohana, that we read Poepoe's "Ka Moolelo o ko Wakea ma Noho ana ma Kalihi—Ka Loaa ana o ke Akua Ulu o Kamehaʻikana," which appeared serially in the nūpepa Ka Naʻi Aupuni from May 2 to June 18, 1906. A small reading group, organized by Kanoa O'Connor, met regularly and was made up of practitioners at Hoʻoulu ʻĀina who were knowledgeable in farming, canoe carving, birthing, lāʻau lapaʻau (traditional medicinal and healing practices), hydrology and waterways, hale building, ʻōlelo Hawaiʻi, and moʻolelo.

Joseph Mokuohai Poepoe was a brilliant writer and newspaper editor who was profoundly knowledgeable about multiple versions of the oral traditions of the moʻolelo he recorded in the Hawaiian-language newspapers. Noenoe Silva provides us with a beautifully meticulous account of Poepoe's dedication to preserving Kanaka Maoli knowledges as they were conveyed in oral traditions. She notes that in his account of the moʻolelo of Hiʻiaka, "Its concentrated focus on the ʻāina and its divine nature, as revealed by the many

FIGURE 5.1 View of Kilohana, home of Wākea and Haumea, from Hoʻoulu ʻĀina, December 6, 2018. Haumeaʻs form as Kāmehaʻikana, a breadfruit tree, in the foreground. Photograph by the author.

spiritual characters who interact with Hiʻiaka, many of whom inhabit kino lau such as plants, animals, land features, forests, and so forth, can inspire us today to envision a more Hawaiian world."[29] She further explains, "I interpret Poepoeʻs assistance [authorial asides] as evidence of his moʻokūʻauhau consciousness as he foresees our generations who grow up deprived of the knowledge of our kūpuna that would allow us to interpret on our own."[30] For this reason, I read his account of Haumea as the culmination of Kanaka Maoli ancestral knowledges of Haumea, who speaks in the moʻolelo as the voice of the land.

In one of the most beautiful moʻolelo of aloha ʻāina, Haumea entangles us in desire for the places below her home at Kilohana (figure 5.1). On a calm summer day, Haumea looks out from Kilohana over the Koʻolau side of the mountains, out over the wide expanse that stretches from the seas of Mōkapu to Heʻeia Kea, and she is ʻono for (craves) limu (seaweed) and the ʻalamihi crabs of the shoreline. She tells Wākea that she will travel down the Koʻolau mountains for these ʻīnaʻi (flavorful accompaniments) for their poi. She descends into Luluku and makes her way to Keʻalohi, the promontory

PLATE 1 The moʻo traversed the flat isthmus plains of Oʻahu, from Waialua in the northwest (left) toward Laeʻahi (Diamond Head) in the southeast (right). Photograph by Kenji Saito.

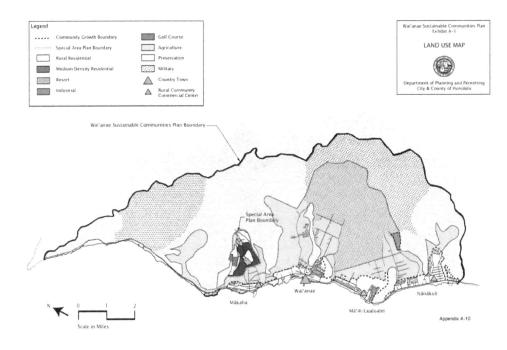

PLATE 2 *Land Use Map*, from City and County of Honolulu Department of Planning and Permitting, Waiʻanae Sustainable Communities Plan, 2012.

PLATE 3   Moʻoʻāina map of the Māui moʻolelo by Joseph Momoa at the Puʻu
Heleakalā Head Start Preschool, 1978. Reproduced with permission of the artist.
Photographic reconstruction by Nate Yuen.

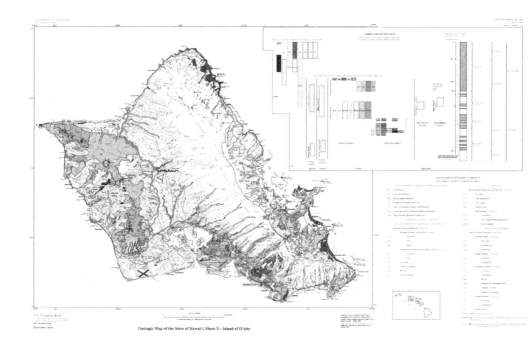

PLATE 4 David R. Sherrod, John M. Sinton, Sarah E. Watkins, and Kelly M. Brunt, *Geologic Map of the State of Hawai'i, Sheet 3—Island of O'ahu* (2007). I have traced in blue the approximate path of the mo'o akua according to waterways and geological formations. Reprint and my modification courtesy of David Sherrod and John Sinton.

PLATE 5 The blaze of light on huakaʻi, Makua Valley. Leandra Wai-Rodrigues, Walterbea Aldeguer, and the author, 2013. The photo was taken on the Mākua Military Reservation on an access day for civilians, who must have military escorts on this land littered with unexploded ordnance. Photograph by Marie Alohalani Brown.

PLATE 6 Mealaaloha Bishop, *Lonoikamahahiki*, oil on canvas, 2019. Mauna a
Wākea in the Makahiki season honoring Lono, the akua of abundance and peace.
Reproduced with the artist's permission.

PLATE 7 Poliʻahu embraced by Kūkahauʻula in his pink cloak. Mauna a Wākea, 2012. Photograph by Deborah Ward.

PLATE 8   Ke Kapuaʻi a Poliʻahu, Poliʻahu's footsteps. Mauna a Wākea, August 2, 2018. Photograph by the author.

PLATE 9 Community mural of Mauna a Wākea at the University of Hawaiʻi, designed by Haley Kailiehu, October 13, 2013. Photograph courtesy of the artist.

PLATE 10 The mana wahine line: Nohea Kawaʻa-Davis, Alohilani Keohuloa, Mehana Kihoi, Kuʻuipo Freitas, Naaiakalani Colburn, and Hōkūlani Reyes. Mauna a Wākea, June 24, 2015. Photograph by Te Rawhitiroa Bosch.

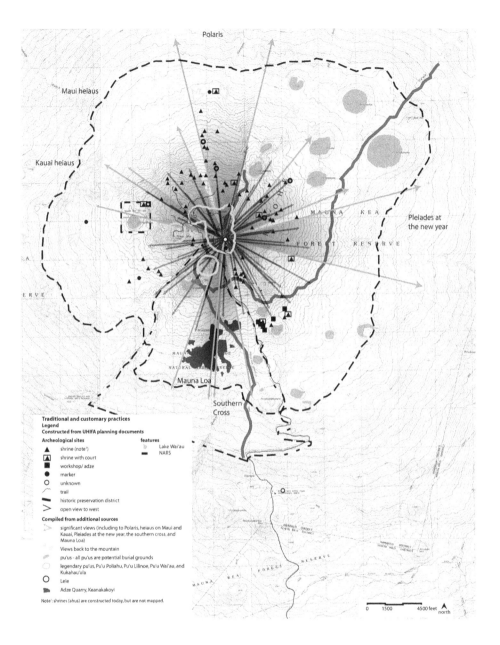

PLATE 11 Kealoha Pisciotta, *Map of Selected Traditional View-Planes at Mauna a Wākea* (2011). Pisciotta maps the star knowledge of her aunt, Kamakahukilani Von Oelhoffen, her Oniha family, and her own kilo hōkū (star practices). Project by Community by Design. Image courtesy of Kealoha Pisciotta.

PLATE 12   Haley Kailiehu, *ReKALOnize Your Naʻau*. Mauna a Wākea, 2015. Image courtesy of the artist.

PLATE 13 Mapping Hau(mea). Kalihi, February 14, 2019. Photograph by the author.

PLATE 14 Mealaaloha Bishop, *Kalo Pa'a o Waiāhole*, mixed media, 1999. Image courtesy of the artist.

PLATE 15   Mealaaloha Bishop, *Palakea ʻEleʻele*, oil on canvas, 2012. Image courtesy of the artist.

PLATE 16 Ashley Hunt, *A World Map: In Which We See . . .* , 2007. Image courtesy of the artist.

between Heʻeia Uli and Heʻeia Kea. Meanwhile, Wākea searches the forest uplands of Kalihi to find the hōʻiʻo (tender fern) and the uhi yams that will flavor their meal, and he comes upon an abundance of wild bananas. As he picks them, he is discovered and called a thief by the guards of the aliʻi (chief) Kumuhonua, taken to Waikahalulu, and tied to a lāʻau ʻulu (breadfruit tree) to be killed. As an akua, Haumea instructs us on the importance of kilo observation and reading the skies, and while she is fishing, she glances above to Kilohana, where she recognizes the hōʻailona of the "piʻo o ke anuenue" (the arching of a rainbow) and "ka halii ana a ka ua koho (koko) a paa pono ka pali" (the spreading of the bloodred rainbow, covering the cliffs completely).[31] A vision of Wākea being led away with hands bound behind his back passes before her eyes.

She makes her way quickly up the mountain, stopping briefly to gird her hips in the war pāʻū (skirt) of pōhuehue (morning glory) flowered vines and to adorn herself with palapalai fern, maile, lehua, and tī—for, as the manifestation of the earth, Haumea carries the mana of Heʻeia and Kalihi with her when she pursues the men who have taken her kāne (man). When she is able to catch up to Wākea, a kind-hearted woman asks the men if Haumea may be permitted to honi (exchange breath with) him one last time.

> Oia hele no ia o ua Haumea nei a mamua pono o ke alo o ke kane, anehe aku la e honi; aole nae i pa ka ihu i ke kane, o kona paʻi aku la no ia i ke kumu ulu. He halulu ka na mea apau o ka lohe ana; he naueue ana hoi o ka honua, o–wa ae la ke kumu ulu a hamama mai la ia me he waha ʼla no kekahi ana nui.
>
> A ia wa no i onou aku ai, o Haumea i ke kane iloko o ua kumu-ulu nei; a oia nei aku nohoi mahope. I lawa no ia laua nei a nalo iloko o ke kumu ulu, o ke olo ae la no ia o na leo hooho pihoihoi o ka lehulehu, e ikuwa ana mai kela peʻa a keia peʻa o ka aha kanaka: "A lilo ke pio—e! A lilo ke pio! He wahine kupua ka keia i hele mai nei. Ka! He keu ka mana! Aohe lua!"[32]

She went, therefore, this Haumea, directly in front of her man's face, stole up to touch her nose to his to exchange breath; she did not, however, touch her man's nose, instead, she struck the breadfruit tree. A thunderous explosion was heard by everyone, the earth swayed back and forth, the ulu tree gaped open like the mouth of a big cave.

At this time, Haumea thrust her kāne into the ulu tree; and she followed immediately after. As soon as they were concealed inside the breadfruit tree, there immediately resounded voices of the crowd exclaiming excitedly, clamoring all over, from one side of the gathering to the other: "The prisoner is lost! The prisoner is lost! This is a supernatural woman who has come here. Oh! So much mana! She is unequalled!"[33]

The ʻulu tree itself is both Haumea and a portal, and Haumea and Wākea emerge on the other side of the tree to make their way back to Kilohana. Their disappearance into the ʻulu tree marks the moment that Haumea takes on a new kino lau (bodily form) as Kāmehaʻikana, the breadfruit tree and a moʻo reptilian water deity.[34] The ʻulu tree bears a pale green breadfruit when ripened, skin textured with an interlocking hexagonal pattern like the armored skin of the moʻo, beauty in geometry.

KE EA O KA ʻĀINA: THE SOVEREIGNTY OF THE LAND

This moʻolelo indulges us in the ʻono of the uplands of Kalihi, the flavors associated with those places, the pleasures of the abundance of delicacies that grow in the wao akua, the realm of the elements. The moʻolelo illustrates for us what Jackson refers to as the sovereignty of the land, described as such because the foods of this realm do not need cultivation by the hands of Kānaka but are grown by the deities who are the elements. The abundance of the sovereign land needs only the rainfall to grow food.

> Ia laua e noho ana ma keia wahi, ua loaa ko laua ola, ma na mea o keia noho kino ana ma o na maia pala-ku i ka nahele, na uhi punapuna moe lepo o ka uka, na kalo aweu manalo a lilo i poi uouo ono; na hooio [hōʻiʻo] me na kika-wai-o e lomi pu iho ai me na opae kala ole o ka uka waokele; na lawalu oopu momona i hele a ala i ka lauki, ame na wahi luau palupalu oia uka iuiu. Pela nohoi me na alamihi kai aala o na kai kohola o kai ae nei o Kalihi, e laa na papaʻi momona, a pela nohoi me na wahi hua opihi mai o na Koolau, ame ko laila mau lau limu. A o keia mau mea a pau inai pu iho me ka poi aweu uouo, he ono mai hoi kau a koe.[35]

While they were dwelling at this place, their living was gotten on the things of this dwelling, on the ripe bananas in the luxuriant forests, the uhi, mealy yams asleep in the soil of the uplands, the firm and tasty wild ʻāweu kalo that is pounded into the sticky poi; the tender young fronds of the upland hōʻiʻo and kikawaiō ferns that are worked together with the fingers with the ʻōpae kalaʻole, the smooth freshwater mountain shrimp of the lush rainbelt of the uplands; the plump ʻoʻopu (goby fish) bound up in tī leaves and cooked until fragrant, and the little tender kalo leaves of the sacred uplands. In this way they lived upon the 'alamihi sea crabs fragrant of the lagoons at the shores of Kalihi, as well as the fat crabs and the little 'opihi (limpets) of the seas of the Ko'olau side of the island and their seaweeds. And all these things were flavored together with the wild sticky poi, so exceedingly delicious.

In particular, the rainfall feeds the upland wild taro called 'Āweu, a variety of kalo considered one of the three kūpuna kalo from which others are derived.[36] According to Jerry Konanui, an eighth-generation kalo farmer, kūpuna are said to prefer the leaves of this kalo because it is particularly tender in the wao akua uplands where it grows under the canopy of trees, whereas leaves grow tough in the direct sunlight of the lowlands.[37] Kūpuna remember being sent into the uplands as children to harvest these leaves for their families.

The abundance of the uplands is also an articulation of Kanaka Maoli sovereignty: not only are the laws of the akua held as a higher authority than the governance of humans, in the capacity of the sovereign land to feed the people, the wild foods themselves became part of the national identity for Kānaka Maoli. By the time the mo'olelo appeared in the newspapers in 1906, the earlier passage of the 1895 Land Grant Act had begun a process for advertising land in Hawai'i for American settlement. This mo'olelo, however, reminded Kānaka that the sovereignty of the land would always exceed the control of settlers. This passage also recalls my argument in chapter 3 regarding the absurdity of Nathaniel Emerson's claim in his footnote that the wao akua are the "waste places of the earth."

The sovereignty of the land and the laws of the akua are manifested in Haumea's voicing the consciousness of the land in a discussion with the farmer Kali'u on the nature of Wākea's "crime": gathering wild bananas. Do wild bananas belong to the ali'i or to the land? Haumea delves into the issue of this offense in depth:

> He maia ulu wale ko ke kuahiwi, he maia maka [sic] nahelehele, he inai na ke kini ame ka puku'i o ka manu. No keaha hoi i kapu ole ia ai ka manu i ka maia a kapu iho la hoi i ke kanaka? Hoouna ka hoi ua 'lii nei o oukou i kona poe kanaka, e kiu i ke kanaka e kii ana i ka mea a kona lima i luhi ole ai; a hoouna ole ka hoi o ia i na kau-kia manu ana e pu-lehua a e ahele i ka manu ai maia? He aha la kana. Ola ka manu ai maia, ola nohoi ke kanaka ai maia. Noonoo ole nohoi ua 'lii nei o oukou, he maia ke kanaka, a kona la nohoi e hua iho ai, hua no.[38]

Bananas growing wild belong to the mountain, bananas in the forest, an accompaniment for the multitudes and the gathering of birds. Why indeed aren't the bananas forbidden to the birds but are forbidden to the people? This aliʻi of yours has sent his people to spy on the man fetching the thing the [aliʻi's] hand has not labored to produce; and neither did he send for the bird snarers to gum lehua flowers for the purpose of snaring the banana-eating birds. What is he doing? The banana-eating birds live, indeed, the banana-eating man lives. Your aliʻi is thoughtless, the man is but a banana, until the day he bears fruit, then he is fruitful.

Haumea in her human form as Papa presents an argument that in the court of the akua, Wākea did not commit a crime and that instead the aliʻi himself is not pono when he seeks to punish Wākea for feeding himself the foods that grow wild and belong to the sovereign land. The aliʻi Kumuhonua has proven himself to be an unjust ruler who does not respect the sovereignty of the land, and he is one to be overthrown. As Noenoe Silva notes in her reading of this passage, "It is likely the banana bunch is a metaphor for the people of the area and that Wākea's taking of the banana is prescient and symbolic of his and Haumea's subsequent takeover of the rule of the island."[39]

In this moʻolelo, as at Mauna a Wākea, the governance of the akua takes precedence over the government of men. Jackson elaborates on the sovereignty of the land to the children she teaches in the summer program at Hoʻoulu ʻĀina, where children learn about the bananas being akua who feed anyone who has a relationship to that land. She explains, "That maiʻa is the maiʻa akua, and if you have relationship to ʻāina that feeds you, there is no aliʻi that can come and tell you that that doesn't belong to you. Because the sovereignty of the land, even in that story, is being challenged by governance, and it is spirituality and spiritual relationship that will perpetuate and make for true abundance."[40] Jackson foregrounds both the sovereignty of the land and the noʻonoʻo ʻole (thoughtlessness, ignorance) of human governance that fails to recognize the sovereignty of the land and the elements. The makaʻāinana are the people who work on the land and attend to the lands' needs; such a spiritual relationship with the land must be recognized, even by aliʻi.

True abundance, as Jackson notes, is the perpetuation of a spiritual relationship to the land that attends to what the lands desire. Haumea asks Kaliʻu if the man should die, and when Kaliʻu says he would rather see him live, she concludes, "Ua like ka hoi kou makemake me koʻu. A ua pono" (Your desire is like mine. And it is morally just). Their makemake, their desire, is the same.

The farmer recognizes the sovereignty of the land, and Haumea, in turn, recognizes him by appointing him as one of her war leaders.

The Hoʻoulu ʻĀina summer program teaches children to attend to the agency of the land and their relationships with the spirits of that land. The Mai Uka Kuʻu Waʻa (My canoe comes from the uplands) Program shows children how the canoes are made of the wood of the forest and teaches them that to understand the spirit of the canoe that will sail on the seas, they must understand the spirit of the upland trees. Jackson explains,

> Summer program, I do the moʻolelo with the keiki, for the naʻau [visceral core and seat of knowledge]. So I take two separate groups into the hale for our canoe program. The little ones are five to seven years old and the older ones are eight to thirteen. As I tell the story of Papa and Wākea, we look from the hale toward Kilohana, the little ones imagining the hale pupupu [humble hut]. So the moʻolelo is really important because with Mai Uka Kuʻu Waʻa, it's not just a canoe program, it's the idea that abundance comes when you understand how to go from uka to kai in the old way. If you understand that the canoe is alive, then you must know the forest, and the carving of the canoe, you have to know all of the different practices if you're going to carve a canoe, you must know lāʻau lapaʻau, you must know the winds, you must know the wai [fresh waters], you must know the kai [the ocean waters], so that's why that is so important because I was using that moʻolelo to help the kids to understand their kuleana, and understand a really specific kuleana. So if you think about Mai Uka Kuʻu Waʻa, we can make waʻa from fiberglass; it doesn't even have to come from uka any more, right? But that one is not alive. If you understand the tree, you understand the spirit of the canoe, you understand the relationship between the uka and the kai, and that ʻuhane that's going to live in the waʻa, all of that is part of the kuleana of the little ones, so their kuleana is to start to see that there was an old way of doing things and there's [a] new way of doing things, and I have kuleana to make sure this lives. I have kuleana to overturn certain things, too.[41]

Jackson explains this lesson is "for the naʻau" and is directed at how the children are cultivating an understanding of their spiritual connectedness to ʻāina, to the lands that grow the food they eat and trees they use to build their canoes (see figure 5.2). Jackson asks the children to make this connection from the forest to the sea, to see the ʻuhane of the tree being honored and being used to navigate on the seas. In this way, young children are being

FIGURE 5.2 Puni Jackson, director of Hoʻoulu ʻĀina, and her son Makulu. Kalihi, June 15, 2016. Still taken by the author from a Mauli Ola Foundation Leo Kupa podcast. Courtesy of Puni Jackson, Kamaka Jingao, and Hans Hagen.

taught that they have the capacity to huli, to overturn, governance that violates their pilina to the land. They can huli human courts of law that ignore the laws of the akua. They can huli the alienation from the land that is driving climate change. They can huli a settler colonial system that plants jet fuel tanks instead of food.

Through this work to huli the systems that harm the land, the invasive albizia tree can be repurposed from an invasive species that drains the land of freshwater into a canoe that sails the saltwaters. That canoe has been named Keaolewaokalihi (The floating cloud of Kalihi), a beautiful canoe carved by Puni's kāne, master carver Casey Jackson. This waʻa was completed in 2013 and sailed on the sea of Keʻehi off the shores of Kalihi. A fundraiser was called He Lau Ke Kino—a beautifully multilayered name, "lau" reminding us that the bodies of Haumea are many and that they are like leaves. The bright yellow sail of the canoe is the color of the hau flowers and leaves loved by the moʻowahine Haumea and her manifestation as Kāmehaʻikana. We then see this canoe, light and swift as a cloud in the sky or as a yellow hau leaf carried on the Haupeʻepeʻe wind, imbued with the mana of Kāmehaʻikana and the forest.

Haumea's creation of the spring Pūehuehu tells us of the importance of invoking the aid of the kūpuna to reveal the waters coursing beneath the land. Haumea needs water to perform an ʻawa ceremony to honor the land and her genealogy and to hoʻomana (grow her mana) as a wahine of Kalihi. The farmer Kaliʻu tells Haumea that during the hot summer months, the people must wait for heavy rains in the mountains for the Waolani Stream to flow. To create a spring, Haumea first finds a pōhaku nui (large stone) at the top of Kilohana. She then chants a pule kūʻauhau kupuna, her ancestral genealogical prayer, by evoking the names of her ancestors who are the cliffs Palikū and Palihaʻi and the other pali (cliffs) before them. She asks of them, "E hiolo, e naueue ka pali, / E lele ka pali a kaa ka pali, / Na kupuna pali oʻu i ka po—."[42] She calls out to the pali to tumble down, to sway back and forth, to fly the pōhaku that is of the pali, and she addresses the cliffs lovingly as "Na kupuna pali oʻu i ka po" (The cliff ancestors of mine in [the ancestral realm of] Pō).

In response to her loving offering of her voice to the pali, the pali recognizes her as a descendant through what Kēhaulani Kupihea describes as a kupuna vibration, discussed later in this chapter. When Haumea chants to her kūpuna pali, the vibration in the chanter's voice achieves a synchronicity with the kūpuna that enables Haumea to access her core mana, intensifying her own mana and enabling wondrous events to occur. The earth vibrates, shudders, and rocks with ancestral life. A blazing tongue of lightning strikes the boulder on all sides, shaking it loose:

> Ia pau ana no o keia kahea ana a ua o Haumea, o ka oni ae la no ia o ua pohaku nei, oia no oe o ka oni ana a ka mea kino ola. He imo ana iho na ka lau lihilihi o na maka o Kaliʻu, pa ana keia makani ikaika, a pakele ua wahi kanaka nei mai olepe pu ia e ka makani, a ke lohe nei hoi ko Waikahalulu ame koia mau kaiaulu apau i nei mea halulu e oni nei iloko o ka lewa: aole i liuliu mahope iho, naue ana ka honua a naka haalulu ae la, me he mea la ua hoonaueia ka honua holookoa e ke olaʻi, a uina pahu ana kekahi mea. He wa pokole wale no, ua ike aku la o Kaliʻu i ka pii ana ae o kekahi ohu pohina mai kahi kahawai ae o Waolani a hala iloko o ka lewa.[43]

As soon as this Haumea had finished calling out, the great rock shuddered, the upward stirring of a living body. Kaliʻu's eyelashes fluttered, the strong winds began to blow, and the man barely escaped from being flung away by the wind, and all of Waikahalulu and the people of that place heard the thunderous explosions, it was as if the earth was being shaken by an earthquake, and something made an explosive splash. It was a short time indeed before Kaliʻu saw the rising of a gray mist from the stream of Waolani, passing into the sky.

Here, we see the ancestral cliffs recognizing Haumea through its vibrations. The naue of the lands shows us that they move, shake, rock, sway, tremble, quake, and vibrate.[44] The ʻoni of the boulder then moves, stirs, shifts, fidgets, squirms, and wiggles. The naka halulu of the earth is a thunderous quaking and shaking of the earth. Kaliʻuʻs eyelashes imo (flutter) in the winds raised by Haumeaʻs voice. All of these movements in that moment show us how Haumeaʻs chanting resonates with kūpuna, activating her cliff ancestors to heave the great rock into the air.

When the boulder responds to Haumeaʻs prayer, it crashes down into the land, forming a deep crater. Water from the Pūehuehu spring sprays up and mists the skies. This wondrous event speaks of Haumeaʻs potential, and the moʻolelo reminds us that there is much more to the ʻāina than what we see.

SUBTERRANEAN PILINA OF MOʻOʻĀINA: SHARKS IN THE MOUNTAINS

Haumea breaks through the lands of Oʻahu to the vast underground cave complex beneath, enclosing its own landscape of lakes, rivers, streams, and broad plains. We can imagine this complex of cave systems as a kalo leaf, and the subterrestrial waterways radiating out from the piko that is the mountain Konahuanui, extending along the backbone of the Koʻolau mountains to the farthest points of the island: from the northern shores of Kahuku and Kualoa, to the mountains of Moanalua, Kalihi, and Nuʻuanu to the southern shores of Puʻuloa and Waipahū, and under the Waiʻanae mountains to the southwestern shores of Keawaʻula. These caverns were so large in places that chanter and master kapa maker Aʻiaʻi Bello describes experts known as the hoʻokele waʻa (navigators) of the caves who traveled through them by canoe.[45]

In the wao (realm) of Kānemilohae, the Papakū Makawalu stewardship law concerns the uninterrupted flows of underground waters. Kanahele describes the significance of Kānemilohae (also known as Kānemilohaʻi) and Kūhaʻimoana, the brothers of Pele, and the phenomena and landforms they represent. She writes,

> Kānemilohaʻi, born from the right palm, is the movement of magma vertically from its source to the earthʻs surface, weaving and twisting its way up through many layers of earth. Kūhaʻimoana, born from the ear, is descriptive of the horizontal movement of magma under the ocean and through the earth. Both male forms take on the physical body of

a shark and are the horizontal and vertical movement of magma. The word "ha'i" in their names means to break through something; in this case it is to break through the earth.[46]

Nu'uhiwa further explains that the kānāwai describes the form of Kānemilohae as "lava tubes that puncture the ceiling."[47] The lava tubes that remain underground are Kūha'imoana, and Nu'uhiwa describes how his birth shapes his form: "Kūha'imoana is born from the ear of Haumea, representing lava tubes that run horizontally like ear canals."

Both deities, Kānemiloha'i and Kūha'imoana, take the form of the shark, and we can see the ways that sharks are remembered in mo'olelo for their great skill in navigating through the underground lava tunnel waterways that are the lava phenomena these two deities embody. An 'ōlelo no'eau referring to the great shark deity of Ke Awalau o Pu'uloa (also known as Pearl Harbor)— "Alahula Pu'uloa, he alahele na Ka'ahupāhau" (Everywhere in Pu'uloa is the trail of Ka'ahupāhau)—reminds us that the sharks knew such caverns and chambers through an embodied form of cartography, and Ka'ahupāhau becomes familiar with every nook and cranny of these labyrinthine lava passageways as she makes her way through them, on the lookout for man-eating sharks who would harm the people.[48] The great shark made her way to pools in the mountains at Kapālama, Moanalua, and Mānana (Pearl City).[49]

The sharks that swim up into the mountains are elemental deities, but osmoregulatory plasticity is an adaptability that enables sharks to move between saltwater and freshwater environments. Juvenile bull sharks are noted for their physiological capacity to retain salinity levels in their bodies while seeking out freshwater environments to avoid predators and find new food sources. The water, too, has its own strata. Graydon "Buddy" Keala, who has worked to restore more than thirty loko i'a, or fishponds, explains that sharks can be found upstream in rivers: "Back in the '60s, my dad was an engineer of Līhu'e Plantation and constructed the Cane Haul Bridge over Wailua River next to where the public bridge is. At the dinner table he explained that he needed to hire extra safety divers to protect the construction dive team from sharks. It was very deep—50 to 60 feet. So, the science is that saltwater is denser and heavier than freshwater, and it stratifies by these properties. The sharks swim along the bottom of the river, where the saltwater is denser, while the freshwater floats to the top."[50]

The presence in Kalihi of Haumea's son Kamohoali'i is one among many reminders of the presence of sharks in the mountains of O'ahu. Wondrous stories of sharks traveling into the mountains illustrate that the underground complex of lava and limestone tunnels gave rise to many different observations of sharks swimming into the mountains to different places on different islands called "Keanakamanō" (The cave of the shark). Some families who lived in the mountains were entrusted with the responsibility of feeding the sharks. One Keanakamanō is the cave in Kalihi where another great shark, Makaliʻi, traveled to through underground lava tunnels. Muriel Lupenui lived on Kahakaʻaulana Island off the shores of Kalihi from 1912 to 1914, and she remembers the shark deity Makaliʻi who would go to Keanakamanō in Kalihi and then return to his cave at Kahakaʻaulana:

> Inā hoʻi mai ʻo Makaliʻi mai Kalihi uka, ʻo ia kēia hele kēia papa piʻi ke one a me kēia, maʻaneʻi nei here channel, kēia one hele there, inā hoʻi ʻo ia pālaha kēia ʻo ia ka mākou.

> (If Makaliʻi returned from the uplands of Kalihi, he [Makaliʻi] was this shark god, if he returned to the island, to our island, you would see this surface, the surface was extended, the sand was stacked like this, right here and here the channel, the sand was moved and stacked on top, it never collapsed in, and the ancestors have returned, and this is good; we stay down there). If he returned the mound of sand would flatten. That's how it was.

> So if you haʻalele this ʻāina, they call Mokauea, well ko mākou nānā ana iluna Ke Ana Ka Manō, that's the cave on top of Kilohana mā. (So if you come to this land they call Mokauea, well if you look upward toward the mountain there was Ke Ana Ka Manō—The cave of the shark, that's the cave on top of the lookout point).[51]

Lupenui describes the presence of Makaliʻi as the great shark who left hōʻailona (signs) for the people to read.

In other accounts the great shark deities, Kaʻahupāhau and her brother Kahiʻukā, also visited a second cave in Kapālama called Keanakamanō, remembered in the name of the road leading up to the Kapālama campus of Kamehameha Schools, called "Kealakamanō" (The pathway of the shark).[52]

In the neighboring valley of Moanalua, there is a third cave called Keanaakamanō, not far from the Red Hill ridgeline where the US military stores of jet fuel are precariously perched today. Kumu hula Nāmakahelu Kapahikauaokamehameha tells us that the ancestors of Moanalua are Kamāwaelualani—the son of Wākea and Papahānaumoku—and Kahikilaulani, a woman who travels from afar.[53] Guided by the winds Kōnihinihi and Kōnahenahe, Kahikilaulani sails in her canoe Kaʻōpua (Pillar cloud), up

Kamananui Stream. Today, the stones of the stream dry in the sun, but Kapa-hikauaokamehameha explains, "The stream, as my father said in those days was wide open from the sea into the mountains so that the canoes could go up. Mullet and ʻāholehole were found in the stream in those days."[54] Ka-hikilaulani sails into Kamana Nui Valley and disembarks at a place called Manō (Shark). She bears a gift of an ʻōhiʻa tree growing from earth bundled in tī leaf, and perched on the tree is a black ʻōʻō bird, a honeycreeper with yellow feathers on its sides, now extinct on Oʻahu. From the union of Kamāwaelualani and Kahikilaulani are born a daughter, Maunakapu, and two sons, Kahoʻomoeʻihikapulani (also spelled Hoomoiihikapulani) and Keanaakamanō, who are a peak, a mountain ridge, and a cave in the valley. Their son Keanaakamanō bore the jaws of a shark on his back, and he reminds us that the sharks knew the ways that the water sources for streams and underground tunnels formed complex subterranean networks.

In these moʻolelo of sharks cruising into the mountains, we see the elemental forms of the shark akua teaching Kānaka about entire worlds of water beneath their feet and the importance of knowing the elemental laws of Kānemilohaʻi and Kūhaʻimoana that the Kīhoʻihoʻi Kānāwai stewards teach us for the protection of our aquifers. Just as the hydrogeologist in the Thirty Meter Telescope contested case hearings failed to provide a comprehensive analysis of the way that water moves in Mauna a Wākea, the military has also failed to provide a comprehensive analysis of the networks of water beneath the jet fuel storage tanks buried in Red Hill. Today, as the US military tries to defend its practice of housing jet fuel tanks underground on an island, we are reminded that sharks may still travel in tunnel complexes under those jet fuel tanks, and the catastrophic release of millions of gallons of jet fuel into our aquifers would be devastating to our interconnected waters of life.

SUBTERRANEAN MONSTERS: THE NAVY'S
PLANTING OF UNDERGROUND FUEL TANKS

The construction of the Red Hill Bulk Fuel Storage Facility violates the Kānāwai of Pahulau, Pahukini, and Kānemilohae concerning the protection of aquifers and watersheds, as well as the free passage of underground waters to the sea; all these kānāwai recognize the "400 chambers" of water in the labyrinthine underground cave system that are now threatened with contamination from the jet fuel tanks. The presence of the jet fuel tanks in Red Hill is emblematic of the operations that enable the broader militarized theater staged by the United States to support its economic policies in Asia and the Pacific.[55] Local operations of US settler colonial power drive and are driven by the interpenetration of the material forces of globalization, militarization, and late liberal settler colonial capital. From the US Pacific Command (PACOM), the United States directs militarized zones across half of the earth's surface to protect what it calls the "liberalizing" of free trade. The United States occupies 25 percent of the land on Oʻahu, seeding unexploded ordnance on what were once the most agriculturally rich lands on the island.

In 2018, the Sierra Club, represented by attorneys Marti Townsend (a settler aloha ʻāina who had represented the Concerned Elders of Waiʻanae in the case against the Purple Spot in chapter 1 and had also represented KĀHEA: The Hawaiian-Environmental Alliance in the first TMT contested case hearing in chapter 3) and David Frankel (a settler aloha ʻāina who has worked for the Native Hawaiian Legal Corporation to protect Haleakalā and many other places in Hawaiʻi), won a major victory in their suit against the Hawaiʻi Department of Health (DOH) for failing to ensure that the Navy replace or upgrade the jet fuel tanks. The DOH had long exempted the Red Hill tanks from rules governing spills and overfill protection. Yet the resulting consent agreement among the Navy, the DOH, and the US EPA gives the Navy *twenty years* to complete the upgrade.

The Navy's arguments rely on yet another iteration of cartographic subdivision. In December 2017, Rear Admiral Brian P. Fort of the Navy sent out a letter stating, "Recently derived hydrogeology data, as well as historic reports, support evidence of a valley barrier. The existence of such a barrier could prove to prevent groundwater in the Red Hill area from reaching the Board of Water Supply drinking water wells."[56] Clearly here, as in the TMT case, the Navy sought to make a case that aquifers are protected by an "impermeable layer" that would isolate the jet fuel. Using particle tracking to map out groundwater flow models in the area, the Navy argued that bedrock layers and valley deposits of saprolite protect the groundwater table.[57] In response to this report, the EPA and the DOH argued that the Navy and its consultants were oversimplifying the hydrostratigraphy of the area.[58] The hydrogeologist hired by the DOH stated even more emphatically that the Navy's studies were "skewed toward investigation of those elements that are protective, but not to the elements that are risk drivers."[59]

Here, the Navy is manufacturing a model of water based on the settler logic of enclosure and containment, one similar to the hydrological schema drawn for Mauna a Wākea. What the Navy fails to disclose in this study is that in any representation of "perched" water, there is always the possibility that these waters can overflow over the bounded area of the impermeable layer, or that the layer itself may have seeps and outlets from which any leakage from the fuel tanks will enter into the aquifer.

The Board of Water Supply has argued that there are two options to remedy this problem: relocating the fuel to a different location, or retrofitting all active Red Hill jet fuel tanks with double walls. The Navy has balked at the cost of these alternatives, citing costs of $2 billion to $5 billion for the tank-within-a-tank option. The Sierra Club released a newsletter stating that a recent study found that 6,000 gallons of fuel already leak annually and that there is a 27.6 percent chance that the Red Hill tanks will collectively leak 30,000 gallons of fuel or more every year.[60] As executive director of the Sierra Club, Townsend is pursuing legal avenues that would force the DOH to take immediate action to shut down the tanks. The urgency of these precarious conditions, however, seems lost on the occupying state as it is paralyzed by the catchphrase "national security," even as that form of security comes potentially at the cost of our wai, the water that is the foundation for our planetary security.

While these jet fuel threats to the aquifers and the indicators of climate change intensify, Hoʻoulu ʻĀina has also faced a decreasing supply of water over the last ten years. Jackson explains that the water table has dropped due to a variety of reasons, including decreased rainfall, increased water use by the Board of Water Supply for the growing population of Honolulu, and the rapid spread of invasive species that absorb three times the water of Native species.

As the director of Hoʻoulu ʻĀina, Jackson has had many conversations about climate change events with Hiʻilei Kawelo, director of Paepae o Heʻeia at the Heʻeia fishpond. Jackson and Kawelo both take the long-term view of these changes within the historical context of succeeding waves of colonialism. As Kānaka Maoli have always done, they are adapting to the changes on their own terms. Jackson tells me that climate change does not trigger panic but is part of the intergenerational work that they do:

> I think that the Native response to climate change is not like this emergency response, like how America perceives that we have to turn the big ship around. The Native response is that every wave that comes to shore—every new wave of people, values—we have to adapt, and so our adapting has to be setting us up for long-term relationships, and that's built in to mālama ʻāina. And the choice-making is based on long-term relationships. I'm not going to put jet fuel in the ʻāina because my

relationship with that ʻāina is long-term. We don't base our planning on short-term studies.[61]

Jackson tells us that it is the act of hoʻomana, of growing collective mana, that is the decolonial work they are doing against climate change. Hoʻoulu ʻĀina opens up a space where all of the peoples of Kalihi, Kānaka Maoli and settler aloha ʻāina and those who identify otherwise, including Samoans, Chuukese, Tokelauans, and other Micronesians, can work together to grow their relationships with each other, to learn about each other's survival strategies in a changing climate. The Pasifika Garden, for example, is a place at Hoʻoulu ʻĀina where the peoples of Kalihi can grow the medicinal plants from their own ancestral lands. The garden is both an illustration of healing abundance and a metaphor for the relationships people are growing with each other, sharing ancestral knowledge with each other in a way that grows Indigenous economies of abundance beyond the limits of capitalism, occupation, and settler colonialism. Just as Setawalese navigator Mau Piailug helped Kānaka Maoli regain the lost art of navigating the Pacific, Kānaka Maoli, Pacific Islanders, and all people who work at Hoʻoulu ʻĀina share ancestral lessons with each other for long-term survival.

TO THE SEA OF KEʻEHI: SEEKING A KUPUNA VIBRATION

In 2013, the aloha ʻāina of Hoʻoulu ʻĀina cheered as Keaolewaokalihi set sail from shores of Keʻehi. The five ahupuaʻa of Keʻehi extend beyond the shores to the outer edge of the extensive Keʻehi lau papa (reef flats). Kēhaulani Kupihea, a cultural anthropologist and director of Hoʻōla Mokauea–Keʻehi, explains that although Keʻehi can be translated as "to tread on," she was taught that Keʻehi means "to embrace the land with your feet."[62] The rich Keʻehi reef system once stretched out around the islands of Kahakaʻaulana, Mokuoeo, and Mokauea, and the kūpuna remember that in times past they would walk all around the area on reefs (see figure 5.3). The abundance of this reef system is documented by chants dating to the 1750s celebrating the ʻanae (mullet) of Keʻehi and Kamehameha III's 1839 designation of Keʻehi as royal fishing grounds.[63]

Kēhaulani's understanding resonates with a moʻoʻāina consciousness of the ways that ecological systems are connected across ahupuaʻa. She explains that we need to see the ahupuaʻa of Mokauea, Kahakaʻaulana, Mokuoeo, and Mauliola as part of the larger reef complex of Keʻehi, not as individual islands spread out over multiple ahupuaʻa (see figure 5.4). These

FIGURE 5.3 The laupapa of Keʻehi, with Mokauea Island in the foreground and Kalihi Valley in the distance, Kilohana rising to the left of the Kalihi saddle and Lanihuli rising to the right. Mokauea, June 26, 2017. Photograph by the author.

islands were known collectively as ipu (gourd containers) for different maritime knowledges:

> The moʻolelo of these islands come together as we map the higher consciousness of Keʻehi. People don't realize that Keʻehi feeds five ahupuaʻa, from Moanalua to Kahauiki, Kalihi, Kapālama, and Nuʻuanu. If your stream is going into Keʻehi, Keʻehi is your makai, and you have to mālama the whole of Keʻehi. Right now, people separate these islands into their different ahupuaʻa and there's no protection for those three islands in relation to each other. My mission is to get protection

FIGURE 5.4 Kēhaulani Kupihea talking about historical maps of Keʻehi. Mauliola, November 11, 2013. Photograph courtesy of Naomi Sodetani.

for them as a preservation historic *district*. They are not individual sites; they make up one area that we use for different purposes. In the Western mindset, they always want to compartmentalize everything. We have to get away from compartmentalizing, putting things in compartments and boxes, and really get back to viewing places organically.[64]

From Mauna a Wākea to Mokauea, we see Kānaka challenging the occupying state's overly narrow focus on individual sites. Through designating these complexes as historic districts, the occupying state would have to recognize that these places cannot be subdivided and isolated from each other in development and urban planning projects. The abundance of each relies on the others.

At Keʻehi, the ʻupena nananana a Papa (spiderweb of Papa) that tracks potentialities corresponds to the string figure woven over the navigational gourds. In the genealogy of Wākea, his youngest child, Makulukuluka-lani, is an astronomer priest. Perhaps he studied the stars at the island Kahakaʻaulana, which Kēhaulani translates as "the floating oracle," a navigational center where the ipu hoʻokele waʻa (navigational gourds) were kept.

The gourd containers were strung by a net of strings and filled with water by which the navigators could see the reflection of the stars in a star compass to read the rising and setting points of the stars on horizons. There is still some mystery about how the ipu hoʻokele waʻa were used, and Kēhaulani has been combing through Hawaiian-language newspapers to recover this knowledge, one line at a time. Her kāne's great-great-uncle, the historian David Malo Kupihea, was interviewed by Theodore Kelsey in 1950 and described the navigational gourd: "Such [a] gourd was partly filled with water to catch the reflection of the stars when two sight-holes on opposite sides were in line with the North Star—thus setting the 'needle' of the Hawaiian compass."[65] Rubellite Kawena Johnson, John Kaipo Mahelona, and Clive Ruggles further explain these notes from Kelsey's interview with Kupihea: at the rim of the gourd, at intervals of forty-five degrees, were double hitches called puʻu mana. A fine olonā cord net was laid over the top of the gourd and tied underneath, forming approximately twenty-four (or alternately, thirty-six) one-inch maka (eyes, squares), each of which was individually named. The nine principal guiding stars, called the Makaiwa (Nine eyes), are each represented by one of the puʻu mana (knots) around the ʻalihi (edge) of the net and gourd rim.

Kaimana Barcarse has woven Nā ʻOhana Hōkū ʻEhā (The four star families), which chart the principal navigational star map, into a composition called "Ka Ipu Hoʻokele," also known as "The Navigator's Chant." Master navigator Nainoa Thompson, who recovered the arts of navigation from Satawalese navigator Mau Piailug, had devised a modern teaching device that organizes the sky into four star-lines, each geometrically taking up a quarter of the celestial sphere: (1) Ke Kā o Makaliʻi (The canoe-bailer of Makaliʻi), (2) Iwikuamoʻo (Backbone), (3) Mānaiakalani (The chief's fishing line), and (4) Ka Lupe o Kawelo (The kite of Kawelo).[66] Barcarse's composition goes,

> Kāhea: E ʻohiʻohi i nā pono!
> Pane: He kā, he iwi, he makau, he lupe!
> Ua lako ka ipu a ka hoʻokele!
>
> Command: Gather up your tools!
> Reply: A bailer, a bone, a fishhook, a kite!
> The gourd of the navigator is provisioned![67]

As the double-hulled canoe Hōkūleʻa sailed on its worldwide voyage, a navigational wonder of the recovered art of wayfinding by the stars, Papa's web continues to show us the potentialities of charting the skies through kilo observations.

The waters of Keʻehi are themselves mapped with an intimate knowledge of the kai (ocean waters) and the life within it. The shoreline was adorned with the beautiful lei of Keʻehi fishponds: Ananoho, Auiki, Pāhouiki, Pāhounui, and ʻĀpili. These once abundant fishponds have since been filled in, and now storage and military facilities occupy these lands, the names of the fishponds memorialized in street names that continue to feed our naʻau and our imaginations.

In 2009, Kēhaulani returned to Mokauea with her kāne, artist Kupihea, to help with the Mokauea Fishermen's Association's efforts to keep the knowledges of Mokauea vibrant. She takes students to the island in a hands-on education effort that enables them to live the moʻolelo in an embodied way. She explains, "Our kūpuna were very, very intimately connected to everything. They named the wind and places on the earth so they could have relationships with them. In one chant, Kahikilaulani talks about this area, she talks about sailing in on her white bird, and then she talks about the wind called Kōnahenahe. So that's the wind that you'll feel out here as you are sailing."[68] Kahikilaulani's two oarsmen are the breezes, Kōnahenahe and Kōnihinihi, that ruffle the waters of Keʻehi.[69]

Kēhaulani defines ea as the moment when we are so attuned to the land that we become synchronized with the kūpuna, and we achieve what she calls a "kupuna vibration." This kupuna vibration is a way for us to access the higher consciousness of the ʻāina and kūpuna:

> As we strive for ea, I feel that our goal, that my goal, is to raise my energy to vibrate on what I call a kupuna vibration. If we can get our vibration to vibrate just for a second on that kupuna vibration, then we can see through the lens of our kūpuna, and we can feel and vibrate with them because they were living in such a different time. They were living in an organic time, and we live in boxed times, dissecting times.
>
> Yesterday, when I went to Kahakaʻaulana, I noticed there were more little corals popping up, and I said, "Wow, she's so happy we're visiting!" And when I took the students to the cultural center on Mokauea, I looked out and I notice there were more colorful corals popping up and little spiky, white, beige, brown rice coral. I think that the more and more you are around, the land speaks to you, and eventually, once we get our vibrations, right now, in this time, to vibrate with our kupuna vibrations, those vibrations merge, and I think that's ea. That organically,

spiritually, physically, the two vibrations are synchronistically in tune. I felt that yesterday.[70]

What is key in Kēhaulani's words is our capacity to access this kupuna vibration. This is also the attunement to the elemental forms that Kanahele describes, and the alignment with the akua that Kealoha Pisciotta describes. When we recall Haumea chanting her Palikū genealogy, we see that she is attuned to the kupuna vibration of her Palikū ancestors and we see the earth's recognition of her oli in the naue (shaking) of the land. Similarly, in the moʻolelo *Keaomelemele*, Keaomelemele's chanting is so powerful that she achieves that kupuna vibration and, with a great roar and shuddering of the earth, the great mountain Konahuanui splits apart from Waolani to create Nuʻuanu Valley.[71] Across the moʻolelo, the pulapula seedling descendants reach out to the ancestral elemental forms, and the land responds. To inhabit the space of ancestral time is to see Haumea returning again and again in fecundity, and the kupuna vibration is what we need to work toward to huli, to overturn, the systems that do not sustain us.

When we gather at the Mauliola shoreline, we chant "E Hō Mai" to wehe (open) ourselves to this kupuna vibration, to open ourselves up to, and to ask for a response from, the phenomena that we will see on the island. Every time we paddle the canoe to Mokauea, the brilliant blue-green waters of Keʻehi evoke powerful historic newspaper images of the residents of Mokauea being evicted from the island, looking back toward the island and watching their homes burn in flames, set on fire by the occupying state. By the 1970s, the "mainland" of Sand Island became a dredged landfill and a sewage treatment plant polluted with the wastes of urban Honolulu. In June 1975, the houseless families who lived on Mokauea were served eviction notices by the occupying state.[72] A public outcry stopped the state's evictions of the Mokauea residents and, three years later in 1978, the state signed a sixty-five-year lease with the fourteen families who were lineal descendants of Mokauea. In 1980, the state arrested nineteen residents of Sand Island and bulldozed 135 homes.

More recently, in 2011, the state presented a proposal for a $30 million Sand Island Ocean Recreation Park with a proposed 25-acre marina that would feature four hundred to five hundred boat slips as a way to generate revenues for the state. The fact that the state's Historic Preservation Division designated Mokauea as an area of important historical concern has staved off the passage of this proposal.

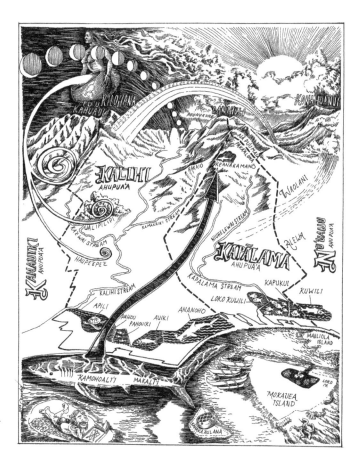

FIGURE 5.5
Kupihea,
"Moʻolelo Map
of Keʻehi,"
2017. A map
of four of the
five ahupuaʻa
whose waters
feed Keʻehi.
Image courtesy
of the artist.

MAPPING THE MOʻOʻĀINA OF KEʻEHI

As part of their restoration efforts, Kēhaulani asked her kāne Kupihea to map Mokauea as a moʻolelo storyboard (see figure 5.5). Kupihea's moʻolelo map allows us to wiliwili, to twist together the strands of the moʻolelo of the five ahupuaʻa connected by the winds, rains, and currents of the sea. He tells me,

> I wanted this map to illustrate that Keʻehi is the piko for Nuʻuanu, Kapālama, Kalihi, Kahauiki, and Moanalua, and all the streams empty out into Keʻehi. The mana of the wai all goes down into this area so the physical result is that there were once hundreds of varieties of limu in the area from the fresh water, not just from the streams but from the springs. And on the old maps, they named some of the springs, and the reefs are named for where certain springs were and where certain limu would grow because of the springs. Our kūpuna were pretty inventive and they

would give names to springs by their characters. Like the one pond that's still at Kahaka'aulana on the side with the Kalihi Channel: when there was a lot of rain up in the mountains, the channel was strong enough to push all the sediment out of the reef, and so they would say that when all the sand piles up, that Makali'i was home. And that could be both references to the actual manō and to the rising of Makali'i, the Pleiades. Our kūpuna were masters of puns, double entendres, riddles, and then— to add to that complexity—there are the actual physical references to plants, mountain peaks, clouds, and other natural phenomena.[73]

In this example of a Kanaka Maoli cartography of resurgence, Kupihea maps the Ko'olau mountain peaks, Pu'u Kahuauli, Kilohana, Lanihuli, and Kona-huanui down to the reef flats of Ke'ehi. Kupihea's map traces the uka (inland) waterways as well, navigated by the shark guardians Kamohoali'i and Makali'i. In this mapping of ea, he illustrates the interconnected ahupua'a through the arching ānuenue (rainbow) and the moon phases of Hina'aimalama (Hina who eats the moon). The abundance of the Ke'ehi fisheries are remembered in the names of the fishponds, fed by the Ka'ewai, Kalihi, and Kamanaiki streams that run across ahupua'a. The Ualipilipi rain and the Haupe'epe'e wind from Hina's 'umeke (bowl) also cross these ahupua'a, as do the fishponds where young men once raced on hammerhead sharks across the fishponds.[74]

On another mo'olelo map of Ke'ehi, Kupihea marks the places of the reefs that are named Pūpū'awa (sea snail with a prickly shell), Keahukūmanō (or alternately, Keahukūmano'o; the standing ahu of the shark, or the ahu at the fountainhead of a stream), Kalaeoni (the jutting promontory, or the promontory that moves about in the sea), and Kaluapuhi (eel's hole). These names are recorded on Registered Map 1138, an 1885 Hawaiian government survey map of the "Kalihi Entrance or Kaliawa Fishery."[75] Freshwater flows feed the fishpond on Mokauea, and the springs feed the places on the reefs where the limu thrive. On Mokauea, the hau grows, a tender promise for the future of the island.

Perhaps the sharks continue to swim through these lava tubes, under the jet fuel tanks of Red Hill, all across the land, navigating around the places where construction has caved in the lava tunnels. The sharks' pathways remind us of Haumea's potentialities, both the possibilites for abundance or destruction. As Haumea's words from the mo'olelo travel across time to us today, it is the sovereignty of the land that endures, and as we see the changes being wrought on the earth by climate change we can choose to materialize our own capacities for regenerating abundance.

CHAPTER SIX

MO‘O‘ĀINA

CASCADES

IN WAIĀHOLE

AND HE‘EIA

A Cartography

of Hau(mea)

The expansiveness of mo‘o‘āina, the relational land divisions that stretch out across islands and the earth, also represents a way to map abundance through envisioning the expansive cascading effects of restoration. Just as environmental degradation caused by late liberal settler capital has exponential effects on contingent ecosystems, an inverse correlation is also true: localized environmental restoration also has exponential effects, and this chapter explores how the restoration of water to streams results in ever-expanding ripples of renewal that move outward across the continuities of mo‘o‘āina.

The regenerative Haumea principle can be seen in these cascading effects: Haumea, who returns again and again, renewed to youth, who multiplies her bodies as women and as mo‘o, plays a key role in this chapter as we see the procession of mo‘o taking the form of the hau flowers that the mo‘o love, the yellow flowers with deep-red hearts that grow along waterways, the passionately intertwined branches of the hau both protecting lo‘i kalo (taro pondfields) long fallow and shading loko i‘a (fishponds). As we will see in this chapter, the yellow path of hau flowers maps the alo (face) stones of ancient structures that feed, now being awakened from their long sleep as mahiʻai (farmers) return to plant kalo and cultivate fish once again (see plate 13).

The awakening of Hāloa (the kalo elder sibling of Kānaka) in the resurgence of kalo cultivation recalls a beautiful description in the moʻolelo of the abundance produced by kalo, who is able to multiply into diverse varieties. In Moses Manu's *Keaomelemele*, Kahānaiakeakua sleeps for one anahulu (ten days), intoxicated by the ʻawa of Ulukaʻa, and he dreams of the healing waters of Kāne. In this vision, he sees a "nani aliali maikai" pool of crystal-clear water with a single kalo plant growing in its center. Two trees stand on the bank of the pool with their branches bending over the surface of the water. Their flowers trill like the kāhuli land shells of the uplands. He sees these things "me ka piha i ka iini nui" (with a fullness of desire for them).[1] Kahānaiakeakua is entranced with wonder, and Kānehūnāmoku (Kāne of the hidden islands) explains to him that he is the keeper of that pool that brings the dead back to life, the elderly to youth, the sick to health.

He then explains that the kalo in the pool is of the Piʻialiʻi variety, and it can produce all vegetable foods without delay ("aia ia ia na pono a pau o na mea ai me ka hikiwawe loa me ka hakalia ole").[2] The red and yellow flowers he had seen are Kanikawī and Kanikawā, bodily forms of his own grandmother, the moʻo Kamoʻoinanea.[3] These flowers, he is told, can assume the forms of women, and from them come flowers of all other varieties. Kānehūnāmiku then tells Kahānaiakeakua, "Nolaila, he nani ia na lakou no i hoike mai la ia oe ma ka moeuhane, nolaila, e hele akua au e hoike aku ia oe i kahi o ua kiowai la i keia wa"[4] (Therefore, since it is their will to reveal themselves to you in a dream, let me go to show you where the pool is now).[5] Mary Kawena Pukui translates this as the "will" of the elements, a recognition of this hōʻailona (sign) as a granting of permission by the elements to be seen. Kānehūnāmoku then takes Kahānaiakeakua to this pool:

> A i ko ia nei ike pono ana'ku, he mea e ke kiowai maikai launa ole. O keia ka wa a Kanehunamoku i kahea aku ai i ke kalo Piialii, aia hoi ua puka koke mai la na mea ulu a pau loa o na ano a pau, a o ka manawa keia i haule iho ai na pua elua mai luna iho o ko laua mau lala iluna o ka ili o ka wai, a hoomaka ae la ua mau pua nei e niniu, a mele mai la me he leo la no ke kanaka maoli, a he mea kupanaha keia i ko Kahanaiakeakua ike ana'ku i ka hana a keia mau pua a me ke kalo Piialii.[6]

When he beheld it, he saw how perfectly beautiful it was. Then Kane-hunamoku called out to the piialii taro and lo, plants of every kind came from it at once. Immediately the trees shed their two blossoms on the surface of the water and they began to whirl and sing with voices that resembled human voices. Those doings of the blossoms and of the piialii taro were wonderful to Kahanaiakeakua.[7]

This is also a story of the lands' recognition of their kahu (guardian): when Kānehūnāmoku calls out to the Pi'iali'i kalo, the kalo and the flowers recognize him and respond to him. It is this reciprocal recognition that is key in this generative moment.

As a mo'olelo tracing the mo'okū'auhau of kalo, this moment begins with kilo (observation and forecasting) of the kūpuna kalo, the oldest generation of kalo. This Pi'iali'i kalo is the kupuna to the kalo today who are hundreds of generations old, and it was treasured as a variety to offer to the akua.[8] From this Pi'iali'i kalo springs hundreds of varieties of kalo, and this mo'olelo also passes on the lesson of growing not just one kind of kalo but a diversity of kalo to survive changes in climate over time.

Eighth-generation master mahi'ai kalo Jerry Konanui also speaks to the problems posed by fantasmatic visions of a singular, genetically engineered kalo, the "superkalo" that can live in all environments. As he argues, because scientists are restricted by funding and time, their focus is too narrow: "They don't know the consequences of what is outside of this lo'i. They don't know that five years from now, that taro they bred will be invasive and will take out the lo'i and choke out the rest of the taro."[9] Instead, he describes the brilliance of kūpuna who have, over generations, cultivated different varieties of kalo to survive a range of conditions:

> The varieties we have that our ancestors passed down to us, is extreme, and when I say extreme: Kalo Paua, the only kalo that can grow in the desert of Ka'ū. Piko Uliuli and Piko o Lono, Piko 'Ele'ele, these are taro that were bred by our ancestors that could tolerate the warm water, the cold water. A variety of taro called Kalo Pa'akai. "Pa'akai" means salt. Why would our Hawaiians call this taro Pa'akai or salt? Some guys say, oh, taste salty. Oh, how come taste salty? The story about Kalo Pa'akai was that was grown in the lihikai, the edge of the ocean where the brackish water comes in. Sometimes pu'uwai [kalo shoot] comes up, so the variation of the salinity, the saltiness of that, these Kalo Pa'akai was bred by our kūpuna that could grow in that. . . . Now I told you about Kalo Pa'akai, we want to find out about the salinity. I also would like, with

my friends, to document all of our taro that have names related to the kai, like 'O'opu Kai, Kai 'Ala, Kai Kea, Kai Uliuli, all those varieties. We wanna kanu [plant] and see if our kūpuna were so deep that these kalo were related to the cultivation near the lihikai, near the beach. How wonderful is that? People are concerned about the rise of the tide and the rise of the sea level. Our kūpuna had that, too! They wen' *breed* this taro for that purpose.

This 'ike kupuna (ancestral knowledge) is encoded in the names of kalo varieties along with the knowledge of where and how to plant them to survive climate change.

I begin with this mo'olelo of kalo to illustrate the importance of kilo to mapping the pathways of cascade effects necessary for vast arrangements of life. The waterways that sustain kalo are also dependent on the people's fight for the restoration of streams from corporate diversions. To set the foundation for a story about water, I return to the mo'olelo of Haumea and Wākea as they take their battle with Kumuhonua to the ko'olau (windward) side of O'ahu. Here, Haumea multiplies her bodies as beautiful women who pack the plains in front of the cliffs of Palikū. Like the procession of the mo'o at Waialua, the multitudes of mo'o wahine provide a mo'o'āina mapping of the iwikuamo'o (backbone) of streams and bodies of water that feed kalo. In this mo'olelo, however, it is the yellow flowers of the hau trees that mark these pathways of the mo'o, bearing witness to the historic theft of water and the fight to restore it.

The people of these windward valleys are the descendants of these mo'o water protectors. Their work to restore kalo terraces and fishponds resonates with the kupuna vibration that Kēhaulani Kupihea speaks of in chapter 5 and as represented in the patterns of Mealaaloha Bishop's sweeping mixed-media oil painting *Kalo Pa'a o Waiāhole*, named for the hard kalo of Waiāhole that is also the name for the resolute people of Waiāhole (see plate 14). Her painting maps the land and the people, layering together the twenty-five-year struggle of farmers, first against eviction by wealthy landowners and developers and later to restore waters to the streams of the Ko'olaupoko valleys. Her son, Hanalē Bishop, plants kalo by the moons and rains, and they complement each other as they each map the choreography of these cycles. The restoration of the Waiāhole and He'eia streams has had ripple effects on the surrounding fishponds, and from the Hale o Meheanu fishpond in He'eia where they are planting hau, we follow the yellow paths of hau(mea)'s restoration up and over the Koʻolau mountains to Keʻehi, where Kēhaulani Kupihea describes the flourishing of corals in chapter 5.

THE MULTITUDINOUS BODIES OF HAUMEA
ON THE PLAINS OF KUALOA

The moʻolelo of Haumea and Wākea continues on the plains fronting the cliffs of Palikū, who are her ancestors. From May 2 to June 18, 1906, *Ka Naʻi Aupuni* ran Joseph Mokuʻōhai Poepoe's "Ka Moolelo o ko Wakea ma Noho ana ma Kalihi—Ka Loaa ana o ke Akua Ulu o Kamehaikana." We recall from chapter 5 that Haumea and Wākea escape through the portal of the breadfruit tree and make their way back up to Kilohana. Haumea knows that war with Kumuhonua is upon them, so they amass their forces on the koʻolau side of the island.

In an astonishing turn in this moʻolelo, we see the wonder of Haumea multiplying her body into thousands of beautiful women who pack the plains before the cliffs of Palikū. In the English translation, I highlight some of the particularly significant ʻōlelo Hawaiʻi terms that I return to below:

> Ua hoihoi aku la o Haumea i ke kane ame ko laua mau ohua apau a loko o ke ana huna o loko o ke kuahiwi o Paliku, oia hoi ke ana o Pohukaina e olelo mau ia nei i keia wa. A koe hookahi iho la o Haumea.
>
> I ka nee ana mai o ka ehu o ke kaua malalo mai o Koolau-loa, a pela nohoi ka ehu o ke kaua ma Koolau-poko mai, ua ike mai la na kanaka i ka paa pono o ke ka-honua mai uka aku nei o kahi i kapaia i keia wa, o Kaahuula Punawai a hele a hoea i ka lae o Kaoio, i ka paa pono i na wahine me na hua kukui ma ko lakou mau lima.
>
> O keia poe wahine a nei poe kanaka e ike aku nei, oia na kino lehulehu o Haumea. A o ia no ke kumu o kona kapaia ana he wahine kino lehu, kino mano, a kino hoopahaohao hoi.[10]

Haumea returned her kāne [Wākea] and all of their attendants inside the hidden cave in the ridge of Palikū, namely, the cave of Pohukaina as it is still said today. And only Haumea remained.

As the dust clouds of the warriors [ka ehu o ke kaua] were moving in [neʻe] below from around the Koolauloa area, likewise, the dust clouds of the warriors from Koolaupoko were also moving in [neʻe], they saw people completely covered [paʻa pono] the flat lands [ke ka-honua] below the cliffs inland of the place now called Kaʻahuʻula Spring, extending to Kaʻōʻio Cape, completely covered [paʻa pono] with women with kukui nuts in their hands.

FIGURE 6.1 View of Kualoa: the cliffs of Palikū, the peak of Kānehoalani, Mokoli'i island, Moli'i and 'Āpua fishponds, and Koholālele pond, March 8, 2017. Photograph by Martin Solhaugen.

> These women that the people were seeing, they were the multitu-dinous bodies [kino lehulehu] of Haumea. And this is the reason why Haumea is called the woman of the multitudinous bodies, the numer-ous bodies four thousand thick, and wondrous bodies as well.[11]

Like the mo'o who pani pa'a loa (completely cover) the plains from Waialua to 'Ewa, here, too, the bodily manifestations of Haumea as beautiful women pa'a pono (completely cover) the plains of Kualoa (see figure 6.1). The repetition of these phrases draws these two mo'olelo together so that they resonate with each other, intensifying the emphasis on the multitudes needed to protect water in these places. Repetitions in mo'olelo enact the rhythms of daily life, from the pounding of the poi to the beating of kapa to, as we will see, the patterning of brushstrokes. Chants are also composed with the understanding that repetition builds a pulsating intensity, a kupuna vibration. For those with 'ike pāpālua, the gift of second sight, they would also see these these beautiful women pulsing between their kino kanaka (human bodies) and their kino mo'o (lizard bodies).

In this beautifully choreographed scene of battle, the movements are mirrored: Kumuhonua's warriors ne'e (surge) across the ko'olau lands, and this is met by the ne'e of the women warriors toward them. When Kumuhonua's warriors see these women, they send messengers to ask for the whereabouts of Wākea. They are answered by "he wahine aiai" (a woman bright as the moonlight), who tells the messengers that their war leader should turn back. When the messengers convey this "pākīkē" (saucy or impudent) reply, the pūkaua (war leader) underestimates the formidable forces of Haumea and orders the warriors to proceed. The women act with swift and deadly force:

> O ka wa no ia i nee aku ai na koa o Kane Kumuhonua, ma ka aoao aku nei ma Kona. I keia wa i ua poe nei i nee aku ai o ka manawa no ia i lele mai ai na hua kukui mai na lima mai o na kino wahine lehulehu o Haumea, oia no oe o na poka-ua hekili e pa ana ma na lae o ua poe koa nei o Kane Kumuhonua. Pa no ka hua kukui i ka lae o ke kanaka, lawe ka hanu i Olepau. He hua kukui ka mea nana i luku i na poe kanaka la; a oia ke kumu i puka ai keia hopunaolelo a kahiko:
> "A-hua-lala-kukui ka make."[12]

> Immediately thereafter the warriors of Kāne Kumuhonua surged forth from the other side, from the leeward side. At this time these women also surged forth, and the kukui nuts flew from the hands of the multitudinous women forms of Haumea, thundering hailstones that struck the foreheads of the warriors of Kāne Kumuhonua. When the kukui nuts struck the foreheads of the people, the breath was taken to Olepau. It was a kukui nut that destroyed the people; and it is the reason this old saying emerged:
> "The dead were scattered like kukui branches in heaps."[13]

The mo'o wahine let fly the seeds of Haumea's potentiality against Kumuhonua's warriors. These seeds then take root in these bodies and grow into groves of kukui nut trees that flourish across the lands of Palikū, now known as Kualoa, memorializing the numbers of men who underestimated Haumea and were killed.

When we map the Haumea story on the ground, we see that, inland from Ka'ahu'ula Spring, said to be at Kalaeoka'ō'io (the promontory or brow of the bonefish), the moʻo bodies of Haumea multiply across the land as guardians of the streams, springs, and other bodies of water. Offshore is the island of Mokoliʻi. In the battle between Hiʻiakaikapoliopele and the moʻo Mokoliʻi, she hurls the moʻo's body into the air: his tail becomes the island, and the body of the moʻo forms the lowlands of Kualoa. Other bodies of water in this area, including the Moliʻi, ʻĀpua, and Koholālele fishponds, would also have been under the protection of moʻo.

KE KALOPAʻA O WAIĀHOLE: THE HARD KALO,
THE PEOPLE OF WAIĀHOLE

In 1916, the loʻi kalo in Waiāhole Valley were forced fallow by the construction of the massive Waiāhole Ditch System, which diverted thirty million gallons of water per day from the streams of Waiāhole, Waikāne, Hakipuʻu, Kahana, Kaʻalaea, and Kahaluʻu to feed the sugarcane plantations on the leeward side of the island.[14] Lincoln McCandless, an industrialist with expertise in oil drilling and mining, was hired by the Oahu Sugar Company to construct the twenty-five-mile tunnel and ditch system, and to do so, he bought much of the land in Waiāhole Valley, leasing it back to farmers. This pattern of water diversion was repeated throughout the valleys in Hawaiʻi, drying up streambeds, forcing Kānaka Maoli and others to leave their ancestral practices of farming kalo.

The stand that the moʻo wahine took in front of Palikū, like the kiaʻi standing in rows along the road to the summit of Mauna a Wākea in chapter 4, is mirrored in the blockade that Waiāhole farmers and their supporters formed against their eviction from their leased farmlands. In 1973, McCandless's daughter Elizabeth Marks was approached by developer Joe Pao and asked to terminate her leases to the farmers so that he could develop a housing subdivision in the valley.[15] The struggle of farmers in Waiāhole and Waikāne Valleys to maintain an agricultural way of life emblematizes the struggles that continue today, as we have seen in Waiʻanae in chapters 1 and 2. The Waiāhole-Waikāne struggle exploded across the newspapers, fueled by a rising consciousness of class disparities, the gains made by the civil rights movement, and the struggle to establish ethnic studies as a field of study at the University of Hawaiʻi. In one iconic moment, the *Honolulu Star-Bulletin* featured a photo of hundreds of people with their linked arms raised in the air in front of the Waiāhole Poi Factory, forming a human blockade against eviction by police.[16] When the landowner and the developer petitioned for a rezoning of the land to urban use, the overwhelming testimonies in support of the Waiāhole and Waikāne farming communities led to the Land Use Commission's ruling to deny the landowner's petition. Governor George Ariyoshi then intervened and purchased the land in the valley for $6 million, leasing it back to the farmers to preserve their rural lifestyle. This was the first significant victory in the struggle of farmers against corporate development.

Yet while the Waiāhole and Waikāne communities had won the battle over land, their fight for water continued. Kapua Sproat and Isaac Moriwake, Earthjustice attorneys for the Waiāhole and Waikāne communities, recount the legal history in which *McBryde v. Robinson* (1973) led the Hawai'i Supreme Court to reinstate the Kanaka Maoli concept of water as a "public trust."[17] In 1976, kalo farmers in Waihe'e Valley, including Charlie and Paul Reppun, sued the Honolulu Board of Water Supply for taking so much water from Waihe'e Stream that little was left for their lo'i kalo.[18] They won their case, and as a result, Governor Ariyoshi tasked a commission to devise a water policy for the state. It was not until 1987, however, that the state legislature adopted the water code to be administered by the Commission on Water Resources Management. Then, in 1993, anticipating the closure of the Oahu Sugar Company, Kānaka Maoli, windward communities, and environmental groups—Waiāhole-Waikāne Community Association, Hakipu'u 'Ohana, Kahalu'u Neighborhood Board, Ka Lāhui Hawai'i, Makawai Stream Restoration Alliance, and Hawai'i's Thousand Friends—petitioned the water commission to restore the waters to the Waiāhole and Waikāne streams. Wealthy and powerful leeward parties, including the Bishop, Campbell, and Robinson estates, Dole, Del Monte, and Castle and Cooke, as well as the military and city, state, and federal agencies—City and County of Honolulu Board of Water Supply, State of Hawai'i Department of Agriculture, and the US Navy—all opposed the return of water: these interests sought to water-bank the thirty million gallons of water a day that were still being diverted to the central plains of O'ahu for future housing development projects. They argued that there was no longer any taro farming and that water would be wasted by dumping it into the ocean.

Farmers from the windward side became parties in the 1995 contested case hearing to restore waters to their streams. When the farmers learned that the ditch operator was dumping millions of gallons of water a day into leeward gulches to avoid returning the water, a six-month agreement was struck that returned half of the water to the streams. Kalo farmer Vivien Lee explains, "When this interim agreement expired and Amfac–Waiahole Irrigation Company—owners of the ditch system—wanted to increase diversions, protesters peacefully blocked company employees from doing so.

Some of the one hundred protesters willing to be arrested were veterans of the earlier Waiāhole struggle; some had worked for twenty years on other land and water issues; and some were young, getting involved for the first time."[19] Like the thousands of Haumea bodies spread out in the plains below Palikū, we see the water protectors of Waiāhole radiating out from the great wheel of the water valve, standing for the return of water to Waiāhole. In the end, the landmark Waiāhole court case returned just under half of the water to windward streams, about twelve million gallons per day.

Lee's husband, kalo farmer Charlie Reppun, raises questions about the underlying logic of capital that underpins state and corporate historical attempts to claim ownership of water, even though water is a public trust:

> When, if ever, does exclusive ownership of water begin? When the water crosses your property line, whether in a stream or underground? Is it yours if it falls from a passing cloud? Would that make the fluffy white cloud directly overhead your cloud? Oh, now the cloud has moved over the land of Bishop Estate. There is a legal theory that says property boundaries go to the center of the earth, so I supposed this sign ["Boundary, State of Hawai'i / Bishop Estate"], located a mere thousand feet beneath the crest of the Ko'olau Mountains, represents only a modest claim to subterranean clouds.[20]

Reppun's allegorical invocation of subterranean clouds foregrounds the element of absurdity in state and corporate historical attempts to claim ownership of water. Reppun begins with the question of *when*, not where, the mathematics of the ownership of water begins, foregrounding temporality as water traverses arbitrary land boundaries set up by late liberal capital and the occupying state.

The determination of the people of Waiāhole to see the water restored to the streams, to the lo'i kalo, and to the estuaries, however, is reflected in their reclamation of the name, Ke Kalo Pa'a, or "the hard taro of Waiāhole." This kalo is not easily pounded into poi, and this is reflected in the phrase "ho'i kalopa'a i Waiāhole," meaning "the people of Waiāhole who are steadfast." B. Kaehuaea recounts the well-known mo'olelo in an 1865 issue of *Ka Nupepa Kuokoa*. The kalo of Waiāhole, Kaehuaea explains, is known as "he paakiki maoli io no ke kalo" (truly hard is the kalo [of Waiāhole]); however, the fame of the kalo of Waiāhole spread due to the hana kupanaha (strange actions) of Kuapunohu, a warrior looking for an adversary to fight in the district of Ko'olaupoko.[21] He arrives at his sister's home and asks her husband Imaole, "Have you two any food?" Imaole replies, "He ai no, aia la iwaena (kaika)" (We have food, it is standing in the kalo patch).[22] Outraged that his brother-in-law refuses to prepare the kalo for him, Kuapunohu uses the tip of his spear to cut the kalo into small pieces and sets them on fire. Kaehuaea provides this description:

> Pela kana hana ana a lilo i mea nui, a pau loa aku loi okoa, & ka (Eka okoa) [*sic*] a pupuhi aku la kela i ke kai o Ukoa, akola, wahi a Kuapunohu, ke heo la kela.

> He worked in this way until there was a great fire and the different loʻi were completely destroyed, and so an entire acre was blown away like the [fish of the] sea waters of Ukoa. "There!" said Kuapunohu, "Bite me!"[23]

The hard kalo burned like wood, and that came to represent the people of the Waiāhole, kūpaʻa (steadfast), tenacious in the face of adversity. Reppun reflects on the way this moʻolelo took on new meaning in the struggle to restore water to streams: "Imaole was unwilling to yield to someone with bad intentions. For this attitude Waiāhole people were characterized as obstinate and called kalo paʻa (hard taro). Obstinacy is a double-edged sword, but it is often the only weapon available to people struggling against entities that are obstinate because of their size, power, and wealth."[24]

The kalo paʻa of Waiāhole sought the return of waters to their streams by planting huli (kalo stalks) and restoring loʻi kalo, but first, they had to find the lands that were formerly in kalo cultivation (see figure 6.2). In 1996, kalo farmers Mealaaloha and Danny Bishop found a map that marked the names of the kuleana grants and the awardees. Their friend Ricky Reppun also found an aerial map from the 1930s that showed lands in cultivation. Meala Bishop told me:

> The most obvious way to identify loʻi is to just look at the viewing plane and lay of the land. A few of us that worked at the local community center, the KEY Project, got together and laid out a map of the valley. Areas that looked like flat expanses we flagged for exploration. We were prompted by a local farmer who had an old aerial map which showed possible loʻi kahiko lining the stream. Climbing into an old Willys jeep, we headed mauka on a hardly used road that led us to an old dry ʻauwai that was still intact. Little did we know we were pioneering a community-based loʻi restoration effort that would span the state of Hawaiʻi, supported by Queen Liliʻuokalani Children's Center, under the name ʻOnipaʻa Nā Hui Kalo.[25]

FIGURE 6.2 Ke Kalo Paʻa o Waiāhole. Kalo farmers Danny, Meala, and Hanalē Bishop. Ben Parker Elementary School Farmers' Market, Kāneʻohe, 2018. Photograph by the author.

In November 1997, ʻOnipaʻa Nā Hui Kalo formed out of a gathering of kalo farmers across the islands and organized thousands of people who helped kalo farmers to clear ancient kalo terraces and restore ʻauwai waterways on all islands.

CARTOGRAPHIC ART: MAPPING STREAM
RESTORATION AND KUPUNA RHYTHMS

Bishop takes up the struggles of the people to protect lands and waters in her sweeping mixed-media oil painting, Kalo Paʻa o Waiāhole (see plate 14). She maps the layered histories of kalo farming, from the collective struggle of farmers against eviction to the fight to restore waters to streams. In a layered palette of translucent greens that captures the effect of sunlight filtering through the fine mesh of capillaries in leaves, the land and kalo vibrate with life.

The veins of the kalo leaves are the arterial streams that feed the valleys, and we see the names of the valleys mapped onto the leaves, a reclamation of

FIGURE 6.3 Leaf detail of Mealaaloha Bishop's *Kalo Paʻa o Waiāhole*, mixed media, 1999. Image courtesy of the artist.

ahupuaʻa names many had forgotten along with the moʻolelo specific to them (see figure 6.3). Bishop explains the impact of lost ahupuaʻa place-names in her own life: "I have lived in Kaʻalaea most of my life. The thing is, I never knew I lived in Kaʻalaea. I thought it was Kahaluʻu. Now we have signs that tell us what the land divisions are, but in the old days, it was just Kahaluʻu."[26] She reminds us of the names: Heʻeia, Kahaluʻu, Waiheʻe, Kaʻalaea, Waiāhole, Waikāne, Hakipuʻu, Kualoa. All of these places, like Keʻehi, must be seen in relation to one another as a complex since the diversion of waters by the Waiāhole Ditch affected the windward coastline and seas, and the restoration of loʻi kalo and loko iʻa are revitalizing the coast as well.

In Bishop's painting, the corm, or the root of the kalo, reflects images of the kalo paʻa—the people who are steadfast in their protection of the land—in an assemblage of newspaper images: people with arms interlinked and raised in front of the Waiāhole Poi Factory, a young girl carrying a sign which reads, "Stop Stealing the Water," an elderly Japanese farmer, a young boy with his arms outstretched in victory, hundreds of people marching to stop police evictions. These images move in the vibrant currents of the Waiāhole Stream that animate the painting.

The taro rises out of the loʻi, red azolla fern fronds floating on the surface of the blue waters, signifying the synthesis of traditional planting methods and contemporary agricultural research—as well as the assertion of a Hawaiian national identification in the water's reflection of the red, white, and blue patterns of the beloved hae Hawaiʻi, the Hawaiian Kingdom flag.

The waters of the loʻi, fed by the Waiāhole Stream, eddy and swirl with the voices of the people telling their own history in the newspaper clippings that appear as palimpsests under green leaves. We hear their voices traveling across time and space: Charlie Reppun describing the widespread support from people who wanted to spend time in the loʻi, voices describing the unity and comradeship of the families deep in the water war, descriptions of the conditions farmers faced on month-to-month leases for two decades, allusions to the David-and-Goliath nature of the struggle of small farmers against corporate interests, concerns about windward water going to feed golf courses, complaints that water flowing to the ocean is a waste. We hear other voices chiming in, telling us that there are few people alive who remember Waiāhole Stream with all of its waters, kalo farmer Calvin Hoe's voice saying that it's a battle of short-term profits versus long-term survival, legal arguments about the public trust doctrine and water being held in trust by the state for the people, children's voices refusing to move from the valley. We hear reports that Governor Ariyoshi will purchase the land and that the water war is not an isolated one but will stand as a model of victory for other rural communities. One of the most beautiful voices of all is George Uyemura's, testifying that the restoration of stream water led to a fantastic return of fish at the Moli'i fishpond.

Bishop's paintings celebrate abundance. Her signature rhythmic brush strokes make her paintings vibrate, and we are reminded of Kēhaulani Kupi-hea's words about how ea is practiced through synchronizing our vibrations with that of the kūpuna. Meala speaks of a similar process in an aesthetic context for her methodology of brushstrokes and her vibrant use of layered colors:

> Working through the folk art of Kanaka Maoli ancestors, I feel I have in-herited their visual interpretations. My perception of the natural world is full of repetitious, geometric shapes and patterns mapped out in the environment affected by the changing light. Beyond the usual docu-mentation and imitation of Hawai'i depicted by many artists, we should be building the Maoli epic. From the heavy pounding of poi, the steady rhythm of kapa beaters, the careful plaiting of lauhala and net weavers, the continuous repetition of chanters, the dependable receding and returning tides, the countless stars and their patterns, to the delightful pleasure of mea 'ai from where the lo'i shows it abundance of wealth, we can be impressed upon by the natural world, as abstract as it might be, and with the hope that Akua is pleased.[27]

The kupuna vibration can be achieved in different ways across the spectrum of Kanaka Maoli practices that all mirror the pulsating rhythms and patterns of the elements.

Bishop's paintings reflect the kilo observations of an artist who farms kalo and is attuned to the elemental patterns of the forces around her. These principles of rhythmic practice can be found in her painting *Palakea 'Ele'ele* (see plate 15). This painting is rooted in the black paint strokes of the hā (petiole or stem) of this kalo cultivar, suffused with a dark, reddish purple. Sometimes the vibrations undulate, like the voice of a chanter, as the twilight-blue and brilliant green strokes for the lau (leaves) reverber-ate, reminding us that Hāloa is the long stalk that trembles in the wind. Sometimes the vibrations are geometric, like the weaving of a makaloa mat, as the horizontal rippling of the blue and green waters of the lo'i, ac-cented with fuschia azolla ferns, or like the vertical energies of the rich, green-gold and lavender mud that pushes up the sprouting huli, like the aloha 'āina rising today. At other times, the vibrations are organic and cascade, like the cold, clear stream water that pours from the ʻauwai into the loʻi, sky-blue and white, recursive brushstrokes tracing the downward rippling movements of water.

In 2016, a replica of Mealaʻs *Kalo Paʻa o Waiāhole* traveled across Moana Nui to connect with the struggles of water protectors at the Standing Rock Sioux Indian Reservation against the construction of the Black Snake, Zuzeca Sapa, the North Dakota Access Pipeline. On September 15, 2016, Kalamokaʻāina Niheu took a canvas replica of *Kalo Paʻa o Waiāhole* to Standing Rock as a gift from Nani Ome to link the water protectors of both places, along with other gifts of healing lāʻau and ʻawa from Puni and Casey Jackson at Hoʻoulu ʻĀina, Rick Barboza at Papahana Kuaola in Waipao, and Danny and Meala at Laukapalili Laukapalala in Punaluʻu. In one photo, Niheu stands with two members of the Sioux Tribal Council on either side of her and Earl DeLeon of the Mauna Kea Kiaʻi behind her. To the far left is Clyde Bellecourt, one of the original American Indian Movement members. To the far right is Everett Iron Eyes, the Oceti Sakowin Camp coordinator. From Kāneikawaiola to Mní Wičhóni, water is sacred.

LANDS EMERGING FROM THE HEI (STRING FIGURES) OF HAU(MEA) AT PUNALUʻU

Just as there are lands being urbanized under settler colonial assault, there are also what Bishop calls "emerging lands," the lands who are being awakened with the flows of water. In June 2013, Danny and Meala Bishop take me to their farm in Punaluʻu, Laukapalili Laukapalala, where they are recovering and restoring loʻi. The valley of Punaluʻu is breathtaking, lush with hau trees that line the cold and clear Punaluʻu Stream. We drive across the plains at the broad mouth of the valley and up into the hills. On foot, Danny leads us deeper into the hau forest, and we see the thickness of the hau, the ways that the roots have entwined, creating an impenetrable thicket (see figure 6.4). The trunks of the hau can grow to a foot and a half in diameter, and the long roots and branches curl around other branches to weave a thick netting. Some branches wind themselves completely around other branches in wild abandon. In moʻolelo, the hau is legendary as a barrier. Pukui explains that the ʻōlelo noʻeau "Kekeʻe hau o Maʻalo" (Crooked are the hau trees of Maʻalo) is a humorous reference to the hau grove of Maʻalo, Maui, that was a well-known as a place for secret love affairs.[28] For fifty years this hau has grown in Punaluʻu, tendrils of roots growing thicker and more densely woven with the passing of time.

FIGURE 6.4 Hau thicket growing over ancient loʻi kalo in Punaluʻu, June 12, 2013. Photograph by the author.

Danny stops, and there, where he has cut away growth with a machete, the hau opens up, revealing the architectural wonders of ancient terraced loʻi, old stone walls hundreds of years old that have lain hidden, overgrown with hau trees (see figure 6.5). Under the dappled sunlight streaming in through the hau branches above, we see the ancient stones, blanketed by dry, papery hau leaves. We can see the stones that line the loʻi as well as the the outflows that allow water to travel by gravity down from terraced loʻi to loʻi. I can see the loʻi kalo walls extending far back, and we follow it as far as we can.

Many had forgotten about these loʻi kalo, hidden by the hau that is considered invasive, but Danny and Mealaʻs son Kanaloa tells me, "Itʻs the

FIGURE 6.5 Lo'i kalo stone walls. Punalu'u, June 12, 2013. Photograph by the author.

hau that has protected these stone walls. The hau has only a few root balls. The roots may hang down, but they don't root in the ground, so they are easy to clear from the earth to recover the lo'i, even if their branches are twisted together."[29] Danny relates the protective nature of hau to long-term planting strategies to replenish nutrients to the lo'i:

> Our people understood long-term fallow and rotation, and that the micronutrients, at some point, would be depleted—and so they needed to let the land rest. They would plant the hau and let it grow for a period of time, sometimes generations, to reinvigorate the soil, and they would plant elsewhere. It's counter to the industrial-mentality management that demands constant planting and does not allow for a more natural

rehabilitation of microorganisms that provide a healthy soil environment. So luckily enough, at this complex in Punaluʻu—I believe the farmers stopped farming in the mid-60s or 70s—the hau that was there had very small root structures, very little disruption. The canopy covered the whole thing and protected it, kept it intact and kept it hidden actually, from most people, especially ranchers and their cattle. Cattle would have trampled the walls down, caused tremendous erosion of rich soil.[30]

The hau revitalizes the land, makes it fertile once again, embodying the re-birthing principles of Haumea.

The hau beloved by the moʻo are entangled, like the hei a Haumea (string figures of Haumea) or the ʻupena nananana a Papa (spiderweb of Papa), creating a sacred space for the survival of Hāloa, the elder brother to Kānaka. I am reminded of Kalei Nuʻuhiwa's words in chapter 5, explaining how Haumea creates hei, string figures that plot the location of the stars and lines of genealogy, preserving knowledge; or Puni Jackson's reference to a chant in the moʻolelo of Wākea and Haumea that references "O Papa la hoi ka nananana," (Papa is indeed the spider), thus enabling us to envision the ʻupena nananana a Papa.[31] As Haumea casts this hei, or webbing, plotting out the stars and potentiality over heiau, we see how a hei or ʻupena of hau has hung over the stone walls of these loʻi kalo, preserving the pōhaku who are the kūpuna holding on to the knowledge and potentiality for their descendants. And here, we see the hau as Haumea plotting resurgence, each nodal point where the hau branches entwine a marker forecasting an abundant future, a gift to descendants who would draw back the hau vines to see this knowledge preserved in the pōhaku who speak of the ways water once moved in this valley.

We walk into the loʻi, across the moʻo (here, the name for the raised pathways that divide the kalo patches). On the other side we see the greater length of the ʻauwai as it curves beyond our sight up deeper into the valley. The ʻauwai is the Kānaka-built waterway that directs the mountain streams to the individual loʻi kalo before returning the water back to the stream to flow down to the seas. The ʻauwai is now dry, but it still stands there, fragrant yellow ginger growing wild along its banks. Danny recalls that in Keʻanae, when they returned the water to the ʻauwai, children ran alongside the water as it slowly made its way along the stone structure, and men shouted in excitement, "It's coming! It's coming!"[32] That is the power of stream restoration, the experience of joy as the freed waters remember the paths they once traveled. We stand there imagining the water running free.

Four years later, I returned to Ānuenue Farm for a workday with fifty other volunteers to help with the clearing of hau. We gather in a circle and are welcomed by ʻAnakala Earl Kawaʻa, who says to us, "I want us all to clear the hau so that we can see those beautiful faces of those rock walls!"[33] Referencing the alo stones, the facing stones on the outside of a rock wall, he reminds us that the pōhaku are kūpuna who are waiting for their descendants to plant kalo again.

The men wielding the power saws slowly cut their way through the forest while the rest of us gather up the branches and logs and pile them in the middle of the cleared loʻi. As kūpuna did hundreds of years ago, we halihali the trunks of the hau, passing the logs hand to hand to build the great pile, while children gather up the leaves and vines on the ground. Hour after hour in the summer sun, we work. Every time we look up we can see the tremendous progress that so many hands make. When the last "HUI!" alerts us that the work is done, Kanaloa Bishop brings in a large hae Hawaiʻi, waves the flag in the air to cheers from us all, and then plants the flag in the hau. This action reminds us that today was an incredible act of ea, a step forward in restoring the loʻi and the lāhui (nation, people) to what they once were. The gathering clouds release the late afternoon rain, and it is the first time in a long time that the stones in the loʻi wall feel the rain on their faces.

A CARTOGRAPHY OF KALO: PLANTING
TO THE RHYTHMS OF THE AKUA

Emerging land is called back into abundance, and Danny and Mealaʻs son Hanalē has a kalo farm that provides such a vision of the possibilities for the Punaluʻu farm. When Hanalē Bishop began leasing lands in Waiāhole, he, too, had to clear the hau to uncover the ancient stone walls that were still there, intact. The ʻauwai, in that case, was running with water, but over the years it had fallen into disrepair and would flood at different points along the way. Hanalē worked to restore the ʻauwai, and he has been milling kalo into his signature Homestead Poi, a rich, floral, and earthy poi that speaks of a light evening rain in the valley, the ʻowē nahenahe a ka wai (soft murmuring of the water) flowing from the ʻauwai into the loʻi.

For Hanalē, the ʻauwai runs, but the pulse events of climate change, including hurricanes that decelerate into tropical storms, have increased torrential flooding from Waiāhole Stream that tears at the rock walls. In April 2018, he sent out a kāhea (call to action) for a community workday to repair

FIGURE 6.6 ʻAuwai repair and restoration day, Waiāhole, April 28, 2018. Hau leaves in the foreground and along stream. Photograph by the author.

the ʻauwai, and hundreds of people showed up to pass stones hand to hand (see figure 6.6). My sixteen-year-old son, Tai, and I worked in the line, passing stones along the historic hau-lined Waiāhole Stream.

Hanalē describes the intimate knowledge of elemental phenomena that comprise a totality, the land having its own sovereign system. He explains, "When you farm, what you're doing is you're taking everything, the totality of that specific place, and you're finding *how you fit into that*. It's greater than just the land itself because it's the winds, the rains, and path of the sun and the moon. It's a connection to totality, and that's a sovereign thing because it's a system."[34] Hanalē plants according to the lunar calendar, ten days of waxing (Anahulu Hoʻonui: Hilo to Hoku), ten days of round moons (Anahulu Poepoe: from Huna to Lāʻaupau), and ten days of waning (Anahulu Hoʻēmi: ʻOlekūkahi to Muku). As he explains, the waxing moon and stronger pull help to open up the leaf; the waning moon and lessening gravity help with root development.

Hanalē describes his loʻi kalo as a beautiful map that resonates with his mother's vibrant paintings. Hanalē is also musician and a songwriter, and each loʻi is his own musical composition, beautiful in symmetry and logic and profound in the meanings of names:

> I'd like to keep the varieties separate, lei style, where you plant all the faster growing kalo on the outside. For me, I got the Pālehua, and that takes real quickly, as well as the Manalauloa, the Pikokea, and the Lenalena. Then I plant the slower-growing Moi in the middle of the patch because then the Palehua grows fast and causes the Moi to stretch up to keep up with the Palehua. Moi provides an abundance, so we plant plenty of Moi. The ones that grow faster on the edge, they can shade out any weeds that grow from the banks into the patches. The kalo that grows very tall, I'll plant on the north side—like the Lihilihi Mōlina, that grows fast. I plant it on the northernmost end so it doesn't shade the other ones because it casts the longest shadow. When you pull the kalo, you try to open up the light. Planting also has to do with the path of sunlight, and kalo facing east and west will get the most sunlight. Any one of these patches, there's an inlet near one corner, and outlet on the opposite corner, and the inlet gets more fresh water and the outlet less, so oftentimes what I'll do is I'll plant the quickest-growing taro by the outlet and that's where I harvest first, working my way from the outlet south to north.[35]

The loʻi reflects the twining of ʻike kūpuna and the kalo practices unique to Hanalē's location and his kilo practices. We see the kalo trembling in the double winds that play on the nearby plain of Makanilua (Two winds), the beading of the Pōʻaihale rain that encircles houses but beads on the leaves of the kalo in the loʻi. Hanalē plants the kalo on the Kūkahi waxing moon, knowing the rains will fall on the ʻOle moons and that one anahulu (ten days) later, the full moon will gently pull out the first leaf, and a new leaf every anahulu (ten days) after that.

The diversity of Hanalē's loʻi also illustrates what Jerry Konanui explains is the importance of planting different kalo varieities to survive changes in climate:

Diversification: our kūpuna understood the need to grow a variety, and so they developed them. That's how we survive. We plant *all* the varieties we can. Because when that wind comes, or that flooding comes, or the drought comes, we going get mea ʻai [food]! Ninety percent of the kalo that is produced today, commercially, is one: the Maoli Lehua. Why are we not planting the others? Our kūpuna had for long, long time, for hundreds of years![36]

Here, Konanui is pointing to the ways that Kānaka have survived by understanding biodiversity, preserving this knowledge in moʻolelo and in plant names as the kalo move to those kupuna vibrations in the waters of Waiāhole.

As a songwriter and a poet, Hanalē began a journal to record the moon phases and how kalo respond to them, how all of the elements in the valley respond to the moon. As he writes, to kilo the moon is to learn that Kānaka respond to the moon as the kalo do:

December 30, 2017: Hua Moon of Makaliʻi
I set out to chronicle
the moon and weather patterns,
planting.
And I did.
And I could fill
another book on those
things, about planting
and the moon, all the revelations
about the seeds and the sky
the rain and heat

Deeper though.

The moon
guides us,
pushes us, pulls us,
into what's important,
into the directions
we should be going.[37]

Reflecting on kilo lessons from his kalo, Hanalē teaches us that some moon phases push us to reach upward, ideas and consciousness unfurling like new leaves, the moon tenderly pulling us out beyond our fears. Other moon phases pull us downward to root us deeper into the earth, in the rich lepo of the places where we live, to remind us that we must care for the lands, waters, and communities who nourish us.

The restoration of Waiāhole streamflows has had a profound impact on fishponds that spread out across the ahupuaʻa depicted on the leaves of *Kalo Paʻa o Waiāhole*, from Waiāhole to Kualoa and beyond. Although he helped to write the state water code, Charlie Reppun explains that the occupying state refuses to acknowledge the importance of the ahupuaʻa system, in which stream flows to the sea are not "wasted" but are ecologically necessary for the estuaries. The State of Hawaiʻi Water Code, chapter 174C-4, arbitrarily fragments the continuities of stream and coastal waters, stating in its regulation of stream waters that "no provision of this chapter shall apply to coastal waters."[38] The return of waters to Waiāhole Stream, however, as George Uyemura testifies in Meala's painting, led to an explosive repopulation of fish at Moliʻi fishpond and along the coast.

Kanaka Maoli fishponds are architectural wonders based on kilo practices that determined the needs of the fish and the needs of the people. Malia Akutagawa, law professor and founder of Sustʻāinable Molokaʻi, an organization that maintains Molokaʻi's cultural legacy of ʻāina momona, describes how the loko iʻa were designed: "The ancestors studied the habits of the fish. They selected those fish lowest in the food chain, knowing that pound for pound, it was more efficient to eat herbivores instead of carnivores roaming the open sea. The kūpuna observed that fish like ʻamaʻama (mullet) and awa (milkfish) feed on limu and graze on micro-algal mats covering the shallow benthos. They observed that these fish search for the 'sweet water,' the freshwater seeps along the shoreline. After careful planning, the kūpuna constructed the loko kuapā (walled ponds) around these springs to create a microenvironment for their selected fish. They built the ponds, and the fish came in droves, multiplied, fattened, and never left."[39] Akutagawa further describes the ways that the akua also create the conditions for healthy fishponds. The great moʻo Kapualei of Kamalō pulverizes stone and lava beneath the mountain to create tunnels through which flowed the waters from the north shore valley of Pelekunu to the Paialoa fishpond on the southeast shore.[40]

At the very forefront of Kānaka mobilizing against global climate change are the kilo insights and practices at the Hale o Meheanu (House of Meheanu) fishpond, also known as the Pihi Loko Iʻa, in Heʻeia Uli, not far from Hanalēʻs loʻi. Meheanu is the moʻo of Heʻeia fishpond who dwells at Luamoʻo, a place known for its many sheltering hau trees.[41] Hale o Meheanu was built about eight hundred years ago by hundreds of Kānaka who passed the stones hand to hand for the massive walls. The 88-acre brackish water fishpond has seven mākāhā, or sluice gates: four on the seaward side used to regulate saltwater flows and three along Heʻeia Stream to regulate freshwater flows.

Hiʻilei Kawelo and Keliʻi Kotubetey are the founders of Paepae o Heʻeia, the nonprofit organization that cares for Hale o Meheanu fishpond. Kawelo explains that Papahulilani researcher Kalei Nuʻuhiwa told her that the moʻolelo of the birth of the first fishpond was most likely a response to climate change, which necessitated the cultivation of fish.[42] Mahi iʻa (fishpond cultivators) look to the moʻolelo of Kūʻulakai and Hinapukuiʻa as providing the roots to their practice. Kawelo explains,

> We are living representations of climate change resiliency. The creation of the first fishpond 1500 years ago was our response to climate change. Hinapukuiʻa and Kūʻulakai are the patrons of fishing, the deities, our gods who lived in Hāna at Lehoʻula. Their son is Aʻiaʻi [pronunciation preferred by descendants].[43] What the story talks about is about famine and the disappearance of fish, which brought about the innovation of fishponds on Maui and Molokaʻi. It attributes the first fishpond ever constructed to one that was built at Lehoʻula in the sea of ʻĀlau off of Haneoʻo. Fishponds were most likely constructed as a direct response and adaptation to a changing climate. It shows us the need to evolve fishing practices.[44]

In the moʻolelo that Kawelo describes, Kūʻula is one who possesses mana kupua (supernatural power) to direct all the fish of the sea. He erects the first stone platform, now named after him, for worshipping the deities of fish. Kūʻula always made an offering of his first catch at this kūʻula, and fishermen today continue to do so. He kept the chief Kamohoaliʻi well supplied with rare fish, no matter the season. When a rival Molokai kahuna befriends Kamohoaliʻi and goes to Kūʻula for fish, Kūʻula tells him, "Eia o Hana la he aina aupehu; o Hana keia ia iki; kai a o Kama; kai a o Lanakila" (This is Hana the aupehu land; Hana of the scarce fish, the fish of Kama; the fish of Lanakila).[45] At this place called Wānanalua (Double prophecy), Kūʻula prophesies the events that will unfold in the moʻolelo, where the Molokai kahuna deceives the chief into sending his people to kill Kūʻula and his family. Embedded in this

FIGURE 6.7 Hiʻilei Kawelo at Hale o Meheanu fishpond. Heʻeia, 2019. Photograph courtesy of Sean Marrs.

moʻolelo is the importance of observation: the aliʻi listened to a stranger and not the enduring evidence of Kūʻulaʻs wondrous mana.

At Hale o Meheanu, Kawelo explains to me that the sovereignty of the land is triggered when Kānaka add their life's breath to working with the land (see figure 6.7). Kawelo looks to the reciprocity between Kānaka and the sovereign ʻāina that enables the lands and seas to flourish:

> You know, I think without us as Kānaka caring for the place, learning about the place as we care for it, restoring it, working through all of those kinks, without us being here, then there is no ea. The ʻāina possesses its own life and exists regardless of whether people are on it or not, but I feel like the ea of it comes through us, through our relationship with ʻāina. We breathe more life into it.[46]

Ea is the intimate reciprocity we see between people and land, the kupuna vibration where people anticipate what the land desires. This is also the lesson of the fishpond, that Kānaka and the ʻāina activate each other, the mutual breathing in and out of the tides and the people.

Kilo observation has led Hale o Meheanu back to traditional forms of cultivating fish after years of using net pens. In 1965, a flood destroyed a 200-foot section of the fishpond wall, so, in order to keep the young fish in the fishpond and to protect them there, caretakers of the fishpond resorted to the use of net pens. As the mahi iʻa (fish cultivators) found, prohibitive state laws concerning the restoration of fishpond walls required permits to repair the wall, and it took the nonprofit years to get the permits approved.

Climate change events made clear the need to return to traditional fishpond methods. In a study of two fish-kills at Hale o Meheanu fishpond, microbial oceanographer Rosie ʻAnolani Alegado and her team found that with changing El Niño weather patterns, modern net pens were immobilizing the fish, causing massive fish-kills.[47] The El Niño Southern Oscillation climate mode is usually confined to the western Pacific, but climate change has resulted in increasing frequency of a Central Pacific El Niño, also known as El Niño Modoki, an anomalous warming of the Central Pacific that extends northeastward to have a dire impact on fishponds in Hawaiʻi. When the tradewinds stop blowing, low tides, increased temperatures, and oxygen depletion cause massive fish-kills. In May 2009, an El Niño Modoki marine heat wave event killed three thousand moi (Pacific threadfin) in net pens, and in October of that same year another heat wave killed ten thousand fish.

To work with these climatic events, the mahi iʻa worked to kilo for solutions, and Kawelo explains that the land's recognition of their work came in the form of a hōʻailona (a sign, portent). She elaborates:

> I think hōʻailona is one way that our ʻāina recognizes our presence, and as Kānaka, we have to be able to interpret those hōʻailona. So after we had the fish-kill, we asked, why are we investing all this time, effort, and resources into restoring the traditional fishpond wall only to not use it? We shouldn't be growing fish in net pens. When there's no oxygen they are confined, whereas if they have eighty-eight acres, they can seek out shaded areas with higher oxygen levels. In 2014, we had a short, seventeen-foot pilot whale that washed up against our wall, and the timing of it wasn't coincidental. Days later our permit got approved to fix the puka [hole] in the wall, a permit that had taken more than five years to get. So when we got the remains of the whale back, we interred

FIGURE 6.8 Pani ka Puka, Hale o Meheanu, Heʻeia, December 12, 2015. Two thousand people lined the fishpond walls to help move stones, hand to hand. Photograph courtesy of Sean Marrs.

the ashes in our ahu. What the ahu does is it activates us as Kānaka. And because the permit was approved, we organized the Pani ka Puka [Close the hole] workday.[48]

On December 12, 2015, two thousand people stood in a massive line stretching out over half a mile, passing stones and buckets of rocks hand to hand to fill in the damaged part of the wall (see figure 6.8). Eight hundred years ago, the people would also have stood in such a line to halihali pōhaku and smaller hakahaka stones in ʻupena olonā (olonā bark nets). It was a community effort that enabled people who had no connection to the fishpond to develop that sense of pilina (connection) and kuleana (responsibility, privilege, purview) to the health of the kuapā (the stone walls). The fishpond is now healthy, with schools of moi (threadfish), pāpio (juvenile trevally), pualu (surgeonfish), ʻamaʻama (juvenile mullet), kākū (barracuda), Sāmoan crab, and moʻala (crab).

The mahi iʻa at the fishpond have composed chants to honor Meheanu that have provided clues to questions that they have about the restoration of the loko iʻa. "Pule no Meheanu" is a prayer that recognizes and celebrates Haumea—specifically "Haumea o ka lehulehu," or Haumea of the multitudinous bodies—and one particular manifestation as the moʻo Meheanu, "Meheanu o ka Paliuli" (Meheanu of the verdant cliffs). The pule maps the Mololani winds important to the aeration and oxygen levels in the fishpond. The celebration of the moʻo recognizes "ka ʻaʻala walewale" (the slimy scent) and the abundance of her kino lau (bodily forms) in the fishpond: the pua ʻama (young mullet), ʻamaʻama (adult mullet), puhi keʻokeʻo (the white puhi), the "pua hau melemele" (the yellow hau flowers), the "lau hau lenalena" (the yellowing leaves of the hau). It names the place of her home at Luamoʻo "i ka malu o ka hau" (in the shade of the hau). And the pule celebrates her life force and knowledge. The pule goes on to tell us, "Kū a paʻa nā pōhaku" (The stones stand firm) in the fishpond, and as the "kuamoʻo o Meheanu" (the backbone or genealogy of Meheanu) lives, so does Heʻeia live.

In this pule, the lines celebrating Meheanu's and Haumea's forms as the yellow hau flowers and leaves indicate that the "malu o ka hau," the shade of the hau around fishponds, is a necessary component of the health of the fishpond. I remember Kanaloa Bishop telling me about the importance of hau, and how he had said, "I always tell the guys at Hale o Meheanu to leave some of the hau in the loko iʻa. They are perfect for flood mitigation as we watch sea levels rise."[49] Kawelo further adds that the hau is important to providing shade to cool the temperature of the fishpond. Traditionally, the fishpond would have had more freshwater input from Heʻeia Stream, lowering the temperature of the water and increasing oxygen levels. The mahi iʻa are working to remove the invasive mangroves that have overrun the shores of the fishpond and blocked Heʻeia Stream, but replanting the hau in the place of mangroves is also necessary to protect the fish:

> I'm sure that our kūpuna ran into low oxygen level problems i ka wā kahiko [in ancient times]. But I haven't come across any moʻolelo that explains what they did in those cases. Maybe increase the vegetation around the perimeter to provide shaded areas. Like hau. Hau doesn't grow into the pond, hau stays here, and the lālā [branches] goes out and shade[s], not like mangrove that grows into the pond. The hau stays

on the edge of the fishpond and just creates the shade. And it's hau, it's Haumea. Hau is Haumea. Meheanu is Haumea.[50]

The elemental form of Haumea as the hau trees that shade the water also illustrates the vital connection of the presence of the moʻo forms to the survival of the fishponds.

The yellowing of the hau leaves around the fishpond is another indicator of the ways that the moʻo activate the reproduction of phytoplankton in the fishponds. When the leaves of the hau tree turn yellow, the people say that Meheanu was present at the fishpond and that it was her urine that yellowed the leaves.[51] Kiana Frank, a microbiologist who studies the microbial dynamics of ecosystems in Hawaiʻi, explains how the moʻo Meheanu activates the nitrogen cycle of the fishpond and the growth of both phytoplankton and fish:

> Nitrogen is a very important nutrient in the fishpond. The forms of nitrogen in the environment are nitrogen gas, ammonium, nitrate, and nitrite. It is cycled by both biological and chemical processes in nitrate production, nitrogen fixation, denitrification, and nitrification. The amount of nitrogen in the fishpond influences the rate of limu growth, as well as decomposition. When Meheanu visits in her moʻo form, her urine causes the hau to turn yellow because it is increasing ammonium concentrations. This increase in the nitrogen causes a bloom in the phytoplankton that the baby pua ʻama can eat. The fish are then well taken care of and guarded by kiaʻi Meheanu, resulting in a thriving loko iʻa.[52]

In this way, we see the ways that the restoration projects look to the moʻolelo to articulate an analytics of life that is the result of generations of observation. As the smallest organisms on the food chain, phytoplankton are necessary for the possibility of all life. Phytoplankton is responsible for producing 50 percent of the earth's oxygen, yet, because of global climate change, phytoplankton levels have decreased 40 percent since 1950.[53] The moʻo, then, are important to the ways we understand our pilina, our connectedness, to interlocking world ecosystems because of the ways that moʻo make possible the blooming of phytoplankton, the tiny creatures necessary to life on this planet.

Kawelo's account about the hau also deepens the complexity of our thinking about trophic webs and moʻoʻāina scalability. She illustrates the moʻoʻāina connectedness of restoration projects that build on one another's abundant effects, which can be traced in what she calls the "corridor of

Haumea," the blooming of the yellow flowers of hau(mea) in a path along water, from the windward side of the Koʻolau mountains up and over to the kona (leeward) side. Contrary to the occupying state's mathematics of subdivision, following the yellow procession of the hau is about the expansion of pilina, of the connectedness over and across the mountains. Kawelo describes the ever-expanding communities that are growing pilina with each other:

> Traditionally, your community was the ahupuaʻa of Heʻeia, but times are different now. Community identity has grown, and now we break these boundaries of ahupuaʻa down. For us, it's Heʻeia ahupuaʻa, then the Koʻolaupoko moku, or district identity, then there's a Koʻolaupoko and Koʻolauloa identity because we share this windward side of the island. Then there's this identity around the story of Kāmehaʻikana that goes up and over the Koʻolau mountains, along Likelike Highway, so we got the Heʻeia action going on, from Hale o Meheanu to Kakoʻo ʻŌiwi [a loʻi kalo restoration project], Papahana Kuaola [a loʻi kalo restoration project], up and over the Koʻolau to Hoʻoulu ʻĀina and the guys down in Mokauea.
>
> And I noticed just in the past two months: *the hau flowering*. Most of the year it's in the vegetative state, but two months ago, I call it the Haumea Corridor, all of the hau from Heʻeia, up and over the mountain, from Hale o Meheanu to all those places up the Koʻolau and then going down over the other side along the Likelike Highway to Hoʻoulu ʻĀina and Mokauea, all flowering yellow.[54]

Following in the footsteps of Haumea, as she travels from her home in Kilohana to Heʻeia and then back to Kalihi to save her kāne, tracks Kawelo's vision of a Kanaka Maoli cartography of the yellow pathways of hau(mea) that stretch across the islands. This cartography maps a radical resurgence along these pathways of hau, protected by Haumea and her capacities for renewal and the birthing of new potentialities.

Kawelo describes these cascade effects as successions of restoration, waves of biological indicators of the restored health of the fishpond. They include the Native plants, seaweeds, and birds that have returned with the restoration of the Heʻeia Stream waters and the cutting back of the mangroves.[55] Kawelo tells me, "The first thing that came back after we cut back the mangrove was the kīpūkai [seaside heliotrope], the ʻākulikuli [sea purslane], and then the mauʻu ʻakiʻaki [sedge] and the ʻahuʻawa [sedge used for straining ʻawa, which helps to control erosion]. We saw the limu [seaweed] come back, especially the ʻeleʻele, and that limu is an indicator for groundwater sufficiency. The increase in freshwater flows into the bay have increased the wai momona, the waters that are full of life, creating estuaries."[56] The restored waters of the Waiāhole and Heʻeia streams bring with them the little freshwater shrimp and crabs that the heʻe (octopus) and other fish like to eat. Where fishermen had begun to think there were no more moi in Kawahaokamanō, they began to see entire schools of moi. The healthy coral spawn during the new Hilo moon, allowing the coral-eating fish to flourish. The ʻūlili (wandering tattler), ʻalaeʻula (mudhens), and aeʻo (Hawaiian stilt) birds have returned to the fishpond and have hatched their chicks. These trophic webs have made it possible for these Native ecosystems to reproduce themselves and the health of the ʻāina.

One of the wondrous things about ʻopihi, coral, and limu is that they grow communities that are dependent on pilina: they are attracted to communities through a process called broadcast spawning. As limu practitioner Billy Kinney notes, "Broadcast spawning shows us how satellite communities or efforts can beget other satellite communities. ʻOpihi broadcast their spawn, but they are attracted to and will attach themselves to rocks where there are communities of ʻopihi. Every ʻopihi on the rock matters in some way, and they attract communities in their waywardness. They would not even land if there were fewer ʻopihi on the rock."[57] This is how the return of a few of these species explodes exponentially; only a few ʻopihi are needed to seed a new community. The restorative effects appear not only in the immediate vicinity, but also miles away where spores and fertilized eggs seed distant limu and ʻopihi communities.

I want to end with a story about the two earliest kūpuna to Kānaka, corals and whales. The restoration of the Waiāhole and Heʻeia streams have been critical to the regeneration of coral in a time of increasing acidification of the oceans. Coral systems are critical to the planet; they sustain 30 percent of marine life. The 2018 United Nations intergovernmental panel reported their prediction that a 1.5-degree Celsius rise in temperature would kill 70 to 90 percent of the coral in the world. With these statistics echoing in my mind, I am walking at low tide on the sandy stretch, where Heʻeia Stream enters Kawahaokamanō (The jaws of the shark, a bay ringed with reefs, also known as Kāneʻohe Bay) on the day after the new moon, Māhoemua, July 12, 2018. We had gathered bags of invasive limu to be repurposed as fertilizer, and as we looked out over the sand, we could see intricate designs, fine threads of coral spawn like the ʻupena nananana a Papa (Papa's spiderweb), laid across the sand, a primordial scent in the air.

Corals are one of the first ancestors of Kānaka Maoli, and to them are accorded great care. In Wā Umikumamahā (the fourteenth era), the birth of the stars is followed by the reappearance of Hinaiaakamalama, the Hina deity who dwells in the "kai koakoa" (coral mounds). She is taken ashore by Wākea, and, we are told,

> Hanau koakoa, Hanau ka puhi,
> Hanau ka inaina, hanau ka wana,
> Hanau ke eleku, hanau ke a
>
> Corals were born and eels were born,
> Sea-urchins were born, sea-eggs were born,
> Blackstone was born, volcanic rocks were born.[58]

Huihui Kanahele-Mossman of the Edith Kanakaʻole Foundation explains that the elemental form of the natural process of coral spawning is embodied in the akua Hinaluaʻikoʻa, and the rising of the gametes to the surface of the water is the elemental form Kūkeapua. To luaʻi is to vomit, to erupt, or more broadly, to bring forth that which is within, and in this case, this manifestation of Hina releases the coral gametes. Kanahele-Mossman writes, "When ocean temperatures increase the lunar cycle cues coral spawning. This specific phenomenon is Hinaluaʻikoʻa. Hinaluaʻikoʻa is partnered with Kukeapua in the story of Hinaiaakamalama. When Hinaluaʻikoʻa commences, male and female gametes combine to form Planulae or baby coral. Kukeapua (or Ku to ascend), rises up, apua spawn, spawn like, is Planulae. The Kukeapua then land on a solid surface and become coral polyps or unukoʻakoʻa."[59]

Hinaʻaimalama is given the moon and the stars for her food, and it is she who ʻaimalama (eats) the moon and causes the moon phases that charge the energies in all living things.[60] And so we see that the removal of the mangroves and the restoration of Heʻeia Stream flows into the fishpond and into Kawahakamanō Bay provide the conditions for healthy coral spawning and the cascading births from coral, evidence of the resilience of life made possible through the practices of kilo.

Out in the deeper oceans, the health of the tiniest coral polyps and phytoplankton are part of the upward cascades that extend to the immensity of whales, such as the pilot whale that washed up on the walls of Hale o Meheanu. Kai Palaoa practitioner Kealoha Pisciotta explains, "The palaoa enter in the second Wā (or epoch of creation). They are a part of the early creation process and are therefore of both a physical and divine consciousness. They are therefore able to exist both in the realms of Pō and that of Ao, the darkness and the light."[61] She tells us that whales are honored as special family members who are able to access Pō, the realm of the ancestors, and the ancestral knowledge in the darkest depths of the oceans. When whales breach, they are sharing this ʻike kupuna with their Kanaka ʻohana. Against ghost nets and the gelatinous smog of the microplastics in the gyres of the Pacific, whales represent the conditions of possibility. Their gifts are the nutrients from the depths of Pō that are brought up in the currents they create when they hoʻowawā, or sound, and their fecal plumes feed phytoplankton and other marine flora that capture carbon in the processes of photosynthesis while producing oxygen.[62] In this way, whales help to stabilize climate change.

On the shores of an island, the burning of the mangroves and the restoration of streams reverberate with these far-reaching planetary effects.

ʻIWAKILOMOKU

Foreseeing a Future

beyond Capital

I f climate change is propelled by our addiction to capital, I want to end by considering the indicators of climate events that are also indicators of the demise of global capitalism and the rising Indigenous economies of abundance that are already taking its place. The lāhui in Hawaiʻi and Indigenous peoples and land protectors around the world are rising as the sea levels in the Pacific rise, and the moʻolelo of Māui pulling up the islands gains new meaning. Kupihea's map, entitled "ʻO MAUI ka ʻIwakilomoku: A Tribute to Mau," depicts the Satawalese master navigator Mau Piailug as the physical embodiment of Māui because he, too, joins the islands in the Pacific through teaching Kanaka Maoli the arts of voyaging once again (see figure C.1). Kupihea writes,

> MAUI is poised with eyes steeled to the horizon. He carries his famous fish hook along with an ʻalae ʻula [mud hen] in preparation to ensnare the great Pimoi [the ʻulua fish who represents land]. He petitions Kāne and Kanaloa for guidance through their heavenly bodies, awaiting the

FIGURE C.1 Kupihea, '*O MAUi ka 'Iwakilomoku: A Tribute to Mau*, pencil and ink, 2010. Image courtesy of the artist.

proper signs to cast his bait. Mahina [the moon] encourages him from above, persuading the tides in his favor. The ʻiwa bird represents the vision and skill of the navigator. She is the gliding night, forecasting from sunrise to sunset.[1]

In this image, Kupihea depicts Māui, the great navigator of the Pacific, wayfinding according to the laws of the akua, practicing kilo, looking to the elemental forms and their signs for guidance. Both Māui and Mau joined together the ancient seas by lifting up the islands from the oceans with the fishhook, Mānaiakalani, also the constellation of Mānaiakalani (Scorpio) on the ʻiwa's wing. Kupihea's portrait of MAUi is a sweeping tribute to both the elements of Moana Nui, the great watery continent of the Pacific Ocean, and to the navigators who know wayfinding by wind patterns, cloud formations, constellations, moon phases, and ocean currents.

As Mau looks to the horizon, what seems like a poetic description of the navigator looking to the future is in fact his kilo practice of reading clouds on the horizon. Kupihea explains:

> You kilo for the cloud forms in the sky. Mau talks about looking to the horizon for certain types of clouds that give off more salt spray than other clouds, so when the sun rises, the salt spray becomes like a filter on the horizon, and it filters out the blue light. So when you have pinks, you have less salt in the air, and the pinks according to Papa Mau, the pinks mean you're going to have good weather, and the stronger the salt spray, that means you're going to have stronger winds, choppy seas, small-craft-warning type weather. The darker the red, the worse the weather is going to be that day. It's the salt crystals in the air, so when the light from the sun pukas (penetrates) from the horizon, then those crystals filter out certain light frequencies. This is all from Mau's teachings.[2]

Even today, Māui inspires us to work against the rising of the seas, connecting the islands all over the world through reminding us of the power of ancestral knowledges of how to observe, how to see, how to learn from our interconnectedness. What Kupihea's map teaches us is that it is the ways of observation that we have to relearn. As Elizabeth DeLoughrey notes in her study, we can focus on allegories of the Anthropocene that "shift the Anthropocene discourse from spectatorship to participation and active engagement."[3] It is in the active practice of recovering clues in the moʻolelo and on the horizon that we are better prepared to find our way to a future we can flourish in.

I began the work in this book inspired by a different map that makes way for Mau's vision. Ashley Hunt's *A World Map: In Which We See . . .* is a dazzling and intricate schematic of globalization and the implosive demise of capital (see plate 16).[4] Like the operations of capital, the processes are overwhelming, seemingly unassailable. The map shows movements from "crisis" to "austerity" to "expansion" to "warfare." Another route takes us to "formations of empire" to "globalization, privatization, economic liberalization." In other places, we see the conditions of those abandoned by capital: "flight," "bodies in flight," "capital flight," "flight of the state," "abstract flight," "physical flight." Many of the currents flow to "social death," which marks the prisoner, the stateless, and the refugee. It is a late liberal settler colonial mapping of death, a slow violence of diminishing.

What is particularly striking to me is that, in the midst of austerity and dispossession, we see the eruptions in the far-flung corners of the map: the "possibility of well-being" and "development of sustainable economic forms." In one particular cluster, we see the "heterogenous systems of grassroots and indigenous explanation, knowledge, self-definition." And even as the currents of capital seek to redirect these energies back into itself through "cultural capital" and "appropriation," the ruptures here generate the possibilities of life that erupt out of the capital's refusal to recognize economies illegible to it in its pursuit of its own ever-expanding growth.

Avery Gordon has a beautiful reading of the human figures in Hunt's map. She argues that he puts the human figures of the criminal, the migrant, the refugee, and the prisoner first, those who are often last or not represented at all. She writes, "But the prisoner or the migrant, the outlaw poor, are not abstractions. They are people: our brothers, sisters, mothers, fathers, aunts, uncles, cousins, friends, foes, strangers, neighbors. . . . They are we who tire and get up again and again. They are we who shout and keep quiet. They are we who are laughing big tomorrow but weeping yesterday. They are we who are busting out of every part of the machine."[5] The sheer exuberance here carries the map beyond the confining channels of flowcharts. They remind us that we have our own agency to pōhuli, to burst out of and overflow the habitualized channels meant to contain the flows of capital, like the children educated in ea, sprouting from the infrastructures of late liberal settler capital with the hae Hawaiʻi, the beloved flag of Hawaiʻi, unfurling in their hands.

As Hunt himself explains, the map is not geographically or place-specific because it is meant as a contingent analytic to identify principles and tactics in the pursuit of power, while enabling audiences to track the operations of capital in their more localized struggles. He writes, "Importantly, the map does not seek to privilege abstract ideas over their lived contexts and effects, but exists as a tool that can be applied to different contexts for the building of local analyses of power and change. . . . Any analysis drawn from it must be seen as imperfect and contingent, used only as a guide for thinking and always reconciled with local realities and history."[6] The settler colonial cartographies I present in this book are repeated the world over by multinational corporations that are busy reiterating the rhetorical regimes of capital in environmental impact statements that are themselves waste-landing the earth, yet the lesson of Hunt's map is that it presages the ruin of capital through localized struggles. Late liberal capital cannot sustain the contradictions of the endless manufacturing of markets. Capital cannot maintain its hold, and eruptions of economies of abundance are busting through every part of the machine.

When the maps of capital become Borges's tattered relics, what will remain?[7]

As I write this conclusion, we are seeing a glimpse of the conditions of possibilities beyond capital in the economies of abundance and aloha in the 2019 stand that kiaʻi mauna are taking to protect Mauna a Wākea from the construction of the TMT International Observatory. On July 10, 2019, Governor David Ige, Attorney General Clare Connors, University of Hawaiʻi President David Lassner, and Department of Land and Natural Resources Chair Suzanne Case announced the partial closure of the Mauna Kea Access Road to the public in order to facilitate the transportation of construction machinery to the summit. The kiaʻi then put their own plans into operation. The members of Hawaiʻi Unity and Liberation Institute (HULI)—Kahoʻokahi Kanuha, Kaleikoa Kaʻeo, Kahele Dukelow, Andre Perez, Camille Kalama, and Kerry Kamakaokaʻilima Long—sent out the kāhea (call to action) for people to gather at the base of the Mauna Kea Access Road at the ahu that the Royal Order of Kamehameha had erected long before as a place of worship, particularly for kūpuna and keiki and others unable to travel to the high elevation of the summit. Piʻikea Keawekāne-Stafford, Kainoa Stafford, my brother Dean Saranillio, and I arrived with the first forty protectors on Friday night, holding space for the thousands of protectors who would later join us. On Saturday, July 13, the Royal Order of Kamehameha declared the kīpuka Puʻuhuluhulu a puʻuhonua (place of refuge). On Sunday, hula hālau gathered to consecrate the puʻuhonua and to set the intentions for the protection of the mauna.

During this time, Puʻuhonua o Puʻuhuluhulu became a marvel of grass-roots, decentralized organizing, providing us with a vision of what the lāhui would look like in a Kanaka Maoli economy of abundance. From the first forty people who spent the night at Puʻuhuluhulu in thirteen cars and trucks, the numbers would later swell to seven thousand and more. The pervading sentiment for all is kapu aloha, defined as a commitment to pono and all that is just, supported by thousands of people who donated food, camping supplies, and services. A food and donation tent was set up with runners who transported all donations from the road to the tents, with kiaʻi volunteering their work where most needed. One of the services we were most grateful for was provided by Hawaiʻi Johns, who installed and maintained first six and eventually thirty portable toilets as the puʻuhonua grew.

On Monday, July 15, we all saw what had been planned by organizers. A banner declaring, "Road Closed Due to Desecration" was positioned at the access road, and we lined up alongside the road, hundreds of kiaʻi holding signs saying "We are here to protect Mauna Kea" and "Crown lands," alluding to the fact that Mauna a Wākea is part of the 1.8 million acres of Crown and government lands seized at the time of the overthrow of Queen Liliʻuokalani in 1893. Behind the banner sat the kūpuna, the cherished elders, longtime activists in the Hawaiian sovereignty movement: Maxine Kahaulelio, William Freitas, Gwen Kim, Richard DeLeon, Noe Noe Wong-Wilson, Hank Fergerstrom, Puanani Ikeda, Mililani Trask, Jonathan Kamakawiwoʻole Osorio, John Keoni Turalde, and Sparky Rodrigues. Further up the road were eight kiaʻi who had chained themselves to the cattle guard in the road: Walter Ritte, Kaleikoa Kaʻeo, Noelani Goodyear-Kaʻōpua, ʻĪmaikalani Winchester, Jamaica Heolimeleikalani Osorio, Adam Mahiʻai Dochin, Malia Hulleman, and Kamuela Park.

When state DOCARE officers and sheriffs arrived at 7:00 in the morning, they were surprised to see the kūpuna on the front line. What would it look like if the world saw the state of Hawaiʻi arresting Kanaka Maoli elders in "paradise"? After three hours of negotiation, the kūpuna agreed to stand aside so that the kiaʻi chained to the cattle grate behind them could be released. At this point, as I stood holding a sign behind the first banner, I remember Aunty Maxine Kahaulelio rushing up to us with tears in her eyes, saying, "They're going to free our brothers and sisters!" Maxine and Walter Ritte in particular had stood together in the 1970s to defend Kahoʻolawe from bombing by the US military. Yet it was hours before the kiaʻi were released. The kiaʻi chained to the cattle guard endured twelve hours of exposure to intense extremes of cold and heat that day.

The next day, the kūpuna were again in place, this time sheltered by tents while hundreds of kiaʻi were lined up on the road (see figure C.2).

FIGURE C.2   Puʻuhonua o Puʻuhuluhulu. Mauna Kea stands behind the vantage point of the viewer. Puʻuhuluhulu, July 15, 2019. Photograph by Valen Ahlo.

The state did not take any action, but on Wednesday, they returned, and a thousand of us bore witness to the state arresting thirty-eight kūpuna. We watched with tears streaming down our faces as the state officers zip-tied their hands and carried or led them to the police vans. They had asked us to stand back and to bear witness, as the whole world did, to the occupying state's criminalization of Kānaka Maoli and settler aloha 'āina elders who are protecting sacred lands. I honor here the names of all the kūpuna who were arrested: Jim Albertini, Sharol Ku'ualoha Awai, Tomas Belsky, Roberta Bennett, Marie Alohalani Brown, Gene Kini Kaleilani Burke, Luana Busby-Neff, Richard Maele DeLeon, Alika Desha, William Freitas, Patricia Momi Greene, Desmon Haumea, Ho'oulualoha Flora Ho'okano, Deena Hurwitz, Keli'i "Skippy" Ioane, Maxine Kahaulelio, Ana Kaho'opi'i, Nohea Kalima, Kalikolehua Kanaele, Pualani Kanaka'ole Kanahele, Deborah Lee, Donna Keala Leong, Daniel Li, Carmen Hulu Lindsey, Leilani Lindsey-Ka'apuni, Abel Lui, Liko Martin, James Naniole, Edleen Peleiholani, Renee Ku'uleinani Price, Hawley Reese, Walter and Loretta Ritte, Raynette Robinson, Mililani Trask, Onaona Trask, John Keoni Turalde, and Noe Noe Wong-Wilson.

When these revered elders were driven away, kia'i quickly regrouped. Seventy-five young women stood with arms locked in the front, singing, "E Aloha ē," and twenty-five men sat on the ground behind them and more kūpuna sat in the tent further back. Many of the kūpuna who had been arrested returned and took their places once again under the tent. This formation with kūpuna on the front lines backed by young women was a way of demonstrating kapu aloha to the law enforcement officers. The kia'i wanted the officers to know that we would not be resisting with force, that we would meet them with kapu aloha. Unlike law enforcement at Standing Rock or Ferguson, here many of the officers were family members or neighbors. A woman officer sent to arrest one kūpuna found that she had been her kindergarten teacher.

The call for the officers to move forward on us never came.

Built on this foundation of kapu aloha, Pu'uhonua o Pu'uhuluhulu has grown, bringing thousands of Kānaka and their allies in closer alignment with the akua. Protocol and ceremony are conducted formally at least four times a day. At the rising of the sun, we chant "E ala ē" and "E Kānehoalani ē" to honor and greet Kānehoalani, the akua who is the sun. At 8:00 protocol, we begin with chanting "E hō mai," asking for 'ike (knowledge) from above and the knowledge in the songs and chants to be revealed to us. We then chant "Nā 'Aumākua," recognizing and honoring all the guardian ancestors from the rising of the sun to the setting of the sun, from the zenith to the horizon, establishing sacred space as Haumea does. We then remind others and ourselves that in "E iho ana," those who are above will be brought down and those below will rise up, as well as the many other meanings of this chant. All these chants we do to remember and honor the elemental forms, to request that they care for us and to promise that we in turn will care for them. It is an affirmation of our commitment to the mauna and to the thousands of elemental forms who inhabit the mauna and are present in our daily lives. When we look for the 'āina's recognition of us, we see a flock of endangered nēnē (geese) flying overhead from their home on Pu'u Nēnē or white rainbows arcing in the mist.

We are growing the abundance that capital fears, and that is making possible new social formations and arrangements of life. Pu'uhuluhulu is also a wondrous kīpuka, a hill around which the lava flows coursed and which stands today as a seed bank of Indigenous koa, 'ōhi'a, and naio trees, uluhe fern, and hinahina moss, preserving that future for seedling descendants. Pu'uhonua o Pu'uhuluhulu is also a kīpuka of knowedge for the many who go there, where teachers share chants, mo'olelo, and 'ōlelo Hawai'i with young people who are hungry for this mea 'ai, this sustenance. Pu'uhonua o Pu'uhuluhulu answers the question Eric Enos asks us with a resounding, "ᴀᴇ!" Yes, the kīpuka is enabling us to bring back entire worlds through the seedbanks that remain, seeding all over the islands the ancestral knowledge that the lāhui is adapting to present conditions.

The Pu'uhonua is also a kīpuka for new modes of governance and collective action, and the kia'i have organized the pu'uhonua on the kauhale system, organized around honoring the kūpuna and feeding the people. The food tent feeds thousands of Kānaka Maoli and their allies. All of the trash is separated by volunteers in a zero-waste system. The Mauna Medic Healers Hui is staffed around the clock by volunteer doctors, nurses, paramedics, lā'au lapa'au practitioners, acupuncturists, and massage therapists, and there are healthcare workers constantly monitoring the health of the kūpuna. The donations tent receives warm clothing, blankets, tents, and many other necessities. Independent media enable the leadership at the Pu'uhonua to hold their own press conferences and to determine for themselves how they are being represented in social and mainstream media.

And on the pā, the flat area surrounded by the pāhochoe lava, we have held classes at what is now being called Pu'uhuluhulu University. As opposed to the problematic claims of University of Hawai'i administrators that ᴜʜ is a "Hawaiian place of learning," organizers extended Kanuha's ᴇᴀducational workshops on Mauna a Wākea after the June 24, 2015, stand by establishing

Puʻuhuluhulu University, one that is, as signs explain, "an ACTUAL Hawaiian place of learning." Puʻuhuluhulu University provides workshops that help us to understand the many dimensions to the stand for Mauna a Wākea and the akua in this time of climate change. Presley Keʻalaanuhea Ah Mook Sang, affectionately titled the "chancellor" of Puʻuhuluhulu University, organizes a brilliant slate of speakers, four sessions of five speakers a day—from activists, farmers, and professors to hula and oli practitioners and māhū (those who embrace feminine and masculine traits) activists already on the mauna—who hold workshops that include "The Hawaiian Kingdom," "Moʻo Akua," "Mana Māhū," "Kaulana Mahina" (Moon Phases), "Moʻolelo o Mauna a Wākea," and "Climate Change."[8] There is a papa ʻōlelo Hawaiʻi (Hawaiian-language class) in every session.

The Puʻuhonua has also been a vital site for teaching the arts of kilo to prognosticate and respond to climate change. Papahulilani researcher Kalei Nuʻuhiwa has held a special two-hour workshop on kilo, teaching kiaʻi the names of the clouds and the weather they portend, and the kaulana mahina (moon phases) and how they direct our actions. Papahulihonua researcher Kuʻulei Higashi Kanahele has held workshops on reading the changes on the land, from the oli that map the flows of lava from time immemorial to the present day. Oceanography professor Noelani Puniwai has spoken on the concepts of climate change and the importance of renewing our intimate relationships with Kanaloa, the deity of the oceans, as we face sea level rise, and our relationships with Kāne, the deity of fresh waters, as we face flood pulse events.

Growing the lāhui at Puʻuhonua o Puʻuhuluhulu has profoundly changed each of us, enabling a seismic shift in our aloha ʻāina imaginaries and material practices. We now think beyond the limitations of the occupying state to the possibilities of land-based governance by a decentralized lāhui—functioning according to the regeneration of abundance—rather than a state-based nation centered on capital's production of scarcity. As Mehana Vaughan writes in her beautiful book, *Kaiāulu: Gathering Tides*, "Communities across Hawaiʻi are engaged not just in environmental protection, but also in strengthening their capacity to govern, independent of the state."[9] We have seen the lāhui living, and we can never go back to anything less. We are also learning the social relationships that enable those of us who are not Kānaka to be settler aloha ʻāina, to enact the intergenerational Kanaka Maoli practices that have sustained life on these lands.

Puʻuhonua o Puʻuhuluhulu is also teaching us what can happen when we face a changing earth by fine-tuning our skills in observing the patterns in interconnected elements around us. Every day in the rainy season of hoʻoilo, we chant on the Ala Hulu Kupuna, under the open sky, to Lonoikamaka-hiki, the akua of cloud formation and rain, and we learn to pay greater attention to the clouds above us, their silhouetted shapes, gradations of color, and fine textures, whether they kolo (creep or crawl) along in deference to the mauna or kiawe (stream) across the sky or hū (rise, swell) as waves as we chant, "E hū ē!" We observe these details, poetically remembered in ʻōlelo Hawaiʻi, and their correlation to weather patterns throughout the day. This is a new language that we are all learning from Papahulilani researcher Kalei Nuʻuhiwa and from the moʻolelo like Keaomelemele.

To map the abundance that capital fears, we are doing the immediate work to huki (to pull out, uproot) the invasive cartographies of capital and to grow in their places the maps of abundance that draw from the past while tracking our growing attunement with the natural world. As we cut down the mangroves, gather invasive seaweed, cultivate loʻi kalo, or make seaweed lei, we are learning a language to describe our deeper relationalities with the natural processes of the earth. The kūpuna have already done so much of the work through naming thousands of winds, rains, and other akua that we are recovering in the moʻolelo and mele that they left for their descendants where the elements themselves speak and act to establish the laws of their world. We strive to know the 400,000 akua. We will learn the old names and haku (compose) new names and new vocabularies for a changing earth.

We are globally connected to other land protectors across the world, learning new metaphors from the different languages, understanding their insights into how they understand and name the elements and how they cultivate their relationships with the elemental forms. At Hale o Meheanu, the megalopa (postlarval stage of crustaceans) are indicators that rains will soon fall. Across the moʻoʻāina, in Madras, the appearance of the megalopa larvae are indicators of the June onset of the southwest monsoon rains and the November onset of the northeast monsoon rains.[10] To reach out toward that kind of finely honed knowledge of the interconnectedness of elemental forms all over the earth is to reach for life. And standing with others who are doing the same, with our feet firmly planted in the cold currents of a stream on mossy rocks, passing stones hand to hand, or in the mud of the loʻi to weed, we gain a sense of purposefulness that fills us and feeds our naʻau, our very core. It's in listening to the knowledge that our human and more-than-human teachers share with us that we learn how we fit into larger webs of life.

As we trace the crises of capital around the world, we see how in the places where capital has failed, economies of abundance sprout, the pōhuli of green life, bursting through abandoned concrete ruins. Like Kailiehu's piece, "Ka Huliau," the huli bursts through the asphalt of the Legendary Crosswalk, the rising of a new generation of leaders. It is a time of overturning, the return of Native kīpūkai, 'ākulikuli, and 'ahu'awa to the shores of the fishponds, a radical resurgence of ancestral knowledges to classrooms on the pā lava, along streams, or in canoes, the glorious sprouting of hae Hawai'i (Hawaiian flags) in trucks across the asphalt highways of occupation and late liberal settler colonialism. All over the world, we see the peoples rising. All we have to do is connect the dots.

Mapping abundance is a mapping of these knots along the string-figures of Haumea, the paths of potentiality laid out like the hau flowers along the land itself. These nodal points are the confluence of repeating images, metaphors, and elemental phenomena that help us to make sense of the correspondences among mo'o, hau, urine, and phytoplankton; among red horizons, 'iwa birds, salt, and thunderstorms; among fog drip, frost heave, stones, and sills; among 405 different clouds and coming floods, king tides, and heat waves. And as we extend ourselves beyond the limits of capital, we open ourselves up to the wonder, the possibilities, and the realization of abundance.

NOTES

INTRODUCTION

Parts of this chapter appeared previously in "Restoring Independence and Abundance on the Kulāiwi and ʻĀina Momona," *American Quarterly* 67, no. 3 (2015): 969–85.

1 Kamakau, *The People of Old*, 83. *Keaomelemele* was first serially published by Moses Manu in *Ka Nupepa Kuokoa* from 1884 to 1885.

2 Manu, "He Moolelo Kaao No Keaomelemele," April 11, 1885. See Note on the Text.

3 Manu, *The Legend of Keaomelemele*, 157.

4 For a discussion of akua as elemental forms, see Kanahele, *The Living Earth*, 5.

5 Lloyd, "The Goal of the Revolution," 209.

6 Kimmerer, *Braiding Sweetgrass*, 115.

7 Lefebvre, *The Production of Space*, 27.

8 Harvey, *Spaces of Capital*, 121, 123.

9 Hawaiʻi Community Foundation, "Wai Maoli Hawaiʻi Fresh Water Initiative," 2013, https://www.hawaiicommunityfoundation.org/strengthening/fresh -water/; Matt Yamashita, "'The Rain Follows the Forest' w/ Jason Scott Lee,"

YouTube, February 10, 2012, https://www.youtube.com/watch?v=4TELmkk -Dpo/.

10 Pukui, 'Ōlelo No'eau, 50. Although not printed in the text, "no" should have a kahakō: "nō."

11 Ka'ahahui 'o ka Nāhelehele, "About Dry Forests," accessed June 4, 2020, http://www.drylandforest.org/about-dry-forests/.

12 Fletcher, Boyd, Neal, and Tice, Living on the Shores of Hawai'i, 124.

13 Gómez-Barris, The Extractive Zone, xix.

14 Berlant, Cruel Optimism, 1–2, 122.

15 Mary Kawena Pukui and Samuel H. Elbert define "lāhui" as "nation, race, tribe, people, nationality," but I am using a more contemporary definition based on the way that Kānaka Maoli are using the term in current stands to protect lands. Pukui and Elbert, Hawaiian Dictionary, 190.

16 Hui Mauli Ola, "Puni Jackson: Leo Kupa Podcast #2," YouTube, June 20, 2016, https://www.youtube.com/watch?v=vQPkfKJeItU/.

17 Tsing, The Mushroom at the End of the World, 42.

18 Whyte, "Indigenous Climate Change Studies," 158.

19 Gómez-Barris, The Extractive Zone, 4.

20 Povinelli, Geontologies, 168, 173.

21 Nu'uhiwa, personal communication, May 2, 2019.

22 Kamakau, "Ka Moolelo Hawaii," December 2, 1869.

23 Kamakau, The Works of the People of Old, 47.

24 Basham, "Ka Lāhui Hawai'i," 50. Goodyear-Ka'ōpua honors Basham's political refusal to translate her words. I will honor that refusal here.

25 Goodyear-Ka'ōpua, introduction, 4–5.

26 Goodyear-Ka'ōpua, introduction, 4.

27 Vogeler, "Outside Shangri-La," 253.

28 Sai, "A Slippery Path toward Hawaiian Indigeneity," 102–3.

29 Goodyear-Ka'ōpua, introduction, 19.

30 Saranillio, Unsustainable Empire, 11.

31 Kauanui, Paradoxes of Hawaiian Sovereignty, 199.

32 Wolfe, Settler Colonialism, 163.

33 Goodyear-Ka'ōpua, introduction, 4.

34 Trask, "Settlers of Color," 20.

35 Byrd, Transit of Empire, xix.

36 Byrd, Transit of Empire, xix.

37 King, The Black Shoals, 59. King writes powerfully about the importance of the "shoaling" of the twinned dates 1441 (commencement of the Portuguese slave trade) and 1492 (Columbus's voyage and the genocide of Indigenous peoples), both marking the ongoing violence of conquest. I disagree with King's subsequent sentence, however, when she argues that Native women like Trask foreground an "emphasis on genocide and slavery rather than coloniality and sovereignty as reigning discourses" (emphasis mine). Trask was making an argument that both sets of discourses are important: slavery and settler

colonialism, abolition *and* decolonization. See Trask, "The Color of Violence," 82, and "Settlers of Color and 'Immigrant' Hegemony," 47. For an essay that illustrates that Black Lives Matter in the Kingdom of Hawai'i and in Oceania, see Enomoto, "Where Will You Be?"

38 Tuck, Guess, and Sultan, "Not Nowhere," 4.

39 Nixon, *Slow Violence*, 2–3.

40 Lê Espiritu, "Vexed Solidarities," 9.

41 Goodyear-Ka'ōpua, *The Seeds We Planted*, 154. See also Aikau, Goodyear-Ka'ōpua, and Silva, "The Practice of Kuleana," 160–62.

42 This is the ethnic breakdown for the 2019 Hawai'i State Legislature that I collected by calling legislators' offices in March 2019.

43 Malo, "I Ku Mau Mau," in *Ka Moolelo Hawaii*, shared by Pualani Kanaka'ole Kanahele and translated by Ainsley Halemau, online at Huapala: Hawaiian Music and Hula Archives, accessed August 6, 2020, https://www.huapala.org /Chants/I_Ku_Mau_Mau.html.

44 Kimmerer, *Braiding Sweetgrass*, 213–14.

45 Hawaii SEED, "Jerry Konanui on Kalo, Biodiversity, Ancient Wisdom, and Modern Science," YouTube, February 6, 2013, https://www.youtube.com /watch?v=bE7K3NXFU1I/.

46 Case, personal communication, July 11, 2019.

47 Louis, *Kanaka Hawai'i Cartography*, xviii.

48 Oliveira, *Ancestral Places*, 94–113.

49 Goeman, *Mark My Words*, 3.

50 Gonschor and Beamer, "Toward an Inventory of Ahupua'a," 79. Beamer explores the ahupua'a in greater depth in *No Mākou ka Mana*, 41–42.

51 Beamer and Duarte, "I palapala no ia aina," 73–74, 78.

52 Bennett, *Vibrant Matter*, 108.

53 Latour, *Facing Gaia*, 98; Chen, *Animacies*, 2; Haraway, *Staying with the Trouble*, 2; and Weston, *Animate Planet*, 10.

54 Povinelli, *Geontologies*, 4.

55 Povinelli, *Geontologies*, 35.

56 Povinelli, *Geontologies*, 40.

57 Apology Resolution, Pub. L. No. 103–150, 103rd Cong. Joint Resolution 19, November 23, 1993.

58 US Department of the Interior, "Procedures for Reestablishing a Government-to-Government Relationship with the Native Hawaiian Community," June 20, 2014, http://www.regulations.gov/#!documentDetail;D=DOI-2014-0002 -0005.

59 Arvin, *Possessing Polynesians*, 160–61.

60 Movement for Aloha No ka 'Āina (MANA), "MANA official press statement regarding OHA governing entity," Facebook, July 16, 2014, http://www .facebook.com/notes/movement-for-aloha-no-ka-%CA%BB%C4%81ina-mana /manaofficial-press-statement-regarding-oha-governing-entity-july-162014 /717387041665365.

61 Coulthard, *Red Skins, White Masks*, 3.

62 Kauanui, "Resisting the Akaka Bill," 319.

63 Leanne Betasamosake Simpson, *As We Have Always Done*, 182.

64 Pukui, Haertig, and Lee, *Nānā i Ke Kumu*, 155.

65 *He Pule Hoolaa Alii*; Liliʻuokalani, trans., *Kumulipo*.

66 Pukui and Korn, *The Echo of Our Song*, 17. I have changed "mountain-son" to "mountain child" since "keiki" is not gendered.

67 Handy, Handy, and Pukui, *Native Planters*, 74, 80.

68 Nākoa, *Lei Momi o ʻEwa*, 22.

69 Kanahele writes, "Mauna Kea is both female and male. Mauna Kea's physical manifestations of rock, soil, water, and ice, are female attributes; his elevation establishes his maleness as it brings him closer to the celestial seat of his father Wākea" (in University of Hawaiʻi at Hilo, *Mauna Kea Comprehensive Management Plan*, i).

70 Manu, "He Moolelo Kaao No Keaomelemele," September 6, 1884; the English translation is in Manu, *The Legend of Keaomelemele*, 100. I discuss this in detail in chapter 2.

71 Young, "Home-Free," 12.

72 Billy Kinney, personal communication, March 4, 2018. "Pulukeke" is "bullshit."

73 Kalei Nuʻuhiwa, opening remarks, ʻAimalama Conference, University of Hawaiʻi, Maui College, Kahului, August 9, 2018.

74 Noelani Puniwai, Kiana Frank, Oceana Puananilei Francis, Rosanna ʻAnolani Alegado, and Kealoha Fox, "Kāne and Kanaloa Are Coming: How Will We Receive Them? A Kanaka Talk (Take) on Climate Change," keynote panel at "Ko Hawaiʻi Pae ʻĀina: Mai ka Lā Hiki a ka Lā Kau," the Third Annual Lāhui Hawaiʻi Research Center Conference, March 30, 2019.

75 Noelani Puniwai, "Climate Change," Puʻuhuluhulu University, Mauna Kea, July 24, 2019.

76 While at Puʻuhonua o Puʻuhuluhulu, I was able to speak with kumu hula Kekuhi Kanahele about beginning this book on mapping abundance with "Nā ʻAumākua," which has been so important to my daily requests for guidance on this project. She said that invoking the akua and their guidance is always a good way to set the intentions and the foundations of a project. Personal communication, November 30, 2019.

77 Kanahele, *Kūkulu Ke Ea a Kanaloa*, 30.

78 Kanahele, *Kūkulu Ke Ea a Kanaloa*, 33.

79 Nuʻuhiwa, Lilly, Nobrega-Olivera, and Huihui, "ʻAimalama," 5.

CHAPTER ONE. MOʻOʻĀINA AS CARTOGRAPHIC METHOD

Epigraph: Eric Enos, testimony sent to Souza and Hammat, February 13, 2007, published in appendix D of Souza and Hammat, "*Cultural Impact Assessment*," 144.

1 Walterbea Aldeguer, bus tour narration, Waiʻanae, May 8, 2010.

2 Pukui and Elbert, *Hawaiian Dictionary*, 253–54.

3 Oliveira, *Ancestral Places*, 110.

4 See Beamer's discussion of kalaiʻāina in *No Mākou Ka Mana*, 32–33. Kamakau describes these land divisions in *The Works of the People of Old*, 6–8.

5 I will refer to some of the elders I work with by their first names. To use their last names would seem disrespectful.

6 Handy, Handy, and Pukui, *Native Planters*, 50.

7 E. Kalani Flores, TMT *Contested Case Hearing*, vol. 32, January 30, 2017, 184–87.

8 City and County of Honolulu, "Master Use Table" (table 21–3), in "Land Use Ordinance" (chap. 21), in *Revised Ordinances of Honolulu*, https://www.honolulu.gov/rep/site/ocs/roh/ROH_Chapter_21_art_3.pdf.

9 City and County of Honolulu, "Waiʻanae Sustainable Communities Plan," A-2.

10 Tropic Land, *Nānākuli Community Baseyard*, 1–2.

11 City and County of Honolulu, "Waiʻanae Sustainable Communities Plan," A-10.

12 *He Pule Hoolaa Alii*, 62–64; Liliʻuokalani, trans., *Kumulipo*, 75–76.

13 As told to Thomas Thrum in Kaaia, "Maui Stories," 248–52.

14 Kamakau, *The People of Old*, 73–74.

15 Beckwith, *Hawaiian Mythology*, 220.

16 Kepelino, *Kepelino's Traditions*, 100–101.

17 Kepelino, *Kepelino's Traditions*, 102. The note about "he kai pueone" is Pukui's, 172.

18 Nuʻuhiwa suggests that there is a deeper political meaning here: Hina is trying to elevate her son to an aliʻinui because she represents the old regime and he represents the establishment of the new regime. Personal communication, June 11, 2020.

19 *He Pule Hoolaa Alii*, 64.

20 *Na Mele Aimoku*, 80–81; Fornander, *Fornander Collection*, 4:370–71.

21 *He Pule Hoolaa Alii*, 64.

22 Liliʻuokalani, trans., *Kumulipo*, 75–76.

23 Shelley Muneoka, personal communication, June 3, 2014.

24 Oahu Metropolitan Planning Organization, "Oahu Regional Transportation Plan 2030," 21.

25 Lucy Gay, personal communication, Environmental Justice in Waiʻanae Working Group meeting, 2010; reiterated on Huakaʻi Kākoʻo no Waiʻanae bus tour, May 25, 2013.

26 Beamer and Duarte, "I palapala no ia aina," 76.

27 Marx, *Capital*, 885.

28 Chang, "Enclosures of Land and Sovereignty," 109, 111. See also Kauanui, *Hawaiian Blood*, 86–87; Barker, *Native Acts*, 53.

29 Hawaii Constitution, art. 12, §7.

30 Camille Kalama, personal communication, December 3, 2010.

31 State of Hawaiʻi Land Use Commission (LUC), transcript, Docket #A09-782 Tropic Land LLC (Oʻahu), December 3, 2010. Archived at the Land Use

Commission Office, Leiopapa a Kamehameha State Office Tower, 235 S. Beretania St., Ste. 406, Honolulu, HI 96813.

32 Tropic Land, *Nānākuli Community Baseyard*, 5–29.

33 Fred Keakaokalani Cachola, interview, Wai'anae, published in Souza and Hammatt, *Cultural Impact Assessment*, 114.

34 Souza and Hammatt, *Cultural Impact Assessment*, 89. Quoted with permission from Souza and Hammatt.

35 LUC transcript, Docket #A09-782 Tropic Land LLC, Honolulu, April 8, 2011.

36 LUC transcript, Docket #A09-782 Tropic Land LLC, Honolulu, April 8, 2011.

37 LUC transcript, Docket #A09-782 Tropic Land LLC, Honolulu, April 8, 2011.

38 I use "houseless" because Kānaka Maoli live on their own homelands.

39 I will use the spelling "Kaolae" as Kamakau does without diacritical marks to keep this name open to different possible translations.

40 Kamakau, "Ka Moolelo Hawaii," October 21, 1869.

41 Kamakau, *Tales and Traditions of the People of Old*, 135–36. It is unclear whether Mary Kawena Pukui or editor Dorothy Barrère added the diacritical marks to "Ka'ōlae," which is not listed in Pukui, Elbert, and Mookini's *Place Names of Hawai'i*.

42 Government of the Hawaiian Kingdom, *Native Testimony*, 403.

43 Alice Kaholo Greenwood, interview, Honolulu, July 3, 2013.

44 Government of the Hawaiian Kingdom, *Native Testimony*, 403.

45 Jason Jeremiah, personal communication, July 11, 2013.

46 M. D. Monsarrat, "Waianae, Oahu," May 1902, Registered Map 2108. Registered maps are located at the State of Hawai'i Survey Division, Department of Accounting and General Services, http://ags.hawaii.gov/survey/map-search/.

47 W. E. Wall, "A Portion of Lualualei, Waianae, Oahu," October 1901, Registered Map 2040.

48 Government of the Hawaiian Kingdom, *Foreign Testimony*, 283.

49 Note that the typewritten script identifies "W" as "Waianae" whereas the handwritten script identifies "W" as "Waialua." Nevertheless, both place-name designations are located in the western direction of the setting sun.

50 Oliveira, *Ancestral Places*, 106.

51 Joseph Momoa, interview, Wai'anae, O'ahu, June 20, 2011.

52 Kamakau, *The People of Old*, 83.

53 I thank Brown for generously sharing with me excerpts from her book manuscript, *Ka Po'e Mo'o Akua: Hawaiian Reptilian Water Deities*.

54 Oliveira, *Ancestral Places*, 110.

55 Oliveira, *Ancestral Places*, 110.

56 Akana and Gonzalez, *Hānau ka Ua*, xv.

57 Manu, "He Moolelo Kaao no Keaomelemele," November 1, 1884; Manu, *The Legend of Keaomelemele*, 116.

58 Manu, "He Moolelo Kaao no Keaomelemele," September 6, 1884.

59 Manu, *The Legend of Keaomelemele*, 99.

60 Manu, "He Moolelo Kaao no Keaomelemele," October 25, 1884; Manu, *The Legend of Keaomelemele*, 114.

61 Manu, "He Moolelo Kaao no Keaomelemele," February 7, 1885; Manu, *The Legend of Keaomelemele*, 143.

62 Alameida, "Waialua," 28; Schill et al., "The Impact of Aerosol."

63 Pukui, *'Olelo Noeau*, 169.

64 Manu, "He Moolelo Kaao No Keaomelemele," April 18, 1885.

65 Manu, *The Legend of Keaomelemele*, 158.

66 "Dictionary of Hawaiian Localities," *Saturday Press*, Honolulu, August 25, 1883. Cited in Sterling and Summers, *Sites of Oahu*, 120.

67 Kamakau, "Ka Moolelo Hawaii," April 28, 1870.

68 Kamakau, *The People of Old*, 84.

69 Manu, "He Moolelo Kaao No Keaomelemele," April 18, 1885; Manu, *The Legend of Keaomelemele*, 158.

70 Akana and Gonzalez, *Hānau ka Ua*, 160, 196.

71 Stearns and Vaksvik, *Geology and Ground-Water Resources*, 91–92.

72 For other descriptions of moʻo, see Kamakau, *The People of Old*, 82–89.

73 Manu, "He Moolelo Kaao No Keaomelemele," April 25, 1885; Manu, *The Legend of Keaomelemele*, 160.

74 McAllister, *Archaeology of Oahu*, 133.

75 "History of Kualii," in Fornander, *Fornander Collection*, 4:390.

76 Kagawa-Viviani et al., "I Ke Ēwe ʻĀina o Ke Kupuna," 4.

77 Schmidt, *Historical Statistics of Hawaii*, 335.

78 Kameʻeleihiwa, *Native Lands and Foreign Desires*, 81; Stannard, *Before the Horror*, 31.

79 Gregory, "USA—Hawaii."

80 Gregory, "USA—Hawaii."

81 DeTroye, personal communication, July 11, 2016.

82 Monsarrat, "Forest Reserve, Waianae Valley, Waianae Kai, Oahu," May 1906, Registered Map 2372.

83 Sproat, "From Wai to Kānāwai," 542, citing Haw. Rev. Stat. §174c State Water Code (2013), specifically Haw. Rev. Stat. §174c-101 Hawaiian Water Rights.

84 Earl Kawaʻa, personal communication, July 15, 2017.

CHAPTER TWO. MAPS IN MOTION

Parts of this chapter previously appeared in "Mapping Wonder on the Māui Moʻolelo on the Moʻoʻāina: Growing Aloha ʻĀina through Indigenous and Settler Affinity Activism," *Marvels and Tales* 30, no. 1 (2016): 46–69; and "Huakaʻi Kākoʻo No Waiʻanae Environmental Justice Bus Tour," in *Detours: A Decolonial Guide to Hawaiʻi*, edited by Hōkūlani K. Aikau and Vernadette Vicuña Gonzalez (Durham, NC: Duke University Press, 2019), 340–49.

1 Kūkauakahi (Clarence Ching), interview, Hilo, August 15, 2012.

2 "He Moolelo Kaao No Kamapuaa," *Ka Leo o ka Lahui*, July 8, 1891. The author is not identified, but Lilikalā Kameʻeleihiwa suggests it could possibly be

John E. Bush, who served in 1888 as president of the Hui Kālai'āina, a patriotic league established to oppose the Bayonet Constitution and to restore power to King Kalākaua. Kame'eleihiwa, *A Legendary Tradition of Kamapua'a*, xviii–xix.

3 Haleole, "Ka Moolelo o Laieikawai," February 14, 1863.
4 Haleole, "Ka Moolelo o Laieikawai," February 14, 1863.
5 Ho'oulumāhiehie, "Ka Moolelo o Hiiaka-i-ka-poli-o-pele," October 30, 1906.
6 Ho'oulumāhiehie, "Ka Moolelo o Hiiaka-i-ka-poli-o-pele," August 24, 1906.
7 Clark, "Kela a me Keia," 38–39.
8 Haunani-Kay Trask has beautiful descriptions of land in her collection of poetry, *Light in the Crevice Never Seen*.
9 Voyles, *Wastelanding*, 10.
10 Franklin, Cooper, and Aoudé, *Life in Occupied Palestine*, vii.
11 I write about Hawaiian independence activists Andre Perez and Kaleikoa Ka'eo wearing keffiyeh in solidarity with Palestinians in Fujikane, "Against the Yellowwashing of Israel," 160.
12 ho'omanawanui, *Voices of Fire*, 42; Perreira, "He Ki'ina Ho'okuana'ike Mauli Hawai'i," 64.
13 Kame'eleihiwa, *Legendary Tradition of Kamapua'a*, ix. See also McDougall, *Finding Meaning*, 23–28.
14 Hooulumahiehie, "Ka Moolelo o Hiiaka-i-ka-poli-o-pele," January 18, 1906; and January 19, 1906.
15 Translation in Nogelmeier, *The Epic Tale of Hi'iakaikapoliopele*, 142, 144.
16 Fornander, *Hawaiian Antiquities*, 6:424.
17 Pukui explains that the proverb "Keke'e hau o Ma'alo" refers to "a humorous saying about the hau grove of Ma'alo, Maui known as a place for illicit love affairs." #1744, *'Ōlelo No'eau*, 187.
18 Osorio, "(Re)Membering 'Upena of Intimacies," 138–39.
19 Māui, the kupua, is spelled with a kahakō (macron); Maui, the island, is not.
20 Tropic Land, *Nānākuli Community Baseyard*, Summary-1.
21 City and County of Honolulu, "Wai'anae Sustainable Communities Plan," 3–11.
22 The older name of Mā'ili'ili is Mā'ili'ili'i; see Sterling and Summers, *Sites of Oahu*, 67.
23 Walterbea Aldeguer, bus tour narration, Wai'anae, May 8, 2010.
24 *He Pule Hoolaa Alii*, 2; English translation in Lili'uokalani, *Kumulipo*, 2.
25 Lucy Gay, bus tour narration, Wai'anae, May 8, 2010. Gay has a copy of the Department of Health document showing the change.
26 Alice Greenwood, bus tour narration, Wai'anae, May 8, 2010.
27 Lucy Gay, bus tour narration, Wai'anae, May 8, 2010.
28 The hawaii.gov site with these figures has been removed. Similar figures are featured in Gregg K. Kakesako, "Lualualei: The Navy Owns More Than 9,000 Acres in the Waianae Valley," *Honolulu Star-Bulletin*, October 5, 1998, http://archives.starbulletin.com/98/10/05/news/story1.html. For a discussion of the militarization of Hawai'i, see Kajihiro, "The Militarizing of Hawai'i"; Gonzalez, *Securing Paradise*.

29 Kelly, "Notes on the History of Lualualei," 32.

30 Stearns and Vaksvik, *Geology and Ground-Water Resources*, 420.

31 Kelly, "Notes on the History of Lualualei," 35.

32 Reiny, "The Lost Land of ʻĀinalani,"46.

33 Jerroll Booth, interview, Waiʻanae, November 20, 2010.

34 State of Hawaiʻi Land Use Commission (LUC), transcript, Docket #A09-782 Tropic Land LLC (Oʻahu), January 6, 2011, 142–44. Archived at the Land Use Commission Office, Leiopapa a Kamehameha State Office Tower, 235 S. Beretania St., Ste. 406, Honolulu, HI 96813.

35 *He Pule Hoolaa Alii*, 63.

36 English translation in Liliʻuokalani, *Kumulipo*, 75.

37 Aldeguer, Huakaʻi Kākoʻo no Waiʻanae bus tour, April 4, 2018.

38 Aldeguer, personal communication, June 21, 2013.

39 Bacchilega, *Fairy Tales Transformed?*, 195.

40 Pukui and Elbert, *Hawaiian Dictionary*, 361.

41 LUC transcript, Docket #A09-782 Tropic Land LLC (Oʻahu), December 3, 2010, 105.

42 Jerroll Booth, interview, Waiʻanae, November 20, 2010.

43 Kimura, *Issei*, 58.

44 Pearl Tavares, interview, Waiʻanae, November 20, 2010.

45 Trask, "The Birth of the Modern Hawaiian Movement," 126.

46 John J. McHugh, "Agricultural Feasibility Report," in *Nānākuli Community Baseyard EIS*, appendix C, 1–12.

47 Sahara, *Detailed Land Classification*, 103.

48 Kukui and Gary Maunakea-Forth to Candace Fujikane, December 15, 2017, author's personal archive.

CHAPTER THREE. MOʻOINANEAʻS WATERWAYS ON MAUNA A WĀKEA

Parts of this chapter previously appeared in "Mapping Abundance on Mauna a Wākea as a Practice of Ea," *Hūlili: Multidisciplinary Research on Hawaiian Well-Being* 11, no. 1 (2019): 23–54.

1 It is possible that the Moʻoinanea of Mauna a Wākea is not the same as the Moʻoinanea who is the matriarch of moʻo. Moʻo have different genealogies depending on the school of knowledge concerned. E. Kalani Flores, personal communication, June 20, 2018.

2 Poepoe, "He Kanaenae no ka hanau ana o Kauikeaouli," February 12, 1906.

3 The Edith Kanakaʻole Foundation, "Cultural Anchor," published in University of Hawaiʻi at Hilo, *Mauna Kea Comprehensive Management Plan*, i.

4 Pukui, Haertig, and Lee, *Nānā I Ke Kumu*, 182.

5 Edith Kanakaʻole Foundation, "Cultural Anchor," ii.

6 Poepoe, "He Kanaenae no ka hanau ana o Kauikeaouli," February 10, 1906; and February 12, 1906.

7 Pukui and Korn, *The Echo of Our Song*, 23. I have revised the translation of "husband" to "man," "wife" to "woman," and "son" to "child" to get closer to the original terms. As I note in the introduction, Kanahele explains that Mauna a Wākea is both male and female.

8 Nā Maka o ka ʻĀina (Puhipau and Joan Lander), "Lake Waiau," Mauna Kea: From Mountain to Sea, accessed June 15, 2020, http://www.mauna-a-wakea .info/maunakea/A2_lakewaiau.html.

9 Haleole, "Ka Moolelo o Laieikawai," January 24, 1863.

10 Kealoha Pisciotta, "Should the Thirty Meter Telescope Be Built?," *Insights on PBS Hawaiʻi*, May 1, 2015, https://www.pbs.org/video/insights-pbs-hawaii -should-thirty-meter-telescope-be-built/.

11 See University of Hawaiʻi at Hilo, "Conservation District Use Application Permit."

12 University of Hawaiʻi at Hilo, *Final Environmental Impact Statement* (FEIS), vol. 1, s-1.

13 University of Hawaiʻi at Hilo, *Mauna Kea Comprehensive Management Plan*, 5–32.

14 NASA, FEIS, xxi–xxii.

15 University of Hawaiʻi at Hilo, FEIS, vol. 1, s-8.

16 Prehearing transcript for the first TMT contested case hearing, May 13, 2011, 27. Archived at the Department of Land and Natural Resources Office of Conservation and Coastal Lands, Kalanimoku Building, 1151 Punchbowl Street, #131, Honolulu, HI 96813, dlnr@hawaii.gov.

17 CCH 2 transcripts, vol. 34, February 13, 2017, 37–38.

18 Estes and Dhillon, *Standing with Standing Rock*, 1.

19 Allen, *Trans-Indigenous*, 244–26.

20 Ahuena, "Ku-Kahau-Ula and Poliahu," 14.

21 Ahuena, "Ku-Kahau-Ula and Poliahu," 15.

22 Kuʻulei Keakealani, interview by Kepā Maly, in Maly and Maly, *Mauna Kea*, 156.

23 Ahuena, "Ku-Kahau-Ula and Poliahu," 15.

24 C. J. Lyons, "Kaohe and Humuula, Hawaii," 1891, Registered Map 1641. Registered maps are located at the State of Hawaiʻi Survey Division, Department of Accounting and General Services, http://ags.hawaii.gov/survey/map-search/.

25 John M. Donn, "Hawaii Territory Survey: Hawaiʻi, Hawaiian Islands," Territory of Hawaiʻi, 1901.

26 Thiongʻo, *Decolonising the Mind*, 3.

27 University of Hawaiʻi at Hilo and TIO, "Joint [Proposed] Findings of Fact, Conclusions of Law, and Decision and Order," case no. BLNR-CC-16-002, May 30, 2017, #646, 102, https://dlnr.hawaii.gov/mk/files/2017/05/671-UHH-TIO-joint-proposal.pdf.

28 Malo, *Hawaiian Antiquities*, xvii. The Emerson footnote in question appears in Malo, *Hawaiian Antiquities*, 17.

29 Malo, *Hawaiian Antiquities*, 17; superscript note in original.

30 Malo, *Ka Moʻolelo Hawaiʻi*, 12.

31 James T. Hayes, written direct testimony, CCH 1, June 2011, and CCH 2, October 11, 2016, 34, https://dlnr.hawaii.gov/mk/files/2016/10/WDT-Hayes-J.pdf.

32 University of Hawai'i at Hilo, FEIS, vol. 1, 3–3.

33 University of Hawai'i at Hilo, FEIS, vol. 1, S-9.

34 For the Hawai'i Supreme Court opinion on the TMT, see *In re Contested Case Hearing re Conservation Dist. Use Application (CDUA) Ha-3568 for the Thirty Meter Telescope at the Mauna Kea Sci. Reserve*, 431 P.3d 752 (2018), https://www.scribd.com/document/392007050/Hawaii-Supreme-Court-Opinion-on-TMT. Justice Michael Wilson, "Dissenting Opinion in the Matter of the Contested Case Hearing Regarding the Conservation District Use Application for the Thirty Meter Telescope," November 9, 2018, 3–4, https://www.courts.state.hi.us/wp-content/uploads/2018/11/SCOT-17-0000777disam.pdf.

35 Pisciotta, closing arguments, CCH 1, September 30, 2011, 124, https://dlnr.hawaii.gov/mk/files/2016/10/B.01i-Kealoha-Pisciotta-Closing-9.30.11.pdf.

36 Prehearing transcript, CCH 1, May 13, 2011, 26–27. See note 16.

37 Prehearing transcript, CCH 1, May 13, 2011, 37–38.

38 Prehearing transcript, CCH 1, May 13, 2011, 33.

39 Kaleikoa testimony to OHA on TMT, April 23, 2015, posted by Occupy Hawaii, YouTube, https://www.youtube.com/watch?v=TmBBvOf-Gbc.

40 Kim TallBear, "Genomic Articulations of Indigeneity," 140–43. For a discussion of the "Indian" as the present absence, the supplement as trace, see Byrd, *Transit of Empire*, 8–11.

41 Pua Case, personal communication, November 29, 2018.

42 Pisciotta, "Meet the Mauna Kea Hui," 6–7.

43 Department of Land and Natural Resources, "Hearing Offificer's Proposed Findings of Fact, Conclusions of Law and Decision and Order," DLNR file no. HA-11-05, November 30, 2012, 8. Archived at the Department of Land and Natural Resources Office of Conservation and Coastal Lands, Kalanimoku Building, 1151 Punchbowl Street, #131, Honolulu, HI 96813, dlnr@hawaii.gov.

44 Salazar, "Multicultural Settler Colonialism," 58–59.

45 Povinelli, *Geontologies*, 16.

46 E. Kalani Flores, written direct testimony, CCH 1, June 2011, 5, https://dlnr.hawaii.gov/mk/files/2016/10/TIO-EXH-C-26.pdf.

47 E. Kalani Flores, written direct testimony, CCH 1, June 2011, 5–6, https://dlnr.hawaii.gov/mk/files/2016/10/TIO-EXH-C-26.pdf.

48 CCH 2 transcripts, vol. 32, January 30, 2017, 184–87.

49 CCH 1 transcripts, August 17, 2011, 98, 102, 176; and August 18, 2011, 107.

50 "Flores-Case Exceptions," July 28, 2017, 53, https://dlnr.hawaii.gov/mk/files/2017/08/806-Flores-Case-Exceptions.pdf.

51 "Flores-Case Exceptions," July 28, 2017, 103–4, https://dlnr.hawaii.gov/mk/files/2017/08/806-Flores-Case-Exceptions.pdf.

52 Haw. Rev. Stat. §183C-1 Conservation District (2016).

53 University of Hawai'i at Hilo, FEIS, vol. 1, section 3.7, 2–16, 2–17.

54 University of Hawai'i at Hilo, FEIS, vol. 1, section 3.7, 3–121.

55 Tom Nance, "Mauna Kea Groundwater Schematic," October 7, 2016, University of Hawaiʻi at Hilo Exhibit A-44, "Demonstrative Exhibits for Tom Nance," CCH 2, https://dlnr.hawaii.gov/mk/files/2016/10/Ex.-A-044.pdf.

56 CCH 2 transcripts, vol. 16, December 13, 2016, 167–68.

57 CCH 2 transcripts, vol. 16, December 13, 2016, 168.

58 CCH 2 transcripts, vol. 16, December 13, 2016, 99–100; emphasis mine.

59 CCH 2 transcripts, vol. 16, December 13, 2016, 116.

60 CCH 2 transcripts, vol. 16, December 13, 2016, 183–84. See also Hunt, "Baseline Water-Quality Sampling."

61 CCH 2 transcripts, vol. 16, December 13, 2016, 205.

62 Kuʻulei Kanahele, written direct testimony, CCH 2, September 16, 2016, 2–3, https://dlnr.hawaii.gov/mk/files/2016/10/B.11a-Kanahele-WDT.pdf. In her oral testimony, Kanahele explains that the lines from the *Kumulipo* are 618 and 619, "Hanau na pahu / O Moanaliha / O Kawaomaaukele ko laua hope mai"; CCH 2 transcripts, vol. 29, January 24, 2017, 146.

63 CCH 2 transcripts, vol. 29, January 24, 2016, 168.

64 Manu, "He Moolelo Kaao No Keaomelemele," November 8, 1884; English translation by Mary Kawena Pukui in Manu, *The Legend of Keaomelemele*, 120.

65 CCH 2 transcripts, vol. 16, December 13, 2016, 179; Scholl, Gingerich, and Trimble, "The Influence of Microclimates," 14.

66 Kalei Nuʻuhiwa, personal communication, May 12, 2019.

67 Kūkauakahi (Clarence Ching), interview, Honolulu, December 3, 2018.

68 Puni Jackson, interview, Kalihi, December 6, 2018. Poepoe, "Ka Moolelo o ko Wakea ma Noho ana ma Kalihi," June 9, 1906. I return to this discussion in chapter 5.

69 Kealoha Pisciotta, personal communication, August 23, 2018.

70 Kanahele, written direct testimony, CCH 2, September 16, 2016, 3, https://dlnr.hawaii.gov/mk/files/2016/10/B.11a-Kanahele-WDT.pdf.

71 Kūkauakahi (Clarence Ching), personal communication, July 18, 2012.

72 Kepā and Onaona Maly discuss this moʻolelo in *Mauna Kea*, 40–49.

73 Wise and Kihe, "Kaao Honiua Puuwai no Ka-Miki," March 12, 1914, 1.

74 I thank Kahikina de Silva for editing my translation of this passage.

75 Wise and Kihe, "Kaao Honiua Puuwai no Ka-Miki," March 12, 1914, 1.

76 Onaona and Kepā Maly translate "pōhaku o Kāne" here as a name, Pōhakuokāne.

77 I thank Kaliko Baker and Kekeha Solis for editing this translation.

78 Pua Case, personal communication, June 2, 2018.

79 Kameʻeleihiwa, *Native Lands and Foreign Desires*, 24.

80 Text taken from the "Community Art" page at Kailiehu's website, accessed June 15, 2020, http://www.haleykailiehu.com/community-art.html.

81 For a history of this diversion, see "Request Approval to Enter into a Memorandum of Agreement (MOA) and Right-of-Entry with the Country of Hawaiʻi on the Transfer of Management for a Portion of the Mauna Kea State Recreational Area (MKSRA)," March 28, 2014, http://files.hawaii.gov/dlnr/meeting/submittals/140328/E-4.pdf.

Parts of this chapter previously appeared in "Mapping Abundance on Mauna a Wākea as a Practice of Ea," *Hūlili: Multidisciplinary Research on Hawaiian Well-Being* 11, no. 1 (2019): 23–54.

1 Silva, *Aloha Betrayed*, 134–35.
2 Elbert and Mahoe, *Nā Mele*, 63–64.
3 Hoʻomanawanui, "This Land Is Your Land," 131.
4 de Silva, introduction for Haunani-Kay Trask, Fall Festival of Writers, University of Hawaiʻi, Honolulu, November 13, 2003.
5 de Silva, introduction, xiv.
6 Peralto, "Hānau ka Mauna," 236.
7 Kikiloi, "Rebirth of an Archipelago," 76.
8 Shelley Muneoka, speech at Mauna Kea rally, ʻIolani Palace, Honolulu, Hawaiʻi, April 13, 2015.
9 For discussion of kapu aloha, see Protect Mauna Kea, "Aunty Pua Case: Kapu Aloha on Mauna a Wākea," YouTube, April 7, 2015, https://www.youtube.com/watch?v=TR-TmM5oXso; and ʻŌiwi TV, "Kapu Aloha 101: Ke Kula o Maunakea," July 3, 2015, Vimeo, https://vimeo.com/132507823. For a discussion of the checkpoint as a place where kiaʻi engaged others in dialogue, see Goodyear-Kaʻōpua, "Protectors of the Future," 190.
10 CCH 2 transcripts, vol. 34, February 13, 2017, 37–38. Archived at the Department of Land and Natural Resources Office of Conservation and Coastal Lands, Kalanimoku Building, 1151 Punchbowl Street, #131, Honolulu, HI 96813, dlnr@hawaii.gov.
11 Kealoha Pisciotta, "Kapu Aloha," presentation at Hālau Kū Māna, Honolulu, August 16, 2019.
12 Kahoʻokahi Kanuha, personal communication, October 28, 2017.
13 ʻŌiwi TV, "Kapu Aloha 101: Ke Kula o Maunakea."
14 For videos of the June 24, 2015, stand, see Mauna Media, "Mauna Media: Lā 91 on the Mauna," YouTube, June 25, 2015, https://www.youtube.com/watch?v=8aub_uJ1-48&feature=share.
15 Ehitu Keeling, no title, video of the Mana Wahine line, public setting on Facebook, June 25, 2015, https://www.facebook.com/ehitu.keeling/videos/724756251117/UzpfSTcxMDU4NTYxMzoxMDE1Mjg3MzgyMDk3MDYxNA/.
16 See Occupy Hawaii, "Mauna Kea Protector Kaleikoa Kaeo Arrested June 24 2015," YouTube, July 3, 2015, https://www.youtube.com/watch?v=AoIu6KoP8bE.
17 These rain names are listed in Ahuena, "Ku-kahau-ula and Poliahu," 14. Kīpuʻupuʻu is both a wind and a rain.
18 ʻŌiwi TV, "ʻĀhaʻi ʻŌlelo Ola: Mauna Momentum: Kapu Aloha," YouTube, September 7, 2017, https://www.youtube.com/watch?v=63mMeMZL43E.
19 University of Hawaiʻi at Hilo, *Final Environmental Impact Statement* (FEIS), vol. 1, 3-19–3-20.

20 CCH 1 transcripts, August 17, 2011, 40. Archived at the Department of Land and Natural Resources Office of Conservation and Coastal Lands, Kalanimoku Building, 1151 Punchbowl Street, #131, Honolulu, HI 96813, dlnr@hawaii.gov.

21 CCH 1 transcripts, August 17, 2011, 29.

22 CCH 1 transcripts, August 17, 2011, 40.

23 See "Conservation District Use Application Permit," 4-1 to 4-3. "SIHP" stands for "State Inventory of Historic Places."

24 E. Kalani Flores, written direct testimony, CCH 2, October 2016, 12, https:// dlnr.hawaii.gov/mk/files/2016/10/B.02a-wdt-EK-Flores.pdf.

25 McCoy and Nees, *Archaeological Inventory Survey of the Mauna Kea Science Reserve*, 4.

26 CCH 1 transcripts, September 30, 2011, 120–21.

27 Kēhaunani Abad, written direct testimony, CCH 2, October 10, 2016, 6, https:// dlnr.hawaii.gov/mk/files/2016/10/B.08a-Abad-WDT.pdf.

28 E. Kalani Flores, written direct testimony, CCH 2, October 2016, 26, https:// dlnr.hawaii.gov/mk/files/2016/10/B.02a-wdt-EK-Flores.pdf.

29 E. Kalani Flores, written direct testimony, CCH 2, October 2016, 26, https:// dlnr.hawaii.gov/mk/files/2016/10/B.02a-wdt-EK-Flores.pdf.

30 For the Hawai'i Supreme Court opinion on the TMT, see *In re Contested Case Hearing re Conservation Dist. Use Application (CDUA) Ha-3568 for the Thirty Meter Telescope at the Mauna Kea Sci. Reserve*, 431 P.3d 752 (2018), https://www.scribd .com/document/392007050/Hawaii-Supreme-Court-Opinion-on-TMT.

31 "Petitioners-Apellants' Motion for Reconsideration," in response to *In re Contested Case Hearing re Conservation Dist. Use Application (CDUA) Ha-3568 for the Thirty Meter Telescope at the Mauna Kea Sci. Reserve*, 431 P.3d 752 (2018), submitted by Richard Naiwieha Wurdeman, Agency Docket No. BLNR-CC-16-002, November 19, 2018, 13.

32 E. Kalani Flores, written direct testimony, CCH 1, June 2011, 8, https://dlnr. hawaii.gov/mk/files/2016/10/TIO-EXH-C-26.pdf.

33 *He Pule Hoolaa Alii*, 59–60.

34 Lili'uokalani, *Kumulipo*, 70–71.

35 Johnson discusses the "Pule Ho'owilimo'o" in *The Kumulipo Mind*, 204–5.

36 I follow the modernized spelling of names with the diacritical marks in Lōkahi Antonio's *He Mo'olelo no 'Aukelenuia'īkū*.

37 Mahalo piha to Marie Alohalani Brown for sharing this Kaunamano version with me. Kaunamano, "He Moolelo no Aukelenuiaiku," November 6, 1862; translation mine.

38 Kapā Oliveira emphasizes the mo'o (continuous) nature of genealogy by referring to the 'ōlelo no'eau, "Ke hi'i lā 'oe i ka paukū waena, he neo ke po'o me ka hi'u" (When you hold on to the middle section [of a genealogy], the head [or the beginning] and the tail [or the ending of the geneaology] are forgotten) (*Ancestral Places*, 22).

39 Antonio, "Ka Waiwai o ka Mo'o," 39.

40 C. M. Kaliko Baker suggests that the name "Kaukihikamalama" references the way that 'Aukelenuia'īkū squeezed the moon, making it puahilohilo (the sliver

of the Hilo moon) and the kupuna lives at the extremity (kihi) of the moon looking on. Personal communication, June 14, 2020.

41 Kaunamano, "He Mooleleo no Aukelenuiaiku," December 4, 1862. C. M. Kaliko Baker suggests that "oi" might be translated as "a contemptuous action" (personal communication, June 7, 2019).

42 Pisciotta, "Meet the Mauna Kea Hui."

43 Pisciotta, "Meet the Mauna Kea Hui."

44 Pisciotta, closing arguments, CCH 1, September 30, 2011, 124, https://dlnr.hawaii.gov/mk/files/2016/10/B.01i-Kealoha-Pisciotta-Closing-9.30.11.pdf.

45 William Freitas, interview, Hilo, December 20, 2018.

46 William Freitas, interview, Hilo, December 20, 2018.

47 William Freitas, interview, Hilo, December 20, 2018.

48 Pua Case, Facebook post, December 30, 2012, https://www.facebook.com/photo.php?fbid=451364538246776&set=pcb.451365618246668&type=3&theater.

49 Nogelmeier, He Lei no 'Emalani, 268–69.

50 Pua Case, available at Occupy Hawaii, "Malana Mai Ka'u—TMT orientation," YouTube, October 5, 2014, https://www.youtube.com/watch?v=kBNaGlb0jeo.

51 Kaho'okahi Kanuha, personal communication, October 28, 2017.

52 Pono Kealoha, "Wakea: BaseCamp Kaho'okahi Kanuha," YouTube, April 26, 2015, https://www.youtube.com/watch?v=BJueh2moX5c&t=101s.

53 This artist's statement was previously available on the artist's website, accessed October 25, 2015, https://www.haleykailiehu.com/.

54 'Ohulei Waia'u, personal communication, June 25, 2015.

55 I thank Kūkauakahi for this comment on a draft of this paper.

56 This quotation was previously available on the artist's website, October 25, 2015, https://www.haleykailiehu.com/.

57 "Kai Palaoa's Mission," KaiPalaoa.com, accessed April 26, 2020, http://kaipalaoa.com/about/.

58 Cited with permission from de Silva and de Silva, "A Maunakea 'o Kalani," 1.

59 de Silva and de Silva, "A Maunakea 'o Kalani," 1.

60 Peralto, "Hānau ka Mauna," 239.

61 Kaukaohu Wahilani, interview, Wai'anae, May 21, 2016.

62 Wang, "Native Hawaiians, Asian Americans Show Support."

CHAPTER FIVE. VERTICAL MAPS OF SUBTERRANEAN WATERS IN KALIHI

1 Board of Water Supply, City and County of Honolulu, "Red Hill Bulk Storage Facility FAQ," accessed June 14, 2020, http://www.boardofwatersupply.com/water-quality/frequently-asked-questions#redhill/.

2 US Environmental Protection Agency, "About the 2014 Fuel Release at Red Hill."

3 Kanahele et al., "Kīho'iho'i Kānāwai," 10–14.

4   Kanahele et al., "Kīhoʻihoʻi Kānāwai," 15–16.

5   Kanahele, *Ka Honua Ola*, 6.

6   Hooulumahiehie, "Ka Moolelo o Hiiaka-i-ka-poli-o-pele," May 5, 1906.

7   Handy, Handy, and Pukui, *Native Planters*, 74, 77.

8   Kamakau, "Ka Moolelo Hawaii," March 31, 1870. See also Beckwith, *Hawaiian Mythologies*, 64.

9   Hooulumahiehie, "Ka Moolelo o Hiiaka-i-ka-poli-o-pele," May 5, 1906.

10 Hooulumahiehie, "Ka Moolelo o Hiiaka-i-ka-poli-o-pele," May 7, 1906.

11 Hooulumahiehie, "Ka Moolelo o Hiiaka-i-ka-poli-o-pele," September 20, 1906.

12 Hooulumahiehie, "Ka Moolelo o Hiiaka-i-ka-poli-o-pele," September 20, 1906.

13 English translation in Nogelmeier, *The Epic Tale*, 366. I have amended the word "chiefesses" to "chiefs" since "chiefess," as Noenoe Silva suggests, is a diminutive form, as is "goddess"; "hulihia" can mean overturned, signalling a shift in power (Silva, personal communication, book launch event for *The Power of the Steel-Tipped Pen*, September 14, 2017).

14 Kanahele, *Ka Honua Ola*, 5.

15 Kanahele, *Ka Honua Ola*, 85.

16 *He Pule Hoolaa Alii*, 57.

17 Translation is a combination of Queen Liliʻuokalani's translation on 68 and Beckwith's on 114. The queen translates "O Haumea kino papamano" as "Haumea in form of a shark," which opens up different interpretive possibilities.

18 Brown, *Ka Poʻe Moʻo*.

19 Kalei Nuʻuhiwa, in ʻŌiwi TV, "Haumea: Establishing Sacred Space, Female Ceremonies, and Heiau," YouTube, February 13, 2012, https://www.youtube.com/watch?v=Z8x7dpp3IME.

20 Nuʻuhiwa, in ʻŌiwi TV, "Haumea."

21 Poepoe, "Ka Moolelo o ko Wakea ma Noho ana ma Kalihi," June 9, 1906.

22 Puni Jackson, interview, Kalihi, December 6, 2018.

23 Johnson, *Kumulipo*, 42.

24 Kanahele, "Haumea lāua ʻo Moemoeaʻaliʻi," in *Ka Honua Ola*, 2–3.

25 The lele of Kapo is identified on an 1883 "Kalihi Valley" map, Registered Map 1017. Registered maps are located at the State of Hawaiʻi Survey Division, Department of Accounting and General Services, http://ags.hawaii.gov/survey/map-search/.

26 Kanahele, *Ka Honua Ola*, 5, 40–41.

27 Hoʻoulumāhiehie, "Ka Moolelo o Hiiaka-i-ka-poli-o-pele," June 4, 1906.

28 Hoʻoulu ʻĀina Nature Preserve, home page, accessed June 12, 2020, https://www.hoouluaina.com/.

29 Silva, *The Power of the Steel-Tipped Pen*, 152.

30 Silva, *The Power of the Steel-Tipped Pen*, 151.

31 Poepoe, "Ka Moolelo o ko Wakea ma Noho ana ma Kalihi," May 7, 1906.

32 Poepoe, "Ka Moolelo o ko Wakea ma Noho ana ma Kalihi," May 18, 1906.

33 This and all subsequent translations from this moʻolelo are mine. I thank Kaliko Baker and Noenoe Silva for editing my translations. All errors are my own.

34 Marie Alohalani Brown discusses the exciting battle between the moʻo Kāmehaʻikana and Lanihuli in *Ka Poʻe Moʻo*.

35 Poepoe, "Ka Moolelo o ko Wakea ma Noho ana ma Kalihi," May 2, 1906.

36 I thank Kalei Nuʻuhiwa for sharing the pule that lists ʻāweu as one of the three kūpuna kalo. Personal communication, June 9, 2018. ʻĀweu is also known as ʻĀweo, ʻĀweoweo, ʻĀweuweu, Māʻauea, Mamauweo, and Maʻāweo (Whitney, Bowers, and Takahashi, *Taro Varieties in Hawaii*, 25).

37 Kupuna Kalo (website), accessed June 20, 2018; http://bentut.github.io/kupunakalo/index.php/kalo_varieties/detail/aweu/index.html/.

38 Poepoe, "Ka Moolelo o ko Wakea ma Noho ana ma Kalihi," May 9, 1906.

39 Silva, "Pele, Hiʻiaka, and Haumea," 170.

40 Puni Jackson, interview, Heʻeia Uli, July 2, 2018.

41 Puni Jackson, interview, Heʻeia Uli, July 2, 2018.

42 Poepoe, "Ka Moolelo o ko Wakea ma Noho ana ma Kalihi," May 11, 1906.

43 Poepoe, "Ka Moolelo o ko Wakea ma Noho ana ma Kalihi," May 12, 1906.

44 All definitions are from Pukui and Elbert, *Hawaiian Dictionary*: "naue" (263), "ʻoni" (289), "naka" (259), "halulu" (55).

45 Aʻiaʻi Bello, personal communication, June 5, 2019.

46 Kanahele, *Ka Honua Ola*, 6.

47 Kalei Nuʻuhiwa, personal communication, December 8, 2018.

48 Pukui, *ʻŌlelo Noʻeau*, 14.

49 Clarice Taylor, "Keana Kamano," *Honolulu Star-Bulletin*, August 19, 1954.

50 Graydon Keala, interview, Loko Ea fishpond, Haleʻiwa, July 11, 2018.

51 Napoka, *Mokauea Island*, appendix A, n.p.

52 Taylor, "Keana Kamano."

53 Damon, *Moanalua*, n.p.

54 Damon, *Moanalua*, n.p.

55 For a discussion of these tactics, see my article "Asian American Critique and Moana Nui 2011."

56 Rear Admiral Brian P. Fort, "Red Hill Update Stakeholder Letter," December 20, 2017, https://www.cnic.navy.mil/regions/cnrh/om/environmental/red-hill-tank.html.

57 US Environmental Protection Agency, "Groundwater Flow Model Progress Report 04," 3.

58 US Environmental Protection Agency, "Regulatory Agency Comments."

59 G. D. Beckett to Ms. Fenxi Grange, Hawaiʻi Department of Health, February 15, 2018, in US Environmental Protection Agency, "Regulatory Agency Comments."

60 Frankel and Townsend, "Water at Risk," 5.

61 Puni Jackson, interview, Heʻeia Uli, July 2, 2018.

62 Kēhaulani Kupihea, interview, Mililani, August 15, 2018.

63 Napoka, *Mokauea Island*, 5.

64 Kēhaulani Kupihea, interview, Mililani, August 15, 2018.

65 Malo Kupihea, quoted in Johnson, Mahelona, and Ruggles, *Nā Inoa Hōku*, 130.

66 "Hawaiian Star Lines and Names for Stars," Hawaiian Voyaging Traditions, accessed June 13, 2020, http://archive.hokulea.com/ike/hookele/hawaiian_star_lines.html.

67 Kaimana Bacarse, quoted in ʻŌiwi TV, "Ka Ipu a ka Hoʻokele," May 9, 2014, https://oiwi.tv/hokulea/ka-ipu-a-ka-hookele/.

68 Kēhaulani Kupihea, interview, Mililani, August 15, 2018.

69 "Damon Notebook XVIII," cited in Napoka, *Mokauea Isand*, n.p.

70 Kēhaulani Kupihea, interview, Mililani, August 15, 2018.

71 Manu, "He Moolelo Kaao no Keaomelemele," February 7, 1885; Manu, *The Legend of Keaomelemele*, 143.

72 Puhipau, "The Ice Man Looks Back," 134.

73 Kupihea, interview, Mililani, December 19, 2018.

74 Clark, "Kēlā a me Kēia," 38–39.

75 J. F. Brown, "Kalihi Entrance or Kaliawa Fishery," Hawaiian Government Survey, 1885, Registered Map 1138.

CHAPTER SIX. MOʻOʻĀINA CASCADES IN WAIĀHOLE AND HEʻEIA

1 Manu, "He Moolelo Kaao No Keaomelemele," May 30, 1885; Manu, *The Legend of Keaomelemele*, 169.

2 Manu, "He Moolelo Kaao No Keaomelemele," May 30, 1885.

3 Here, the name in the moʻolelo is Kamoʻoinanea, while elsewhere her name is recorded as Moʻoinanea, Moʻoianea, and Moʻoʻīnanea. These can be different names for the matriarch of the moʻo or, as Kalani Flores suggests, are different historical figures. See chapter 3, note 2.

4 Manu, "He Moolelo Kaao No Keaomelemele,"May 30, 1885.

5 Manu, *The Legend of Keaomelemele*, 170.

6 Manu, "He Moolelo Kaao No Keaomelemele,"May 30, 1885.

7 Manu, *The Legend of Keaomelemele*, 170.

8 See "Piʻialiʻi" at Kapunakalo.com, accessed June 20, 2018, http://kupunakalo.com/index.php/kalo_varieties/detail/aweu/ (site is private).

9 Hawaiʻi SEED, "Jerry Konanui on Kalo, Biodiversity, Ancient Wisdom, and Modern Science," YouTube, February 6, 2013, https://www.youtube.com/watch?v=bE7K3NXFU1I.

10 Poepoe, "Ka Moolelo o ko Wakea ma Noho ana ma Kalihi," June 7, 1906.

11 This and all subsequent translations from this moʻolelo are mine. I thank Kaliko Baker for editing my translations. All errors are my own. Baker suggests that "ka ehu o ke kai" evokes the phase "kuehu lepo," the dust-raising wind of Oʻahu. The following phrase, "ke ka-honua," evokes the striking of the earth, or the feet kicking up the dust, and this is a beautiful echo of Pūehuehu, the spray of water that rises up into the skies when Haumea creates the spring Pūehuehu. Personal communication, June 7, 2019.

12 Poepoe, "Ka Moolelo o ko Wakea ma Noho ana ma Kalihi," June 8, 1906.

13 The proverb "Ahu a lālā kukui" (The kukui branches lay about in heaps) describes "the strewing of dead bodies after a battle" (Pukui, *'Ōlelo No'eau*, 4).

14 Sproat and Moriwake, "Ke Kalo Pa'a o Waiāhole," 253.

15 Geshwender, "Lessons from Waiāhole–Waikāne," 146.

16 "Waiahole Tenants, Supporters, Block Kam Highway for an Hour," *Honolulu Star-Bulletin*, January 5, 1977.

17 Sproat and Moriwake, "Ke Kalo Pa'a o Waiāhole," 255; Sproat, "From Wai to Kānāwai," 534–38.

18 Lee, Reppun, and Piliamo'o, "Ho'i ka Wai," 122.

19 Lee, Reppun, and Piliamo'o, "Ho'i ka Wai," 123.

20 Lee, Reppun, and Piliamo'o, "Ho'i ka Wai," 122.

21 Kaehuaea, "Na mea Kaulana o Waiahole," September 16, 1865.

22 Translations of this mo'olelo are mine.

23 The 'ōlelo no'eau (proverb or poetical saying) referenced here is "pupuhi ka i'a o 'Uko'a" (the fish of 'Uko'a have vanished [blown away]), said of the famous pond in Waialua to describe "something quickly taken." Pukui, *'Ōlelo No'eau*, 301. I had translated the last phrase as "Serves you right!" but Baker suggests "Bite me!" since "kola" references an erection and "heo" the tip of the penis. C. M. Kaliko Baker, personal communication, June 7, 2019.

24 Lee, Reppun, and Piliamo'o, "Ho'i ka Wai," 125.

25 Meala Bishop, interview, Punalu'u, June 11, 2013.

26 Meala Bishop, interview, Punalu'u, June 14, 2013. Signs on O'ahu identifying ahupua'a were established by the Ko'olaupoko Hawaiian Civic Club with the Kailua and Waimānalo Civic Clubs in 2011. Ko'olaupoko Hawaiian Civic Club, "Ko'olaupoko Ahupua'a Boundary Markers—An Historic Event!," accessed June 14, 2020, http://www.koolaupoko-hcc.org/ahupuaa-boundary-marker-project/.

27 Bishop, "Meala," 94.

28 Pukui, #1735, in *'Ōlelo No'eau*, 187.

29 Kanaloa Bishop, personal communication, November 10, 2017.

30 Danny Bishop, interview, Kāne'ohe, December 29, 2018.

31 Poepoe, "Ka Moolelo Hawaii Kahiko," June 9, 1906. For a fuller discussion, see chapter 5.

32 Danny Bishop, interview, Punalu'u, June 12, 2013.

33 Earl Kawa'a, personal communication, Punalu'u, July 15, 2017.

34 Hanalē Bishop, interview, Kāne'ohe, September 30, 2018.

35 Hanalē Bishop, interview, Kāne'ohe, September 30, 2018.

36 Jerry Konanui, available at Hawaiian Voice, "Mālama Hāloa: Protecting the Taro," YouTube, March 12, 2012, https://www.youtube.com/watch?v=RxX33qqCaFY.

37 Hanalē Bishop, "Moon Following," unpublished manuscript.

38 Haw. Rev. Stat. §174C-4 State Water Code: Scope (2013).

39 Akutagawa, "Nā Kai Po'olo'olo'u O Moloka'i," 31–32.

40 Akutagawa, "Nā Kai Poʻoloʻoloʻu O Molokaʻi," 34.

41 McAllister, *Archaeology of Oahu*, 173.

42 Hiʻilei Kawelo, interview, Heʻeia Uli, July 25, 2018.

43 Kalei Nuʻuhiwa explains that the descendants of this family prefer the pronunciation "Aʻiaʻi" to "ʻAiʻai." Personal communication, August 11, 2018.

44 Hiʻilei Kawelo, interview, Heʻeia Uli, July 25, 2018.

45 Manu, "Ku-ula, the Fish God of Hawaii," 220–21.

46 Hiʻilei Kawelo, interview, Heʻeia Uli, February 9, 2019.

47 McCoy et al., "Large-Scale Climatic Effects," 2.

48 Hiʻilei Kawelo, interview, Heʻeia Uli, July 25, 2018.

49 Kanaloa Bishop, personal communication, November 10, 2017.

50 Hiʻilei Kawelo, interview, Heʻeia Uli, July 25, 2018.

51 Kelly, *Loko Iʻa o Heʻeia*, 2.

52 "Meheanu and the Nitrogen Cycle," YouTube, June 22, 2017, https://www
.youtube.com/watch?v=r2m_g6mFrxA.

53 Watts, "Global Warming Is Putting." See also Boyce, Lewis, and Worm, "Global
Phytoplankton Decline," 591.

54 Hiʻilei Kawelo, interview, Heʻeia Uli, July 25, 2018.

55 Möhlenkamp et al., "Kū Hou Kuapā," 161.

56 Hiʻilei Kawelo, interview, Heʻeia Uli, February 9, 2019.

57 Billy Kinney, interview, Honolulu, November 30, 2018.

58 *He Pule Hoolaa Alii*, 61; Liliʻuokalani, trans., *Kumulipo*, 72.

59 Edith Kanakaʻole Foundation with the help of Huihui Kanahele-Mossman,
"Hinaluaʻikoʻa," Instagram, May 20, 2020, https://www.instagram.com/p
/CAWhAaCA389/. Cited with permission of Kanahele-Mossman.

60 Fornander, *Hawaiian Antiquities*, 5:268–69.

61 Kealoha Pisciotta, "Kai Palaoa: Spirit and Traditions," Kai Palaoa: Kinolau o
Kanaloa, accessed June 14, 2020, https://kaipalaoa.com/nana-i-ke-kumu-look
-to-the-source/.

62 Balaraman, "Whales Keep Carbon out of the Atmosphere."

CONCLUSION

1 This quotation from the artist's statement was previously available on Kupihea's website, accessed July 9, 2016, http://www.kupiheahawaiianart.com/art
-work/pencil-and-ink.

2 Kupihea, interview, Mililani, December 19, 2018.

3 DeLoughrey, *Allegories of the Anthropocene*, 196.

4 Ashley Hunt, *A World Map: In Which We See . . .*, one of ten maps with the
accompanying text, *An Atlas of Radical Cartography*, edited by Lize Mogel and
Alexis Bhagat.

5 Gordon, "A World Map," 144.

6 Hunt, "A World Map," 146.

7 Borges, "On Exactitude in Science," 286.

8 For a discussion of "māhū," see *A Place in the Middle*, story by Hinalei-
   moana Wong, directed by Dean Hamer and Joe Wilson, 2015, https://
   aplaceinthemiddle.org/.

9 Vaughan, *Kaiāulu*, 157.

10 Subramoniam and Gunmalai, "Breeding Biology," 167.

BIBLIOGRAPHY

Ahuena (Emma Ahuena Davison Taylor). "The Betrothal of the Pink God and the Snow Goddess: The Pink Snow Is Always Seen upon Mauna Kea." *Paradise of the Pacific* 44, no. 7 (1931): 13–15.

Aikau, Hōkūlani K., Noelani Goodyear-Kaʻōpua, and Noenoe Silva. "The Practice of Kuleana: Reflections on Critical Indigenous Studies through Trans-Indigenous Exchange." In *Critical Indigenous Studies*, edited by Aileen Moreton-Robinson, 157–75. Tucson: University of Arizona Press, 2016.

Aikau, Hōkūlani K., and Vernadette Vicuña Gonzalez. *Detours: A Decolonial Guide to Hawaiʻi*. Durham, NC: Duke University Press, 2019.

Akana, Collette Leimomi, with Kiele Gonzalez. *Hānau ka Ua: Hawaiian Rain Names*. Honolulu: Kamehameha Publishing, 2015.

Akutagawa, Malia. "Nā Kai Poʻoloʻoloʻu o Molokaʻi: The Turbulent Seas of Molokaʻi." In *Nourish: The Revitalization of Foodways in Hawaiʻi*, edited by Gillian Bostock Ewing and Clare Gupta, 26–37. San Francisco: ExtraCurricular Press, 2019.

Alameida, Roy Kakulu. "Waialua: Voices from the Past." *Hawaiian Journal of History* 28, no. 1 (1994): 21–34.

Allen, Chadwick. *Trans-Indigenous: Methodologies for Global Native Literary Studies.* Minneapolis: University of Minnesota Press, 2012.

Antonio, ʻIolani. "Ka Waiwai o ka Moʻo: The Transformative Mana of Moʻo ʻŌlelo in Maui Water Battles and Kanaka Maoli Resurgence Movements toward Ea." Master's thesis, University of Hawaiʻi, 2016.

Antonio, Lōkahi. *He Moʻolelo no ʻAukelenuiaʻīkū.* Honolulu: Hale Kuamoʻo, 1993.

Arvin, Maile. *Possessing Polynesians: The Science of Settler Colonial Whiteness in Hawaiʻi and Oceania.* Durham, NC: Duke University Press, 2019.

Bacchilega, Cristina. *Fairy Tales Transformed? Twenty-First-Century Adaptations and the Politics of Wonder.* Detroit, MI: Wayne State University Press, 2013.

Balaraman, Kavya. "Whales Keep Carbon out of the Atmosphere." *Scientific American,* April 11, 2017. https://www.scientificamerican.com/article/whales-keep -carbon-out-of-the-atmosphere/.

Barker, Joanne. *Native Acts: Law, Recognition, and Cultural Authenticity.* Durham, NC: Duke University Press, 2011.

Basham, Leilani. "Ka Lāhui Hawaiʻi: He Moʻolelo, He ʻĀina, He Loina, a He Ea Kākou." *Hūlili: Multidisciplinary Research on Hawaiian Well-Being* 6, no. 1 (2010): 37–72.

Beamer, Kamanamaikalani. *No Mākou Ka Mana: Liberating the Nation.* Honolulu: Kamehameha Schools Publishing, 2014.

Beamer, Kamanamaikalani, and T. Kaʻeo Duarte. "I palapala no ia aina: Documenting the Hawaiian Kingdom—A Colonial Venture?" *Journal of Historical Geography* 35, no. 1 (2009): 66–86.

Beamer, Kamanamaikalani, and Lorenz Gonschor. "Toward an Inventory of Ahupuaʻa in the Hawaiian Kingdom: A Survey of Nineteenth and Early Twentieth Century Cartographic and Archival Records of the Islands of Hawaiʻi." *Hawaiian Journal of History* 48, no. 1 (2014): 53–87.

Beckwith, Martha. *Hawaiian Mythology.* Honolulu: University of Hawaiʻi Press, 1970.

Beckwith, Martha. *The Kumulipo: A Hawaiian Creation Chant.* Honolulu: University of Hawaiʻi Press, 1951.

Bennett, Jane. *Vibrant Matter: A Political Ecology of Things.* Durham, NC: Duke University Press, 2010.

Berlant, Lauren. *Cruel Optimism.* Durham, NC: Duke University Press, 2011.

Bishop, Mealaaloha. "Meala." In *Nā Maka Hou: New Visions, Contemporary Native Hawaiian Art,* edited by Momi Cazimero, David J. de la Torre, and Manulani Aluli Meyer, 94–95. Honolulu: Honolulu Academy of Arts, 2001.

Borges, Jorge Luis. "Of Exactitude in Science." Translated by Norman Thomas di Giovanni. *Antioch Review* 30, nos. 3–4 (1970–71): 286.

Boyce, Daniel G., Marlon R. Lewis, and Boris Worm. "Global Phytoplankton Decline over the Past Century." *Nature* 466, no. 1 (July 29, 2011): 591–96.

Brown, Marie Alohalani. *Ka Poʻe Moʻo: Hawaiian Reptilian Water Deities.* Honolulu: University of Hawaiʻi Press, forthcoming in 2021.

Brown, Marie Alohalani. "Mauna Kea: Hoʻomana Hawaiʻi and Protecting the Sacred." *Journal for the Study of Religion, Nature, and Culture* 10, no. 2 (2016): 155–69.

Byrd, Jodi A. *The Transit of Empire: Indigenous Critiques of Colonialism*. Minneapolis: University of Minnesota Press, 2011.

Chang, David A. "Enclosures of Land and Sovereignty: The Allotment of American Indian Lands." *Radical History Review* 109 (2011): 108–19.

Chang, David A. *The World and All the Things upon It: Native Hawaiian Geographies of Exploration*. Minneapolis: University of Minnesota Press, 2016.

Chen, Mel Y. *Animacies: Biopolitics, Racial Mattering, and Queer Affect*. Durham, NC: Duke University Press, 2012.

City and County of Honolulu. "Waiʻanae Sustainable Communities Plan." Honolulu: Department of Planning and Permitting, March 2012.

Clark, John. "Kela a me Keia." *Lawaiʻa Magazine* 3 (October 2009): 38–39.

Coulthard, Glen S. *Red Skins, White Masks: Rejecting the Colonial Politics of Recognition*. Minneapolis: University of Minnesota Press, 2014.

Damon, Gertrude MacKinnon. *Moanalua Valley, Kamananui. From the Writings of Gertrude MacKinnon Damon on Moanalua, as Told to Her by Namakahelu and Other Older Inhabitants*. Honolulu: Moanalua Gardens Foundation, 1971.

DeLoughrey, Elizabeth M. *Allegories of the Anthropocene*. Durham, NC: Duke University Press, 2019.

de Silva, Kīhei. "Introduction." In Kapulani Landgraf, *Nā Wahi Kapu o Maui*, xiii–xiv. Honolulu: ʻAi Pōhaku Press, 2003.

de Silva, Kīhei, and Māpuana de Silva. "A Maunakea ʻo Kalani." Translation by Kawena Pukui. 2006. Pukui Collection, Kaleinamanu Literary Archive. http://apps.ksbe.edu/kaiwakiloumoku/kaleinamanu/he-aloha-moku-o -keawe/maunakea_o_kalani.

Donn, John M. "Hawaii Territory Survey: Hawaiʻi, Hawaiian Islands." Honolulu: Territory of Hawaiʻi Land Office, 1901.

Elbert, Samuel H., and Noelani Mahoe, eds. *Nā Mele o Hawaiʻi Nei: 101 Hawaiian Songs*. Honolulu: University of Hawaiʻi Press, 1970.

Enomoto, Joy. "Where Will You Be? Why Black Lives Matter in the Hawaiian Kingdom." *Ke Kaupu Hehi Ale*, February 1, 2017. https://hehiale.wordpress .com/2017/02/01/where-will-you-be-why-black-lives-matter-in-the-hawaiian -kingdom/.

Estes, Nick, and Jaskiran Dhillon, eds. *Standing with Standing Rock: Voices from the #NoDAPL Movement*. Minneapolis: University of Minnesota Press, 2019.

Fletcher, Charles H., Robynne Boyd, William J. Neal, and Virginia Tice. *Living on the Shores of Hawaiʻi: Natural Hazards, the Environment, and Our Communities*. Honolulu: University of Hawaiʻi Press, 2010.

Fornander, Abraham. *Fornander Collection of Hawaiian Antiquities and Folk-Lore: The Hawaiian Account of the Formation of the Their Islands and Origin of Their Race, with the Traditions of Their Migrations, Etc., as Gathered from Original Sources*. Facsimile edition. Vols. 4–6, *Memoirs of Bernice Pauahi Bishop Museum*. Bilingual edition. Honolulu: Bishop Museum Press, 2004.

Frankel, David Kimo, and Marti Townsend. "Water at Risk as Navy Seeks Another 25 Years of Leaky Fuel Tanks at Red Hill." *Mālama i ka Honua: A*

Quarterly Journal of the Sierra Club of Hawai'i, January–March 2020, 8. https://static1.squarespace.com/static/5e28fa5870afe4486a9e6a2d/t /5e8b8c81707a3c095b726afe/1586203793787/Malama_January2020_WEB .pdf.

Franklin, Cynthia G., Morgan Cooper, and Ibrahim G. Aoudé, eds. "Life in Occupied Palestine" (special issue). *Biography* 37, no. 2 (2014).

Fujikane, Candace. "Against the Yellowwashing of Israel: Liberatory Solidarities across Settler States." In *Flashpoints for Asian American Studies*, edited by Cathy Schlund-Vials, 150–71. New York: Fordham University Press, 2017.

Fujikane, Candace. "Asian American Critique and Moana Nui 2011: Securing a Future beyond Empires, Militarized Capitalism and APEC." *Inter-Asia Cultural Studies* 13, no. 2 (2012): 189–210.

Fujikane, Candace. "Introduction: Asian Settler Colonialism in the U.S. Colony of Hawai'i." In *Asian Settler Colonialism: From Local Governance to the Habits of Everyday Life in Hawai'i*, edited by Candace Fujikane and Jonathan Y. Oka-mura, 1–42. Honolulu: University of Hawai'i Press, 2008.

Fujikane, Candace. "Mapping Abundance on Mauna a Wākea as a Practice of Ea." *Hūlili: Multidisciplinary Research on Hawaiian Well-Being* 11, no. 1 (2019): 23–54.

Fujikane, Candace. "Mapping Wonder in the Māui Moʻolelo: Growing Aloha ʻĀina through Indigenous and Affinity Activism." *Marvels and Tales* 30, no. 1 (2016): 45–69.

Fujikane, Candace, and Jonathan Y. Okamura, eds. *Asian Settler Colonialism: From Local Governance to the Habits of Everyday Life in Hawai'i*. Honolulu: University of Hawai'i Press, 2008.

Fujikane, Candace, and Jonathan Y. Okamura, eds. "Whose Vision? Asian Settler Colonialism in Hawai'i" (special issue). *Amerasia Journal* 26, no. 2 (2000).

Geschwender, James A. "Lessons from Waiahole-Waikane." *Social Process in Hawaii* 28, no. 1 (1980): 121–35.

Goeman, Mishuana. *Mark My Words: Native Women Mapping Our Nations.* Minneapolis: University of Minnesota Press, 2013.

Gómez-Barris, Macarena. *The Extractive Zone: Social Ecologies and Decolonial Perspectives.* Durham, NC: Duke University Press, 2017.

Gonzalez, Vernadette Vicuña. *Securing Paradise: Tourism and Militarism in Hawai'i and the Philippines.* Durham, NC: Duke University Press, 2013.

Goodyear-Ka'ōpua, Noelani. Introduction to *A Nation Rising: Hawaiian Move-ments for Life, Land, and Sovereignty*, edited by Noelani Goodyear-Ka'ōpua, Ikaika Hussey, and Erin Kahunawaika'ala Wright, 1–33. Durham, NC: Duke University Press, 2014.

Goodyear-Ka'ōpua, Noelani. "Protectors of the Future, Not Protestors of the Past: Indigenous Pacific Activism and Mauna a Wākea." *South Atlantic Quarterly* 116, no. 1 (2017): 184–94.

Goodyear-Ka'ōpua, Noelani. *The Seeds We Planted: Portraits of a Native Hawaiian Charter School.* Minneapolis: University of Minnesota Press, 2013.

Goodyear-Kaʻōpua, Noelani, Ikaika Hussey, and Erin Kahunawaikaʻala Wright, eds. *A Nation Rising: Hawaiian Movements for Life, Land, and Sovereignty.* Durham, NC: Duke University Press, 2015.

Gordon, Avery. "A World Map." In *An Atlas of Radical Cartography*, edited by Alexis Bhagat and Lize Mogel, 139–44. Los Angeles: Journal of Aesthetics and Protest Press, 2008.

Government of the Hawaiian Kingdom. Board of Commissioners to Quiet Land Title (also known as the Land Commission). *Native Testimony (1846–1853)*. Vol 9. Honolulu: Government of the Kingdom of Hawaiʻi, 1853.

Government of the Hawaiian Kingdom. Board of Commissioners to Quiet Land Title (also known as the Land Commission). *Foreign Testimony (1846–1853)*. Vol. 9. Honolulu: Government of the Kingdom of Hawaiʻi, 1853.

Gregory, Regina. "USA—Hawaii—Restoring the Life of the Land: Taro Patches in Hawaiʻi." *The EcoTipping Points Project: Models for Success in a Time of Crisis*, August 2014. http://ecotippingpoints.org/our-stories/indepth/usa-hawaii -mao-organic-farmempower-youth.html (accessed July 5, 2017; no longer available).

Haleole, S. N. "Ka Moolelo o Laieikawai." *Ka Nupepa Kuokoa*, November 29, 1862–April 4, 1863.

Haleole, S. N. *Lāʻieikawai.* Edited by Dennis Kawaharada, Richard Hamasaki, and Esther Mookini. Translated by Martha Warren Beckwith. 1863. Honolulu: Kalamakū Press, 2006.

Handy, E. S. Craighill, Elizabeth Green Handy, and Mary Kawena Pukui. *Native Planters in Old Hawaii: Their Life, Lore, and Environment.* Bernice P. Bishop Museum Bulletin no. 223. Rev. ed. Honolulu: Bishop Museum Press, 1991.

Haraway, Donna J. *Staying with the Trouble: Making Kin in the Chthulucene.* Durham, NC: Duke University Press, 2016.

Harvey, David. *Spaces of Capital: Towards a Critical Geography.* New York: Routledge, 2001.

Hawaiian Studies Institute. *Oʻahu: Pre-Māhele Moku and Ahupuaʻa.* Honolulu: Kamehameha Schools, 1987.

Hawaii Territory Survey. *A Portion of Lualualei, Waianae, Oahu.* Map by F. E. Harvey. Registered Map 2165. April 1902.

He Pule Hoolaa Alii: He Kumulipo Ka I-amamao, a ia Alapai Wahine. Honolulu: Hui Paʻipalapala Elele, 1889.

Hoʻomanawanui, Kuʻualoha. "'This Land Is Your Land, This Land Was My Land': Kanaka Maoli versus Settler Representations of ʻĀina in Contemporary Literature of Hawaiʻi." In *Asian Settler Colonialism: From Local Governance to the Habits of Everyday Life in Hawaiʻi*, edited by Candace Fujikane and Jonathan Y. Okamura, 116–54. Honolulu: University of Hawaiʻi Press, 2008.

Hoʻomanawanui, Kuʻualoha. *Voices of Fire: Reweaving the Literary Lei of Pele and Hiʻiaka.* Minneapolis: University of Minnesota Press, 2014.

Hoolumahiehie. "Ka Moolelo o Hiiaka-i-ka-poli-o-pele." *Ka Naʻi Aupuni*, December 1, 1905–November 30, 1906.

Hunt, Ashley. "A World Map: In Which We See . . ." In *An Atlas of Radical Cartography*, edited by Alexis Bhagat and Lize Mogel, 145–47. Los Angeles: Journal of Aesthetics and Protest Press, 2007.

Hunt, Charles D., Jr. "Baseline Water-Quality Sampling to Infer Nutrient and Contaminant Sources at Kaloko-Honokōhau National Historical Park, Island of Hawai'i, 2009." *US Geological Survey Scientific Investigations Report 2014–5158*. Reston, VA: US Geological Survey, 2014. https://pubs.usgs.gov/sir/2014/5158/downloads/sir2014-5158_report.pdf.

Johnson, Rubellite Kawena. *Kumulipo: The Hawaiian Hymn of Creation*. Vol. 1. Honolulu: Topgallant Publishing, 1981.

Johnson, Rubellite Kawena. *The Kumulipo Mind: A Global Heritage in the Polynesian Creation Myth*. Honolulu: n.p., 2000.

Johnson, Rubellite Kawena, John Kaipo Mahelona, and Clive Ruggles. *Nā Inoa Hoku: Hawaiian and Pacific Star Names*. West Sussex, UK: Ocarina Books, 2015.

Kaaia. "Maui Stories: Fishing Together the Islands (O'ahu Version)." In *More Hawaiian Folk Tales*, edited by Thomas G. Thrum, 248–52. Chicago: A. C. McClurg, 1923.

Kaehuaea. "Na mea Kaulana o Waiahole." *Ka Nupepa Kuokoa*, September 16, 1865, 3.

Kagawa-Viviani, Aurora, Penny Levin, Edward Johnston, Jeri Ooka, Jonathan Baker, Michael Kantar, and Noa Kekuewa Lincoln. "I Ke 'Ēwe 'Āina o Ke Kupuna: Hawaiian Ancestral Crops in Perspective." *Sustainability* 10, no. 12 (2018): 1–36.

Kajihiro, Kyle. "The Militarizing of Hawai'i: Occupation, Accommodation, and Resistance." In *Asian Settler Colonialism: From Local Governance to the Habits of Everyday Life in Hawai'i*, edited by Candace Fujikane and Jonathan Y. Okamura, 170–94. Honolulu: University of Hawai'i Press, 2008.

Kamakau, Samuel Manaiakalani. "Ka Moolelo Hawaii." *Ke Au Okoa*, January 7, 1869–February 2, 1871.

Kamakau, Samuel Mānaiakalani. *The People of Old: Ka Po'e Kahiko*. Translated by Mary Kawena Pukui. Edited by Dorothy B. Barrère. Honolulu: Bishop Museum Press, 1993.

Kamakau, Samuel Mānaiakalani. *Tales and Traditions of the People of Old: Nā Mo'olelo a ka Po'e Kahiko*. Translated by Mary Kawena Pukui. Edited by Dorothy B. Barrère. Honolulu: Bishop Museum Press, 1993.

Kamakau, Samuel Mānaiakalani. *The Works of the People of Old: Nā Hana a ka Po'e Kahiko*. Translated by Mary Kawena Pukui. Edited by Dorothy B. Barrère. Honolulu: Bishop Museum Press, 1992.

Kame'eleihiwa, Lilikalā, trans. and ed. *A Legendary Tradition of Kamapua'a, the Hawaiian Pig-God: He Mo'olelo Ka'ao o Kumupua'a*. Honolulu: Bishop Museum Press, 1996.

Kame'eleihiwa, Lilikalā. *Native Lands and Foreign Desires: How Shall We Live in Harmony? (Ko Hawai'i 'Āina a Me Nā Koi Pu'umake a Ka Po'e Haole: Pehea Lā E Pono Ai?)*. Honolulu: Bishop Museum Press, 1996.

Kanahele, Pualani Kanakaʻole. *Ka Honua Ola: ʻEliʻeli Kau Mai: The Living Earth: Descend, Deepen the Revelation*. Honolulu: Kamehameha Publishing, 2011.

Kanahele, Pualani Kanakaʻole, Huihui Kanahele-Mossman, Ann Kalei Nuʻuhiwa, and Kaumakaiwapoʻohalahiʻipaka Kealiʻikanakaʻole. *Kūkulu Ke Ea a Kanaloa: The Culture Plan for Kanaloa Kahoʻolawe*. Hilo, HI: Edith Kanakaʻole Foundation, February 9, 2009.

Kanahele, Pualani Kanakaʻole, Kekuhikuhipuuone Kealiikanakaoleohaililani, Huihui Kanahele-Mossman, Kalei Nuʻuhiwa, Kuʻulei Kanahele, and Honuaiākea Summit Group. *Kīhoʻihoʻi Kānāwai: Restoring Kānāwai for Island Stewardship*. Hilo, HI: Edith Kanakaʻole Foundation, September 21, 2016. http://nomaunakea.weebly .com/uploads/1/0/2/2/102246944/kanahele_kihoihoi_kanawai_final.pdf.

Kauanui, J. Kēhaulani. *Paradoxes of Hawaiian Sovereignty: Land, Sex, and the Colonial Politics of State Nationalism*. Durham, NC: Duke University Press, 2019.

Kauanui, J. Kēhaulani. "Resisting the Akaka Bill." In *A Nation Rising: Hawaiian Movements for Life, Land, and Sovereignty*, edited by Noelani Goodyear-Kaʻōpua, Ikaika Hussey, and Erin Kahunawaikaʻala Wright, 312–30. Durham, NC: Duke University Press, 2015.

Kaunamano. "He Moolelo no Aukelenuiaiku." *Ka Hoku o ka Pakipika*, November 6, 1862–December 25, 1862.

Kelly, Marion. *Loko Iʻa o Heʻeia: Heeia Fishpond*. Honolulu: Department of Anthropology, Bernice Pauahi Bishop Museum, 2000.

Kelly, Marion. "Notes on the History of Lualualei and Honouliuli." In *Research Design for an Archaeological Survey of Naval Magazine, Lualualei; Naval Communication Area Radio Transmission Facility, Lualualei; and Naval Air Station, Barber's Point, Oʻahu, Hawaiʻi*, by Alan E. Haun, 31–55. Honolulu: Dept. of Anthropology, Bernice Pauahi Bishop Museum, 1984.

Kepelino. *Kepelino's Traditions of Hawaii*. Translated and edited by Martha Warren Beckwith. Bilingual edition. Honolulu: Bishop Museum Press, 2007.

Kikiloi, Kekuewa. "Rebirth of an Archipelago: Sustaining a Hawaiian Cultural Identity for People and Homeland." *Hūlili: Multidisciplinary Research on Hawaiian Well-Being* 6 (2010): 73–115.

Kimmerer, Robin Wall. *Braiding Sweetgrass: Indigenous Wisdom, Scientific Knowledge, and the Teaching of Plants*. Minneapolis: Milkweed Editions, 2013.

Kimura, Yukiko. *Issei: Japanese Immigrants in Hawaiʻi*. Honolulu: University of Hawaiʻi Press, 1988.

King, Tiffany Lethabo. *The Black Shoals: Offshore Formations of Black and Native Studies*. Durham, NC: Duke University Press, 2019.

Latour, Bruno. *Facing Gaia: Eight Lectures on the New Climatic Regime*. Translated by Catherine Porter. Medford, MA: Polity Press, 2017.

Lee, Vivien, Charlie Reppun, and Piliāmoʻo. "Hoʻi ka Wai: The Waiāhole Stream Restoration, A Portfolio by Piliāmoʻo." *Mānoa* 9, no. 1 (1997): 119–36.

Lê Espiritu, Evyn. "Vexed Solidarities: Vietnamese Israelis and the Question of Palestine." *LIT: Literature Interpretation Theory* 29, no. 11 (2018): 8–28.

Lefebvre, Henri. *The Production of Space*. 1974. Translated by Donald Nicholson-Smith. Malden, MA: Blackwell Publishing, 1991.

Liliʻuokalani, trans. *The Kumulipo: An Hawaiian Creation Myth*. Honolulu: Pueo Press, 1978.

Lloyd, David. "'The Goal of the Revolution Is the Elimination of Anxiety': On the Right to Abundance in a Time of Artificial Scarcity." In *Critical Ethnic Studies: A Reader*, edited by the Critical Ethnic Studies Editorial Collective, 203–14. Durham, NC: Duke University Press, 2016.

Louis, Renee Pualani, with Aunty Moana Kahele. *Kanaka Hawaiʻi Cartography: Hula, Navigation, and Oratory*. Corvallis: Oregon State University Press, 2017.

Malo, Davida. *Ka Moʻolelo Hawaiʻi: Hawaiian Traditions*. Translated by Malcolm Nāea Chun. Bilingual edition. Honolulu: First People's Productions, 2006.

Malo, David. *Hawaiian Antiquities: Moʻolelo Hawaiʻi*. Translated by Nathaniel B. Emerson. Honolulu: Hawaiian Gazette, 1903.

Maly, Kepā, and Onaona Maly. *Mauna Kea: The Famous Summit of the Land* [Mauna Kea: Ka Piko Kaulana o ka ʻĀina]; *A Collection of Native Traditions, Historical Accounts, and Oral History Interviews for Mauna Kea, the Lands of Kaʻohe, Humuʻula and the ʻĀina Mauna on the Island of Hawaiʻi*. Prepared for the Office of Mauna Kea Management, March 30, 2005. Excerpts included in *Final Environmental Impact Statement: Thirty Meter Telescope*. Vol. 3. *Appendices*. University of Hawaiʻi at Hilo, May 8, 2010. Accessed April 26, 2020. https://dlnr.hawaii.gov/occl/files/2013/08/2010-05-08-HA-FEIS-Thirty-Meter-Telescope-Vol3.pdf.

Manu, Moke. "Ku-ula, the Fish God of Hawaii." Translated by M. K. Nakuina. In *Hawaiian Folktales: A Collection of Native Legends*, edited by Thos. G. Thrum, 215–29. Honolulu: Mutual Publishing, 1998.

Manu, Moses. "He Moolelo Kaao no Keaomelemele." *Ka Nupepa Kuokoa*, September 6, 1884–June 27, 1885.

Manu, Moses. *The Legend of Keaomelemele: He Moolelo Kaao no Keaomelemele*. Edited by Puakea Nogelmeier. Translated by Mary Kawena Pukui. Bilingual edition. Honolulu: Bishop Museum Press, 2002.

Marx, Karl. *Capital*. Vol. 1. Translated by Ben Fowkes. New York: Penguin, 1990.

McAllister, J. Gilbert. *Archaeology of Oahu*. Bernice P. Bishop Museum Bulletin 104. Honolulu: Bishop Museum, 1933.

McCoy, Daniel, Margaret A. McManus, Keliʻiahonui Kotubetey, Angela Hiʻilei Kawelo, Charles Young, Brandon D'Andrea, Kathleen C. Ruttenberg, and Rosanna ʻAnolani Alegado. "Large-Scale Climatic Effects on Traditional Hawaiian Fishpond Aquaculture." *PLoS One* 12, no. 11 (2017): e0187951. doi:10.13371/journal.pone.0187951.

McCoy, Patrick C., and Richard C. Nees. *Archaeological Inventory Survey of the Mauna Kea Ice Age Natural Area Reserve, Kaʻohe Ahupuaʻa, Hāmākua District, Island of Hawaiʻi*. Vol. 1, *Inventory Survey Report*. Prepared by Pacific Consulting Services for the State Department of Land and Natural Resources, Division of Forestry and Wildlife. Honolulu: Pacific Consulting Services, 2013.

McCoy, Patrick C., and Richard C. Nees. *Archaeological Inventory Survey of the Mauna Kea Science Reserve, Kaʻohe Ahupuaʻa, Hāmākua District, Island of Hawaiʻi.* Prepared by Pacific Consulting Services for the Office of Mauna Kea Management, University of Hawaiʻi at Hilo. Honolulu: Pacific Consulting Services, 2010.

McDougall, Brandy Nālani. *Finding Meaning: Kaona and Contemporary Hawaiian Literature.* Tucson: University of Arizona Press, 2016.

Möhlenkamp, Paula, Charles K. Beebe, Margaret A. McManus, Angela H. Kawelo, Keliʻiahonui Kotubetey, Mirielle Lopez-Guzman, Craig E. Nelson, and Rosanna Alegado. "Kū Hou Kuapā: Cultural Restoration Improves Water Budget and Water Quality Dynamics in Heʻeia Fishpond." *Sustainability* 11, no. 1 (2019): 61–85.

"Moʻolelo of Moanalua." Educational pamphlet published by Pacific American Foundation and Moanalua Gardens Foundation, 2012. http:// moanaluagardensfoundation.org/wpcontent/uploads/2015/10/Lesson-1 -Moolelo-of-Moanalua.pdf.

Muneoka, Lauren. "Meet the Mauna Kea Hui: Kūkauakahi (Clarence Ching)." *KĀHEA: The Hawaiian-Environmental Alliance* (blog), August 14, 2011. http:// kahea.org/blog/mk-vignette-kukauakahi-clarence-ching.

Nākoa, Sarah Keliʻilolena. *Lei Momi o ʻEwa.* Honolulu: ʻAhahui ʻŌlelo Hawaiʻi, 1979.

Nā Maka o ka ʻĀina (Puhipau and Joan Lander). "Lake Waiau." Mauna Kea: From Mountain to Sea. Accessed April 26, 2020. http://www.mauna-a-wakea.info /maunakea/A2_lakewaiau.html.

Na Mele Aimoku, Na Mele Kupuna, a me Na Mele Ponoi o ka Moi Kalakaua I: Dynastic Chants, Ancestral Chants, and Personal Chants of King Kalakaua I. 1886. Hawaiian-Language Reprint Series, buke 1. Honolulu: Hawaiian Historical Society, 2001.

National Aeronautics and Space Administration (NASA), Universe Division. *Final Environmental Impact Statement for the Outrigger Telescopes Project.* Vol. 1. Mauna Kea Science Reserve, Island of Hawaiʻi. Washington, DC: NASA, 2005.

Ngũgĩ wa Thiongʻo. *Decolonising the Mind: The Politics of Language in African Literature.* London: Heinemann, 1986.

Nixon, Rob. *Slow Violence and the Environmentalism of the Poor.* Cambridge, MA: Harvard University Press, 2013.

Nogelmeier, Puakea, ed. *The Epic Tale of Hiʻiakaikapoliopele: Woman of the Sunrise, Lightning-Skirted Beauty of Halemaʻumaʻu; As Told by Hoʻoulumāhiehie.* Translated by M. Puakea Nogelmeier. Honolulu: Awaiaulu Press, 2006.

Nogelmeier, Puakea, ed. *He Lei no ʻEmalani: Chants for Queen Emma Kaleleonālani.* Translated by Puakea Nogelmeier. Honolulu: Queen Emma Foundation, 2001.

Nuʻuhiwa, Kalei. "Papakū Makawalu: A Methodology and Pedagogy of Understanding the Hawaiian Universe." In *The Past before Us: Moʻokūʻauhau as Methodology,* edited by Nālani Wilson-Hokowhitu, 39–49. Honolulu: University of Hawaiʻi Press, 2019.

Nuʻuhiwa, Kalei, Olani Lilly, Malia Nobrega-Olivera, and Micky Huihui. "ʻAimalama: E Mauliauhonua; Readapting to Ancestral Knowledge for Survival." ʻAimalama.org, May 1, 2016. http://www.aimalama.org/wp-content/uploads/%CA%BBAimalama-%E2%80%93-E-Mauliauhonua.pdf.

Oahu Metropolitan Planning Organization. "Oahu Regional Transportation Plan 2030." Honolulu: Oahu MPO, 2006.

Oliveira, Katrina-Ann Kapāʻanaokalāokeola Nākoa. *Ancestral Places: Understanding Kanaka Geographies*. Corvallis: Oregon State University Press, 2017.

Oliveira, Katrina-Ann Kapāʻanaokalāokeola Nākoa, and Erin Kahunawaikaʻala Wright, eds. *Kanaka ʻŌiwi Methodologies*. Honolulu: Hawaiʻinuiākea School of Hawaiian Knowledge, University of Hawaiʻi Press, 2016.

Oppenheimer, Nathan E., and Nathan Napoka. *Mokauea Island: A Historical Study*. Honolulu: Historic Preservation Office, Department of Land and Natural Resources, 1976.

Osorio, Jamaica Heolimeleikalani. "(Re)Membering ʻUpena of Intimacies: A Kanaka Maoli Moʻolelo beyond Queer Theory." PhD diss., University of Hawaiʻi, 2018.

Osorio, Jonathan Kay Kamakawiwoʻole. *Dismembering Lāhui: A History of the Hawaiian Nation to 1887*. Honolulu: University of Hawaiʻi Press, 2002.

Peralto, Leon Noʻeau. "Hānau ka Mauna, the Piko of Our Ea." In *A Nation Rising: Hawaiian Movements for Life, Land, and Sovereignty*, edited by Noelani Goodyear-Kaʻōpua, Ikaika Hussey, and Erin Kahunawaikaʻala Wright, 232–43. Durham, NC: Duke University Press, 2014.

Perreira, Hiapokeikikāne Kichie. "He Kiʻina Hoʻokuanaʻike Mauli Hawaiʻi ma ke Kālailai Moʻokalaleo." *Hūlili: Multidisciplinary Research on Hawaiian Well-Being* 9 (2013): 53–114.

Pisciotta, Kealoha. "Meet the Mauna Kea Hui: Kealoha Pisciotta." KĀHEA: *The Hawaiian-Environmental Alliance* (blog), August 14, 2011. http://kahea.org/blog/mk-vignette-kealoha-pisciotta.

Poepoe, Joseph M. "He kanaenae no ka hanau ana o Kauikeaouli" in "Ka Moolelo Hawaii Kahiko." *Ka Naʻi Aupuni*, February 10 and 12, 1906.

Poepoe, Joseph M. "Ka Moolelo o ko Wakea ma Noho Ana ma Kalihi: Ka Loaa ana o ke Akua Ulu o Kamehaʻikana," in "Ka Moolelo Hawaii Kahiko." *Ka Naʻi Aupuni*, May 2, 1906–June 18, 1906.

Poepoe, Joseph M. "Ka Moolelo Kaao o Hiiaka-i-ka-Poli-o-Pele." *Kuokoa Home Rula*, January 10, 1908–January 20, 1911.

Povinelli, Elizabeth A. *Geontologies: A Requiem to Late Liberalism*. Durham, NC: Duke University Press, 2016.

Puhipau. "The Ice Man Looks Back at the Sand Island Eviction." In *A Nation Rising: Hawaiian Movements for Life, Land, and Sovereignty*, edited by Noelani Goodyear-Kaʻōpua, Erin Kahunawaikaʻala Wright, and Ikaika Hussey, 126–36. Durham, NC: Duke University Press, 2014.

Pukui, Mary Kawena, ed. *ʻŌlelo Noʻeau: Hawaiian Proverbs and Poetical Sayings*. Collected, translated, and annotated by Mary Kawena Pukui. Honolulu: Bishop Museum Press, 1983.

Pukui, Mary Kawena, and Samuel Elbert. *Hawaiian Dictionary*. 1957; reprint, Honolulu: University of Hawai'i Press, 1986.

Pukui, Mary Kawena, Samuel H. Elbert, and Esther Mo'okini. *Place Names of Hawaii*. 1966; reprint, Honolulu: University of Hawai'i Press, 1974.

Pukui, Mary Kawena, E. W. Haertig, and Catherine A. Lee. *Nānā I Ke Kumu: Look to the Source*. Vol. 1. Honolulu: Hui Hānai, 1972.

Pukui, Mary Kawena, and Alfons L. Korn, eds. *The Echo of Our Song: Chants and Poems of the Hawaiians*. Honolulu: University of Hawai'i Press, 1973.

Reiny, Samson. "The Lost Land of 'Ainalani: The Heavenly Land." *Flux Hawaii* (winter 2010): 42–47.

Sahara, Tamotsu. *Detailed Land Classification: Island of Oahu*. LSB Bulletin No. 11. Honolulu: Land Study Bureau, University of Hawai'i, 1972.

Sai, David Keanu. "A Slippery Path towards Hawaiian Indigeneity: An Analysis and Comparison between Hawaiian State Sovereignty and Hawaiian Indigeneity and Its Use and Practice in Hawai'i Today." *Journal of Law and Social Challenges* 10, no. 1 (2008): 68–133.

Salazar, Joseph A. "Multicultural Settler Colonialism and Indigenous Struggle in Hawai'i: The Politics of Astronomy on Mauna a Wākea." PhD diss., University of Hawai'i, 2014.

Saranillio, Dean Itsuji. *Unsustainable Empire: Colliding Futures of Hawai'i Statehood*. Durham, NC: Duke University Press, 2018.

Saranillio, Dean Itsuji. "Why Asian Settler Colonialism Matters: A Thought Piece on Critiques, Debates, and Indigenous Difference." *Settler Colonial Studies* 3, nos. 3–4 (2013): 280–94.

Schill, Steven R., Douglas B. Collins, Christopher Lee, Holly S. Morris, Gordon A. Novak, Kimberly A. Prather, Patricia K. Quinn, et al. "The Impact of Aerosol Particle Mixing State on the Hygroscopicity of Sea Spray Aerosol." *ACS Central Science* 1, no. 3 (2015): 132–41. https://doi.org/10.1021/acscentsci.5b00174.

Schmitt, Robert C. *Historical Statistics of Hawaii*. Honolulu: University of Hawai'i Press, 1977.

Scholl, Martha A., Stephen B. Gingerich, and Gordon W. Trimble. "The Influence of Microclimates and Fog on Stable Isotope Signatures." *Journal of Hydrology* 264, nos. 1–4 (2002): 170–84.

Sherrod, David R., John M. Sinton, Sarah E. Watkins, and Kelly M. Brunt. *Geologic Map of the State of Hawai'i, Sheet 3—Island of O'ahu: US Geological Suvey Open-File Report 2007–1089*. Washington, DC: US Department of the Interior, US Geological Survey, 2007. https://pubs.usgs.gov/of/2007/1089/Oahu_2007.pdf.

Silva, Noenoe K. *Aloha Betrayed: Native Hawaiian Resistance to American Colonialism*. Durham, NC: Duke University Press, 2004.

Silva, Noenoe K. "Pele, Hi'iaka, and Haumea: Women and Power in Two Hawaiian Mo'olelo." *Pacific Studies* 30, nos. 1–2 (2007): 159–81.

Silva, Noenoe K. *The Power of the Steel-Tipped Pen: Reconstructing Native Hawaiian Intellectual History*. Durham, NC: Duke University Press, 2017.

Simonson, Mindy, and Hallett H. Hammatt. "Cultural Impact Assessment for the Thirty Meter Telescope (TMT) Observatory Project." Prepared for the *Final Environmental Impact Statement: Thirty Meter Telescope.* Vol. 3, *Appendices.* University of Hawai'i at Hilo, May 8, 2010. Accessed April 26, 2020. https://dlnr.hawaii.gov/occl/files/2013/08/2010-05-08-HA-FEIS-Thirty-Meter-Telescope-Vol3.pdf.

Simpson, Leanne Betasamosake. *As We Have Always Done: Indigenous Freedom Through Radical Resistance.* Minneapolis: University of Minnesota Press, 2017.

Souza, Kehaulani E., and Hallet H. Hammatt. "Cultural Impact Assessment of 179 Acres for the Proposed Nānākuli B Composting and Solid Waste Landfill Facility, Lualualei Ahupua'a, Wai'anae District, Island of O'ahu, Hawai'i." Kailua, HI: Cultural Surveys Hawai'i, 2007.

Sproat, D. Kapua'ala. "From Wai to Kānāwai: Water Law in Hawai'i." In *Native Hawaiian Law: A Treatise,* edited by Melody Kapilialoha MacKenzie, Susan K. Serrano, and D. Kapua'ala Sproat, 522–610. Honolulu: Kamehameha Publishing, 2015.

Sproat, D. Kapua'ala, and Isaac H. Moriwake. "Ke Kalo Pa'a o Waiāhole: Use of the Public Trust as a Tool for Environmental Advocacy." In *Creative Common Law Strategies for Protecting the Environment,* edited by Clifford Rechtschaffen and Denise Antolini, 247–84. Washington, DC: Environmental Law Institute, 2007.

Stannard, David E. *Before the Horror. The Population of Hawai'i on the Eve of Western Contact.* Honolulu: Social Science Research Institute, 1989.

Stearns, Harold T., and Knute N. Vaksvik. *Geology and Ground-Water Resources of the Island of Oahu, Hawaii: Prepared in Cooperation with the U.S. Geological Survey.* Wailuku, HI: Maui Publishing Company, 1935.

Sterling, Elspeth P., and Catherine C. Summers. *Sites of Oahu.* 1962; reprint, Honolulu: Bishop Museum Press, 1978.

Subramoniam, T., and V. Gunmalai. "Breeding Biology of the Intertidal Sand Crab, Emerita (Decapoda: Anomura)." *Advanced Marine Biology* 46 (2003): 91–182.

TallBear, Kim. "Genomic Articulations of Indigeneity." In *Native Studies Keywords,* edited by Stephanie Nohelani Teves, Andrea Smith, and Michelle H. Raheja, 130–55. Tucson: University of Arizona Press, 2015.

Trask, Haunani-Kay. "The Birth of the Modern Hawaiian Movement: Kalama Valley, O'ahu." *The Hawaiian Journal of History* 21, no. 1 (1987): 126–53.

Trask, Haunani-Kay. "The Color of Violence." In *Color of Violence: The Incite! Anthology,* edited by Incite! Women of Color against Violence, 81–87. Cambridge, MA: South End Press, 2006.

Trask, Haunani-Kay. *From a Native Daughter: Colonialism and Sovereignty in Hawai'i.* Honolulu: University of Hawai'i Press, 1999.

Trask, Haunani-Kay. *Light in the Crevice Never Seen.* Honolulu: University of Hawai'i Press, 1999.

Trask, Haunani-Kay. "Settlers of Color and 'Immigrant' Hegemony: 'Locals' in Hawai'i." 2000. Reprinted in *Asian Settler Colonialism: From Local Governance* to the *Habits of Everyday Life in Hawai'i*, edited by Candace Fujikane and Jonathan Y. Okamura, 45–65. Honolulu: University of Hawai'i Press, 2008.

Tropic Land. *Nānākuli Community Baseyard: Final Environmental Impact Statement*. Prepared by Kimura International for Tropic Land LLC, Lualualei, O'ahu, Hawai'i, April 2010. Accessed April 26, 2020. http://oeqc2.doh.hawaii.gov/EA_EIS_Library/2010-06-23-OA-FEIS-Acceptance-Nanakuli-Comm-Baseyard.pdf.

Tropic Land. *Nānākuli Community Baseyard: Final Environmental Impact Statement: Appendices*. Prepared by Kimura International for Tropic Land LLC, Lualualei, O'ahu, Hawai'i, April 2010. Accessed April 26, 2020. http://oeqc2.doh.hawaii.gov/EA_EIS_Library/2010-06-23-OA-FEIS-Acceptance-Nanakuli-Comm-Baseyard-App.pdf.

Tsing, Anna Lowenhaupt. *The Mushroom at the End of the World: On the Possibility of Life in Capitalist Ruins*. Princeton, NJ: Princeton University Press, 2015.

Tuck, Eve, Allison Guess, and Hannah Sultan. "Not Nowhere: Collaborating on Selfsame Land." *Decolonization: Indigeneity, Education and Society*, June 26, 2014. https://decolonization.wordpress.com/2014/06/26/not-nowhere-collaborating-on-selfsame-land/.

Tuck, Eve, and K. Wayne Yang. "Decolonization Is Not a Metaphor." *Decolonization: Indigeneity, Education and Society* 1, no. 1 (2012): 1–40. https://jps.library.utoronto.ca/index.php/des/article/view/18630.

US Environmental Protection Agency. "About the 2014 Fuel Release at Red Hill." November 8, 2017. https://www.epa.gov/red-hill/about-2014-fuel-release-red-hill/.

US Environmental Protection Agency. "Groundwater Flow Model Progress Report 04, Red Hill Bulk Fuel Storage Facility." Naval Facilities Engineering Command Hawai'i, April 5, 2018. https://www.epa.gov/sites/production/files/2018-04/documents/red-hill-gw-model-progress-rpt04-rev00_2018-04-05.pdf.

US Environmental Protection Agency. "Regulatory Agency Comments on Groundwater and Fate Transport Model Development." February 23, 2018. https://www.epa.gov/sites/production/files/2018-02/documents/regulatory_agency_comments_on_groundwater_and_fate_transport_model_development_23_february_2018_.pdf.

University of Hawai'i at Hilo. *Mauna Kea Comprehensive Management Plan: UH Management Areas*. Prepared by Ho'akea LLC for the University of Hawai'i, Hilo, April 2009. http://www.malamamaunakea.org/uploads/management/plans/CMP_2009.PDF.

University of Hawai'i at Hilo. "Conservation District Use Permit Application: Thirty Meter Telescope Project." Hilo, September 2, 2010. https://dlnr.hawaii.gov/mk/files/2016/10/A023.pdf.

University of Hawai'i at Hilo. *Final Environmental Impact Statement: Thirty Meter Telescope Project*. Vol. 1. Hilo, May 8, 2010. https://dlnr.hawaii.gov/occl/files/2013/08/2010-05-08-HA-FEIS-Thirty-Meter-Telescope-Vol1.pdf.

University of Hawaiʻi at Hilo. *Final Environmental Impact Statement: Thirty Meter Telescope Project*. Vol. 2. Hilo, May 8, 2010. https://dlnr.hawaii.gov/occl/files/2013/08/2010-05-08-HA-FEIS-Thirty-Meter-Telescope-Vol2.pdf.

University of Hawaiʻi at Hilo. *Final Environmental Impact Statement: Thirty Meter Telescope Project*. Vol. 3. *Appendices*. Hilo, May 8, 2010. https://dlnr.hawaii.gov/occl/files/2013/08/2010-05-08-HA-FEIS-Thirty-Meter-Telescope-Vol3.pdf.

Vaughan, Mehana Blaich. *Kaiāulu: Gathering Tides*. Corvallis: Oregon State University Press, 2018.

Vogeler, Kūhiō. "Outside Shangri-La: Colonization and the US Occupation of Hawaiʻi." In *A Nation Rising: Hawaiian Movements for Life, Land, and Sovereignty*, edited by Noelani Goodyear-Kaʻōpua, Erin Kahunawaikaʻala Wright, and Ikaika Hussey, 252–66. Durham, NC: Duke University Press, 2014.

Voyles, Traci Brynne. *Wastelanding: Legacies of Uranium Mining in Navajo Country*. Minneapolis: University of Minnesota Press, 2015.

Wang, Frances Kai-Hwa Wang. "Native Hawaiians, Asian Americans Show Support for the North Dakota Pipeline Protest." *NBC News*, September 26, 2016. https://www.nbcnews.com/storyline/dakota-pipeline-protests/native-hawaiians-asian-americans-show-support-north-dakota-pipeline-protest-n654321/.

Watts, Sarah. "Global Warming Is Putting the Ocean's Phytoplankton in Danger." *Pacific Standard*, December 29, 2017. https://psmag.com/environment/global-warming-is-putting-phytoplankton-in-danger/.

Whitney, Leo D., F. A. I. Bowers, and M. Takahashi. "Taro Varieties in Hawaii." *Hawaii Agricultural Experiment Station of the University of Hawaiʻi Bulletin* No. 84. Honolulu: University of Hawaiʻi, 1939.

Whyte, Kyle. "Indigenous Climate Change Studies: Indigenizing Futures, Decolonizing the Anthropocene." *English Language Notes* 55, nos. 1–2 (2017): 153–62.

Whyte, Kyle. "Indigenous Lessons about Sustainability." In *Sustainability: Approaches to Environmental Justice and Social Power*, edited by Julie Sze, 149–79. New York: New York University Press, 2018.

Wise, John, and J. W. H. I. Kihe. "Kaao Honiua Puuwai no Ka-Miki." *Ka Hoku o Hawaii*, February 5, 1914–December 6, 1917.

Wolfe, Patrick. *Settler Colonialism and the Transformation of Anthropology: The Politics and Poetics of an Ethnographic Event*. London: Cassell, 1999.

Yamashiro, Aiko, and Noelani Goodyear Kaʻōpua, eds. *The Value of Hawaiʻi*. Vol. 2, *Ancestral Roots, Oceanic Visions*. Honolulu: University of Hawaiʻi Press, 2014.

Young, Kalaniopua. "Home-Free and Nothing (. . .)-Less: A Queer Cosmology of Aloha ʻĀina." *Hūlili: Multidisciplinary Research on Hawaiian Well-Being* 11, no. 1 (2019): 9–21.

INDEX

blockade: at Kualoa, 177–81; at Mauna a Wākea, 117, 120–23, 213–15; at Waiāhole, 181–83

Borges, Jorge Luis, 212

Boycott, Divest, and Sanction (BDS) movement, 64

Brathwaite, Kamau, 13

Brown, Marie Alohalani, 50–51, 148, 215, 226n53

Busby-Neff, Luana, 121–22

Byrd, Jodi, 13

Cachola, Fred Keakaokalani, 42, 77

capital, 3; accumulation by dispossession 4, 6, 39, 56, 82, 211; alienation from land, 5, 62; cartographies of, 3–4; contentment as a radical proposition, 5; climate change and, 143, 174, 208; crises of, 99, 211; dissipating possibilities of life, 13, 19, 97; economies of scarcity, 11, 86, 166, 217; as factory of fragmentation, 5; failure of, 218; fear of abundance, 4, 216, 218; imaginaries of, 86, 151; implosive demise of, 15, 208, 211–12; industrialism and militarization, 8, 164; localized struggles against, 83, 212; neoliberalization of free trade, 164; planetarity and, 12; privatization of land, 34, 56, 183; rejection of, 116, 142, 158, 211; rhetorical regimes of, 97, 124, 212; seemingly unassailable, 211; spatial economies of, 5; statehood and, 71–72. *See also* cartographies, settler colonial; infrastructure, settler colonial

cartographies, critical settler, 4; abundance and, 7, 30, 75, 114; aloha ʻāina as foundation for, 15, 18, 62, 64–66, 152, 217; critique of colonial wastelanding arguments, 94–96; critique of the mathematics of subdivision, 42, 49, 110–12, 125–26, 130–31, 164–65; decolonized STEM (science, technology, engineering, and mathematics) and, 26; embodied experience of land, 30; exposing logics of settler colonial maps, 17–18, 165; methodology of, 17–19; presenting evidence of past and present abundance, 3–4, 32, 75, 83; relationality-based, 12, 46–47, 61–62, 79, 109–10; rooted in Kanaka

Maoli cartographies, 16–19; schematic of globalization, 210–11; tracking settler colonial omissions, 82–83; using settler colonial maps as evidence against the state, 57–58, 82–84

cartographies, Kanaka Maoli, 1–2, 4; abundance and, 9, 30, 80, 88, 112, 114, 137; ahupuaʻa as organizing principle, 19–21, 26–27, 150, 167, 187; akua as natural processes shaping, 26–27, 52–53, 55–56, 60–61, 86; aloha ʻāina as foundation for, 18, 24–25, 64–66; of ecosystems as, 8, 203–6; climate change and, 80, 85, 142, 165–66; ea and, 7–10, 135–37, 185–88, 215–18; embodied on huakaʻi (traveling across the land), 30, 59, 62–64, 109–10, 114; genealogical connectedness to the natural world, 18, 23–24, 27–28; governance and, 9–10, 136, 156–58, 216–17; kilo and, 197; Land Commission Awards as, 46–49; kino lau (bodily forms) of land, 29, 61–62, 78, 147–48, 151–52; landforms as ʻohana (family), 42–43; moʻo, 55–56; moʻoʻāina expansiveness of, 35, 37–38, 47–49, 111–12, 130–31, 174, 177; moʻolelo as, 1–3, 32, 91–94, 110–12, 119, 178–81; moʻolelo conventions, 64–66; in motion, 29, 60–62, 77–79, 87, 120; Oliveira and "sense abilities," 50–51, 118; protocol and, 18, 102; regeneration and, 61, 203–4; relational, 19, 129; vertical cartographies of papa (strata), 29, 35, 143–47, 161; of waterways, 1–2, 55, 179–81, 185–86. *See also* moʻoʻāina

cartographies, settler colonial, 3–4, 17–18; climate change and, 3, 29; "empty" maps, 39–40, 104–5, 124; global circuits, 212; historical trace, 57–58; as invasive species, 218; land as a bucket of dirt in, 41–42; obscure evidence of impact, 104; Purple Spot industrial zoning, 36; reflecting modes of capitalist economies, 5; refusal to consult Indigenous practitioners, 126; representing abundant lands as wastelands, 3, 5, 32, 68, 75, 82–83, 94; static representations of land, 32, 39, 78–79; tactic of omission, 82–84, 107, 124–25; "telescoping," 125–26; US Navy's Red Hill Bulk Fuel Storage Facility hydrological study, 164–65. *See also* mathematics of subdivision

cascades, 7; of climate change effects, 97; counters mathematics of subdivision, 97; moʻoʻāina and, 174; of restorative effects, 7, 137, 177, 204, 206

Case, Pua, 90; on joy, 133–35; on kapu aloha, 119; memory of water in puʻu, 112; on protocol, 103; on the refusal to grant Moʻoinanea standing, 99, 103; at Standing Rock, 143

caves, 144, 145; limestone, 73; navigation of, 160; Oʻahu complex, 160; sharks and, 161–63; water in, 106

"ceded" lands (also known as seized lands). *See* Crown and government lands

ceremony, 8, 17, 27; ʻawa ceremony, 159; Kanaka Maoli cartographic practices and, 18, 102, 103; naming of akua (elements and natural processes), 34; protocols for permission, 23, 102–3, 132; at Puʻuhonua o Puʻuhuluhulu, 215–16; solstice and equinox, 130–31

Chang, David A., 39–40

chants, prayers, songs, 17, 119; "Nā ʻAumākua," 215; bearer of kānāwai (laws), 145; chanting for permission to enter, 102; "E ala ē," 215; "E Hō Mai," 215; "E Hū ē!" 218; "E iho ana o luna," 17, 216; "E Kānehoalani ē," 215; "E Ō E Maunakea," 107; Haumea's pule kūʻauhau kupuna (ancestral genealogical prayer), 159; "Ka Ipu Hoʻokele" ("The Navigator's Chant"), 169; "Kahuli Aku, Kahuli Mai," 107; Kūaliʻi chant, 108, 149; "Mālana Mai Kaʻū," 117, 122, 134–35; "Manu ʻŌʻō," 66–67; "A Maunakea ʻo Kalani," 140–41; "Mele Hānau no Kauikeaouli," 24, 122; power of the voice to split mountains, 152, "Pule Hoʻowilimoʻo," 128; "Pule no Meheanu," 201; reciprocity and, 132; vibration and activation, 27, 120, 122–23, 159–60, 188. See also "Kaulana Nā Pua"

Chen, Mel Y., 21

Ching, Clarence. *See* Kūkauakahi

civil rights movement, 80, 181

climate change, 1–4, 5, 8; acidification of the ocean, 3, 27, 205; ancestral knowledges across the earth, 166, 218; capital, impacts on, 5, 64, 143, 174, 208; capital's inability to survive, 3; cascading effects of, 97; classes on at Puʻuhuluhulu University on Mauna a Wākea, 217; creating microclimates, 80; driven by cartographies of capital, 3, 5, 32, 97; El Niño Modoki marine heat wave, 200; flood pulse events, 26–27, 193, 196, 217; indicators of, 2, 6, 165; Indigenous regenerative approaches to 6, 12, 26, 28, 80, 90, 165–66; as intensification of colonialism, 8, 29; Kanaka Maoli cartography of, 1–2; kilo at fishponds, 197–98, 200–201; kilo for planting, 80, 176–77, 193–94, 195–96; need for biological diversity, 175–76, 195–96; phytoplankton and, 203, 206. *See also* sea level rise

clouds, 1, 6; akua of cloud formation, Lonoikamakahiki, 218; captured as fog drip, 53; cloud akua names, 8, 19, 52; follow forests, 6, 19, 53; 405 subcategories of, 51; hydrological cycle, 20; Kaʻōpua (Pillar cloud; a canoe), 162; Keaolewaokalihi (The floating cloud of Kalihi; a canoe), 158; kilo and, 25, 27, 107, 209–10, 217–18; Leialoha, 62; love mountain summits, 70, 106; moʻo migration from cloud islands, 1; names of, 218; seeding, 21, 53; subterranean, 21, 183; wayfinding, 210. *See also* "He Moolelo Kaao no Keaomelemele"

community activism, 17, 38, 68–69; community murals, 112–13; Concerned Elders of Waiʻanae, 32, 38, 68–69, 73, 75, 84; for demilitarization, 114; Environmental Justice in Waiʻanae Working Group, 45, 68–69; giving testimony, 31, 44, 59, 83–84, 92, 101; Hawaiʻi Unity and Liberation Institute (HULI), 212–15; huakaʻi as, 62; Kaʻala Farms, 57–59; KĀHEA: The Hawaiian-Environmental Alliance, 38, 68–69; Kalama Valley, 81–82; Makawai Stream Restoration Alliance, 182; on Mauna a Wākea, 120–23, 212–15; ʻOnipaʻa Nā Hui Kalo, 184–85; Pani ka Puka at Hale o Meheanu, 201; for water in Waiāhole, 182–85. *See also* aloha ʻāina

community benefits package, 69, 84

Concerned Elders of Waiʻanae, 32, 33, 68; cartographic strategies, 84; on environmental injustice hotspots in Waiʻanae, 69, 73–79; organized political bus tours, 69, 80; protecting the birthplace of Māui and agricultural lands, 38, 45, 47–48

coral, 9, 205; abundance and, 170; akua natural processes Hinaluaʻikoʻa and Kukeapua, 206; ancestors in the Kumulipo, 24, 206, 71; broadcast spawning, 205–6; dwelling of Hinaiaakamalama, 206; global warming impacts, 205; limestone made into cement for Waikīkī hotels, 71; moon phases and, 28, 205; spawn resembles ʻupena nananana a Papa (spiderweb of Papa), 205

Coulthard, Glen, 22–23

Crown and government lands, 99; designated as "public trust lands," 99; Mauna Kea, 99, 213; in Waiʻanae, 75, 151

Dawes Act (1887 General Allotment Act), 39

decolonization, 10, 222n37; ally work focuses on, 14–15; decolonial joy, 17, 28, 66–67, 133–35, 192; decolonial love, 4, 12–16, 18, 24–25, 60, 62, 132; decolonization of the Anthropocene, 8; false thresholds, 99; independence and, 11–12; intergenerational, 17; political process for, 10. *See also* aloha ʻāina; EAducation; resurgence, radical

degradation principle, 96–97

DeLoughrey, Elizabeth M., 210

desecration, 67; of ahu (stone altars), 133; ʻai pōhaku (stone eaters) speak out against, 117; of iwi kupuna (ancestral remains), 67; of Mauna a Wākea, 101, 113, 117–18, 122, 213; of water as sacred, 143

de Silva, Kahikina, 116–17

de Silva, Kīhei, 117; Māpuana de Silva and, 140–41

desire, 3, 25; for capital's imaginary plenitude, 4; cartographies of ʻiʻini (desire) for places, 18, 25, 55, 65–66, 79, 152, 175; beyond cissettler and heteronormative desire, 25; between Haumea and Wākea, 150; growing the desire for decolonial work, 17, 216–18;

between Hiʻiaka and Kaʻanahau, 65–66; between Kamapuaʻa and Pele, 61; land as a referent for beauty, 25; of lands, voiced in moʻolelo, 8, 156–57, 200; Kanaloa as desiring principle, 146; settler desire, 11, 38–39; between women, 66–67

DeTroye, Butch, 16, 57–58

directionals, 19, 46–49, 130–31, 149

Duarte, T. Kaeo, 20, 39

Dukelow, Kahele, 212

ea (life, breath, political sovereignty), 4, 10, 21; as an active state of being, 10; daily practices of, 114, 193, 196; as foundation for the lāhui (nation, collective), 12, 155; fullest expression of, 123; growing ea, 17, 173; intergenerational, 133; kupuna vibration and, 27, 170–71, 188; Mauna Kea and, 118, 139, 212–18; piko of, 139; refusal to recognize the settler state, 91; in relationship between Kanaka and land, 199–200; settler allies and, 14. *See also* EAducation

EAducation, 117; Aha Aloha ʻĀina organizing in communities across Hawaiʻi, 138; children rising, 136–37; Kanuha on, 135–36; at Puʻuhonua o Puʻuhuluhulu on Mauna a Wākea, 216–18

education, 28; through art, 136–37; huakaʻi as embodied education, 170; in kilo, 27–28, 217; at MAʻO Organic Farms, 85; at Puʻuhuluhulu University, 216–18; under settler colonialism, 67; testimony as pedagogical practice, 84. *See also* EAducation

Elbert, Samuel H., 33, 79, 222n15

elements. *See* akua

Emma, Queen, 109, 140–41

enclosure, 4, 39, 164. *See also* mathematics of subdivision

Enomoto, Joy, 223n37

Enos, Eric, 31, 35, 57–59, 79, 215

Enos, Kamuela, 80

environmental impact statements, 17; cultural impact assessments in, 41–43, 45, 92, 101; as evidence, 123; omissions from, 45, 80, 82, 123–26; rhetorical dissipation of impact in, 96–97, 211; for the Thirty Meter Telescope,

89, 96–97, 123–26; wastelanding of the earth, 32, 40–41, 80, 82–84, 212

governance (continued)
and the governance of markets, 8; occupying state's naturalization of, 11; statist and
nonstatist forms of governance, 12, 135
Greenwood, Alice Kaholo, 44, 68; on bus
tour, 69, 75–76; community organizer, 45;
documenting Māui's birthplace, 44–49;
on impacts of toxic waste dumping, 73; research on Land Commission Awards, 33, 45
Guess, Allison, 13

Hae Hawaiʻi (Hawaiian flag), 136; in *Kalo Paʻa
o Waiāhole*, 187; at restoration of loʻi kalo,
193; sprouting from the infrastructures of
capital, 140, 211, 219
Hale, Lydia, 116
Haleole, S. N. *See* Lāʻieikawai
Hale o Meheanu (Pihi Loko Iʻa) fishpond,
30, 177; cutting back mangrove, 202–3,
204; home of Meheanu, 198; megalopa as
indicator, 218; oxygen levels in, 202; Pani ka
Puka (Close the Hole) event, 201; restoration of Heʻeia Stream, 204–5; restoration of
Kawahaokamanō (Kāneʻohe Bay), 204–5
Hāloa, 24; awakening of Hāloa, 175, 192;
moʻolelo of, 112–13; mural of, 112–13;
relationship to Mauna a Wākea, 87–88;
vibration, 24, 188
Haraway, Donna J., 21
Harvey, David, 5
hau, 17, 29–30, 50, 150; flood mitigation, 202;
flower beloved by moʻo, 158, 174; forests
of places for love affairs, 66, 189; Haumea
Corridor of hau, 203–4; as indicators of
waterways, 174–75, 177, 189; like the hei
a Haumea or spiderweb of Papa, 192; of
Luamoʻo, 198; manifestation of Haumea,
203; necessary for health of fishponds, 174,
202–3; procession of, 177–78, 203–4, 219;
protection of fishponds, 202–3; protection
of taro pondfields, 174, 189–93; yellowing
leaves of, indicator of moʻo presence, 203
Haumea, 27, 29–30; births children from
different parts of her body, 150, 159–60;
consciousness of the earth, 147, 152,
155–58; genealogy of, 129, 150; Haumea

Corridor, 203–4, 219; "hei a Haumea"
(Haumea's string figure), 148–49, 192,
219; as Kāmehaʻikana, 153–54, 158; kilo
and, 153; laws of the sovereign land,
155–57; as Meheanu, 202–3; as moʻo, 48; as
Moʻoinanea's daughter or granddaughter,
148; moʻolelo of Wākea and Haumea living
in Kalihi, 151–60; multiplies her bodies,
148, 155, 174, 177–80, 183; Palikū and Palihaʻi
ancestors, 159, 171, 178; as Papahānaumoku,
148, 149; as potentiality, 148–49, 180, 192;
principle of birthing and regeneration, 145,
147, 150, 171, 174, 192; Pūehuehu Spring,
creation of, 158–60; sacred space, establishes, 148, 216; as shark, 236n17; the ʻupena
nanana a Papa (Papa's spiderweb), 107–8,
149–50; vibration of her voice, 159–60
Hawaiian flag. *See* Hae Hawaiʻi
Hawaiian language. *See* ʻōlelo Hawaiʻi
Hawaiʻi Supreme Court: on conservation district use permit for the Thirty Meter Telescope, 90, 97, 120, 127; on Native Hawaiian
traditional and customary rights, 43–44;
stay of Thirty Meter Telescope construction, 143; on water as a public trust, 182
Hawaiʻi Unity and Liberation Institute
(HULI), 212; inspired by KŌKUA Hawaiʻi, 82
hei (string figure) a Haumea, 148–48, 192, 219;
ipu maoloha (net filled with food), 149;
See also spiderweb of Papa
Hiʻiakaikapoliopele, 61; divine nature of ʻāina
and, 151; finds water below sand, 146; lover
Kaʻanahau on their birthplaces and, 65–66;
Mokoliʻi and, 181; strata of the earth and,
146–47
Hina (mother of Poliʻahu), 92, 102
Hinaʻaikamalama (Hina who devours the
moon, also Hinaiaakamalama), 37, 173,
206
Hinaakekā (Hina of the canoe bailers), 37
Hinakawea (Māui's mother, also Hinaakeahi),
32, 36, 42–43, 67; in Kamakau's account of
Māui, 45; in the Kumulipo, 38, 77–78; in
Momoa's mural, 50
Hinaluaʻikoʻa (Hina who releases coral
gametes), 206

Hinapukuiʻa (patron of fishing), 198

Hinawelelani, 25

hōʻailona. *See* signs

Hōkūleʻa, 134, 166, 169–170, 208

Hoʻōla Mokauea-Keʻehi, 166

Hoʻoulu ʻĀina, 147, 151; albizia canoe, Keaolewaokalihi, 158, 166; decreasing water supply, 165; growing mana with all peoples of Kalihi, 166; Mai Uka Kuʻu Waʻa Program, 157–58; moʻolelo of Haumea and Wākea incorporated into work, 151–57; Pasifika Garden, 166; repurposing invasive species, 158

huakaʻi (intellectual, spiritual, embodied journeys), 29, 30, 33; comparison with political tours in the West Bank and Belfast, 64; connecting generations, 60; to feed the naʻau, 59; growing aloha ʻāina with those grown on the land, 61–62, 64, 67; inviting decision makers on, 62, 63; kaʻapuni mākaʻikaʻi as practice, 63, 109; mapping conditions of occupation and settler colonialism, 63; moving aloha ʻāina to direct action, 62, 68; to remap lands, 62; widespread movement to grow broad base of support, 64, 69; wonder on, 59, 60–62, 77–80, 107–9, 114, 205–6. *See also* Huakaʻi i Nā ʻĀina Mauna; Huakaʻi Kākoʻo no Waiʻanae bus tour

Huakaʻi i Nā ʻĀina Mauna, 102, 108–10, 114

Huakaʻi Kākoʻo no Waiʻanae bus tour, 62, 88, 95–107

Hui ʻAimalama, 28

Hui Kū Like Kākou, 59

Hulleman, Malia, 143, 213

Hunt, Ashley, 211–12

Indigenous economies of abundance, 3–5; ancestral knowledges and, 80, 166; demise of global capitalism and, 208, 211; farming kalo and, 194–96; at Hoʻoulu ʻĀina, 151, 157–58; kilo and, 197–205, 206; laws of in Kīhoʻihoʻi Kānāwai stewardship plan, 145–46; on Mauna a Wākea 86–88, 216–17; the sovereign land and, 155–56. *See also* abundance

Indigenous peoples: activism in Belyuen aboriginal community, 136; American Indian Movement, 189; climate change and settler colonialism, 8; critiques of capital, 5, 8; critiques of federal or state recognition, 7, 22–23; debates over term in Hawaiʻi, 10–12; enclosure and the Dawes Act (1887), 39–40; on front lines of climate change movement, 3, 8, 26–27, 143; murders of land defenders, 6; Nishnaabeg practices of reciprocal recognition, 23; Pacific Islander knowledges as, 166; settler cartographies of enclosure and, 5, 39–40; settler state and, 40, 56, 63–64; threshold of impact and "vanishing" Indian figure, 99, 231n40; trans-Indigenous alliances, 9, 91, 120, 143, 166, 189, 208

infrastructure, settler colonial, 38–39, 70, 211; concrete channelization of streams, 70; limestone quarries and cement plants, 71–72; roads, 38–39; settler colonial infrastructures, 70, 211; Waiāhole Ditch system and diversion of water, 5, 181; water banking, 182

invasive species, 6, 151, 158, 205

ipu hoʻokele waʻa (navigational gourd), 108, 168–70

Islamophobia, 13–14

Jackson, Casey, 158, 189

Jackson, Puni: "abundant-mindedness," 6–7; on climate change, 165–66; on hoʻomana (collectively growing spiritual life force), 166; on kuleana, 157–58; relationship between uka (uplands) and kai (seas), 157; sovereignty of the land, 154, 156–58; spider-web of Papa (ka ʻupena nananana a Papa), 107–8, 149, 192; trans-Indigenous alliance, 189

Jeremiah, Jason, 46

Johnson, Rubellite Kawena, 119, 128, 149–50, 169

Kaaia, 36

Kaʻala, 2, 19, 34, 52; abundance of water at, 70; home of Keaomelemele, 53; Luakini fishpond and Kamaʻoha, 56. *See also* Kaʻala Cultural Learning Center

language, Hawaiian. *See* ʻōlelo Hawaiʻi

Latour, Bruno, 21

laws, 2, 8; of the akua, 15, 22–23, 90–91, 210; community education in land use laws, 69; on conservation land use, 100, 103, 125; court of the akua (elements) and, 98, 140, 155–58; "degradation principle" in, 96–97; enclosure, 39–40; environmental, 97; fishpond repair, 200; Hawaiian customary and traditional rights, 41, 59–61; international law and occupation, 10, 22; Kanaka Maoli conservation kānāwai (laws), 2, 6, 160–61; Kīhoʻihoʻi Kānāwai stewardship laws, 145–146, 162; Land Grant Act (1895), 155; land use ordinances, 36; mathematics of subdivision in, 5, 42; *McBryde v. Robinson* on water as a public trust, 182; *Ka Paʻakai o ka ʻĀina v. Land Use Commission*, 43; *Public Access Shoreline Hawaiʻi (PASH) v. Hawaiʻi County Planning Commission*, 43; on standing in contested case hearing, 90; US Public Law 103–150 (the Apology Resolution), 22; Waiāhole Combined Contested Case Hearing, 183; water code, 58

Lee, Vivien, 182

Lê Espiritu Gandhi, Evyn, 14

Lefebvre, Henri, 5

liberalism, late, 8, 17–18; distinctions between life and nonlife, 21–22, 94, 97, 100, 211; governing of difference, 13–14, 164

Līlīnoe, 88, 91, 106; as hōʻailona (sign), 102, 122, 141; as a puʻu (cinder cone), 124; sister of Poliʻahu, 113

Liliʻuokalani, Queen, 38, 75, 77, 80, 115, 213

literary devices (meiwi moʻokalaleo), 64–66

Lloyd, David, 4–5

Long, Kerry Kamakaokaʻilima, 113, 122, 212

Lonoikamakahiki, 218

Louis, Renee Pualani, 18

Lupenui, Muriel, 162

Māhele (1848), 20, 34, 75

Mākālei tree, 65–66

Makaliʻi: Pleiades, 128, 169, 173; punning, 173; shark, 161–62, 173

Makawai Stream Restoration Alliance, 182

Malo, Davida, 94–96

mana (spiritual life force), 61, 65; of Haumea, 15354, 159–60; hoʻomana (to grow mana), 159, 166; of Kāmehaʻikana, 158; of Kūʻula, 19899; in the leo (voice), 132; mana māhū, 217; mana wahine (power of women), 122, 215; on Mauna a Wākea, 123; of places, 153; sharing moʻolelo and, 79; of stones, 116–17, 132; of wai, 172

Manu, Moke (Moses), 53, 56, 175

MAʻO Organic Farms, 80, 84–85

maps, 4; aerial, 83, 184; of ahupuaʻa, 20; ʻape leaf as a, 129; Bishop, *Kalo Paʻa o Waiāhole*, 185–88; of condominiumization, 40; as contingent analytics, 211; critical settler map exposing wastelanding, 82–84; of decentralized leadership, 137–39; empty map of settler colonial hydrology, 104–5; of Haumea's women's bodies, 178–79; huakaʻi map of the Concerned Elders' activism, 69–77; Hunt, *A World Map: In Which We See . . .*, 211–12; ipu hoʻokele waʻa (navigational gourd), 168–69; Jefferson and grid mapping, 39; Kailiehu, *ReKALOnize Your Naʻau*, 139–40; of land as a bucket of dirt, 41–42; land as a, 83, 78–79; of lands lovers are from, 65–66; of leadership, 137–38; of a loʻi kalo (taro pondfield), 195; "Mālana Mai Kaʻū" as a, 134–35; of Māui moʻolelo, 31–32; mele as, 188; of moʻo, 55–56; moʻoʻāina map, 47–49; moʻoʻāina map of the moʻolelo of Kamiki, 110–12; moʻolelo map of Keʻehi, 172–73; in motion, 77–78; murals as, 49–50, 112–13; on the naʻau, 109–10; of Pele's pursuit of Kamapuaʻa, 61; place names preserved in street names, 39, 170; of the Purple Spot representing industrialization, 36; of reefs, 173; registered maps, 46–47, 49, 57, 173; Ring of Shrines, 125–26; star map, 126–27, 149, 169–70; settler colonial map of Mauna Kea, 94–95; vertical map of the papa (strata) of Kīlauea, 146–47; vertical map of the wao (horizontal realms), 145–45; of view planes, 130–31; Waiau as a, 87; of water diversions, 57–58

Marx, Karl, 39

mathematics of subdivision, 5, 19, 29; agricultural feasibility and 32, 82–84; archaeological boundary lines and, 41–42, 125–26; bucket of dirt emblematic of, 41–42; condominium property regime as, 39; "containment" of water on Mauna Kea and, 104–5; deploying moʻoʻāina cartographic method against, 29, 33, 130; enclosure, juridical precedent of, 39–41; fragmenting of land, 32–33, 44; fragmenting of stream-flows, 197; gridding of land illustrating, 39; in "impermeable layer" and perched waters, 93, 105, 111, 164–65; individual sites vs. a regional complex (or historic district), 41–42, 123–26, 166–68, 187; phased archaeological inventory surveys, 5; subdivision of practice, 130–31; "telescoping effect," 125; thresholds of impact, 5, 96–97; urban spot zoning, 5, 35–36, 39, 81

Māuiakalana: 29, 31–32, 36; finding the birthplace of, in Waiʻanae, 41, 43–49, 74, 85; gifts, 36, 80; on Mauna a Wākea, 109; moʻolelo of his fishing up islands in Waiʻanae, 36–38; moʻolelo illustrates integrity of papa (foundation), 42–43; moʻolelo of, on island of Maui, 67; mural of genealogical continuities, 49–50; navigator bringing together the Pacific peoples, 67, 94, 208–10; slowing the sun, 31–32; unfolding of birth along Puʻu Heleakalā ridgeline, 62, 77–79; wonder and, 68–69, 79–80, 84

Mauna a Wākea (Mauna Kea or Maunakea), 29; as all three piko (fontanel, umbilicus, genitalia) of Hawaiʻi island, 87–88, 117, 127, 131, 140–41; aquifers, 103; archaeological studies of, 124–27; customary and traditional practices, 127, 130–31; decentralized leadership on, 137–39; "degradation principle" and, 97; desecration of Ahu o ka Uakoko, 133; designated as Crown lands, 99; elder sibling of Kānaka Maoli, 87–88; fog drip as water source, 107–9, 116; frost heave, 108–9; genealogy, 24, 87; Huakaʻi i Nā ʻĀina Mauna cultural monitoring of, 109–10, 114; huliau, a time of change growing from, 136; hydrology of, 104–9, 110–12; Kailiehu's

artwork on, 112–13, 136–39; Kanaka Maoli ancestral knowledge of water on Mauna a Wākea, 107–9; kapu aloha as protocol on, 118–19; kūpuna pohaku (stone ancestors) and, 141–42; as lei ʻōpuʻu (whale tooth pendant symbolizing sovereignty), 118; is male and female, 25; Moʻoinanea testifies against the Thirty Meter Telescope, 100–103; moʻolelo of Kamiki, 110–12; moʻolelo of Poliʻahu and Kūkahauʻula, 92–94; mural of and censorship, 112–14; observatories on, 89; as pahuwai (water container), 107; Ring of Shrines, 123; settler state represents as a wasteland, 88–89, 94–96; standing for with decolonial joy, 17, 134–35; star maps, 126–27; Supreme Court decision on the Thirty Meter Telescope, 97; as symbolic sealant in making of a canoe, 134; Thirty Meter Telescope proposed for, 89; Thirty Meter Telescope threat to aquifers on, 103–6; "threshold of impact" and, 96–97, 99; trans-Indigenous solidarity, 64, 143; University of Hawaiʻi applicant on behalf of the Thirty Meter Telescope, 89; view planes, 117, 130–31; water deities of, 88. *See also* ea; Moʻoinanea; Poliʻahu; Thirty Meter Telescope; Waiau

Mauna a Wākea, protector stands and arrests for: April 2, 2015, stand, 120, 131–32; June 24, 2015, stand, 117, 120–23, 141–42; July 15, 2019, kūpuna stand, 212–215; July 17, 2019, stand, 214–15

Maunakea-Forth, Kukui and Gary, 84–85

McCandless, Lincoln, 75–76, 181

Meheanu, 102, 202–3. *See also* Hale o Meheanu

migrants, 13–16, 84

Moanalua, 55; fed by Keʻehi, 167, 172; moʻolelo of Kahikilaulani, 162–63; moʻolelo of Keanakamanō, 163; moʻolelo of sharks in the mountains, 147, 161–63

Mokauea, 162, 166–67, 170–73, 204

Mokoliʻi, 56, 179, 181

Momoa, Joseph, 49–50

moʻo (reptilian water deities), 1, 33; Alamuki, 53–56; antithetical to settler colonial logic

27–28; Kānāwai Kānemilohae, 145, 160[61]; Kīhoʻihoʻi Kānāwai stewardship plan, 145, 163; Papahulihonua and Mauna a Wākea, 107; Papahulilani, 26, 148, 198, 217–18. *See also* Hui ʻAimalama

Parsons Brinckerhoff (wsp), 96–98

Pele (Peleʻaihonua), 31; birthing new lands, 61; born of Haumea, 149; Hiʻiakaikapoliopele and, 66, 146–47; Kamapuaʻa and, 61; threatened by Namakaokahaʻi, 146

Peralto, Leon Noʻeau, 118, 140–41

Perez, Andre, 113, 122, 143, 212, 228n11

permission, 23, 102; of akua and other guardians, 100–103, 175; cartography and, 18, 23, 102; hōʻailona (signs) granting or denying, 23, 103, 175; in *Keaomelemele*, 175–76; kilo practices and, 23; Nishnaabeg practices of requesting, 23; oli kāhea (chant requesting permission to enter), 102; protocols for, 17, 27, 102–3, 132, 215–16; of stones, 132–33

Perreira, Hiapo, 64

phytoplankton, 203, 206–7, 219

Piailug, Mau, 166, 169, 208–10

piko (three piko: fontanel, navel, genitalia), 29, 87; junction of kalo stem and leaf, 88; Keʻehi as, 172; Mauna Kea as, 87–88, 101, 117, 127, 131, 139–41; pōhaku as, 131; Thirty Meter Telescope blocking piko, 101, 127; Waiau as, 130–41

Pisciotta, Kealoha, 27, 90; on activating, to hoʻopōhuli, 139–40; on alignments with akua, 119–20, 149, 171; on the effects of "increments," 98; on frost heave, 109; on kapu aloha, 119–20; on the laws of the akua, 91; on view planes to sacred places, 130–31; whales' ability to access Pō, the ancestral realm, 206–7

place-names, 55, 63, 186–87

planetarity, 3–4, 6, 8; cascading effects, 207; Indigenous movements against climate change, 3, 6, 12, 90–91, 143; interconnected life systems and globalization, 12; restoring Indigenous land bases and, 12; thresholds of life and nonlife and, 98; water and planetary security, 4, 6, 103, 143, 165, 189

Pō (ancestral realm), 10, 158: in the Kumulipo, 23–24; Waiau and, 140–41; whales and, 207

Poepoe, Joseph Mokuohai, 208. *See also* "Ka Moolelo o ko Wakea ma Noho Ana i Kalihi"

pōhaku, 29, 116; alo (face) stones, 175, 192–93; building foundations that feed (taro pondfields, fishponds, altars), 116, 192, 202; fog drip and, 107; as food, 57, 115–16, 117; frost heave and, 108–9, 116–17, 132; halihali pōhaku, 131, 133, 142, 193–94, 201; as kūpuna, 29, 123, 129, 141–43, 192–93; living, 159–60; manifestations of Papahānaumoku, 115; Mauna a Wākea guardian associated with, 126; moʻo and, 117; planting pōhaku, 123, 142; protectors as, 117, 131–32, 142; stone eaters (ʻaipōhaku), 116–17, 142; "Stone-Eating Song" ("Mele ʻAi Pōhaku," also known as "Mele Aloha ʻĀina" and "Kaulana Nā Pua"), 42; uhauhumu pōhaku (stonemason), 131

Pōhakuloa, 91; akua kiaʻi (elemental guardian) 110; gulch, 193; Hawaiʻi Supreme Court case regarding the US military's lease for, 114; live-fire training and, 112, 114; in the moʻolelo of Kamiki, 110–12; Pōhakuloa Training Area subterranean waterways, 112

Poliʻahu, 88, 106, 110; footsteps of, 108–9; heiau, 130; lover, Kūkahauʻula, and, 24, 91–94, 102–3, 122; part of canoe, 134; sisters of, 114; testimony of, 100–101

portals, 65–66, 153–54, 178

Povinelli, Elizabeth, 8, 21–22, 90, 100

prayer (pule). *See* chants, prayers, songs

precarity, 7, 28, 144–45, 162, 165

protectors (kiaʻi) of land and waters, 1, 15–17, 64; as ʻai pōhaku (stone eaters), 116–17; at Hale o Meheanu, 200–203; intergenerational, 113, 133–34, 138, 177; at Kalama Valley, 82; in Kalihi, 151, 157–58, 165–66; at Keʻehi, 167–68; on Mauna a Wākea, 120–23, 131–32, 141–43, 212–15; protectors, not protesters, 118; at Red Hill, 164; trans-Indigenous alliances, 9, 91, 143, 189, 208; in Waiāhole, 177, 180, 182–89; in Waiʻanae, 38, 57–59, 68–69, 80–81. *See also* aloha ʻāina

Pukui, Mary Kawena, 33; on the fishes of
'Uko'a, 54, 239n23; on hau, 189; on the
lāhui, 222n15; on low tide 37; on mo'o'āina,
34; 'ōlelo no'eau about hau, 189, 228n17; on
rain, 80; on the will of the elements, 175
Puniwai, Noelani, 26–27, 217
Purple Spot, 35–39, 69; abundance of, 75; the
birthplace of Māui and, 47, 49; farmed,
75–76; microhistory of occupation, 75–76;
represented as a wasteland, 41–42, 83; resistance to, 42–43. *See also* urban spot zoning
Pu'u Heleakalā, 31–32, 36–37, 43–44, 46–47,
49–50, 77–79
Pu'uhonua o Pu'uhuluhulu, 212–13, 216
Pu'uhuluhulu University, 216–17

racism, 13–14; anti-Black, 13; discrediting of
Kanaka Maoli cultural practitioners in
archaeological surveys, 126; environmental,
63, 72–73; Hawai'i Supreme Court ruling
on Thirty Meter Telescope conservation
permit, 127; racialization of Kanaka Maoli
communities, 68; racial value systems in settler colonial systems, 11; reliance on white
translations of 'ōlelo Hawai'i texts, 94–96
rainbows (ānuenue), 92; drawing together
ahupua'a, 173; elemental alignments,
119–20; frost heave and, 108–9; as hō'ailona,
92, 103, 153, 216; at Mauna a Wākea, 216
rains, 6, 51; as gifts, 36, 80; as hō'ailona (signs),
65; Kaniko'o (He'eia Uli), 17; Kīpu'upu'u
(Mauna a Wākea), 92, 122, 233n17; Kolowao
(Ka'ala), 71; Kuauli (Mauna a Wākea),
92, 122; Leialoha, 61; Līlīlehua (rain of
Waialua), 55; Lonoikamakahiki, akua of
cloud formation and rain, 218; megalopa as
indicators for, 218; misty rains, 102; Nāulu
(Kemo'o), 55; 'ōlelo no'eau (proverb),
"Rains always follows the forest," 5; as part
of the hydrological cycle in the ahupua'a
land division, 20; Pō'aihale (Waiāhole),
195; Po'aipuni (Kemo'o), 55; rainy season
(ho'oilo), 108; sign of Wākea making love to
Papahānaumoku, 62; Ualipilipi (Kalihi), 173
reciprocal relations, 8, 16; consent and, 23,
66–67, 99, 102; land and Kānaka activate

each other, 156, 199–200; long-term relations, 25–26, 165–66; radical resurgence
and, 23; requesting permission, 102–3
recognition, 8; of abundance, 5; abundance
as a form of recognition by the akua (elements), 9, 59, 188, 197; of and by akua, 22,
98, 102, 132, 158–59; in ceremony, 34; of
descendants, 159–60; earth's recognition
of us, 7, 102, Haumea's recognition of the
farmer Kali'u, 156–57; hō'ailona (signs)
of recognition by the land, 23, 26, 170–71,
175–76, 200–201; international recognition
of Hawai'i as an independent nation-state,
20; Kanaka Maoli refusal to recognize the
settler state, 91; performative recognition,
100; reciprocal recognition, 23, 132, 147,
155–58, 175–76; rejection of federal recognition, 22–23; of settler colonial difference, 15;
state's refusal to recognize akua, 90, 99
Red Hill Bulk Fuel Storage Facility, 144–45;
exempted from rules governing spills and
overfill protection, 164; Navy on impermeable layer, 164; Sierra Club lawsuit, 164;
annual leakage, 165
Reiny, Samson, 75
relationality, 3, 12; to 'āina (land, seas, skies),
24, 60–61, 199–200; with akua (elemental
forms), 23, 86, 102, 128, 156, 170; between
akua, 27, 157, 217; between ancestral knowledges and decolonized STEM (science,
technology, engineering, and mathematics),
26; between settler allies and Indigenous
peoples, 14–18, 67, 79, 120, 218; cartography
as relational, 4, 18–19, 34, 47; decolonization
based on, 14, 166, 194, 215–18; distributional
archaeology, 125–26; of ecosystems, 3, 21,
28; expansive Kanaka Maoli genealogical relationalities, 18; hō'ailona (signs) as
index of, 23; ho'omana (growing collective
life force) and, 166; kilo and, 26–28, 102,
145; land-based lāhui (nation, collective)
and, 12; mo'o'āina lessons in, 19, 29, 34,
47; Mo'oinanea as principle of, 91–92, 103;
mo'olelo conventions and, 64–65; piko
of Mauna a Wākea establishes, 117; pilina
(connectedness) as, 37, 66, 201; of places to

each other, 42–43, 55, 64–65; pleasures of, 86, 216–18; simultaneity of overlapping positionalities, 14; view planes and sightlines, 130–31. *See also* alignments; vibration

Reppun, Charlie, 182–84, 187, 197

restoration, 3–4; ʻauwai, 192, 193–94; cascading restorative effects, 7, 187–88, 204–5; climate change, 6; in a decolonial present, 12; each restoration project builds on others, 203–4; of fishponds, 55, 200–203, 204–5 ; of Hawaiʻi's independence, 22–23, 135–36, 193, 215–19; of Heʻeia Stream, 204; of Indigenous land bases, 12, 118; Kīhoʻihoʻi Kānāwai stewardship plan, 145, 163; of loʻi kalo, 35, 56–59, 174–75, 189–97; ʻOnipaʻa Nā Hui Kalo, 184–85; queer love as a restorative force, 25; rethinking scale, 7, 25–26, 84, 203–4; of water, 58–59, 182–89

resurgence, radical, 4, 23; EAducation as, 136–37, 216–17; Haumea plots, 192, 204; of kalo farming, 184–97; of Kanaka Maoli ancestral ways of knowing, 18, 63, 101–2, 173, 145, 219; kilo renewal of relations with akua, 8, 26–28, 107–8, 145; mapping of, 204; reKALOnizing the naʻau as, 139–40. *See also* education; kilo

Ritte, Walter, 213–15

rocks. *See* pōhaku

Royal Order of Kamehameha I, 212

sacred, 28, 63; astro-architectural alignments of heiau, 149; channels of energy between sacred places, 130–31; developers identify for "easements," 44; Haumea establishing sacred space, 148–49, 192, 215–16; kapu aloha as an ancestral protocal of conduct, 119; Mauna a Wākea as sacred, 87–88, 91; permission to enter sacred realms, 100–103; piko as sacred, 87, 127; to protect water, 109; sacred as lifegiving, 117; spiral as a sacred pattern, 139–40; water as sacred, 189

Sai, David Keanu, 10

Salazar, Joseph (ʻIokepa) A., 99

Sand Island (Mauliola), 171

Sang, Preseley Kaʻalaanuhea Ah Mook, 216

Saranillio, Dean Itsuji, 11, 16

scalability, 7, 97, 203

sea (kai), 3, 19; of ʻĀlau, 198; cultivation of kalo on the lihikai (edge of the saltwaters), 176; estuaries, 71, 182, 187, 197; of ʻEwa, 55; joining of nā kai ʻewalu (eight seas or channels), 38, 50; Kanaloa, 26–27, 146; Kāne (freshwater stream flows) mitigating acidification, 26–27, 205; kaulana mahina (moon phases) and, 28; Kīhoʻihoʻi Kānāwai stewardship plan for the health of, 145–46, 160; kilo and, 26–27, 37, 206, 210–12, 217; of Kualoa, 56; lands rising from, 37–38, 210; of Mōkapu, 152; of Polea, 25; revitalization of, 187; seeding clouds, 21, 53; sewage contamination of, 106; subterranean passages to, 54, 73, 161, 163; thermal expansion of, 97; of Ulehawa, 32, 36, 49–50. *See also* ocean

sea level rise, 3, 26; hau for flood mitigation, 202; Kanaloa, return of, 26, 217; Māui pulling up the islands and, 36–38, 208

seaweed (limu), 2, 33, 152–53; gardens, 71, 73; groundwater indicator, 205; in the Kumulipo, 24; moon phases and, 28, 205; planting, 30; repurposing invasive, 205; restoration of, 30, 204–5; Waimānalo Limu Hui, 30

seed banks. *See* kīpuka

settler allies, 12; agency, 13; growing aloha ʻāina consciousness, 60–61; imaginative possibilities for, 14; kuleana of, 18; opposition to all forms of state oppression, 13–14; protecting Mauna a Wākea, 113; refugee settlers, 14; settlers of color, 13, 16

settler aloha ʻāina, 12, 14; against the settler state, 18, 164; arrests of, 121–22, 215; Asian settlers as, 16, 120; on being a Japanese settler aloha ʻāina, 12, 14–15, 67–68, 121; embodied experience of the land, 30; foundation for critical settler cartography, 16–17; Goodyear-Kaʻōpua on, 14; hoʻomana (growing collective mana, life force), 166; joining protocol, 17; kuleana of, 18; land-based consciousness, 16–17; in restoration projects, 30; at stands on Mauna a Wākea, 29, 120, 215; statist and non-statist forms of organizing, 134; work of deoccupation and decolonization, 15–16

temporality. *See* ancestral time

Thirty Meter Telescope (TMT) 29, 87, 89–91; astronomers on, 89, 100; conservation district use permit for, 89–90; contested case hearings, 98–103, 104–6, 107, 114, 124–27; and degradation principle, 97; desecration, 133, 213; environmental impact statement for, 89, 96–97, 101, 107, 123–24; and failure to gain consent, 102–3; impacts of, 97–98, 101, 126–27, 130–31; and the juridical underpinning of the settler state, 97; Justice Wilson's dissenting opinion on, 97; and mathematics of subdivision, 104–6, 110, 124–25; 128; Mauna Kea Groundwater Schematic, 104–5; Supreme Court ruling on, 97, 127; threat to aquifers, 103–6, 111; and "threshold of impact," 96–97, 99; and title to land, 97, 118; University of Hawaiʻi's representation of, 89, 112–13; and the wastelanding of Mauna Kea, 94–97. *See also* Mauna a Wākea, protector stands and arrests for

threshold, 5, 29; apocalyptic, 4; of colonial impact for Native peoples, 90, 99; "degradation principle" and, 96–97; distinction between life and nonlife, 29, 90; of impact, 96–97; for Moʻoinanea's standing in the contested case hearing, 98–99; raising, 73; tactic in settler colonial mathematics of subdivision, 5; in the wastelanding of the earth, 97

title to land, 99, 118

topography, 19, 29; and elements of each ahupuaʻa, 19; environmental hotspots as part of, 74; erasure of, 104; of moʻo along the land, 35, 52–56; in mural of Māui moʻolelo, 50

Torres, Jada Anela, 142

tourism, 68, 74, 82, 151

tours, political. *See* huakaʻi

Townsend, Marti, 38, 69, 90, 164

toxic waste, 3, 15; in food chain, 73; increasing legal thresholds, 73; landfills and, 71–73; legally disposable on agricultural lands, 35, 62, 74; on Mauna a Wākea, 89, 104, 106

Trask, Haunani-Kay: as an ʻai pōhaku (stone eater), 116–17; differentiates Blacks from settlers of color, 13; on Kalama Valley land struggle, 82; Lākea Trask and, 121; poetry of, 228n8; on slavery, 13, 222n37

Tsing, Anna Lowenhaupt, 7

Tuck, Eve, 13

ʻUkoʻa fishpond, 1–2, 53–55

Ulehawa Stream, 32, 36–37, 42–45, 49–50, 77

University of Hawaiʻi, 17, 89; community struggle to establish ethnic studies at, 181; manages the Mauna Kea Science Reserve, 89, 103; representation of the Thirty Meter Telescope, 89, 94–96, 100, 104–5, 113, 124; students and faculty opposed to the Thirty Meter Telescope, 112–14, 216–17

urban spot zoning, 5, 35–36, 39

US Department of the Interior on recognition of a Native Hawaiian governing entity, 22–23

US Environmental Protection Agency, 164

US military, 6, 82; bombing of Kahoʻolawe, 25, 67, 213; diversions of water, 6, 74, 114, 182; leaking jet fuel storage tank, 145, 163–65; live-fire training at Pōhakuloa Training Area, 112, 114; Lualualei Naval Radio Transmitter Facility and Naval Magazine Lualualei, 74; occupation of agricultural lands, 164; role in the overthrow of Queen Liliʻuokalani, 22, 75, 115; unexploded ordnance, 164; US Pacific Command, 164; water banking, 74, 182

Vaughan, Mehana Blaich, 217

vibration, 27; attunement, 28; kupuna, 147, 170–71, 177, 179–80, 188–89; repetitions in moʻolelo, 179–80; rhythmic patterns in art, 188–89; of voice, 119–120, 159–60, 171, 188

view planes, 31–32; identifying loʻi kalo, 184–85; relationships between landforms, 109, 117, 130–31; stories remembered in, 63, 78–79

Vogeler, Kūhiō, 10

Von Oelhoffen, Kamakahukilani, 119–20, 130

Voyles, Tracy Brynne, 62

CPSIA information can be obtained
at www.ICGtesting.com
Printed in the USA
BVHW092020221022
649779BV00003B/12

9 781478 011682